M000247956

ADVENTURES IN MUNILAND

A Guide to Municipal Bond Investing in the Post-Crisis Era

Michael F. Comes • David R. Kotok • John R. Mousseau

Foreword by Alexandra Lebenthal

Cumberland Advisors Publishing
Sarasota, Florida

Dedication

This book is dedicated to the memory of our late business partner, Peter Demirali. Peter was a shareholder, managing director, and portfolio manager at Cumberland Advisors until his sudden death due to an aneurysm in 2012. Peter's expertise in the course of his professional career was in the taxable fixed-income arena. He pioneered the evolution of the use of Build America Bonds in Cumberland's portfolios. Peter was with Cumberland Advisors for over a decade.

The authors of this book worked with Peter and knew him as a colleague and personal friend. He was a mentor to the primary writer of this book, Michael F. Comes, who heads muni research at Cumberland and is also a portfolio manager. As an associate and business partner, Peter participated at the very highest levels of Cumberland Advisors' management.

Peter invested his life in helping others through his management of their assets. In addition, he advocated for those unable to care for themselves. After Peter's first visit to the Columbus Community Center, he was moved to see the obstacles that young adults with intellectual and physical disabilities face in making their way in the world. This visit impressed on Peter the good fortune and opportunities available to his family, and his first response was to reach out and ask how he could make a difference in the lives of other families. Columbus had just launched a small scholarship program for this special population—one of the first of its kind in the country, and Peter was one of the early supporters of the program. In 2012, an endowed scholarship was established in Peter's name so that young men and women with disabilities have a way to pursue their goals of finding meaningful work in the community where they live. Through this endowment, young adults with disabilities and their families will have doors of opportunity open to them that would have otherwise been unavailable without this scholarship.

A portion of the sales from this book will be donated to the Peter Demirali Scholarship Fund to ensure that the legacy of his many influences, accomplishments, and commitments will live on. Visit *http:www.cumber.com* or *http:www.columbusserves.org/peterdemirali/* for more information about this scholarship fund.

Table of Contents

Preface

My colleagues acceded to my request to write a preface for our newest book. There is a reason for this preface. The book that we have created is for the benefit of modern investors, state and local governments, and anyone with an interest in municipal bonds. Our book focuses on the last seven years, but municipal bond history starts with the issues of states over two centuries ago.

Since I am the oldest dog in the Cumberland kennel, I am using that prerogative to include a few personal observations here. When I encountered my first tax-free municipal bond at age 10, it was a physical piece of paper, issued to the bearer. The owner of that bond was a local physician in Vineland, New Jersey. He was Dr. Charles Cunningham, an icon in what was then a small town in southern New Jersey.

On his way to the bank one day, Dr. Cunningham stopped in to say hello to my father, who ran the family business, a produce market in the middle of town. In those days, the place was the true Vineland town center, and everyone dropped by Kotok's Market on the corner of Sixth Street and Landis Avenue.

Dr. Cunningham showed me the tax-free bond he was carrying in the pocket of his jacket. He said, "Son, when you get older and save money, you are going to want to have some of these." He smiled, winked at my father, and walked off in the direction of the bank.

This bond was a very strange-looking piece of paper, as seen through the eyes of a 10-year-old child in the 1950s. I learned that he used a pair of scissors to cut off the coupon, because that coupon was payable on demand to the bearer of the bond, and it was the same as cash in those days. The cash to make the payment was held in the bank by the "paying agent." The arrangement then was a form of trust, and the safety of the payment was sacrosanct. If someone had robbed Dr. Cunningham of his bonds, the thief could have gone to the bank and cashed in the coupons as the holder of the bonds. There was no written or electronic record of ownership.

We have come a long way since then. Bonds and their payment streams are now electronic. Capital markets also function electronically. There are no bearer bonds anymore. Nothing is hidden in the legal structure, supervision, or regulation of tax-free and other bonds. Privacy, as we knew it in the old days, has vanished from Muniland.

In the world of municipal bonds, there have also been numerous changes in the tax code over the years. We have bonds that are subject to the AMT (Alternative Minimum Tax). This means that a tax-free bond in the AMT category can become a taxable bond, depending on the tax status of the holder. Think about that for a minute. About the worst thing a bondholder could possibly have to deal with would be a tax-free bond that becomes taxable. The bond would carry a lower interest rate because it would be tax-free under so many circumstances, yet in the hands of certain holders it would be taxed at AMT rates. That is a legal construction that did not exist in the days of Dr. Cunningham.

There are now many and varied forms of municipal credit. Credit structures have become very complex and are discussed in detail in this book. As a result of the financial crisis of the last seven years, Muniland is no longer an easy place in which to live and invest.

For decades, assumptions about municipal bonds were relatively straightforward. Taxes were not paid on the interest. There was little worry about a capital gain on which taxes might have to be paid if the bond was sold before its maturity. Most people who bought bonds did hold them until maturity and used them as an alternate way to invest their savings. They did not think very much about those bonds. As bond insurance developed, they thought less about specific bonds. The assumption was, "It is AAA and insured; I don't need to know any more than that."

That was the world of the bond buyer and issuer. If bond issuers could satisfy the requirements and obtain bond insurance, they could sell their bonds with an AAA rating to people who were willing to buy them. People buying the bonds assumed those bonds were rock-solid and safe. All that changed during this financial crisis. The world of municipal bonds as we knew it for half a century has been permanently altered.

This book addresses the alterations that have taken place during and after the financial crisis. It extracts thousands of hours of work we have done in Muniland over this period. It has been a pleasure and an honor for me, the old dog in the kennel, to work with the younger dog, John Mousseau. John has been a senior participant in the management of Cumberland Advisors for more than a decade.

John and I have also had the pleasure of working with our even younger colleague Michael Comes. He joined us after graduation from college and has been with us a number of years, obtaining his CFA along the way. Working as a portfolio manager, he has honed his skills in the area of municipal bond and credit research and has developed prestigious credentials in this Muniland space. Michael shouldered the greatest load of work on this book and deserves the applause.

If there is anything that readers need to know as they peruse our *Adventures in Muniland*, it is that any errors that crop up belong to John Mousseau and me. Now let's take a trip into this fascinating 3.7-trillion-dollar world. We hope you enjoy the book.

David R. Kotok
Sarasota, Florida
June 2015

About the Authors

Michael F. Comes, CFA, serves Cumberland Advisors as Vice President of Research and Portfolio Manager. He joined Cumberland Advisors in 2008 after graduating with a B.A. in economics from Dickinson College. His responsibilities include research of current and prospective bond holdings, both tax-exempt bonds and Build America Bonds (BABs), as well as trading of tax-exempt bonds and BABs on Cumberland's fixed income desk. In addition, Mr. Comes works with Cumberland's IT department and assists Cumberland's Vice Chairman and Chief Monetary Economist, Robert Eisenbeis, in developing Cumberland's proprietary rating and forecasting models.

Mr. Comes was born in Paris, France and grew up in Millburn, New Jersey. He is a member of the Global Interdependence Center (GIC), *www.interdependence.org*, whose mission is to encourage the expansion of global dialogue and free trade in order to improve cooperation and understanding among nation states, with the goal of reducing international conflicts and improving worldwide living standards. Mr. Comes also is a member of the Tampa Bay chapter of the CFA Institute.

David R. Kotok cofounded Cumberland Advisors in 1973 and has been its Chief Investment Officer since inception. He holds a B.S. in economics from The Wharton School of the University of Pennsylvania, an M.S. in organizational dynamics from The School of Arts and Sciences at the University of Pennsylvania, and an M.A in philosophy from the University of Pennsylvania.

Mr. Kotok's articles and financial market commentaries have appeared in *The New York Times*, *The Wall Street Journal*, *Barron's*, and other publications. He is a frequent contributor to Bloomberg TV and Bloomberg Radio, Fox Business, and other media. Mr. Kotok has served as Program

Chairman and currently serves as a Director of GIC. Mr. Kotok chaired its Central Banking Series and organized a five-continent dialogue held in Cape Town, Chile, Hong Kong, Hanoi, Milan, Paris, Philadelphia, Prague, Rome, Santiago, Shanghai, Singapore, Tallinn, and Zambia (Livingstone). He has received the Global Citizen Award from GIC for his efforts.

Mr. Kotok is a member of the National Business Economics Issues Council (NBEIC), the National Association for Business Economics (NABE) and served on the Research Advisory Board of BCA Research. Mr. Kotok has served as a Commissioner of the Delaware River Port Authority (DRPA) and on the Treasury Transition Teams for New Jersey Governors Kean and Whitman. He has also served as a board member of the New Jersey Economic Development Authority and as Chairman of the New Jersey Casino Reinvestment Development Authority. He has authored or co-authored four books, including the best selling second edition of *From Bear to Bull with ETFs*.

John R. Mousseau, CFA joined Cumberland Advisors in 2000. He is currently an Executive Vice President and the Director of Fixed Income, as well as a portfolio manager for municipal bond investments. In this capacity, Mr. Mousseau and his team manage portfolio construction, trading, and research for both tax-free and taxable bond accounts.

Mr. Mousseau has over 30 years of investment management experience. Prior to Cumberland, he was the Director of Municipal Bond Investments for Lord Abbett & Company. He also worked previously for Shearson Lehman Brothers and its predecessor firm, E.F. Hutton. His comments and analyses have appeared in *The Bond Buyer*, *Barron's*, *The Wall Street Journal*, *Bloomberg*, *Forbes*, *The New York Times*, the *San Francisco Chronicle*, and the *Newark Star-Ledger*. In addition, he has appeared on Bloomberg TV and Bloomberg Radio, Reuters, and CNBC for commentary on fixed-income markets. He has also been a speaker at various industry conferences, and a guest lecturer at Florida International University. Mr. Mousseau holds an A.B. in economics from Georgetown University and an M.A. in economics from Brown University.

Mr. Mousseau is a member of the Philadelphia Council for Business Economics (PCBE), the National Federation of Municipal Analysts (NFMA), the National Association for Business Economics (NABE), the Washington Association of Money Managers (WAMM), and the National Economists Club (NEC). He is also a member of the New York Society of Security Analysts, where he served on the Society's High Net Worth Investors Committee. He is a past chair of the Municipal Bond Buyers Conference. In addition, he has served as an instructor at the New York Institute of Finance and Bond Market Association. Mr. Mousseau resides in Sarasota, FL, and is active in alumni affairs at Georgetown University. He was involved with the Rotary and YMCA in Maplewood, New Jersey, and is an active member of the Sarasota Southside Rotary Club. He is also a member of the Tampa Bay chapter of the CFA Institute.

Foreword

Author Tom Wolfe, no stranger to the financial markets, once suggested that a book on the municipal bond market should be called *The Dark Continent.* There is wisdom in that observation, because the municipal bond market is a vast place. There are more than 90,000 municipal entities, and some 50,000 have issued municipal bonds. There are about 1 million different bond issues currently outstanding, totaling approximately $3.6 trillion in value, and anywhere from 10 to 15 thousand new issues come to market every year. And while there is some general conformity across different issues—all general obligation bonds and revenue bonds are structured similarly, and as fixed-income instruments they all generally track the price movements of the overall bond market—municipal bonds are, as investor Paul Isaac wryly observed, "particular and specific to a remarkable degree."

It is the distinctiveness of each municipal bond issuer that makes it so very dangerous to generalize about the market as a whole, as Meredith Whitney and those who agreed with her found out in the years since her call for imminent—and sizable—credit disasters. The muni meltdown never happened. (Thank you, Joe Mysak, for that phraseology.) The current woes of Detroit, Jefferson County, or Puerto Rico are unique to them, and their experiences cannot be extrapolated to other issuers. The relative wealth of an issuer's citizens is no guarantee of creditworthiness—just ask the bondholders of Orange County, California, which went bankrupt in 1994, or Nassau County, New York, which has had a state monitoring board controlling its finances since 2011. Nor is geographical proximity a predictor of bond performance: the state with the lowest credit rating in the union, A-minus-rated Illinois, is surrounded on three sides by triple-A-rated Iowa, Indiana, and Missouri. So do your homework if you are looking to invest in municipal bonds, and trust that your advisors and mutual fund managers are doing theirs.

This is where Michael Comes, David Kotok, and John Mousseau of Cumberland Advisors come in. John Mousseau and David Kotok have been doing their homework for decades, and the book you are holding is testament to their unparalleled experience and market savvy. They have protected and grown their clients' capital—there is no higher praise on Wall Street—through all of the adventures in Muniland they describe. I have learned over the years that whenever they proffer an opinion in their market commentaries, it pays to listen; and that was particularly true during the period on which they focus their book.

The financial crisis and its aftermath was a game changer in global markets: systemic weaknesses were exposed; liquidity proved to be fickle; unintended consequences of misguided regulatory regimes came to fruition; historical market truths could no longer be trusted; huge sums of money were lost (and made); venerable firms were gobbled up or went under; and the ensuing finger-pointing and recrimination has led to a period of regulatory activism rarely seen in global finance. Global central banks, using all tools at their disposal, are still executing Herculean feats of monetary policy to create the illusion of recovery. The municipal bond market, mostly a bystander during this period, nevertheless suffered unprecedented market and reform repercussions. In particular, Muniland was beset by a firestorm of headline risk, tax-reform saber rattling, bond insurer troubles, and some high-profile credit catastrophes. It takes a cool head to weather this kind of storm, and there are few heads cooler than Messrs. Comes, Kotok, and Mousseau.

It wasn't always this way in Muniland. There typically hasn't been too much to say about municipal bonds, because the vast majority of them are money-good. Default rates for munis have historically been below those of similarly rated corporate bonds. And their utility in supporting the structural and financial stability of our nation's states, cities, and towns is beyond question. I can't count the number of times my father, Jim Lebenthal, would talk about the three main things he learned about munis from his mother, Sayra Lebenthal, the co-founder of Lebenthal & Company: they are safe, they don't fluctuate much, and they are tax-free. Or he'd talk about the infrastructure projects and other public works that were made possible through public finance. "Tax-exemption isn't an end in itself," he said; "it is an important [tool] for rebuilding the country. And rebuilding infrastructure is the way a civilized society shows it has got a future.... I am gung ho for municipal bonds because it is the only instrument we have in hand for refinancing the building of the country."

So why do we need another book on the municipal bond market? It is arguable that if anyone wanted to read about the workings of the municipal bond market, they could find pretty much all they needed to know in *A B C of Municipal Bonds*, written by my grandfather, Louis S. Lebenthal, in 1937. (It's long out of print, so no danger of its outselling this fine tome.) That's how sleepy Muniland used to be. But the financial crisis changed all that. Just as the Vietnam War catalyzed a generation to question authority and expose government corruption, the financial crisis prompted this generation to re-examine the structure and function of every corner of the financial markets, from money market funds to banks, from mortgages to securitizations, from executive compensation to consumer financial protection. It has been a worthwhile exercise (even if it is sometimes pursued with a zealousness that does more harm than good), because we do not want to go through another preventable financial crisis. After all, a little sunlight never hurt anybody.

Adventures in Muniland is an absolute necessity for investors and practitioners in this market at this time. Consider it a source of sunlight shining on the vast, dark continent of municipal bonds.

Alexandra Lebenthal,
CEO, Lebenthal Holdings, LLC
February 2015

Acknowledgments

The preparation of a book is a complex task. This book has three co-authors, all from Cumberland Advisors. Michael Comes, Vice President of Research and Portfolio Manager, is the lead author. Michael performed a great deal of the research in assembling the book and drafted many of the book's chapters. David Kotok and John Mousseau also participated in writing the book, assisting Michael in the heavy lifting that he undertook and in fleshing out the topics that developed into the sections and chapters of the book. All three and others were involved in writing the second section of the book, which reproduces the last seven years of Cumberland Advisors' commentaries that were concerned with the muni market.

Many thanks go to Samantha Jackson, Administrative Assistant, for receiving drafts, organizing texts, copy editing, and performing a substantial list of administrative functions in assembling the book. Sharon Prizant, Director of Marketing and Managing Director, managed communications with our publisher. Steven Hall, Director of IT, assembled the information technology materials that were needed for the book. DonnaMarie Valles, Portfolio Manager and ETF Analyst, guided the process from rough draft to galley. Matt McAleer, Senior Vice President and Portfolio Manager, made edits and aided in the intellectual process. Charley and Lisa Sweet also did substantial copy editing.

Others in the Cumberland Advisors' Fixed Income and Marketing departments were involved as well. They include Robert Malvenda, Vice President and Portfolio Manager; Shaun Burgess, Analyst & Portfolio Manager for Fixed Income; Daniel Himelberger, Analyst and Portfolio Manager for Fixed Income; Amy Raymond, Portfolio and Trading Assistant; Nannette Sabo, Vice President of Taxable Fixed Income Trading and Portfolio Manager; Pam Scott, Sales Support Manager; Julie Takeda, Administrative Assistant; and Brenda Venditti, Head Trader. The rest of the Cumberland Advisors' family was also helpful.

Robert A. Eisenbeis, PhD, Vice Chairman and Chief Monetary Economist, and Michael D. McNiven, PhD, Managing Director & Portfolio Manager, at Cumberland Advisors both offered suggestions on citations and reviewed text.

Joe Mysak, Editor and Columnist at Bloomberg, and author of *Encyclopedia of Municipal Bonds: A Reference Guide to Market Events, Structures, Dynamics, and Investment Knowledge*, guided in construction of our glossary and the municipal market profile we discuss in Chapter 2. Mr. Mysak also provides valuable market insights with his daily contributions to the *Bloomberg Brief Municipal Market* newsletter. We are also grateful to Joe for writing a testimonial for this book.

The published research of Moody's Investors Service, Standard & Poor's, and Fitch Ratings helped guide our thinking for the development of chapters on New Jersey, Puerto Rico, Illinois, and municipal bankruptcy. We have developed historical narratives using their work. The importance of the role these entities have played as information providers for the development of this book and the municipal market in general cannot be overstated.

The authors would like to credit *The Bond Buyer* for its daily reporting on events transpiring within the marketplace. Specifically, beat reporting by Paul Burton, Yvette Shields, and Shelly Sigo have informed us about financial strains in places like Illinois, Harrisburg, and Jefferson County. Aaron Kuriloff, Staff Reporter at *The Wall Street Journal*, and Luciana Lopez, Senior Correspondent at Reuters, provided in-depth analysis and insight on events pertaining to Puerto Rico and New Jersey.

Several municipal market professionals aided in helping us formulate a narrative true to events as they occurred. We would like to thank Mikhail Foux, George Friedlander, and Vikram Rai for their ongoing research efforts at Citigroup Global Markets and Michael Zezas, Executive Director and Fixed Income Strategist at Morgan Stanley. The Municipal Market Analytics Team—Thomas G. Doe, Robert Donahue, Matt Fabian, and Lisa Washburn—contributed with its ongoing missives detailing daily market trends.

We thank Natalie Cohen, Managing Director and Head of Municipal Research at Wells Fargo Securities, for guiding our thoughts on market events such as Detroit and Puerto Rico, providing valuable content suggestions and edits, and writing a testimonial for this text.

John Dillon, Managing Director at Morgan Stanley Wealth Management, offered valuable guidance on content edits and wrote a testimonial for this text.

We would also like to thank our other testimonials authors for their willingness to put pen to paper with their thoughts; namely, Dennis W. Archer, former mayor of Detroit; Thomas G. Doe, President and Founder, Municipal Market Analytics; and Thomas H. Kean, former governor of New Jersey.

Robert D. Klausner, Esquire, provided valuable insight into the statutes governing the interaction between states and local governments.

Frank Comes, lifelong editor, journalist, and father of Michael Comes, reviewed text and made helpful suggestions when necessary.

R. David Heekin, MD and Joshua M. Stone advised on citation formatting, changes in the healthcare industry, and the impacts of weather-related events on regional economies.

Andrea Wherry and Aikta Wahi, friends of Michael Comes, offered support, tough love, and helpful suggestions.

We would like to give special thanks to Alexandra Lebenthal, CEO of Lebenthal Holdings, LLC, whose foreword perfectly captures the essence of this book's message.

Last but not least, we would like to thank Chris Angermann of Bardolf & Company, whose publishing expertise, wisdom, and professional judgment guided this book's development from start to finish.

Disclaimer

The materials contained herein represent the opinions of the authors and should not be construed as a recommendation to buy or sell securities. Any statements nonfactual in nature constitute only their current opinions, which are subject to change without notice. The opinions expressed herein do not necessarily represent the opinions of all the authors or of any institution with which the authors have been, are now, or will be affiliated; nor do they represent the views of any firm named in this book. Nothing contained in this book is to be considered as the rendering of any form of investment advice. In addition, neither the authors nor the publisher are engaged in rendering tax or legal advice through this book. Readers are responsible for obtaining such advice from their own competent professional.

All information published herein is gathered from sources that are thought to be reliable; however, mistakes can be made. Readers are invited to verify data independently and are cautioned not to act based on a surmise that the work done to prepare this book is flawless.

Introduction

This book is written for municipal bond investors, whether they are institutions, trusts, or individuals, large or small; state and local governments; and anyone with an interest in municipal bonds. The idea is straightforward: If moneys are invested in debt issues from state and local government issuers, the authors of this book plan to discuss those investments.

The book focuses on the years during and immediately after the financial crisis. Prior to that, the municipal bond arena was relatively quiet, somewhat boring, and fairly well understood by most investors. Municipal bonds appealed to some institutions, mutual funds, other organizations, and approximately 10% of the U.S. population. The rest of the population may have had a casual interest in them. There was certainly a very serious benefit from municipal bonds, but that benefit did not apply to every investor. In order to justify investment in tax-free municipal bonds, an investor had to be in a higher tax bracket. All that changed when the financial crisis started to unfold at the end of 2007. Since then, the playing field in tax-free municipal bonds, and municipal bonds generally, has been altered in a substantial way.

Chapter 1 of this book traces the structural changes that have taken place in the municipal bond market. There are many questions for us to answer. What happened in those seven years that was so different from the previous half century? What was the nature of this transition and how did it unfold? Why was it a shock? Why did it alarm the investor class? How and why did it alter the concept of safety in municipal bonds? In this chapter, we attempt to summarize the grand transition.

Chapter 2 classifies the types of municipal bond issuers and profiles the market. It is important for bond buyers to discern the differences that proliferate among munis and to understand the claims and security that can offer assurance that the bonds they invest in will pay them back. We think of this in the following context: The bond investor is a lender who takes money, decides to exchange it today for a promise to be paid tomorrow, and obtains a rate of interest that is determined in a marketplace and may not be subject to federal income taxation. Under many circumstances, depending on the structure of the bond, it is also not subject to state and local taxation. Other bonds may be subject to taxation but still be issued by municipal entities rather than corporate entities.

Municipal bonds are securities broadly owned by millions of Americans but idiosyncratic in nature. We like to sit back and use the terms *munis, Muniland,* and *municipal bonds* and to think of them as an asset class in which there are great similarities. But the homogeneity lies in the income tax code and its treatment of municipal bonds, not in the bonds themselves. The types of issues and numbers of issuers are extraordinarily diverse. As a practical matter, there are substantial differences among them. Painting the municipal bond arena with a broad brush ignores these idiosyncrasies at the peril of the investor who chooses to disregard the differences. On the other hand, Muniland also affords opportunities for the investor who takes the time and effort to pay attention. Chapter 1 addresses these broad topics and what they mean for the investor.

Chapter 3 delves into the notion of a general obligation (GO) bond. What does a general obligation pledge mean? How well does it protect the bond investor? This question was easy to answer prior to 2008. Before the financial crisis there was a basic assumption that a GO pledge was the strongest type of promise a municipal bond issuer could make. Institutions and investors depended upon it.

The financial crisis changed that game. We see cities in bankruptcy, like Detroit. We see the GO pledge of a bond issuer under attack. We are not sure that this unlimited commitment to pay principal and interest on indebtedness is as sound, valid, and strong as we thought for half a century. It is important for investors to understand the GO pledge. They need to understand the positives, negatives, the entity that is making it, and how the pledge is backed up.

Chapter 4 deals with a different type of bond, one secured by specific revenue—whether airport landing fees, water utility revenues, turnpike tolls, or something else. These bonds tied to revenue streams were originally thought to be of secondary creditworthiness—GOs came first; specific revenues came second. That notion has now been tested in the financial crisis and may be reversed. In some jurisdictions we see the specific pledges of revenue tied to an absolute claim on that revenue as offering higher credit quality than the GO pledge. In troubled jurisdictions like Puerto Rico and

Detroit, revenue bonds are now believed to be stronger than GO bonds when it comes to getting paid. In jurisdictions that have been through reorganizations, the revenue pledge has been sustained even as other forms of direct debt or pledges to secure direct debt have had to take "haircuts" on the amounts that were paid back to bondholders.

In Chapter 5 we discuss the ratings agencies—now a subject of intense debate. In the past, investors viewed the ratings agencies as the most reliable credit surveillance mechanism one could have. They are the traditional U.S. ratings agencies—Standard & Poor's, Moody's, and Fitch. There are additional ratings agencies that are less well known because of the narrowness of their ownership or purpose, such as Kroll Bond Ratings and Egan-Jones. These ratings agencies also play a role when it comes to certain institutional investors and others who need to delve deeply into the creditworthiness of a bond issue. The financial crisis exposed the ratings agencies to criticism because they failed to respond quickly to changes and subsequently instituted dramatic changes in their ratings.

A good example was insured bonds: Before the crisis, nearly all bonds of the major bond insurers were deemed to be AAA-rated securities. History shows that not to have been the case. The ratings agencies have changed the way they view the ratings of bond insurers as a response to the criticism they received when those highly rated securities started to perform poorly.

With regard to other bond characteristics, ratings agencies had fairly well-established standards of creditworthiness. In Chapter 5, readers will find descriptions of the ratings and what they mean. The terms AAA, AA, A, BBB, and so forth mean different things to different ratings agencies. Ratings generated by the agencies are not identical. They may be close, and they parallel each other, but there are nuances of difference that are important. In this book, we have articulated what various ratings mean to each of the ratings agencies. That information has been drawn from the ratings agencies themselves.

Chapter 6 explores the issue of bond insurance. The issue is actually credit enhancement. In the past, a municipal bond issuer had to make a choice: Do I issue the bond without a bond insurer's imprimatur? If so, the bond would be priced in the marketplace without insurance and based upon the ratings and information that was available to bond buyers, who would then have to dig into a very difficult and complex array of data to determine whether the bond was creditworthy. The alternative was to obtain bond insurance, get the AAA rating from the ratings agency, and present the bond to the market as a very high-quality security. Until the financial crisis, bond buyers accepted this construction. They determined that the insurance company would essentially scrutinize for them. When the insurance company agreed to insure the bond, the purchaser of the bond could depend on this very high-quality rating. The issuer would then pay the insurance company a premium in order to obtain bond insurance. During the financial crisis, this entire scheme of bond insurance, its pricing, and investors' notions about the ratings attached to bonds changed dramatically. Some insurers, once rated AAA, are no longer in existence.

Chapter 7 examines municipalities in recessions. What do they do with the promises they have made for benefits, pensions, post-employment benefits, and healthcare? How do those pledges and promises impact the budgets of municipalities? How do they expose bond investors to attacks on the issuer's creditworthiness? What can bond investors do to protect themselves? How can they obtain the information they need in order to assess their level of risk? Chapter 7 explores these liabilities of issuers and what they mean for investors.

Chapter 8 focuses on a topic we did not think about before the financial crisis: municipal bankruptcy. As the post-crisis period unfolds and mounting liabilities continue to haunt some issuers, headlines announce the bankruptcies of cities and the risk of bankruptcies elsewhere. We explore the use of Chapter 9 municipal bankruptcy in Chapter 8.

In the subsequent chapter, we delve into case studies of distressed municipalities. Detroit is the latest example; Harrisburg is another, along with cities in California, Jefferson County in Alabama, and others. In each case, we assess what went wrong and how it happened. How much time did the process take to unfold? What were the warning signs, if any? Were they heeded?

We intend to focus on these warning signs. The idea for muni investors is to act on early warnings when credit is deteriorating. At Cumberland Advisors, we have consistently attempted to do that. We would rather sell 20 bonds and have 19 of them end up paying perfectly than to hold 20 bonds and have one of those fail to pay. We make our errors on the side of credit tightness and surveillance. No longer can a bond investor rely on AAA insurance. No longer can a bond investor take payments for granted. Chapter 9 may help investors determine what to look for in order to avoid losses in the event of weakening credit in Muniland.

Chapter 10 describes a form of municipal bond, the Build America Bond, which is part of the class of taxable municipal bonds that has been around for many years. The difference between tax-free and taxable municipal bonds is determined by the Internal Revenue Service Code and acts of Congress. As the laws change, that definition changes. Not well understood, taxable municipal bonds remained mostly off investors' radar screens, and issues were usually small. Then in 2009 a newly designed program called Build America Bonds (BABs) became tremendously successful and opened the market to non-traditional municipal investors such as sovereign wealth funds and credit hedge funds. Regrettably, Congress did not extend the program, which ended in 2010. There is less than $200 billion in outstanding Build America Bonds, but these represent a valuable component of the $3.7 trillion municipal bonds asset class.

Chapter 11 discusses headline risk. This is a big issue for investors. Munis spent decades off the front pages and TV radar screens, but all that has changed. Detroit's is the largest city bankruptcy in American history. It and other events have scared investors in munis. Munis also succumbed to intense selling pressure when TV personalities offered punditry about the asset class. One commentator took to national television and predicted "hundreds of billions of dollars of defaults in a single year."

The issue of headline risk is important because it affects investors' behavior. We estimate that about 10% of the U.S. population falls into tax brackets high enough for them to consider the use of tax-free municipal bonds in their portfolios. These folks also follow markets, watch TV, and read news stories about the financial markets. They are exposed to headline risk. And when they sell out of fear, they usually move in a herd-like fashion and thus exacerbate the volatility of market shifts. Examples of headline risk and its aftermath will be examined in Chapter 11.

Chapters 12 and 13 detail challenges facing two major municipal bond issuers: the Commonwealth of Puerto Rico and the State of Illinois. These entities were dealt a difficult hand with the onset of the Great Recession and have been slow to enact reforms to shore up their finances. Because they have $120 billion in combined debt outstanding, news regarding the fiscal health of these entities has far-reaching implications for other issuers in the market. In Chapters 12 and 13 we discuss the current problems facing these two behemoths, how they got where they are, and the road ahead.

Chapter 14 discusses a special topic that has arisen in the aftermath of the recession: What many have called America's "infrastructure cliff" and the role of state and local governments in paying for infrastructure projects. Contrary to what media and pundits say, public infrastructure spending on transportation infrastructure is the highest it has ever been and is poised to continue increasing. We address this hot-button topic at length in this chapter.

Chapter 15 discusses the problems impacting New Jersey and the state's ongoing failure to make contributions to its pension system. We discuss the state's unaffordable spending trajectory and use of debt as a palliative to solve its budgetary shortfalls over the course of decades. Like Illinois, the Garden State has large unfunded liabilities that will most likely be resolved with litigation.

All these bond-related issues, their nuances, descriptions, and details make up thousands of matters that require study and surveillance. They make up Muniland.

In the back of this book is a glossary of terms that may be helpful to readers. It is not complete, but it is instructive. It will hopefully assist readers as they make their way through their adventures in Muniland.

In the second section of the book, there is a compilation of the Muniland research pieces published by Cumberland Advisors during the last five years. We have not cherry-picked some and avoided others, nor have we changed the content in view of subsequent developments. This section of the book shows how we saw the Muniland events as they unfolded in real time. Financial markets are always functioning as a discounting mechanism and with some uncertainty. That is true for all asset classes. It is certainly true for Muniland. The commentaries section of the book is designed to show the investment process from the perspective of a real money manager who is making buy, sell, and hold decisions in the muni space.

Section I

The Transformation of an Entire Asset Class

1
The Changing Face of the Municipal Bond Market

The linkages between financial market entities prior to the collapse of Bear Stearns in the spring of 2008 were more complex than anyone could have predicted. The municipal bond market, once thought of as a tranquil silo within the modern financial system, was dominated by an insulated retail buyer base that traded bonds relatively infrequently. A buyer, in his search for bonds, sought out AAA insurance with the understanding that credit risk was de minimis and large changes in market value would never occur. Little did muni market participants know that the collapse of two Bear Stearns hedge funds in June 2007 would set in motion a series of events that would eventually impact all municipal market entities.

The financial crisis impacted munis through financial market disruptions and the negative feedback loop into the real economy. State and local governments faced revenue shortfalls and higher pension contributions. Dealer trading desks lost market-making liquidity because of a lack of confidence and losses in other business lines. Tender-option bond (TOB) programs lost short-term money market investors who refused to roll their short-term debt.[1] The confluence of financial market impacts and the negative feedback loop into the real economy impacted all market players in some way.

Municipal Market Analytics (MMA), a municipal bond market research firm, has written extensively on the subject of spillover effects from other asset classes into municipal bonds. We rehash some of their thoughts here and highly recommend that interested readers look into their work.[2]

Bond insurers were the canary in the coal mine for stresses that would later present themselves in munis.[3] Their exposure to subprime mortgages and collateralized debt obligations (CDOs) created a downward spiral. This led to the insurers' reduced capital levels and resulted in credit rating downgrades and a reduced perceived value by investors of their bond insurance policies. In 2007, the trouble began in the municipal auction rate market where long-term bonds were sold at an auction rate and re-priced at a short-term rate that rose until a price would clear the market. At one point, the Port Authority of New York and New Jersey was priced at 20% interest for short-term, auction-rate securities before falling back.[4] These troubles soon affected the short-term, variable-rate demand bond (VRDO) market and would later impact all insurance-wrapped issues. Once a VRDO was put back to the remarketing agent and could not be remarketed, these bonds would become obligations of letter of credit (LOC) providers, and interest rates would reset to upwards of 12%, creating liquidity pressures for these issuers. This problem would eventually correct itself as these issuers later refinanced these bonds. From the start of the crisis to 2012, the number of monolines actively writing new business declined from 10 to 1. Bonds that initially traded as risk-free now traded with risk premiums based on their underlying ratings.

Starting in early 2008, hedge funds and levered TOB programs were unable to roll their short-term debt, either because of downgrades or money market fund liquidity constraints. They were forced to sell bonds into a market without any buyers.[5] Retail investors, always the last to the party, amplified the selling pressure in their reaction to negative events. The sell-off occurred in all gradations of municipal bond debt, including high-grade issuers such as the State of Utah and New York City Municipal Water Finance Authority. At this point, municipal issuers had not yet felt the brunt of the recession on their balance sheets: The financial crisis was purely a loss of liquidity, which would later cause widening reverberations into the real economy. This loss of liquidity increased volatility and created difficult conditions for both secondary market participants and issuers. Chapter 11, "Headline Risk in the Municipal Bond Market," discusses loss of liquidity as a result of headline risk in greater detail.

To better grasp the stagnation that occurred during this period, consider the relationship between 30-year municipal bonds and Treasuries. During normal times, municipal bonds will trade at lower yields than Treasuries, reflecting their tax-exempt status while Treasuries are taxable.[6] Prior to the financial crisis, the ratio of these two asset classes averaged roughly 90%. When tax-exempt bond yields increased to more than 100% of Treasuries, taxable mutual funds, arbitrage desks, and other "tactical" buyers would step in to purchase muni bonds and drive yields back down to their historical equilibrium levels. In late December 2008, due to panic selling, muni yields spiked to 223% of Treasury yields, a 5.4 standard deviation move. We map this out in Figure 1.1.

Figure 1.1

Panic Selling in Municipal Bonds

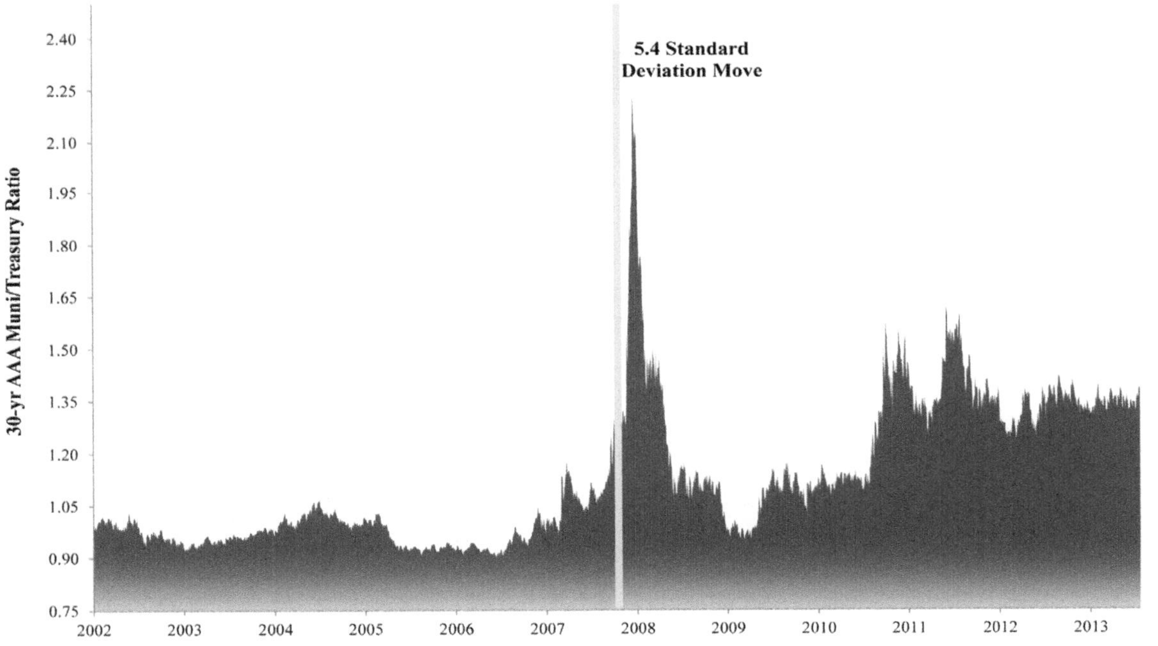

Source: Cumberland Advisors, Bloomberg, Municipal Market Advisors

As the chart indicates, prior to 2008, the ratio remained range-bound without major swings. Since the crisis, to the right of the vertical line, the ratio of muni to Treasury yields has stayed elevated. The financial crisis, which decreased use of borrowed money, reduced the amount of players in the space, and by extension, the amount of capital in the municipal bond market. Arbitrage came to a standstill. Market dislocation ensued. This reduction in capital had major ramifications for the rest of the public finance sector. How do state and local governments invest in new projects, pay personnel, or fund their operations in the short-term when the credit channel is broken?

Lack of market activity meant that intra-market yield and correlation relationships broke down. Consider the yield spread relationship between general obligation bonds and revenue bonds. Prior to 2008, these two bond sectors traded in close proximity with the average spread ranging anywhere from 10 to 15 basis points. Indeed, in Figure 1.2 we see a close relationship in the years leading to the financial crisis, with a divergence in the post-crisis period. The post-crisis spread has averaged 40 basis points. The rolling 30-day average correlation between the two declined substantially after the financial crisis, from 0.93 before the crisis to 0.73 afterwards. Correlation is still significantly positive, but much less so after the crisis. When markets function properly, correlation is possible.

Figure 1.2 **Breakdown in Intra-Market Yield Relationships**

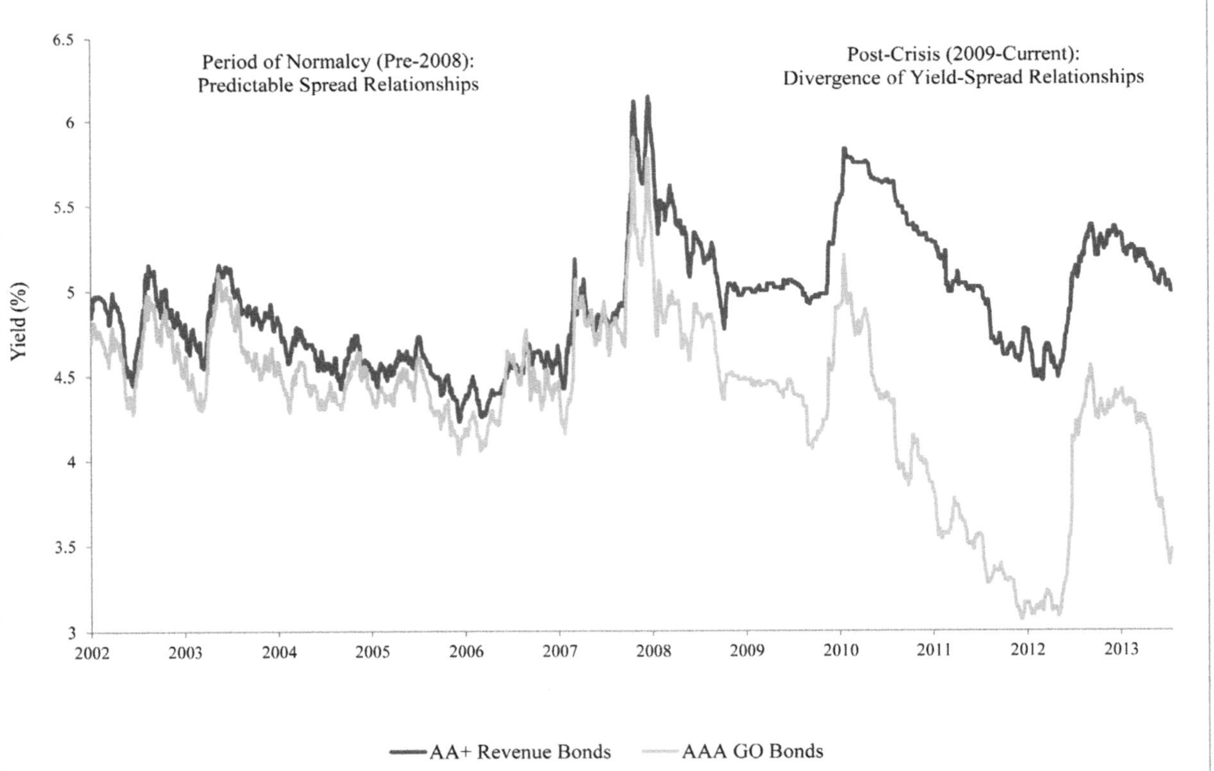

Source: Bloomberg, Cumberland Advisors

Muni market volatility has increased post-crisis as well. Headline risks, both in the U.S. and abroad, have created a fear-driven marketplace, marked by panic selling. Post-crisis, volatility has increased during such market events as the European sovereign debt crisis in early 2012, the "Credit Scare of 2010-2011," Fed tapering fears starting in mid-2013, and the Puerto Rico sell-off in late 2013. We discuss these headline-risk sell-offs in Chapter 11. In Figure 1.3, we see the historical one-month volatility of the 30-year, AAA-rated GO bond increasing from 11% pre-crisis to 17% post-crisis. We attribute this rise to overreaction by the muni market's large retail investor component, since roughly 70% of outstanding municipal debt is owned by individuals through retail accounts, mutual funds, or money market funds.

Figure 1.3 **Heightened Volatility from Retail Selling**

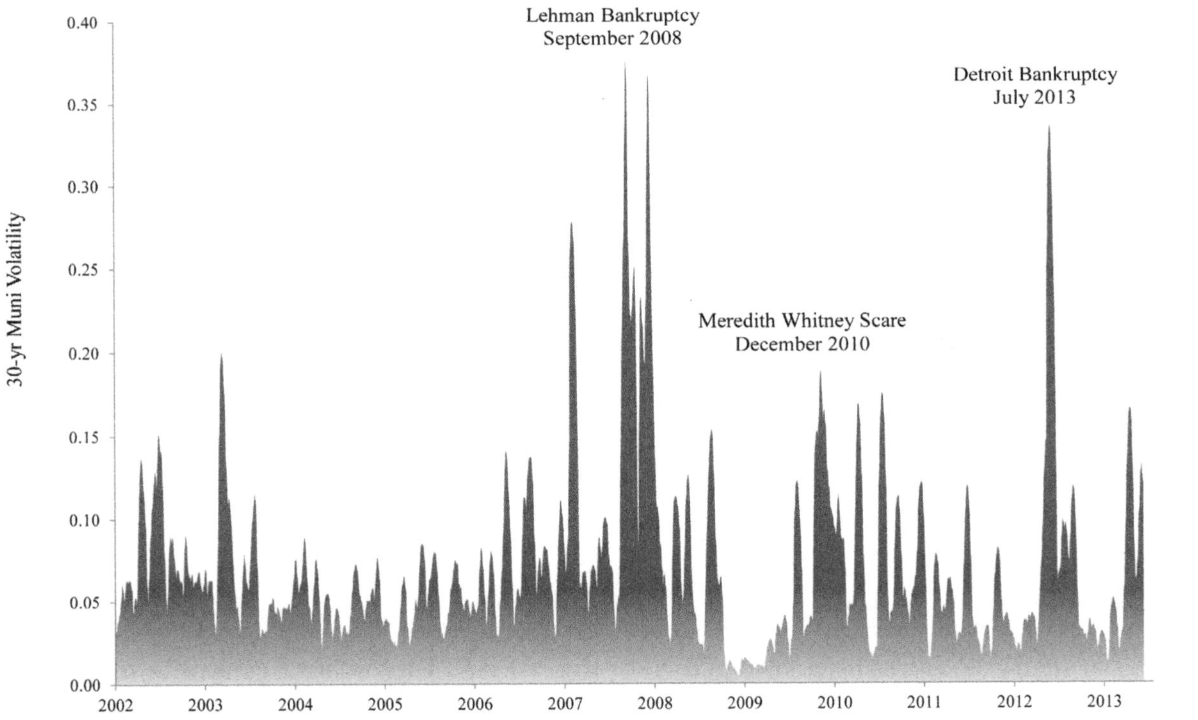

Source: Bloomberg, Cumberland Advisors

This post-crisis volatility is present in securities considered to be virtually credit risk free and not just in low-rated securities, hence our choice in graphing the yield of a security rated AAA versus the yield of a distressed credit. During periods when investors sell for liquidity, they sell off high-grade securities because that is all they can sell. This is counterintuitive because, as Figure 1.3 demonstrates, isolated credit risks in distressed parts of the market such as Detroit, Puerto Rico, and Harrisburg result in news headlines that spook retail investors and cause selling throughout the entire market, including the market's highest-grade securities. A missed interest payment by a distressed city such as Detroit will not impact the ability of AAA-rated Washington Suburban Sanitation District to provide water and sewer services to residents of Montgomery and Prince George's counties in Maryland. Hence, headline risk specific to the muni market is a new risk we see in the post-crisis market and one that is very difficult to guard against or hedge.

We find that the market is much more diffuse than it was prior to the crisis; sources of returns have changed; and investor behavior and attitudes are different.

Until the demise of bond insurers in 2007, roughly 50% of municipal bond issuance was insured, and the market was considered a "rates-driven" market. By "rates-driven," we mean that munis traded with little compensation for credit risk and there was little credit-spread differentiation between securities. Little due diligence was required on the part of the investor for two reasons: (1) the low historical default risk of the asset class as a whole, which has been *de minimis* (1/40th of that in corporates) and (2) the majority of the actively traded bonds in the market were insured.

The line of thinking went as follows: A bond was either AAA-rated or it wasn't. Buyers purchased these "riskless" commoditized investments because of the insurance policy "wrapping" them.[7] Market supply, demand, and monetary policy were often the primary determinants of yield in the markets. If you did your homework on the handful of insurers wrapping the municipal bonds, you had an understanding of the fundamental credit factors that would ultimately determine the value of 50% of the market. Credit quality was not a concern except in distressed scenarios.

The downgrading of the monolines changed all of this. Several insurer ratings were ultimately downgraded to distressed levels. There were 10 bond insurers actively writing new bond insurance business in 2006. Of those rated AAA during this time, three entered bankruptcy; five became insolvent and had their ratings withdrawn; and only two are actively writing new bond insurance policies.[8]

Figure 1.4 shows the current ratings versus the ratings of bond insurers in 2007.[9] Investors' distrust in bond insurance diminished the role of bond insurance in the market to the point that, currently, only 12% of issuance is insured. Credit analysis once entrusted to the bond insurers shifted over to buy-side institutions as investors looked to each underlying issuer's creditworthiness.[10] Whereas little compensation was given in the past for purchasing AAA-wrapped bonds with BBB underlying ratings, as opposed to AAA-wrapped bonds with AA underlying ratings, investors' attitudes toward risk have changed. We are now in a marketplace where defaults and major stresses have occurred in major cities such as Detroit and Harrisburg.

Figure 1.4

	Moody's		**S&P**	
	Original	*Current*	*Original*	*Current*
Ambac	Aaa	NR	AAA	NR
Assured Guaranty	Aaa	A2	AAA	AA-
Assured Guaranty Municipal	Aaa	A2	AAA	AA-
Build American Mutual	NR	NR	AA	AA
Berkshire Hathaway	Aaa	Aa1	AAA	AA+
CIFG	Aaa	NR	AAA	NR
FGIC Corp	Aaa	NR	AAA	NR
Municipal Assurance Corp	NR	NR	AA+	AA+
National Public Finance Guarantee	Aaa	Baa1	AAA	A
Radian	Aa3	Ba1	AA	B+
Syncora Guarantee	Aaa	NR	AAA	NR
Syncora Capital Assurance	Aaa	NR	AAA	NR
ACA Capital	NR	NR	A	NR

Source: Raymond James

In its 2014 outlook for local governments, Moody's paints a picture of the future given the state of the economy as of late 2014. Weak disposable personal income growth of roughly 1.5% annually (versus 3% annually prior to the recession), higher savings rates, and lower consumer spending have created stresses for municipalities and their related entities.[11] Low income growth and higher savings have reduced income and sales tax revenues, while high joblessness has created pressures on states' abilities to fund social welfare programs.[12] According to Moody's, in the past few years, municipal entities have been able to raise fees to make up for these revenue deficiencies.[13] While states have been able to cut expenditures more easily due to their role as a funding and disbursement mechanism of moneys, local municipalities, which are charged with provision of services, have faced higher deficits. Because the services they provide, such as public safety and K-12 education, are essential, it is likely that local municipalities will continue to run deficits. We believe these trends will impact not just local governments but all issuers in the space. Cuts on the state level have been down-streamed, and rebalancing has been difficult. The costs of labor union contracts have risen steadily. Continual provision of social programs and services in the face of rising costs and a declining revenue base are themes we will continue to see.

As of June 2015, Moody's describes trends as being consistent with the "new stable," stating that "credit quality is not as benign as it was before the crisis, nor will be anytime soon." A "new stable" era in munis does mean, however, that "credit risks are more visible and predictable."[14] As most local governments have done the dirty work of rationalizing their cost structures by reducing employee headcounts and negotiating benefit packages to cope with constrained resources, conditions are no longer getting worse; but neither are they returning to what they were prior to 2008.[15]

State and local governments were stronger and more able to withstand economic pressures than they had been at any time in the past. The regions that fared the best during this time were states rich in energy resources.[16] Regions that fared the worst were mostly concentrated in the Midwest, in places that did not benefit from the economic expansion.[17] Some of the stresses in the housing sector began to spread to the broader economy, slowing tax revenues and impacting high-growth states, such as Florida and California, which were heavily exposed to real estate development.[18] Declines in construction employment hit these states as well, leading to long-term unemployment of many construction workers.[19] Just as revenues declined as a result of slowed business activity, demand for Medicaid and public assistance programs increased because of the larger number of unemployed workers. With the expansion of Medicaid under the Obama Administration, Medicaid increased from 16% of states' budgetary expenditures to 25%.[20] Unemployment insurance programs were also a continued source of stress.

The 2008 stock market decline also took its toll in unexpected ways. Those states, such as California, that derive a substantial amount of their revenues from capital gains and income taxes saw steep declines in tax revenues.[21] In Figure 1.5, we show the steep drop in California income tax collections, which declined from their peak of $65 billion in 2008 to a low of $52 billion in 2010. Income tax collections, the state's primary source of revenues, have since recovered because of tax increases and strong stock market performance.

Figure 1.5

California Income Tax Collections: Steep Drop and Recovery

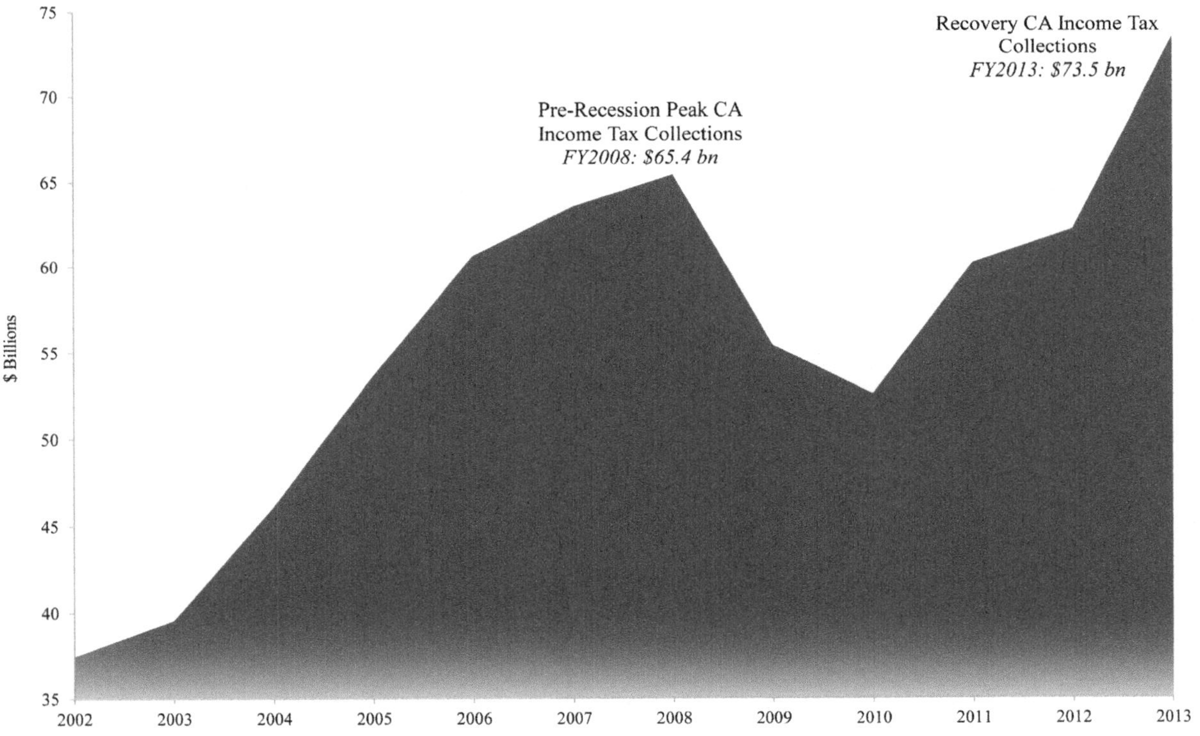

Source: Bloomberg

On the cost side, the stock market decline in 2008 reduced the value of pension fund assets securing workers' retirement benefits, increasing required contributions at a time when state and local governments could least afford them.[22] In the years following the financial crisis, renegotiation of collective bargaining agreements governing pension benefits and employee wages were highly contentious issues that were heavily litigated, costing municipalities a lot of money to fight in court.

As we continue in this post-recession, uneven-growth environment, there are many unanswered questions and unforeseen risks to state and local governments. Will heightened joblessness force municipalities to further cut staffs to reduce deficits?[23] Will sequestration cuts to states reduce revenues to local governments for funding important policy priorities such as K-12 education? What will be the impacts of state and local government entitlement reforms, and how will entitlement beneficiaries fare versus bondholders in distressed scenarios?[24] The answers to these questions will impact not only investment decisions for market practitioners but also the daily civic lives of all Americans. In the chapters that follow, we discuss these trends and the sea change we have seen in the municipal bond market since the crisis.

2

A Profile of the Municipal Bond Market

The municipal bond market is dispersed and varied.[1] There are roughly 50,000 issuers of municipal debt across some 40 or so sectors, with different legal structures, in different states, serving diverse regions of the country.[2] Indeed, it may at first seem implausible to find a tie that binds these different issuers. Given that municipal issuers are impacted by the varying regional industry, demographic, and business trends endemic to the areas they service, how are any two separate entities operating in different states related at all? How is the fiscal health of local utilities operating in California, for example, related to special-purpose financing districts in Florida, or even California, for that matter?

The answer to these questions is "Federalism" and the hierarchical structure of the municipal market. Figure 2.1 shows the structure of municipal market issuers, highlighting the verticality of issuing entities at the various tiers of government. At the top of the hierarchy is the federal government, followed by states, who derive their power from the federal government via the U.S. Constitution. All other entities within the governmental sector (e.g., towns, counties, toll roads, and airports are creatures of their states).[3] To the right of the government hierarchy in Figure 2.1 are organizations that operate for exempt purposes under section 501(c)(3) of the Internal Revenue Code. These entities are able to issue debt securities exempt from federal taxation and are therefore lumped into the "municipal bond asset class," despite having little in common with state and local governments.

Figure 2.1

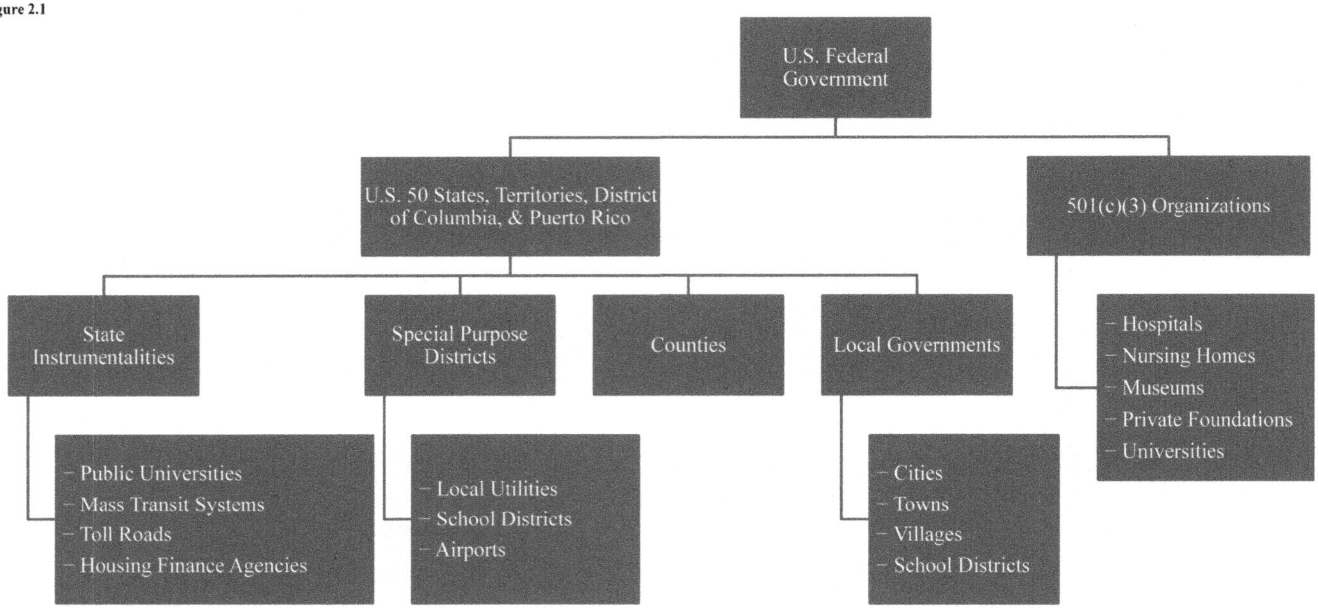

Source: Cumberland Advisors

There is a complex web of fiscal and regulatory relationships that form the basis of both state and local governments as we know them today. Local governments are "creatures" of their states, and states somewhat resemble the federal government, but are independent from the federal government under the American concept of dual federalism.[4] The idea that local governments are "creatures" of their states was penned by American jurist John Forrest Dillon, who wrote extensively in court rulings on the powers given to municipalities by states.[5]

What constitutes a government in the United States is a very complex matter governed by federal and state law, court decisions, and an analysis of facts and circumstances; it is open to legal interpretation and depends on the regulatory environment and taxation.[6] The IRS, the Federal Unemployment Tax Act (FUTA), and the Federal Insurance Contributions Act (FICA) all define the term "government" differently for purposes of taxation. It is really not as straightforward as most people would think.[7]

We classify governmental issuers of tax-exempt debt into three broad categories. Our classification comes from IRS code:[8]

1. States, which operate as sovereign entities with broad powers defined under the U.S. Constitution
2. Instrumentalities, which are public benefit corporations closely related to state and local governments by ownership or control, serving a defined and narrow purpose such as operating a mass transit system or a public university
3. Political subdivisions, which are state-chartered municipal corporations (e.g., cities, towns, villages, and school districts) that exercise the three primary sovereign powers of government: policing and law enforcement, taxation, and eminent domain

Fiscal and statutory interdependencies bind governmental issuers to their enabling governments. Local governments depend on states primarily for the funding of K-12 education, while state governments fund social welfare programs such as Medicaid from federal mandatory outlays. Such relationships create vertical interdependencies. The United States is a country comprised of 50 separate republics, five inhabited territories, and one district, all with their own statutes and administrative laws governing the bodies politic operating within their borders.[9] State governments are vertically integrated entities that receive federal outlays for means-tested welfare and social insurance programs that increase during business-cycle contractions, providing a buffer against falling tax revenues.[10]

The American dual federalist system, as spelled out in the U.S. Constitution, specifies the legal apparatus that governs the interplay between each of the 50 states and the federal government. The dual federalist system originated from the need for a central government to defend itself from foreign adversaries while preserving the sovereignty of the 13 colonies that fought for freedom against the centralized authority of the British Empire.[11] Preserving state sovereignty was essential to win votes for the ratification of the Constitution from anti-federalist colonies such as Virginia, New York, and Rhode Island.[12]

Aside from the federal government, the states are the only governmental units other than the federal government addressed by the U.S. Constitution.[13] Figure 2.2 lists the powers of states versus the federal government. The powers of states are more involved with practical matters impacting the daily civic lives of U.S. citizens (e.g., licensure or setting smoking ages), while the federal government is involved with items that affect the collective interests of citizens on a broader scale (e.g., declaring war).[14]

Figure 2.2

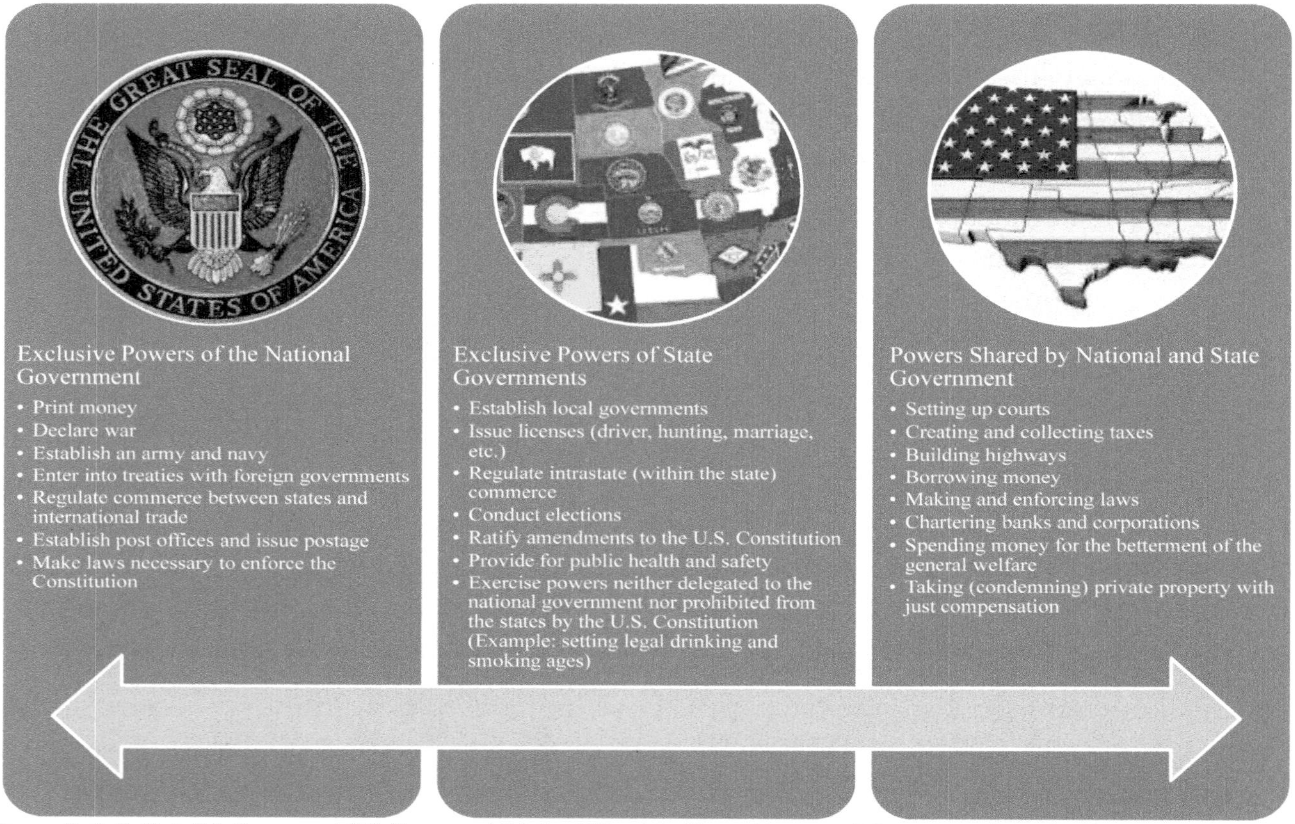

Exclusive Powers of the National Government
• Print money
• Declare war
• Establish an army and navy
• Enter into treaties with foreign governments
• Regulate commerce between states and international trade
• Establish post offices and issue postage
• Make laws necessary to enforce the Constitution
Exclusive Powers of State Governments
• Establish local governments
• Issue licenses (driver, hunting, marriage, etc.)
• Regulate intrastate (within the state) commerce
• Conduct elections
• Ratify amendments to the U.S. Constitution
• Provide for public health and safety
• Exercise powers neither delegated to the national government nor prohibited from the states by the U.S. Constitution (Example: setting legal drinking and smoking ages)
Powers Shared by National and State Government
• Setting up courts
• Creating and collecting taxes
• Building highways
• Borrowing money
• Making and enforcing laws
• Chartering banks and corporations
• Spending money for the betterment of the general welfare
• Taking (condemning) private property with just compensation

Source: Ben's Guide to U.S. Government, U.S. Government Printing Office <http://bensguide.gpo.gov/6-8/government/federalism2.html>

The federal government can exert substantial control over state governments. The executive branch acts as both regulator and transmission mechanism through which fiscal policy that is passed by Congress is implemented via the 15 executive-branch departments and several independent regulatory agencies, such as the Department of Transportation and the Environmental Protection Agency. Through the passage of continuing resolutions by Congress, U.S. federal outlays are allocated to pay for major budgetary items such as defense spending, Medicaid, and interest on debt.[15]

A definitive piece published by the Congressional Budget Office (CBO) in 2013 entitled *Federal Grants to State and Local Governments* shows that historically, approximately 12% of federal outlays were transferred to U.S. states, primarily to provide grants for social safety net programs such as Medicaid and Temporary Assistance for Needy Families (TANF).[16] Figure 2.3 depicts this historical level of federal support. As the chart indicates, outlays to state and local governments have increased substantially since 1980. This chart describes in a nutshell one of the primary problems currently pressuring both federal and state budgets: rising entitlement spending.

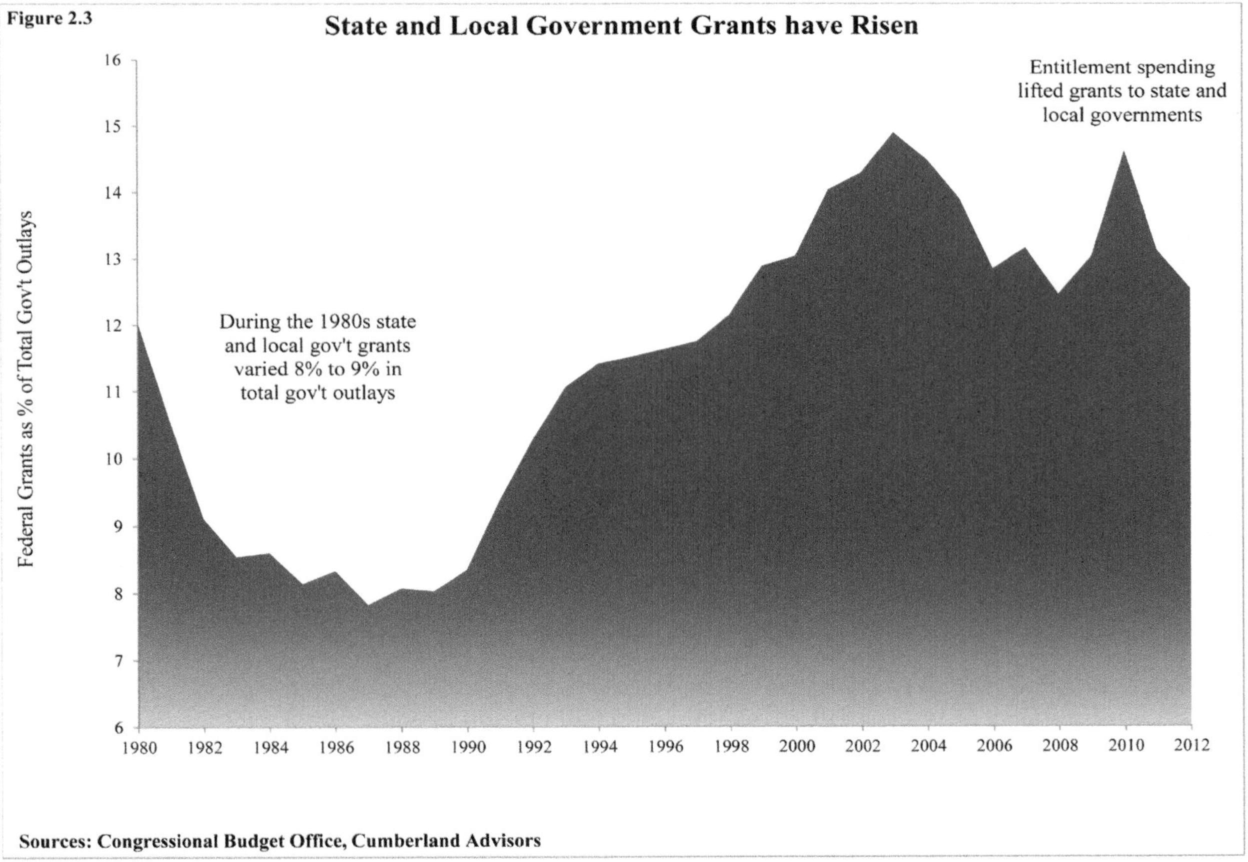

The CBO states that providing grants to states for these programs is the primary way in which U.S. federal government fiscal policy impacts states. Through such programs, the financial health of U.S. states is strongly linked with U.S. fiscal policy and U.S. politics at the federal level. In 2012, on average, 28% of total state governmental revenues came from federal government fiscal transfers.[17] Fiscal transfers amounting to 90% of this amount were then paid out to political subdivisions and instrumentalities within the states, with the balance used to pay for welfare programs such as unemployment insurance and various other subsidies on the state level.[18]

The CBO study also points out that federal grants typically finance activities that state and local governments fund out of their revenues, thereby having a direct impact on state expenditures.[19] As a result, the growing cost of administering federal fiscal policy via entitlement programs delivered on the state level adds to state budgetary expenditures.[20] Healthcare spending on Medicaid by states and the federal government is the primary culprit for these growing costs. Figure 2.4 depicts this rise, which is dominated by healthcare spending.

Figure 2.4

Medicaid Spending Dominated Rise in Entitlements

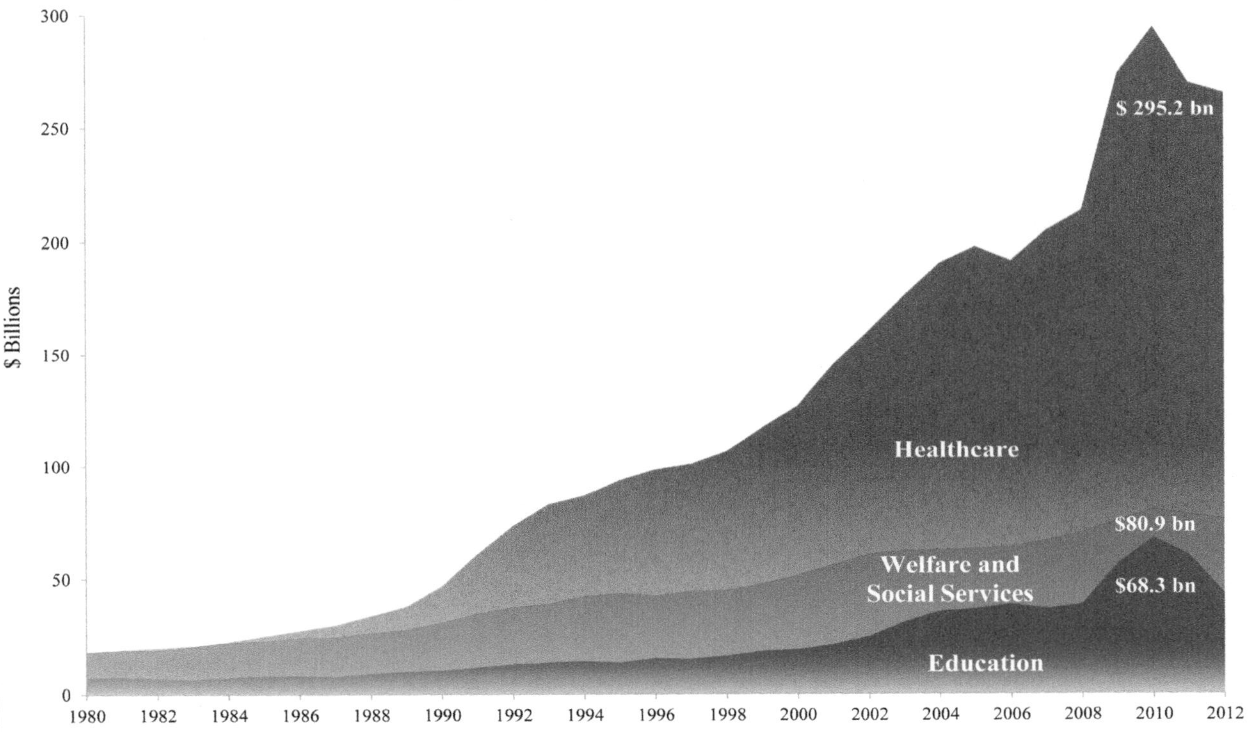

Sources: Federal Reserve Bank of St. Louis FRED Database, Congressional Budget Office, Cumberland Advisors

Grants to state governments are mandatory spending (i.e., the outlays for those programs are governed by state statutes and not annual appropriation acts).[21] State entitlement spending is non-discretionary, similar to interest payments on debt. Paraphrasing from CBO, "spending on so-called entitlement programs is controlled by eligibility and benefit criteria established in the programs' authorizing legislation," and people may enroll in these programs if they meet state-established eligibility requirements.[22] The burden of funding those programs often falls more heavily on state governments during economic downturns, when these programs are utilized the most.

The belief that the federal government administers all fiscal policy is only half true; states also play a role, namely for open-ended programs such as Medicaid and Food Stamps (SNAP—Supplemental Nutrition Assistance Program). According to CBO, "federal government grants to state and local governments" act as "automatic stabilizers" because spending increases when the economy contracts.[23]

National Association of State Budget Officers (NASBO) states, "The federal government is the banker to states during recessions."[24] Fiscal transfers from the federal government to states increase during recessionary periods, when tax revenues decline, to make up the deficiency in tax revenues used to pay for current expenditures. When unemployment increases during recessionary periods, demand for means-tested and social safety net programs increase.[25] The federal government increases funds allocated to states during these times because it can more easily borrow money during periods of economic weakness.[26]

CBO states that these grant programs "with open-ended funding commitments," such as SNAP or Temporary Assistance for Needy Families, tend to smooth peaks and troughs of the business cycle, providing economic stimulus by boosting incomes and expenditures.[27] In contrast to states, the federal government is able to spend more than it collects through taxes because it is a "monetary sovereign" with the ability to influence the money supply to avoid insolvency.[28]

State credit quality has declined in recent years because of the greater responsibility shouldered by states to pay for mandatory expenditures. Federal transfers for entitlements have increased by 28% in the last six years, from 24% of total revenues in 2006 to 28% in 2012.[29] Figure 2.4 shows that although healthcare spending by the federal government started increasing in the late 1980s, it really took off in 2009 and 2010.[30] Sales taxes, and personal and corporate income taxes, which together constitute 42% of total state revenues, have increased by only 11.5% during the same period.[31]

Federal government transfers vary widely by state, depending on the matching percentages that are determined by Federal Medical Assistance Percentages (FMAP). FMAP determines funding amounts based on need-based metrics such as per capita income levels. For example, the state with the lowest per capita income, Mississippi, receives 45% of its revenues from the federal government, while Virginia receives just 25%.[32]

According to the Center on Budget and Policy Priorities (CBPP), government programs often match dollars of state funding with three to five times the amount in federal funding to entice states to enact federal policy priorities.[33] In 2013, there were over 900 such federal government programs administered by 30 federal instrumentalities and agencies for specific projects or programs.[34] None of these programs provide general fund assistance; instead, they target specific projects and federal policy priorities.[35] The largest such federal program administered by states, Medicaid, has grown rapidly and has crowded out other policy priorities such as continuing highway investment, higher education, and even income security programs such as TANF. According to CBO, Medicaid will dominate state and federal government spending in the coming decade and will increase as a share of the economy.[36] To the extent that eligibility, enrollments, and healthcare costs increase, states will shoulder, on average, 50% of these cost increases.[37]

Higher education and K-12 education expenditures are the second largest state budgetary priority after means-tested welfare and social insurance programs. Public higher education is available in the United States, with funding coming primarily from state and local governments, and with specific policies for K-12 education set by local school districts. In 2013, the total amount spent on public education by state and local governments was \$580 billion—approximately \$500 billion for K-12 education and \$80 billion for higher education—more than the federal government spent on national defense.[38] These costs to state and local governments have increased as well, but in a more controlled fashion, mimicking the rate of inflation.

Figure 2.5 graphs the growth in these costs since the late 1970s. Education spending has increased consistently since that time but started to decline in 2008, consistent with fiscal belt-tightening on the state and local level as a result of state tax revenue declines.

Figure 2.5 **Decline in K-12 Education Spending**

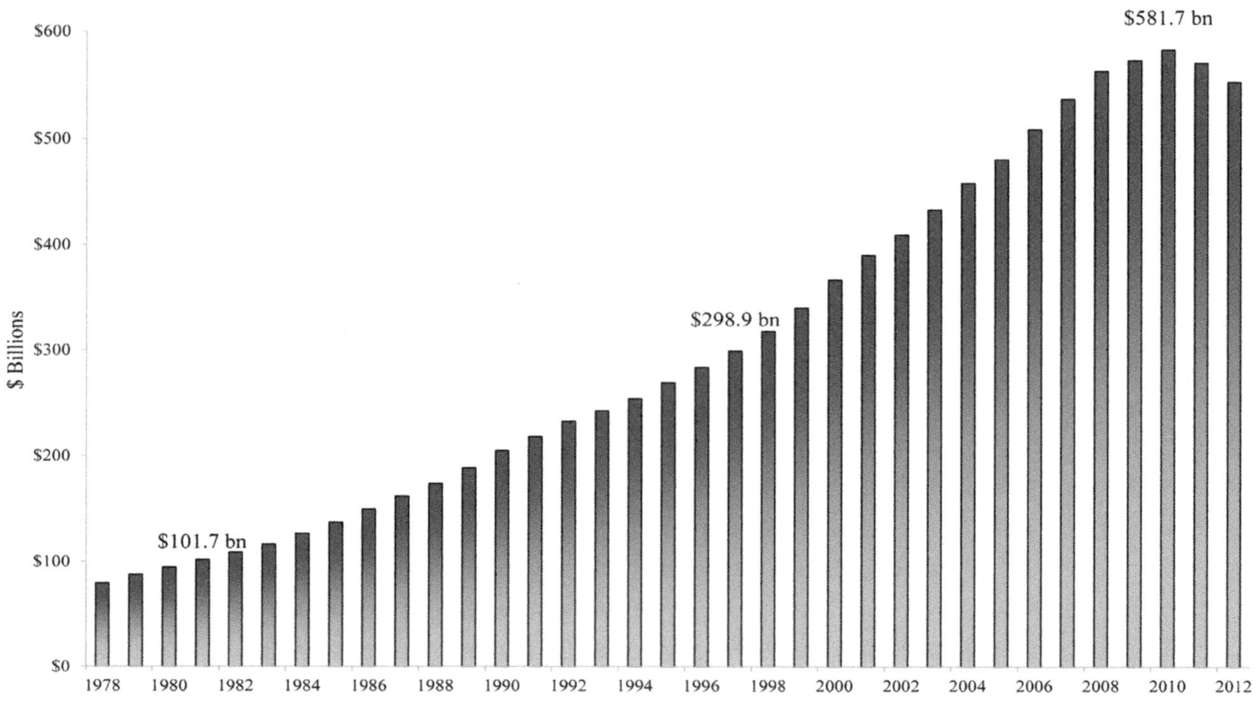

Sources: Federal Reserve Bank of St. Louis FRED Database, Census Bureau Government Finance Statistics

Public higher education has been an important component of public policy and a necessity for upward mobility. It is funded primarily by states, and like other areas of state spending, has experienced funding declines in the current budgetary environment. Higher education programs are unique, however, because they can be paid for with other revenue sources, such as tuition and student fees, in addition to state appropriations.[39]

According to the State Higher Education Executive Officers Association (SHEEO), competing budgetary priorities, current economic conditions, and demographic trends often determine "policies and decisions about the financing of higher education."[40] States fund 90% of grants and appropriations to higher education out of general fund expenditures, with the balance coming from local governments.[41] These funding streams amount to approximately 50% of the operating expenses of higher education institutions, with the balance paid for by tuition revenues.[42]

SHEEO states that the 2008 recession dramatically reduced state and local support of higher education, consequently shifting a "larger" burden "of the cost of higher education" to students through tuition increases between 30% and 43% annually from 2008 to 2012 while cutting state-sourced higher education expenditures by 40% during this period.[43] Our friend Natalie Cohen points out that *total spending* didn't decline, but the state portion of it.[44] Such draconian measures have been possible because higher education is seen as a "soft" budgetary item that can be easily cut during periods of economic weakness in an environment of declining tax revenues.[45] Shifting more higher education costs to college students while minimizing actual "cuts" to personnel or programs is seen as more politically palatable than cutting K-12 funding (thereby precipitating teacher layoffs) or services to Medicaid beneficiaries. As demand for higher education typically increases during recessionary periods, students have little choice but to pay these increased costs, as public higher education remains the lower-cost alternative to private higher education.[46]

The steep decline and subsequent depressed growth in sales and income tax revenues from 2008 to 2012 occurred (perhaps coincidentally) in conjunction with an increase in demand for higher education, resulting in part from a 13% increase in the 18- to 24-year-old population.[47] Figure 2.6 shows that state tax collections declined nationwide by 10% from 2008 to 2010. The decline in tax revenues during that period is a theme we revisit in this book when we discuss the states of Illinois and New Jersey in Chapter 13, "Pension Problems and The Land of Lincoln," and Chapter 15, "A Tale of Broken Promises: Trouble in the Garden State," respectively.

Figure 2.6

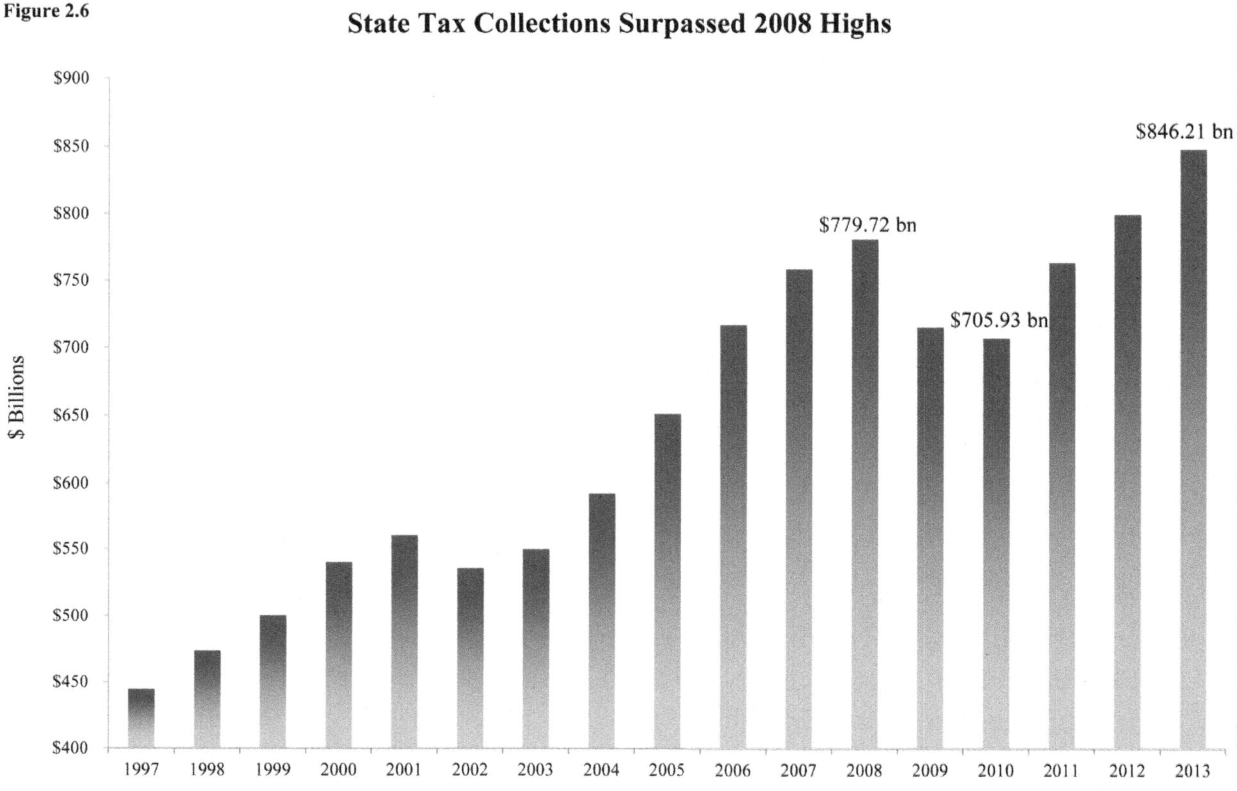

Sources: Federal Reserve Bank of St. Louis FRED Database, Census Bureau Government Finance Statistics

Although collections have since recovered due to higher rates, the steep decline pressured budgetary expenditures, especially on discretionary items such as higher education. SHEEO states that the confluence of both lower collections and higher demand forced universities to spread higher education appropriations revenues more thinly to serve a much larger student body, thus creating a deflationary scenario where universities were forced to consolidate their operations, cutting faculty and course offerings while charging higher tuition.[48] The 40% decline in appropriations to higher education during this period has been met with increased tuition rates of roughly 30%.[49] The trend is both pro-cyclical and secular, and it is exacerbated during recessionary periods.

According to NASBO, K-12 education commands a considerably larger slice of state budgets than higher education.[50] In 2012, states spent $80 billion on higher education versus $327 billion for K-12 education—the "largest single component of state general fund spending."[51] K-12 funding levels by state and local governments have typically been four to five times the amount spent on higher education. There are obvious reasons for this disparity: K-12 education encompasses 13 grades instead of just 4 years, and K-12 school districts lack the tuition revenues that colleges, universities, and technical schools collect. Nonetheless, this underscores the relative size of funding K-12 education versus other priorities, and its importance as a policy priority.

CBPP does an excellent job of summarizing the U.S. system of funding of K-12 education in an article titled, "Overview of K-12 Education Finance." In it they state the following:

> *There are over 14,000 active school districts in the United States, governing approximately 90,000 individual schools. The districts vary considerably in size, ranging from the New York City public school system, which enrolls over one million students, to more than 1,000 primarily rural school districts educating less than one hundred students each. The primary expense every school district incurs is the cost of hiring its share of the nation's 2.9 million public school teachers.*[52]

According to CBPP, whereas in the past 20 years the state share of spending on higher education has declined 22% on average, its share of funding for K-12 education has doubled.[53] Most states transfer funds to school districts in amounts based on specific factors relating to a district's tax base and ability to raise taxes, and they distribute proportionately more of those funds to districts most in need.

Wealth levels and the number of students enrolled in a given school district will determine school funding amounts to some degree.[54] Higher transfers to less wealthy school districts, using property values as a proxy for wealth, ensure nearly equal treatment of students in underprivileged areas. This concept is known as "equalization."[55] CBPP states that "In recent years approximately 50% of K-12 education funds have come from state-level appropriations, 44% have come from local revenues and 7% from the federal government," with the exact percentages paid by states determined by these equalization formulas allowing for increased transfers to lower-wealth school districts.[56]

Local taxes are used, in part, to fund education because they are a predictable funding source and easy to collect. Many states distinguish between education funding for capital expenditures and operating expenses. States are more likely to provide support and equalization for operating expenses because the "cost, schedule, design, scope and financing" of capital expenditures are locally controlled.[57] State funding for K-12 education from 2008 to 2012 declined only 5.5% versus close to 28% for public higher education institutions, suggesting that states value K-12 as an important component of discretionary spending.[58] But the rising school-age population and the inability to shift costs by raising tuition forced cuts downstream to school districts, effectively reducing the funding per student that states provided. Since the recession, a number of states have moved toward increasing their share of funding K-12 by substituting state funds for local funds in order to reduce local governments' reliance on property taxes.

We have discussed the fiscal interrelationships between the federal government and states, and between states and local governments. While the linkages in terms of dollar amounts are great, the practical function of states in public finance and in daily life is quite small. In the past decade, state governments have issued only 10.4% of total muni bond issuance, with the remainder from other political subdivisions such as cities, counties, towns, and state or local-sanctioned instrumentalities such as local authorities and utilities.[59] Constitutional limitations on general fund debt issuance have forced much of the responsibility of providing services and servicing debt onto the plates of political subdivisions and instrumentalities, a trend exacerbated in recent years by greater entitlement funding needs and budget imbalances.[60] States function as "resource allocators," while local subdivisions and instrumentalities are the "service providers" or the "doers."

Because there are 50 state constitutions, each one delineating the rights of its municipalities, there are often important distinctions between the municipalities of different states. According to the National League of Cities, the authorities granted to municipalities by states can be broken down into four categories:[61]

1. Structural: The power to choose a given form of government such as Council-Manager or Mayor-Council forms
2. Functional: The power to exercise self-governance

3. Fiscal: The power to levy taxes
4. Personnel-related: The power to hire, set salaries, and negotiate collective bargaining contracts[62]

Political differences governing the enactment of laws over time have created competing philosophies over the interaction between states and local government. Ten states treat local governments as sovereign entities, giving them the power to legislate independently from the state as long as their laws do not conflict with state law. Municipalities with this independence are known as "home rule" municipalities. Home rule is employed by Alaska, Iowa, Massachusetts, Montana, New Jersey, New Mexico, Ohio, Oregon, South Carolina, and Utah.[63] The National League of Cities states that the powers and limits of home rule are defined on a state-by-state basis; provisions are "defined by each state's constitution" and enacted into law by state legislatures.[64] Municipalities given only explicit powers are known as "Dillon's Rule" municipalities.

The primary funding of local governments comes from property taxes and intergovernmental transfers from states. Property taxes, which are more stable than state sales or income taxes, are an important funding source because they ensure the stability of essential services provided on the local level (e.g., road maintenance, police and fire protection, and K-12 education).[65] State budget cuts do not disrupt essential services to the same extent as local government cuts.

There are many different types of local political subdivisions with differing powers. The powers and limits of these local political subdivisions are defined by the states. It is difficult to make generalizations about political subdivisions, as different states delegate different powers to political subdivisions similar in name but dissimilar in function. For example, while counties typically perform state-mandated duties such as property assessment, record keeping, and road maintenance,[66] counties in Florida have the power to levy property taxes to fund K-12 education. Counties in New Jersey typically levy taxes and fees to pay for correctional facilities, parks, and utilities, and have no such control over funding and providing education. Natalie Cohen states that "counties are typically responsible for social welfare programs for the indigent—and often run public 'safety-net' hospitals."[67]

A review of individual states shows that New Hampshire counties spend the majority of their revenues on public welfare services, while Virginia counties spend most of their revenues on education.[68] Maine counties spend the majority of their budgets on public safety.[69] The tie that binds counties is their position as intermediate, quasi-state entities without the autonomy of local governments, operating within a Dillon's Rule framework, with only those powers explicitly given to them by states.

On the local level, villages, towns, and cities are the basic forms of municipal government. The term "municipal government" refers to those entities granted the three primary powers of sovereign government by their states: policing and law enforcement, taxation, and eminent domain.[70] Whether a municipality is a village, town, or city depends on each state's laws regarding incorporation.[71] In a given state, municipalities termed to be "cities" will usually provide mixed-use zoning of residences, businesses, and industrial areas; and they meet population thresholds distinguishing them from smaller municipalities such as towns and villages.[72]

The population thresholds distinguishing cities, towns, and villages vary by state. Typically, villages are located in rural areas with small populations (usually less than 5,000 residents) and have fewer powers than towns, whereas a town will differ from a village based on population or whether or not it is incorporated. Towns are typically larger than villages; but in some states, for example North Carolina, there is no statutory distinction between the two.[73] In some instances, variation is purely due to different naming conventions. With such variations in mind, we use the term "municipality" as a catch-all to refer to all of these entities endowed with the three powers of government.

Local governments are responsible for providing general public services such as public safety, education, road maintenance, and health and welfare services to residents. State fiscal transfers are the primary funding source for these operations, constituting, on average, 33% of revenues, followed by property taxes (29%), user fees and charges (22%), with sales and income taxes, corporate income taxes, and federal aid making up the balance.[74] These services are deemed "highly essential," in that they lay the necessary groundwork for the basic daily needs of citizens. They are so essential that if someone were to take them away, the basic needs of a modern economy and society would likely be compromised. Effective law enforcement, for example, deters crime that might otherwise undermine civil order; K-12 education provides the required foundation for skills essential in an information-driven economy; good roads and traffic infrastructure are needed for the efficient transportation of goods and services.[75]

State and local governments govern the incorporation of towns, cities, and villages for the provision of some of these services. These services and other business-like functions can also be provided through the creation of "special districts." Special districts are given the power to levy taxes for particular needs, whereas instrumentalities are given the authority to charge user fees such as tolls and ticket fares. For example, fire districts can be created to levy taxes and borrow to finance the purchase of fire trucks and to provide fire safety to residents located within a special district's borders. These districts have been utilized heavily in Illinois and Rhode Island. The most widely used districts, although not technically considered "special districts," are school districts, which levy taxes to provide K-12 education to children. Mass transit systems such as Bay Area Rapid Transit (BART) in San Francisco and the New Jersey Turnpike Authority are examples of state-chartered instrumentalities that charge ticket fares and tolls to system users.

These governmental entities, which can be contiguous or overlapping, each have specific purposes not defined within typical charters granted to local general-purpose governments. They also lack the three sovereign powers of local government discussed above. They combine with general-purpose governments to provide these services both to residents living within district borders and to the general public. Instrumentalities have issued twice as much debt as general-purpose state and local governments have in the past decade, as state and local governments have looked to dedicated revenues instead of general obligation debt as a financing alternative.[76] The distinguishing feature of instrumentalities is that some portion of their revenues comes from the operation of "business-like" entities. We include a list of governmental instrumentalities below. We continue the discussion of instrumentalities in Chapter 4, "Revenue Bonds: How America Builds Infrastructure."

- Airports
- Electricity/public power
- Parking facilities
- Seaports/marine terminals

- Single- and multi-family housing
- Toll roads
- Universities
- Water/sewer systems

Instrumentalities are also products of their states. Their ability to set tolls, fares, tuition, rates, and fees is delineated in state charters.

Entities in the municipal market exist to meet the needs of citizens by enforcing laws and providing essential services and infrastructure. It is sometimes hard to pinpoint the functions of municipal issuers as a whole. They serve diverse needs and are subject to different sets of facts and circumstances. After the financial crisis, all issuers were impacted by declining revenues and tightening budgets on the state and federal levels. The result is that governments have been forced to accomplish more with less. Tax revenues are now more volatile. Economic growth is slower, and entitlement spending is growing. The role of government in the lives of citizens is changing. The goal of this book is to trace a historical narrative and examine how these changes impact bondholders.

3

General Obligation Bonds: The Backbone of the Municipal Bond Market

General obligation bonds are issued by states, local governments, and their instrumentalities to pay for public improvements and to provide essential services to their residents. They serve as the backbone of the municipal bond market, as the single largest credit type, making up roughly 34% of all municipal bond issuance.[1] Most general obligation bonds, or "GO bonds," are known as "unlimited tax" bonds, meaning that the bond issuer is required to raise taxes by as much as needed to repay the obligation. Holders of GO bonds are effectively given a blank check by the issuer with the promise to commit all its resources into repayment. The strength of this "unlimited tax pledge" is what distinguishes GO bonds from other bonds in the market.

Those GO bonds without an unlimited tax pledge are considered "limited," in that the issuing entity is subject to legal limits as to how much it can raise taxes to repay the bonds, usually because of voter-imposed limitations on debt.

Taxpayer bill of rights provisions in certain jurisdictions, such as Colorado, also impose fiscal discipline on municipalities in order to protect residents. As will be discussed in Chapter 4, "Revenue Bonds: How America Builds Infrastructure," debt limitations, in actuality, have unanticipated consequences. They lead to increased "special revenue issuance" and other non-general obligation bonded indebtedness in order to circumvent these restrictions. For example, the State of New Jersey has relied on appropriation-backed debt to circumvent its constitutional debt limitations. In theory although never in practice, governments with general obligation unlimited-tax bonds could be forced by creditors to raise taxes to infinite amounts to repay indebtedness; however, taken to the extreme, this pledge is difficult to enforce.

Historically, annual general obligation bond issuance has totaled between $100 billion and $150 billion, or roughly 40% to 60% of that of revenue bond issuance.[2] Figure 3.1 shows that general obligation issuance during this cycle peaked at $154 billion in 2010 and has since fallen roughly 18%, a reflection of shifting policy priorities from investing in projects to cutting expenses.[3] The peak in issuance lagged two years behind the start of the recession in 2008 because of the lagged nature of tax revenues, which are levied on prior-year incomes and property values.[4]

Figure 3.1 **GO Debt Issuance Declined Since the Recession**

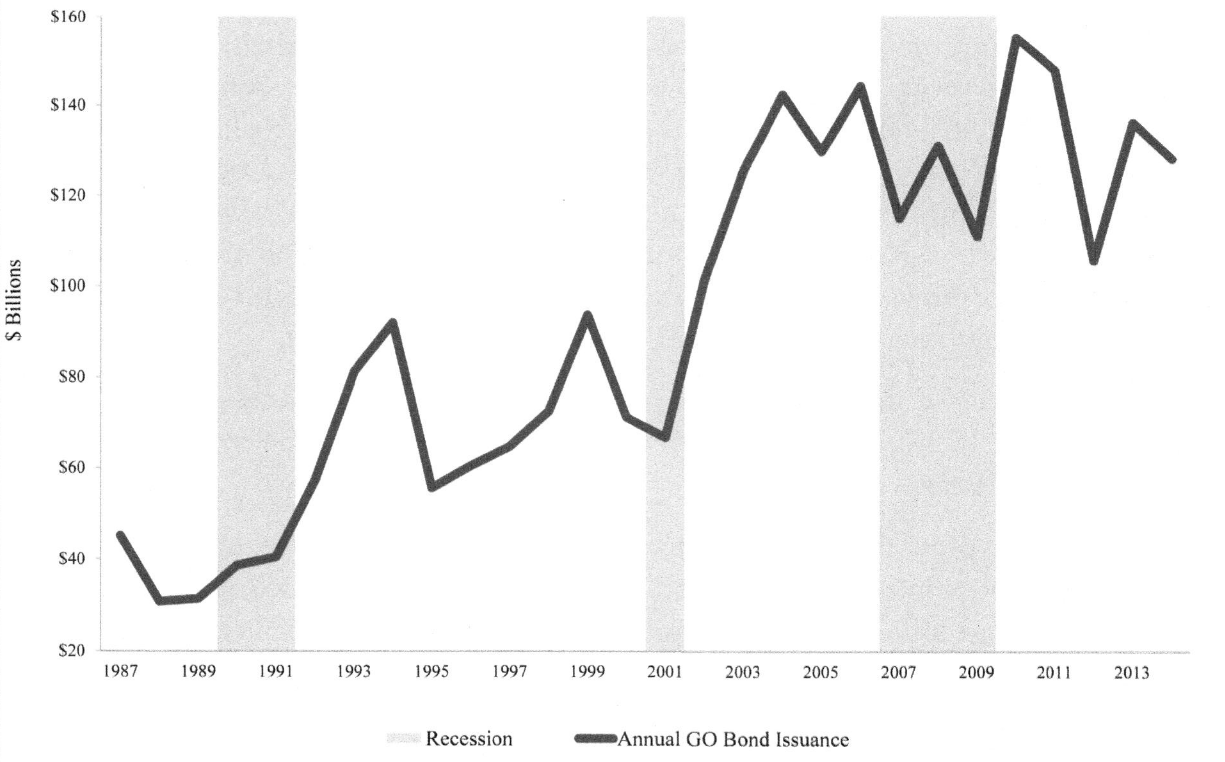

Source: The Bond Buyer

During normal economic times, the general obligation pledge has been considered sacrosanct for its safety. It is a "full faith and credit" pledge. The pledge to raise taxes for bond repayment is a unique security structure that no other type of obligation within the municipal bond market confers. We also know of no other type of obligation in other asset classes, with the exception of other government bonds, that has this type of backing.

In distressed situations such as Chapter 9 municipal bankruptcy, the general obligation pledge, specifically the unlimited-tax variant, is senior to other obligations in the capital structure of municipal issuers for the waterfall of debt repayment.[5] In the Detroit bankruptcy, for example, GO unlimited-tax bondholders recovered 74 cents on the dollar, whereas limited-tax bondholders recovered only 40 cents on the dollar.[6] Because of Chapter 9 Bankruptcy cram-down provisions, the GO recovery was less than 100%. Most bankruptcy judges have honored the pledge to increase taxes as a form of security, and general obligation bonds often trade higher in price than other obligations within the capital structures of municipal issuers as a result. In other bankruptcy scenarios, recoveries on general obligation debt have been higher than those on limited-tax bonds and special revenue bonds.[7]

GO bonds are paid out of an issuer's general fund, the primary fund into which revenues flow and from which expenditures are paid. They are also paid out of an issuer's debt service funds, a discussion of which is beyond the scope of this writing.[8] These non-earmarked revenues are used to pay for "general expenses" of the issuer, such as public safety or roads and other basic infrastructure. Typically, general obligation bonds will be issued to finance projects with non-discrete cash flows such as school construction, local road repair, and miscellaneous police and fire expenses. A general fund can be simple and account for inflows of tax revenues, intergovernmental transfers from other entities (such as states), and charges for fees and services (motor licensing fees, for example). It can also be complex, as would be the case for a state with large-scale operations and multiple operating units.

Figure 3.2 shows the revenue structure of the 50 states based on U.S. Census Bureau classification during fiscal year 2012.[9] As you can see, the revenue streams from which states pay their general obligation bonds are quite diverse.

Figure 3.2

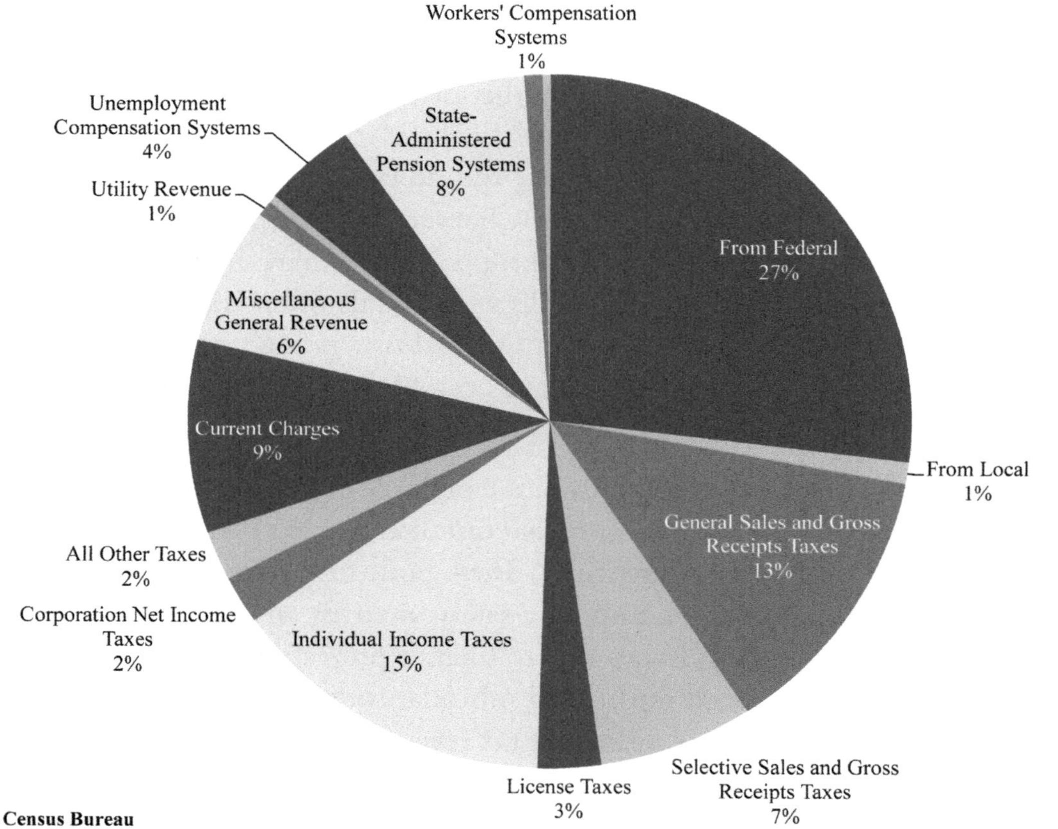

Source: Census Bureau

Although some of these revenues are dedicated only for specific purposes (e.g., federal Medicaid transfers), the vast majority of taxes are derived from a variety of transaction types (e.g., income taxes, taxes on select sales of certain goods). As an example, Figure 3.3 depicts the revenue structure of the City of Tampa for fiscal year 2013.

Figure 3.3

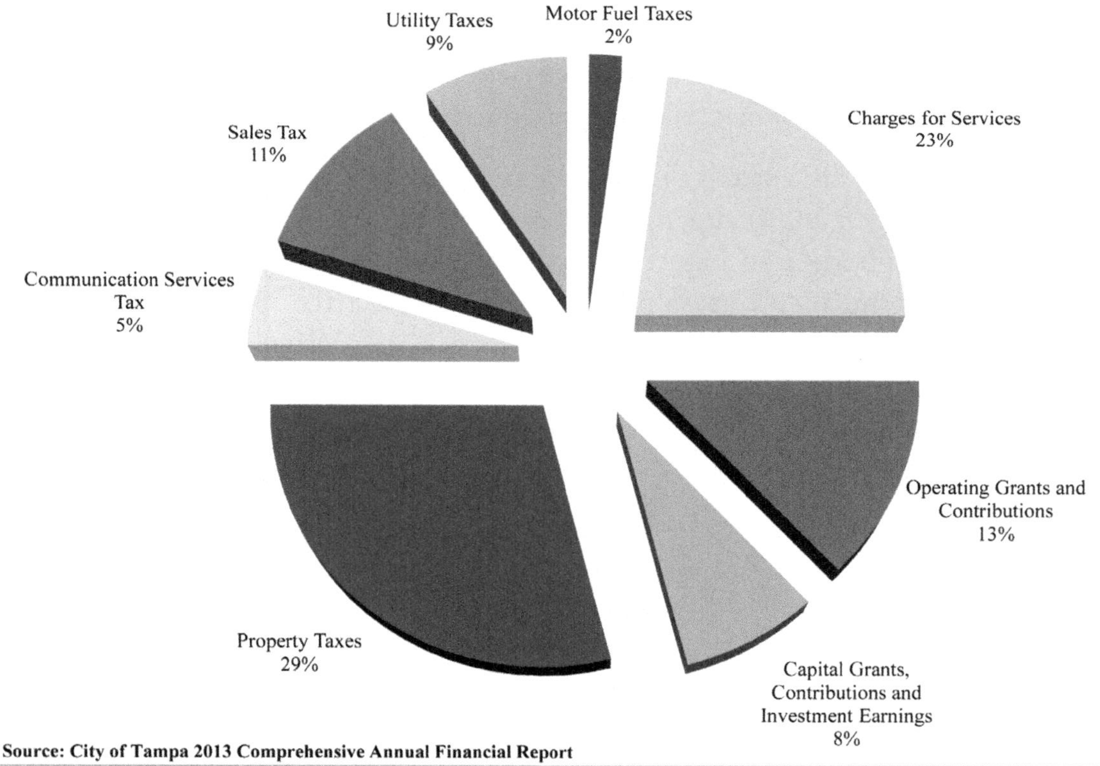

Source: City of Tampa 2013 Comprehensive Annual Financial Report

The pie chart shows that, for the City of Tampa, property tax revenues are by far the single largest tax revenue at 29% of revenues, followed by sales taxes at 11%.[10] The City of New York's general revenue stream is comprised of property taxes (41%), income taxes (36%), and sales taxes (14.4%).[11] The revenue streams are different, but both are heavily reliant on property taxes to fund operations. The City of Camden, New Jersey, derives a substantial portion of its general fund revenues from the State of New Jersey in the form of state fiscal assistance payments. The State of Florida receives a large portion of its revenues from state sales taxes and Medicaid transfer payments from the U.S. federal government. No two general obligation bonds are exactly comparable, because, as the examples show, each entity's revenue mix is different.

The property tax revenue stream is very stable because it is property-based as opposed to transaction-based and is set on a "budget-to-levy basis" by local municipalities.[12] *Budget-to-levy*, a term we borrow from Moody's, refers to the fact that local governments will budget for a certain amount of general fund revenues and levy the required millage needed to extract those revenues. Sales taxes ebb and flow with the level of economic activity generated in a certain region.

The stability of property taxes is a strength for holders of local GO bonds.[13] In spite of the large decline in property values in 2008 during the Great Recession, property tax collections remained very stable. As can be seen in Figure 3.4, which graphs the total local government property tax collections versus the S&P Case-Shiller 20-City Home Price Index from 2002 to 2012, property tax collections increased by 6.5% from 2008 to 2012.[14] The 20-City Index, however, declined from a high of 206.61 to a low of 137.44, or 33%, during the same time period,[15] This stability also serves another function: it allows local governments to better plan for expenditures on a multi-year basis.

Figure 3.4

Property Tax Collections: Stable

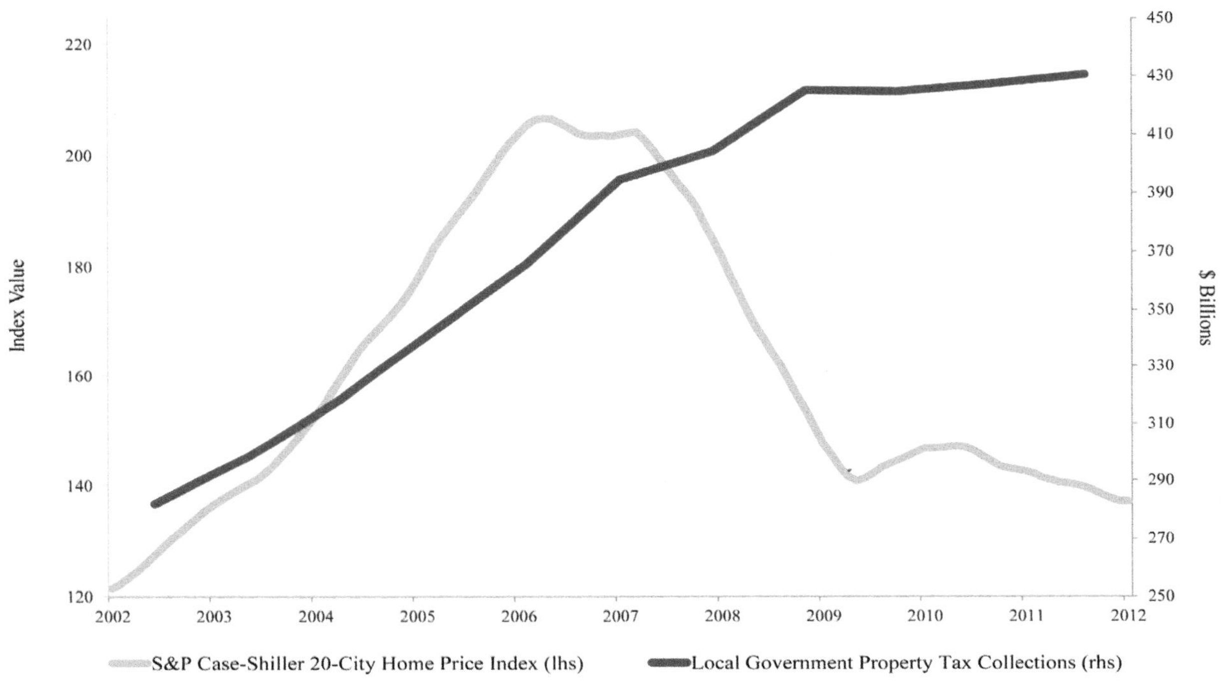

Sources: Moody's Investors Service, Cumberland Advisors, S&P Dow Jones Indices, Census Bureau Qtrly Summary of State and Local Taxes

Each municipal issuer's classification of revenues and expenses in its general fund is discretionary based on its structure and accounting preferences. The Governmental Accounting Standards Board (GASB), which sets generally accepted accounting principles for state and local governments, grants issuers substantial discretion in the classification of these items. Consider, for example, that the State of Illinois uses over 600 funds to account for its various activities.[16] It has created separate funds from the general fund to reclassify expenses so that it may more easily "balance its budget." In the case of Illinois, the general fund from which the state's full faith and credit is pledged accounts for less than 50% of its expenditures.[17] The Commonwealth of Puerto Rico has taken similar measures. In conjunction with a $3.5 billion general obligation debt issue, the Commonwealth capitalized a large portion of the $3.5 billion in order to pay $500 million in debt service. Because the $3.5 billion was a refinancing of existing indebtedness, the Commonwealth was able to remove $500 million of interest costs from its general fund to its capitalized interest account. The Commonwealth has stated that it will achieve a "balanced budget" by 2015; however, a portion of this "balance" will have been achieved through the use of accounting tricks.

State general obligation bonds are much safer credits than local general obligation bonds because states have sovereignty to raise taxes by the amount needed to repay debt. It is true that states derive their revenues from much less stable sources than local governments rely upon, but local governments may be subject to tax limitations and do not have the implicit federal backstop of greater federal transfers during difficult times.[18] States derive their sovereignty, a cornerstone of the U.S. federalist system, from the U.S. Constitution and are able to manage their fiscal affairs with a high degree of independence.[19] As noted earlier, local governments are creatures of their states, and their specific rights are delineated in each state's constitution.[20]

On a sector-wide basis, states rely much less than local governments do on general obligation debt as a tool to fund their operations or finance new projects. Debt service is a relatively minor budgetary item for states versus their larger spending priorities. For most states, annual debt service on outstanding general obligation debt amounts to less than 4% of revenues and is prioritized over other expenditures by state statute.[21] The low usage of general obligation debt by states means that debt service is not a burden on their operations. For example, the 50 states took in $1.9 trillion in revenues in 2012 and paid $50 billion in interest expense, or roughly 2.6% of total revenues, a small amount compared to $188 billion paid into pension systems or $588 billion spent for education.[22] Given the need for continued access to capital markets both on the state and local level, states are likely to target these other expenditures to balance their budgets.

Many states, such as the Commonwealth of Pennsylvania, micromanage the affairs of their municipalities, setting strict limitations on general indebtedness and providing voluntary assistance to municipalities in distress.[23] The State of Alabama's Constitution (the longest constitution of any government in the world, with 883 amendments) micromanages individual municipalities and limits the usage of general obligation debt.[24] States are not subject to such limitations by the federal government.

States such as Illinois and New Jersey that are burdened by large long-term liabilities like other post-employment benefits (OPEB) and underfunded pension systems are especially unlikely to fail to pay on their general obligation indebtedness because they depend on access to capital markets to fund these obligations. Such states have looked to discretionary spending, and not entitlements, for cuts. Many entitlements are protected under state constitutions; therefore it is very difficult for states to legislate entitlement reforms to whittle costs. At the end of 2013, the State of Illinois attempted to reform its pension system, only to have the reforms struck down by a circuit court judge.

The recession's impact on all state operations was great. NASBO has compiled valuable information on the subject. According to NASBO's *Fiscal Survey of the States: 2013*, higher outlays for Medicaid and unemployment compensation in 2008 and 2009, coupled with a 17% decline in tax revenues from the near-unprecedented contraction in the national economy, pressured state budgets on both the cost and the revenue side, forcing across-the-board reductions in other budget areas such as K-12 education funding, appropriations for higher education, transportation, and corrections.[25] Without help from the federal government under the American Recovery and Reinvestment Act (ARRA), state budget cuts and tax increases would have been much more substantial.[26] Among the 50 states, the accumulated budgetary shortfall from 2009 to 2011 was $431 billion. States received approximately $140 billion in stimulus funds from 2009 to 2011, most of it distributed in 2010 when the total state budgetary shortfall was $191 billion, allowing states to temporarily maintain most of their funding levels.[27] When stimulus funding expired, governors were forced to raise income and sales taxes and cut expenditures in the face of weak sales and income tax collections.

States have each acted much differently from a policy standpoint in the face of declining tax revenues;[28] specific policy decisions have typically been made based on a state's political environment: progressive states often choose to place the burden of balancing the budget on the wealthy by raising taxes (e.g., California), while conservative states rely on reducing K-12 and higher education funding, while raising tuition rates for public universities (e.g., Florida). From time to time, important decisions have been kicked down the road because of a political stalemate or an unwillingness to make difficult decisions.

In many cases state financing needs are mostly met by component units that operate as businesses outside the purview of the state's direct oversight and management.[29] Financing for the most capital-intensive state-level instrumentalities such as mass transit systems, toll roads, and public universities is done on a project-specific basis utilizing revenue bonds to match the cash flows of these projects, with debt service on the bonds.[30] General obligation bonds have typically been used only to cover revenue shortfalls, as was the case during the 2009 and 2010 budget cycles, or to fund the expansion of entitlement programs. General obligation bonds have been used in Illinois, New Jersey and elsewhere to pay higher costs associated with collective-bargaining agreements. These trends may reverse as states continue to plug budget holes with higher taxes, headcount reductions, and general obligation debt.

Provision of police and fire protection and education constitute the lion's share of local government expenditures and require debt financing for the construction of schools, purchases of police and fire equipment, and payment of benefits to those local employees. During the 2009 and 2010 budget cycles, cities were less able to provide these services because of depressed revenues, and many were forced to issue debt to meet these expenditure needs.

In the years following the financial crisis, many practitioners and prognosticators voiced concern regarding the status of the general obligation pledge as a security "superior" to revenue bond pledges. Declining property values in weak housing markets, the argument went, would reduce property tax revenues pledged to local general obligation bondholders. As shown in Figure 3.4, declining property values do not translate into declining property tax revenues.

Detroit's bankruptcy filing concerned some investors because Detroit Water and Sewerage Department (DWS) bondholders were unimpaired in the city's bankruptcy plan. Detroit's holders of unlimited-tax bonds, thought of as the highest-ranking creditors in the capital structure, recovered only 74 cents on the dollar. This reorganization plan, submitted by the city's emergency manager in June 2013, caused a fear-driven sell-off in Michigan local general obligation debt.

The astute investor understood that DWS bonds were issued by a completely separate entity with separate charter and were therefore not part of the bankruptcy estate. Any attempt to impair general obligation bonds and water and sewer bondholders in the same plan would not have passed muster with a bankruptcy judge.

When city officials attempt to use bankruptcy as a strategic tool, the rules of the game change. In these scenarios, city officials attempt to suspend or haircut payments to GO bondholders while preserving claims of pension funds and other personnel costs. This is typically done because it is the most politically expedient course. We have seen these attempts in many distressed scenarios, notably Harrisburg, Stockton, and San Bernardino. There haven't been consistent outcomes for general obligation bondholders versus collective bargaining agreements: GO bondholders have recovered as much as 100% and as little as 50% of principal, while pension payments have been kept intact in some cases and reduced in others.

Since the Great Recession, the general obligation pledge has performed better than other revenue and tax-backed pledges. Sales and dedicated tax bonds are secured only by specific tax streams dedicated to debt service. If revenues fall short of these amounts, for reasons such as lower business activity and high unemployment, the local government is under no obligation to raise sales taxes to pay these bonds. Almost by definition, if a state or local government dedicates a stream of revenues to pay a certain bond issue, for example a sales tax bond issue, it may not have the legal authority to raise taxes to repay these bonds should the dedicated revenue stream prove inadequate. The primary reason for dedicating taxes to repay these bonds in the first place is to segregate them from the general fund either in order to circumvent voter-approval requirements or potentially get capital at a lower cost. Raising taxes would effectively make these obligations GO bonds.[31]

Another challenge to the general obligation pledge has been the perceived superiority and essentiality of water and sewerage services securing the claims of revenue bondholders versus those of GO bondholders. As an example, the monthly household cost of water is a fraction of what is paid in property taxes and therefore much less vulnerable to lower usage or missed payments from customers. There was a trend toward purchase of essential service revenue bonds as safer credits in 2009 and 2010. This trend, however, did not manifest itself in lower yields for revenue debt and, we think, offers an attractive relative value opportunity. Most investors still perceive the general obligation pledge as being superior to that of revenue bonds. As shown in Figure 3.5, in the years leading up to the financial crisis, yields on general obligation debt traded in lockstep with those of revenue bonds, after controlling for credit quality. The average yield spread between revenue bonds and general obligation bonds was 7.67 basis points. In 2008, after the downgrades of the monolines and signs of stress started to appear, spreads between revenue and GO debt averaged

36.8 basis points. State and local governments that issue GO debt are typically able to operate free from the oversight of the federal government. This enhances their security and investment merit. Water and sewer services are typically provided by local utilities whose boards often overlap with those of cities.

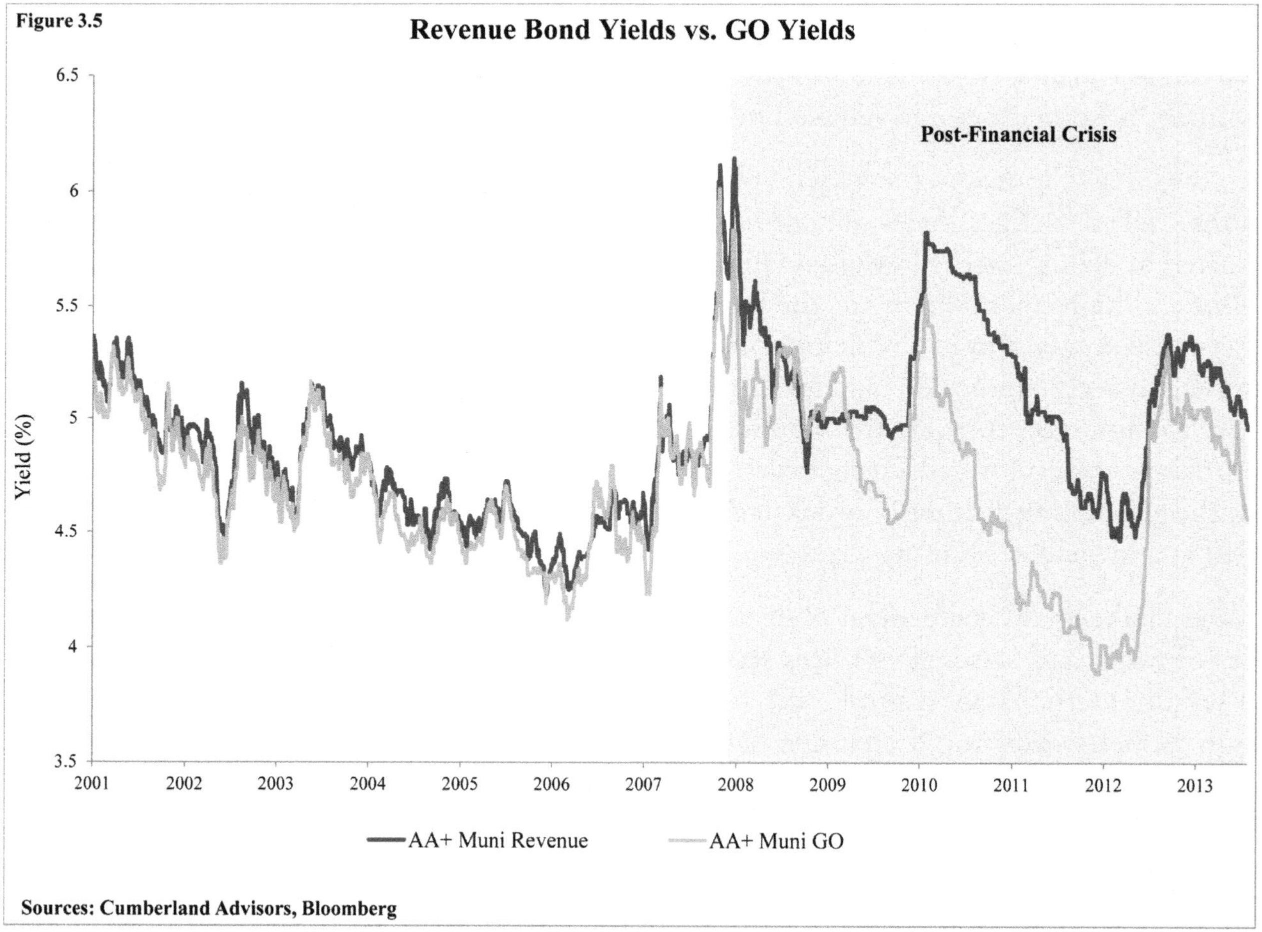

In spite of the strong credit quality and stability of the GO pledge, we believe the municipal market has made a secular shift toward relying on other sources of financing. During the post-recession deleveraging and the accompanying difficult political environment, many state and local governments have shied away from taking on more general obligation debt for both political and constitutional reasons.[32] Voters are less likely to approve new debt issuance as a result of the general social distaste for debt voiced by groups such as the Tea Party, and many state and local government issuers are running up against constitutional limitations after reliance on general obligation debt for deficit financing in the years leading up to and even since the recession. States like Colorado do not utilize general obligation debt in the first place, while states like California allow municipalities to issue debt only with voter approval. As the population in many of these regions has expanded and financing needs have increased, state and local governments have turned to other financing sources as an alternative to GO bonds, in order to circumvent these limitations.

Instead of utilizing the general obligation pledge, many issuers will sell bonds backed by user fees or appropriation-backed lease pledges. These alternatives have been a popular financing tool for states, such as Illinois, that are able to achieve much lower financing costs for sales tax financings versus GO financings.

The general obligation pledge has been tested many times over the last few years, given declines in real estate values, high unemployment, and escalating state and local government cost pressures. It is the backbone of the municipal market and has succeeded in being a stable source of financing for both state and local governments for important policy priorities. In the few instances where the strength of this pledge has been challenged or compromised by government officials, there has inevitably been a negative market reaction that served to discourage such behavior. The vast majority of rational officials will choose the prudent path of preserving payments to general obligation bondholders in order to maintain continued access to affordable financing. In later chapters we explore that attempts to subvert the general obligation pledge do not end well.

4

Revenue Bonds: How America Builds Infrastructure

A revenue bond is any bond that is not a general obligation bond. This overly simplistic definition is the result of the diversity of bond structures in the muni market that happen not to be general obligation bonds. Hospital debt, various forms of appropriation-backed bonds, and water and sewer bonds are all revenue bonds. Bonds issued by 501(c)(3) organizations are also classified as revenue bonds. Typically issued by business-like entities, revenue bonds are secured by an explicit revenue stream that matches the project or asset that it is financing. Revenue bonds make up 67% of total municipal bond issuance and are a more popular financing structure than general obligation bonds because they do not require voter or legislative approval.[1] For example, the New Jersey Turnpike Authority is given legislative authority to issue revenue bonds to fund its capital improvement program on an ongoing basis without voter approval. Because the bonds will be payable out of revenues of the authority as opposed to revenues of the state, the debt is considered "self-supporting" and technically not an obligation of the root entity, such as a town, city, or state.[2] Although neither legislation nor a referendum is needed to issue revenue bonds (unlike GO bonds), states have enacted legislation that allows for their issuance as needed.[3]

Revenue bonds are possible based on the idea that the cash flows of the asset being financed will roughly match the debt service and amortization of the outstanding bonds.[4] Thus the bonds issued tend to be level-amortizing, with annual debt service payments matching to some extent the cash flows of the asset being financed.[5] Dr. Alan W. Steiss, a professor of urban planning at the University of Michigan, states that in contrast to general obligation bonds, "there is no claim on the government's general credit and taxing power" and no "unlimited" or open-ended commitment of all revenue-producing powers to meet debt service.[6] Revenue bonds typically have a closed flow of funds structure particular to the individual revenue bond indenture.[7]

The number of municipal issuers of revenue bonds is vast. We list below the most common issuers that rely on revenue bond financing. Revenue bond issuers make up a diverse group of entities that often bear little economic relation to one another. We have used geographical comparisons at previous times in the book to highlight the municipal bond market's idiosyncrasies and its potential diversification of idiosyncratic risk. Nowhere is this more true than in the revenue bond sector. Airplane traffic at Lambert-St. Louis International Airport does not directly impact water revenues of the City of Los Angeles Department of Water and Power (LADWP).

Issuers Dependent on Revenue Bond Financing

- Airports
- Bridges
- Hospitals
- Issuers of special/miscellaneous tax bonds
- Mass transit systems
- Parking facilities
- Public power projects
- Public housing programs (single-family and multifamily)
- Stadiums
- Toll roads
- Tunnels
- Universities
- University dorms
- Water and sewer systems

Each of the above revenue bond issuer types falls into one of the six sectors that we will discuss in this chapter: special tax revenues, higher education, healthcare, housing, transportation, and utilities. We note that none of these entities have the power to tax.[8] These are either 501(c)(3) organizations or public corporations that are run by municipal entities on a within-arms-length basis.

Miscellaneous/Special Tax Bonds

Miscellaneous tax bonds (or special tax bonds—we use the two terms interchangeably) occupy a gray area between revenue bonds and general obligation bonds. While unlimited tax bonds are backed by a pledge to raise taxes to repay bondholders, the miscellaneous tax pledge is much narrower.[9] A miscellaneous tax bondholder receives a specified percentage of a revenue stream, while a GO bondholder is given what amounts to a blank check. Miscellaneous tax revenues may be used to subsidize projects or enterprises, or they can be used as an alternative financing mechanism for general state and local governments that do not have voter approval to issue debt. New Jersey Transit, for example, is heavily reliant on sales tax revenues, a type of miscellaneous tax revenue stream, to finance its operations; as such, bonds issued by New Jersey Transit are backed by a combination of ticket fares and sales tax revenues.

New York State issues personal income tax (PIT) bonds as a financing vehicle for its general purpose needs. The security pledge of these obligations is confined to these revenues.[10] These bonds are also likely isolated from the operations risk of the issuing entity, if the revenue stream backing the bonds is segregated from the general revenues of the issuer. In recent years, Illinois and Puerto Rico have relied on sales tax debt as a financing alternative to general obligation debt when their general obligation debt was downgraded. Moody's has taken the view that sales tax debt is linked to general fund debt, whereas S&P has viewed the two as separate.[11] Miscellaneous tax bonds are backed by multiple tax types. We list typical miscellaneous tax bond types below:

Types of Special Tax Bonds

1. Hotel/motel taxes
2. Income taxes

3. Insurance policy taxes
4. License fees
5. Motor vehicle fuel taxes
6. Payroll taxes
7. Real estate transfer taxes
8. Stadium and convention center taxes
9. Tobacco and cigarette excise taxes

Usually miscellaneous tax bonds, which tend to be more highly levered than general fund obligations, are backed by narrow transaction-based income, sales, or excise taxes.[12] Because they are "transaction-based" as opposed to "property-based," they tend to be pro-cyclical and more volatile than property-based taxes.[13] As indicated in Figure 4.1, even though local sales tax collections declined by roughly 10% from 2008 to 2009, property taxes increased by 10% during the period. Property taxes dipped slightly from 2010 to 2011, but only by 1%, a testament to their resiliency versus more volatile miscellaneous taxes.

Moody's, in their ratings methodology on special tax bonds, states that special tax bonds have "been more prevalent in years when the national economy was expanding and utilized more heavily in states that have property tax caps or other tax-rate caps."[14] In the years leading up to the recession, population growth and an economy based on consumer spending contributed to increased use of special tax bonds secured by "dedicated sales, gas, hotel, and utility taxes."[15] Given the widespread usage of tax bonds and the variety of revenues being securitized, an explanation of this financing source is not cut and dried.

Figure 4.1

Local Sales and Property Tax Collections

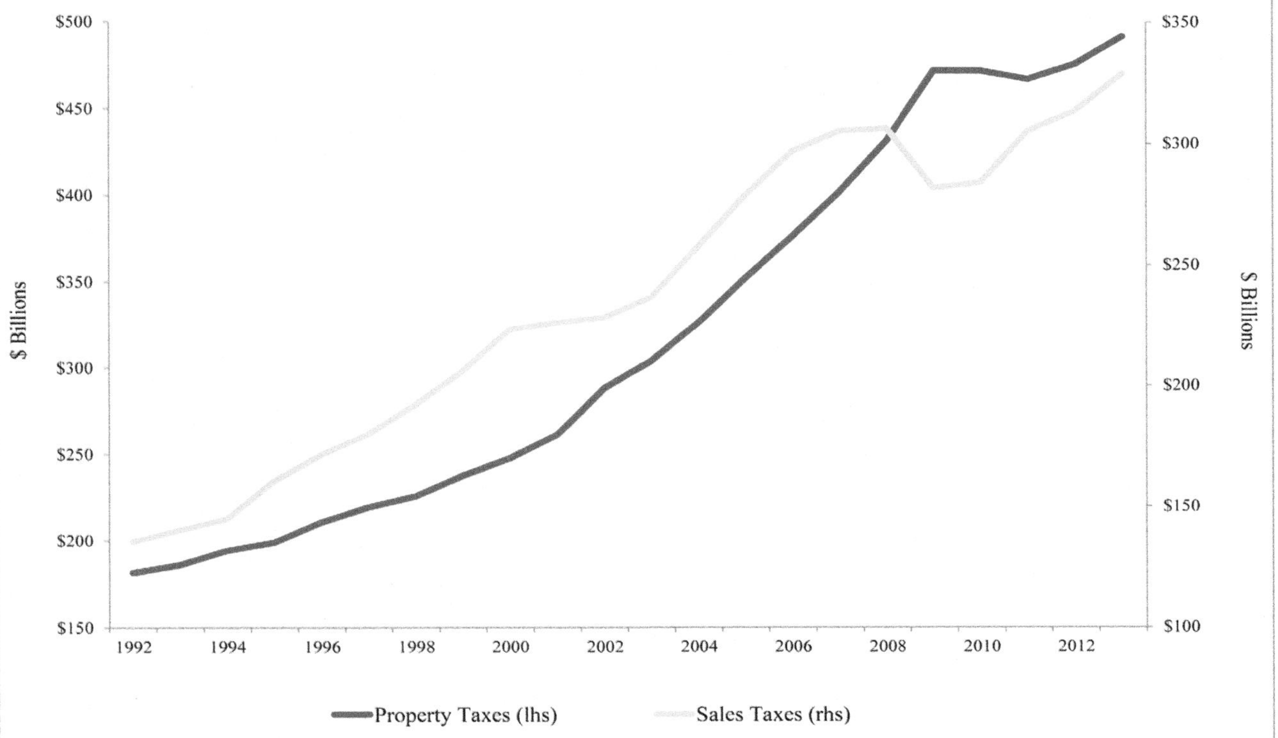

Source: Moody's Investors Service, Cumberland Advisors

An example of a hybrid structure having both miscellaneous revenue and business-type revenue qualities are GARVEEs, Grant Anticipation Revenue Vehicles—which, according to Moody's, are backed "solely by anticipated highway or transit grants or paid first by those revenues, with a secondary pledge of other revenue" (e.g., gas/fuel or other motor vehicle taxes).[16] GARVEEs have been used heavily by state governments to fund ongoing improvements to the interstate highway system. GARVEE bonds have come under pressure because of their exposure to sequestration should revenues for these programs not be reauthorized by Congress during the annual appropriations process.[17] Given their closed structure, states are not obligated to raise taxes to make bondholders whole if grants from the federal government decrease; hence the narrowness of the GARVEE pledge, illustrative of typical risks associated with miscellaneous tax bonds.[18] According to the American Association of State

Highway and Transportation Officials (AASHTO), GARVEE activity has increased 54-fold since the program's inception in 1998.[19] Figure 4.2 illustrates this rapid rise.

Figure 4.2

GARVEE Issuance: Increased 54-fold since 1998

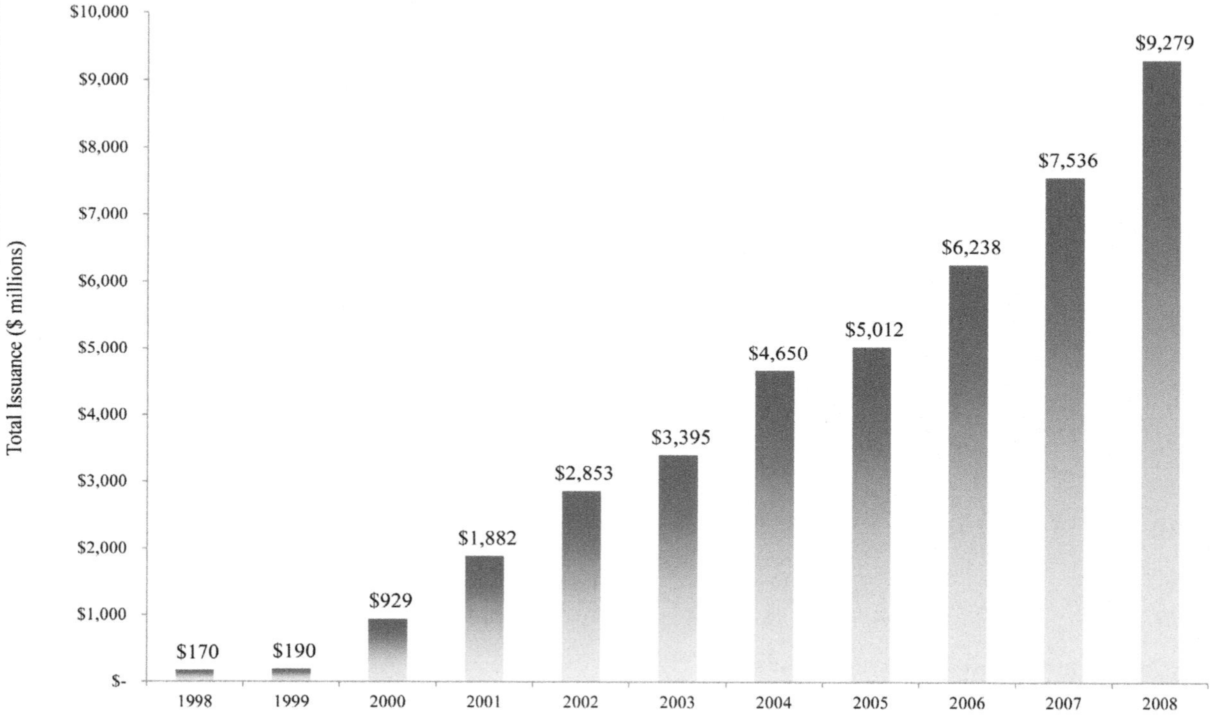

Source: AASHTO

In February 2014, Moody's downgraded the ratings of 17 GARVEE programs, citing the following as their rationale[20]:

> *The downgrades reflect changes in federal liquidity management which increase the risk of interruption of timely payments of federal transportation aid due to states and transit entities. These include the government's recurring episodes of threatened debt ceiling expirations, government shutdowns, and the threat of depletion of the highway trust fund balance later this year due to the fund's persistent structural imbalance.*

The state-federal linkages distinguish GARVEEs from other revenue bond structures. The financing structure's popularity stems from the fact that states are able to receive upfront payments from the federal government as an alternative to coming up with multiple rounds of financings for what are multi-year capital investments.[21] AASHTO states that GARVEEs also "enable a state to accelerate construction timelines and spread the cost of a transportation facility over its useful life rather than just the construction period."[22] As states have continually looked to revenue-based financing structures to avoid use of balance sheet, AASHTO states that GARVEEs also "expand access to capital markets as an alternative or in addition to potential general obligation or revenue bonding capabilities."[23] Uncertainty over federal funding of discretionary expenditures will likely mitigate the use of this structure in the near future.

A type of special revenue bond somewhat resembling general obligation bonds, special assessment bonds are backed by a narrow "special assessment" on a type of property. The special assessments are usually levied for a specific purpose on residents living within a designated area. For example, fire, hospital, and park districts can issue bonds backed by their specified revenue streams. They lack the broad taxing power of general-purpose governments, such as towns, but are still given limited authority to levy specific taxes.[24] Mello-Roos bonds were issued in California to construct streets, schools, and water and sewer systems after voters approved property tax limitations under Proposition 13 in 1978.[25] Property owners paid annual assessments backing these bonds in addition to their property tax bills.[26]

Typical revenue bond structures that do not fall into the category of "miscellaneous tax bonds" operate as business-like enterprises with revenues derived from user charges, tolls, and fees from the operation of these businesses. Entities such as toll roads or mass transit systems are typically run by the public sector in the U.S., whereas they are run by the private sector in other countries. In the U.S., these entities operate under state charters to conduct their operations and collect revenues sufficient to pay their operating expenses. Because they operate as tax-exempt organizations, their service charges are cheaper than if they were profit-seeking entities. Their tax-exempt financing status and their mandate to provide essential services at the lowest possible cost make the government-run model an attractive value proposition.

From start to finish, each entity has a different structure for the order in which bondholders are paid versus other costs. For example, will a mass transit system's bondholders be paid before or after operations and maintenance expenses? The order in which revenues are applied to operations and maintenance expenses, debt service, working capital, and reserves is specified in the "flow-of-funds" section of the bond indenture.

The flow-of-funds structure is an important component of revenue bond issues regardless of sector because it specifies the hurdles that rate revenues must overcome in order for bondholders to receive payment. It is most relevant in distressed scenarios where revenues are likely to fall short of the amount needed to pay all fixed and variable costs and to make deposits to reserve funds. Whether or not debt service on a particular bond issue comes before or after debt service on other bond issues or operations and maintenance expenses determines the likelihood of full and timely repayment and recoveries during insolvency.

Figure 4.3 shows the flow-of-funds structure for a Puerto Rico Electric Power Authority (PREPA) bond issued in 2008. This flow-of-funds structure was established in 1974 and is used for all financings under the general revenue bond indenture. No two flow-of-funds structures are the same. We chose this indenture because it is unique: revenues of the power system are deposited into the Commonwealth of Puerto Rico's general fund prior to payment of debt service on the authority's bonds. In this instance, the subordination of debt service to the Puerto Rico general fund gives the Commonwealth a blank check to use PREPA's revenues to subsidize its own operations—a weakness for bondholders. A close analysis of the flow-of-funds structure allows investors to identify these weaknesses.

Figure 4.3

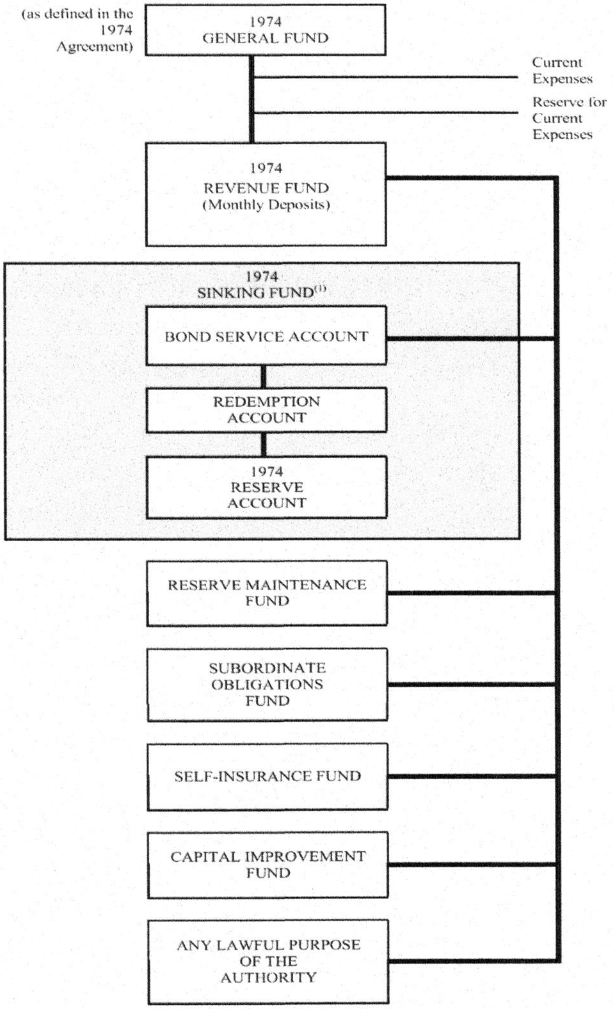

(1) Monthly deposits to the Bond Service Account and the Redemption Account for all Power Revenue Bonds bearing interest at a fixed rate are capped at 1/6 of the interest due on the next interest payment date and 1/12 of the principal due on the next principal payment date and 1/12 of Amortization Requirements for the current fiscal year.

Source: Puerto Rico Government Development Bank

Another issue clarified in the flow-of-funds structure is whether payment of debt service will come before or after payment of operating expenses. In this particular case, debt service is paid from "net revenues" after expenses. While it is true that without paying expenses the authority will lack revenues to pay debt service, the legal protection of a gross revenue pledge forces issuers to reduce expense in order to pay debt service in the event of a shortfall, and not the other way around.

Looking at the PREPA flow-of-funds structure, we see that, after payment of debt service, funds are deposited into a reserve account that can be used in the event of a revenue shortfall to pay bondholders. Dipping into reserves buys an issuer time to adjust its revenues and expenses in the event that revenues have a "one-off" bad year or shortfall. After reserves are replenished, the funds are used to pay off other bonds; funds that remain are then available to the authority to use for other purposes. Flow-of-funds structures are shown in diagrammatic fashion similar to that of Figure 4.3 for a variety of bond structures, including sales tax bonds and water and sewer bonds.

Issuers of revenue bonds also promise to maintain policies that ensure the timely and full repayment of principal and interest. These promises, or "covenants" as they are formally known, variously require the issuing entity to levy a certain level of fees and charges to keep facilities in working condition, or to purchase insurance to protect against losses. Arguably, the most important type of covenant for bondholders is the "rate covenant," which specifies the rates an issuer must charge to maintain revenues at some multiple of annual debt service and to provide a buffer if revenues fall short.

For example, oftentimes rate covenants will require an issuer to levy fees at a rate sufficient to generate revenues that exceed 1.25 times MADS, or maximum annual debt service; if revenues fall short of this amount, the issuer is in what's known as "technical default" for non-compliance with the covenant and must therefore raise fees or hire a consultant to create a plan to bring MADS coverage above the covenanted amount. Rate covenants differ by bond issue and specify a different coverage ratio for compliance. The higher the rate-covenant-required ratio, the greater the protection afforded to bond holders. Rate covenants apply to various types of indebtedness but are most common in water and sewer revenue bond transactions. For example, an issuer will be forced to charge rates for water such that revenues exceed debt service by 1.25 times.

Water and Sewer Utilities

Bonds issued by water and sewer systems and other utilities have been favored during and after the financial crisis because they are insulated from the local political process and unlikely to be affected by declining property values. Since the vast majority of bond-issuing utilities in the municipal bond market happen to be local water and sewer systems, we will focus on this subsection of the market. As Moody's states, because water and sewer systems are essential to their local municipalities and to the health of citizens and the local economy, they function as well-secured monopolies with substantial autonomy for setting rates.[27]

As was the case with the water and sewer system of Jefferson County, Alabama, local utilities are subject to EPA regulations that may prove onerous, imposing financial stress on smaller utilities. Utilities are often forced to invest considerable amounts of money in capital improvement programs to comply with these regulations.[28] The costs are ultimately borne by ratepayers in the form of higher water and sewer rates. Regulatory approval to set rates, which can be highly politicized, is often needed to enable water and sewer districts to charge higher rates in order to pay for these capital expenditures.

The water and sewer bond sector is one of the largest sectors within the tax-exempt market, accounting for approximately 10% of issuance within a given year.[29] As discussed earlier, heavy regulation under the Clean Water Act (CWA) is the greatest source of cost pressure impacting these entities, somewhat understandably, because drinking water quality and the health of the service area population are of primary importance.[30] The large costs associated with treatment, distribution, and transmission have meant that these systems have typically been regulated and operated as natural monopolies (similar to electric utilities).[31] Eighty percent of wastewater systems in the United States are owned by or operate under the control of local municipal governments and service 72% of the U.S. population, with the remainder served by privately owned systems or individual households.[32]

Subdued economic growth is not likely to impact utilities in the future, nor is low consumer confidence or political uncertainty. Generally, utilities are self-reliant, funded solely by user charges. The kinds of cuts to state aid that strained school budgets in the aftermath of the financial crisis had little effect on utilities. Challenges for utilities are not economy-related but are linked instead to capital expenditures and weather conditions. For example, U.S. droughts in 2012 reduced water and sewer bond issuance by 28% in 2013 and pushed back capital spending.[33] In 2013 issuance increased as weather conditions facilitated greater water usage and additional revenues to support higher debt service costs from project-financing. S&P states that water and sewer services were not cut during the recession, whereas library and park systems were cut the most.[34] This is a testament to the sector's essentiality and resilience. The relatively low cost of water and sewer services, often less than 3% of consumers' after-tax income, means that these services are highly affordable and that most utilities have margin to increase rates to pay bondholders in the event of revenue shortfalls.[35]

Water and sewer systems are often established as local units of government, either as a separate entity or consolidated with the related general-purpose local government. The New York City Municipal Water Finance Authority is a component unit of the City of New York. Its ability to set rates is governed by the New York City Water Board, which is independent from the city's leadership.[36] The distinction between a component unit and an entirely independent system is important during times of fiscal distress. If the water system's revenues are commingled with those of the city, the city may have access to those revenues, reducing revenues to bondholders. If the two entities are legally distinct, however, the local government would not have access to those revenues.

In distressed scenarios these can be contentious issues. During the ongoing bankruptcy process with the City of Detroit, the emergency manager made the claim that the city should be able to access revenues from the DSWD, even though the system derived 80% of its revenues from surrounding municipalities and the funds of both entities are not commingled. This plan was ultimately scrapped in favor of a "grand bargain." The City of Chicago is an example of a water system whose operating revenues are commingled with those of the city, as city funds are not separate from the water utility's funds.

Higher Education

Funding for higher education comes primarily from tuition, fees, and state appropriations, as opposed to ad valorem taxes for K-12 education. Bonds backed by such revenues are considered revenue bond indebtedness. This chapter on revenue bonds will focus on higher education and not K-12 education.

Higher education institutions have a combined $200 billion of debt outstanding.[37] Moody's states that the sector itself is highly diffuse, with thousands of colleges and universities operating in different niches and competing at difference price points.[38] Typically those universities with strong market positions (e.g., Ivy League schools or land-grant institutions) will perform better than others during weak economic periods because of strong demand for their brand and reputation.[39] The best indicator of demand for a university is student preference, which is usually dictated by a school's brand but also by course offerings that provide skills relevant to the hiring needs of employers.[40] Demand, as measured by the number of applications divided by matriculations, will often dictate a university's ability to raise tuition and fees. For public universities this is an important attribute, as state appropriations in recent years have been cut back due to budgetary stresses.

In the years since the financial crisis, the U.S. higher education sector has faced multiple challenges. The affordability of college tuition has been called into question, and demand has shifted to public higher education as a low-cost alternative to private schools. Cost pressures for middle-income families mean that small private schools will be forced to cut tuition to attract students, while public schools are faced with greater demand for services. Regardless of these trends, the demand for higher education will likely continue to rise because desirable careers require special training and education in an increasingly knowledge-based society. Students graduating from college still have higher incomes than those holding only high school diplomas, reinforcing the value of undergraduate education.[41]

Despite some of the short-term changes in enrollments at universities, the trend is still for greater enrollment. S&P states that education attendance is not likely affected by economic conditions due to families' long-term planning and savings over the course of decades.[42] However, we note that employment trends impact enrollment in graduate schools.[43] The contra-cyclical nature of graduate school enrollment reflects the fact that enrollments will increase during weak economic periods when jobs are sparse and the opportunity cost declines because of the weak labor market.[44] High unemployment can both help and harm higher education institutions: while high unemployment reduces the ability of working families to pay tuition costs, it prompts re-enrollments when the job market is weak.[45] High unemployment over long periods of time hurts universities because it reduces consumer spending and the willingness of students to take on tuition payments and debt.[46]

John Quinterno, in his work "The Great Cost Shift: How Higher Education Cuts Undermine the Future Middle Class," published by *Demos.org*, describes the impacts of cuts to higher education on median incomes over time. The college-age demographic cohort (18- to 24-year olds) has grown from 26.7 million to 30.7 million between 1990 and 2010. During that time, per-pupil funding from states increased by only $10.5 billion—a 26.1% drop, when we adjust for inflation. In real terms, however, tuition rates have increased by 71%, creating a much larger funding burden for the middle class. To bridge the gap, students have taken on increasing levels of student debt. Quinterno's research shows that "student loan debt has increased by a factor of 4.5 from 1999 to 2013."[47]

Government involvement in higher education is necessary because of public need and our society's desire for equality of opportunity. The State Higher Education Executive Officers Association (SHEEO) has stated that "in the past decade, the two recessions and larger macro-economic challenges" in the U.S. have created a "new normal for state funding of public higher education."[48] In this scenario, retirement and healthcare costs, which "must compete with education for limited public resources," have driven up the cost of higher education dramatically.[49] That said, accessible and affordable higher education will be an increasingly crucial priority in a global, knowledge-based economy; thus we believe that higher education will remain an important part of state and federal government policy.[50] The requirement that public higher education be relatively low cost means that it will have to be subsidized in some manner by state and local governments.

In the years leading up to the financial crisis, many universities engaged in debt transactions that have gone sour in the years after the financial crisis. Instead of issuing level fixed-rate debt, many issued short-term variable-rate debt while entering interest-rate swap transactions to synthetically convert the variable-rate debt to long-term debt. When the universities were unable to remarket their short-term debt because of a lack of buyers, the bonds became "bank bonds" with penalty rates as high as 12%. With the increase in short-term rates, the interest-rate swap transactions fell far out of the money (a liability for the schools) as the short-term interest rates on the bonds greatly exceeded the payments they were receiving from dealers on the floating leg of the swaps. This same scenario forced Jefferson County into bankruptcy. Universities were required to post collateral, per the swap contracts, when the positions were marked to market, creating liquidity needs. Since that time, most schools have refinanced these transactions and have made the onerous payments needed to terminate them. The presence of variable-rate debt in a university's capital structure is a cause for concern and should be watched closely.

Overall, the credit quality of public universities tends to be higher than that of private universities. Public higher education institutions have an implicit state backstop as part of a state's mission to provide affordable education to its residents. To fund the majority of their operations, they rely on tuition revenues, student fees, and state appropriations—more stable funding sources than endowment spending.[51] Enrollments at public institutions increase during recessions, a reflection of both state budgetary pressures and greater demand for lower cost education. As enrollments increase, institutions' revenue mixes shift toward more stable tuition and fee revenues and away from state appropriations, which can be volatile and driven by politics. In general, those universities with little reliance on state support are more viable credits.

Standalone financings to construct student dormitories have been accomplished without using university general-revenue pledges. These bond issues, backed by rent payments, student fees, or a combination of both, tend to be riskier and less secured than general revenue obligations of universities; they should be treated similarly to mortgage debt of private commercial real estate transactions. An analysis of university enrollment trends, competition from surrounding dormitories, and vacancy rates is needed to assess the viability of these projects. These bond issues, which are often sold under the guise of being related to their contiguous university, are anything but, and are often subject to idiosyncratic risks that may be unknown to the ordinary retail investor.

As an example, a bond issued in 2000 by a large university in Florida defaulted on an interest payment in 2011 because of mold found in the dormitory's basement. The dorm had to be evacuated during mold remediation efforts. Remediation efforts eventually succeeded, meeting the approval of an independent health inspector; and the facility, now inhabitable under a new name, continues to make payments in full. However, the issuer's default on interest payments in 2011, the result of a severe drop in occupancy and subsequent downgrade to junk, subjected investors to substantial loss of capital.

Housing Bonds

Revenue bonds issued by state housing finance agencies, or state HFAs as they are called, tend to be backed by well-entrenched, state-sponsored entities charged with the mission of expanding home ownership to low-income buyers. These issuers finance mostly single-family mortgages for first-time homebuyers, through the issuance of tax-exempt bonds. Some HFAs have separate multifamily programs to finance loans for low-income multifamily projects; however, most multifamily loan financings are done on the local level and without the broad diversification and strength of single-family programs.[52] HFAs function much like conservatively levered banks, with the ability to issue short-term tax-exempt debt to purchase whole loan pools or both privately and federally-insured mortgage-backed securities (MBS).

Typically, the safest housing revenue bonds have high levels of assets to outstanding debt (greater than 1.05 times) and conservative loan portfolios with low delinquencies. The typical HFA program has high Moody's and S&P ratings, usually Aa2 or AA.[53] That rating is a reflection of the sector's high credit quality and the ability of HFA programs to require private insurance on the loans they hold or government insurance from the Federal Housing Administration (FHA) or U.S. Department of Veternans' Affairs (VA).[54] Loans may also be repackaged into MBS and guaranteed by the U.S. Department of Housing and Urban Development (HUD), Fannie Mae, or Freddie Mac. HFA programs are stronger now, post-crisis, despite declines in home values and negative impacts on financing from the financial crisis.[55] Given a large exposure to the federal government via collateral guarantees, the credit quality of these programs has been more closely linked to that of the U.S. government.

State HFA programs have maintained conservative underwriting standards, purchasing only 30-year fixed-rate debt instead of exotic variable-rate products; and they never lowered their standards prior to the crisis. As a result, loan performance has remained stable, and both equity and reserves have continued to increase since the recession.[56] Like universities, a few state HFAs utilized variable-rate debt financing, which added to the complexity of cash flow projections, exposing them to rollover risk and early termination payments when marking positions to market.

Since 2012, only three state HFAs reported losses, versus five in 2011 and seven in 2010.[57] As they are entities similar to banks, which fund most of their operations with short-term debt, yield curve risk is a concern for state HFAs. Higher long-term interest rates and a return to normalcy in tax-exempt bonds relative to taxables will increase profitability by increasing the spread between assets and liabilities. Low interest rates hurt HFAs' profitability and created the need for federal intervention through the New Issue Bond Program (NIBP), which allowed HFAs to sell securities out of their portfolios to the U.S. Treasury. In spite of some of the troubles HFAs have endured, equity as a percentage of assets and credit quality have continued to increase in this sector. In their role as social safety net providers, state housing authorities continue to fulfill their mission of financing affordable housing.

Transportation Bonds

A much larger and more capital-intensive responsibility for state and local governments is the provision of transportation services, whether that is the construction and operation of airports, toll roads, mass transit systems, or ports. These entities are the most business-like of all issuers in the municipal bond market and are typically self-sustaining, with the ability to fund themselves out of operating revenues and dedicated taxes. Slow growth has impacted transportation issuers because they operate based on demand.

Transportation sector issuers include airports, toll roads, parking systems, mass transit systems, and ports. The public transportation sector, like other sectors, was faced with uncertainty in 2013 when usage levels of services dropped as a result of the subdued economic recovery.[58] The federal funding environment was also bleak due to sequestration.[59]

On the local level, capital requirements have gone unnoticed while existing infrastructure has aged, and rehabilitation and expansion needs have gone unaddressed. Budgetary stresses as a result of low revenue growth and higher personnel costs have crowded out infrastructure needs.[60] The ability of transportation issuers to raise revenues has diminished, as higher toll and fee rates have already been used as a stopgap budgetary measure in recent years. Given that these entities have already gone through rounds of higher service charges, the willingness to raise toll and user rates has declined; as a result, operating margins in this sector are expected to remain thin.[61]

Since the recession, revenue-producing transactions such as ticket fees, tolls, and fares have increased modestly. Modest economic growth and slow growth in employment have provided a margin adequate to service existing expenses but not large enough to resolve uncertainties over funding new projects.[62] We expect that some of these concerns will lessen as recovery continues and state and local governments shift gears from targeting budget cuts to funding new investments. The U.S. economic growth story, which increasingly depends upon the shipment of oil and gas produced by hydraulic fracturing, also lends itself to infrastructure and transportation investment.[63] Given the uncertain funding environment on the federal level, the rise of public partnerships in recent years is an example of a shift away from revenue bond usage and exclusive government funding.

The two largest issuer types within the transportation sector are airports and toll roads.

Airports are similar to other issuer types within this sector, as they derive their revenues from ticketing fees, oil sales to airlines, various land leases on airport property, and various charges to carriers. They are thus exposed to airline industry trends and consumer sentiment. Since the funding of airport capital expenditures is subsidized by the government under various federal airport improvement programs, airports are exposed to federal budget pressures, as are other capital-intensive transportation sector issuers. As of this writing, demand at airports still lags 5% below pre-recession levels, and air traffic has grown roughly 1% to 2% annually.[64] With the slow growth environment, capital plans have been put off, affording airports some breathing room.[65] Because airports are heavily impacted by consumer sentiment, their financial performance has been pro-cyclical and somewhat shaky ever since airline deregulation in the late '70s.[66] When airlines fail or restructure, as has been the case with major airline consolidations since 2009, airports are inevitably affected.

In the coming years, as airports cut unprofitable flights to reduce costs, smaller airports with concentrated exposure to single airlines will come under pressure. Large airports with multiple airlines conducting operations will continue to function as essential service providers and international gateways to major cities.[67] The strongest airports are those situated in major cities that have a substantial amount of origin and destination traffic.[68]

Toll roads, another major capital-intensive issuer within the revenue bond sector, are also subject to economic trends as the major determinant of traffic levels. A rising economy lends itself to higher levels of discretionary and business travel and allows toll road issuers to increase tolls to pay greater capital needs.[69] As can be seen in Figure 4.4, up until 2007, national vehicle miles traveled has tracked closely with U.S. nominal GDP.[70] Lower discretionary and commercial travel in the years after the recession created a divergence between trends in vehicle miles traveled and nominal GDP where vehicle miles traveled declined and nominal GDP continued to increase.[71] Vehicle travel is very much a function of economic activity.

Figure 4.4

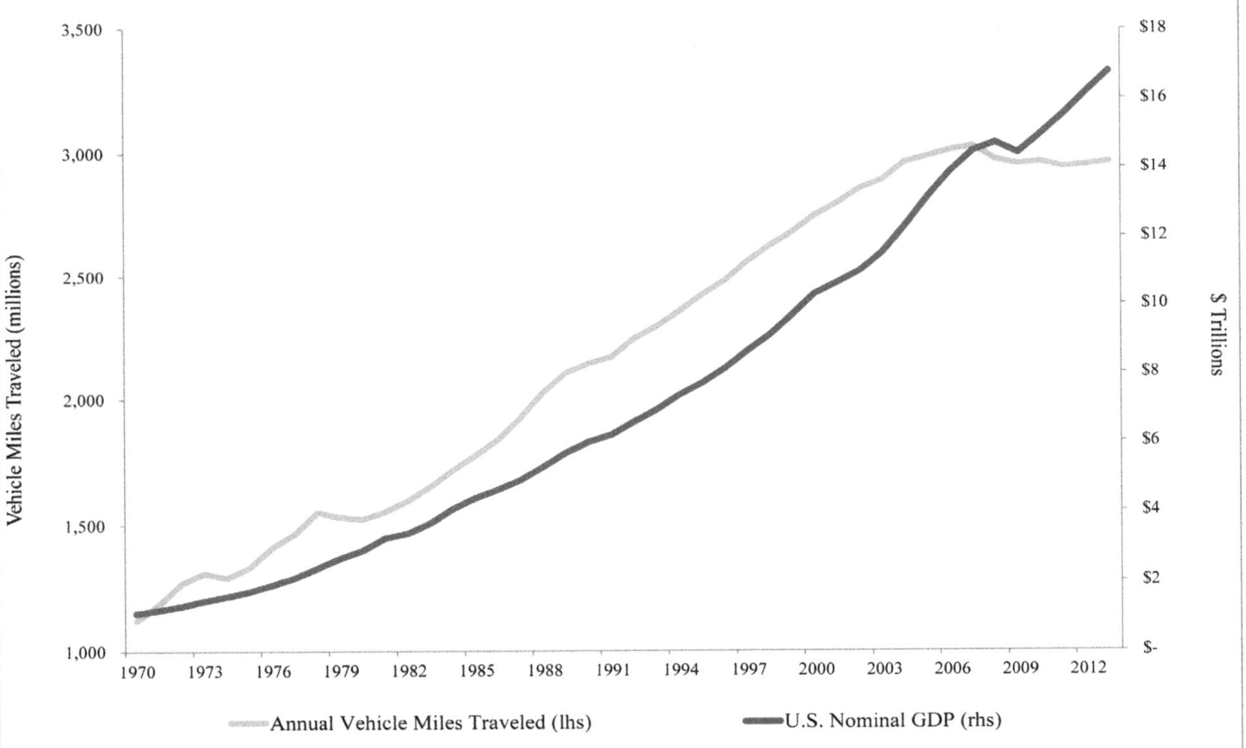

Source: U.S. Department of Transportation Federal Highway Administration

Those toll roads in areas with large population bases and diverse service areas are the most stable credits and benefit from consistent traffic trends.[72] Toll roads range greatly in size, from large, statewide, multi-road systems like the New Jersey Turnpike to smaller, single-road systems such as the Tampa Hillsborough Expressway Authority (THEA), which operates the Selmon Expressway.[73] Despite the sector's stability, vehicle traffic has not reached pre-recession levels. In addition, fuel prices will often impact vehicle traffic trends.

The longer a toll road has been in operation with stable traffic trends, the stronger its market position will be.[74] The larger the population base and the stronger its service area, the better position a toll road authority will be in to withstand economic declines. Many state and local governments have used toll roads as their "cash cows," transferring revenues from the operation of toll roads to their general fund to subsidize their budgets.[75] The implications are obvious: outside control over a toll road's expenditures can impact its finances.[76]

A final issuer type in this sector is mass transit systems, which variously involve the operation of buses, subways, trains, light rails, and trolleys. Mass transit systems function similarly to toll roads and airports in that they are sensitive to economic cycles and derive a substantial portion of their revenues from appropriations of dedicated taxes. The largest mass transit issuer is the New York Metropolitan Transportation Authority (MTA), which operates train and bus service in the New York metropolitan area. The most utilized mass transit service is bussing, with a total of 5.3 billion rides in 2013, followed by heavy rail at 3.8 billion rides during that time.[77] Heavy rail is much more capital-intensive than other forms of mass transportation; to illustrate the scale of the largest systems, we show the 10 largest systems by average weekly heavy-rail ridership in the first quarter of 2014.[78] Figure 4.5 shows the 15 largest mass transit systems operating in the United States.

Figure 4.5

Heavy Rail
Public Transportation Ridership Report
Fourth Quarter 2014

State and Primary City	Transit Agency	Average Wkdy (000's)
CA - Los Angeles	Los Angeles County MTA	153.0
CA - San Francisco	San Francisco Bay Area RTD	447.2
DC - Washington	Washington Metro Area TA	829.2
FL - Miami	Miami-Dade Transit Agency	74.6
GA - Atlanta	Metro Atlanta Rapid Tr Auth	232.1
IL - Chicago	Chicago Transit Authority	753.6
MA - Boston	Massachusetts Bay Tr Auth	560.5
MD - Baltimore	Maryland Transit Admin	48.0
NJ - Jersey City	Port Authority of NY & NJ	250.7
NJ - Lindenwold	Port Authority Transit Corp	35.3
NY - New York	MTA New York City Transit	9,060.8
NY - New York	MTA Staten Island Railway	26.9
OH - Cleveland	Greater Cleveland Reg TA	NA
PA - Philadelphia	Southeastern Penn TA	342.6
PR - San Juan	Puerto Rico DOT	33.7

Source: American Public Transportation Association

Figure 4.6 shows the cumulative change in ridership by mode of mass transit since 1990. As can be seen in the chart, light rail ridership has increased by more than 250% since 1990, a reflection of urbanization and change in consumer tastes toward living in cities.[79] Going forward, smaller cities without underground tunnel infrastructure will look to light rail for mass transit needs.

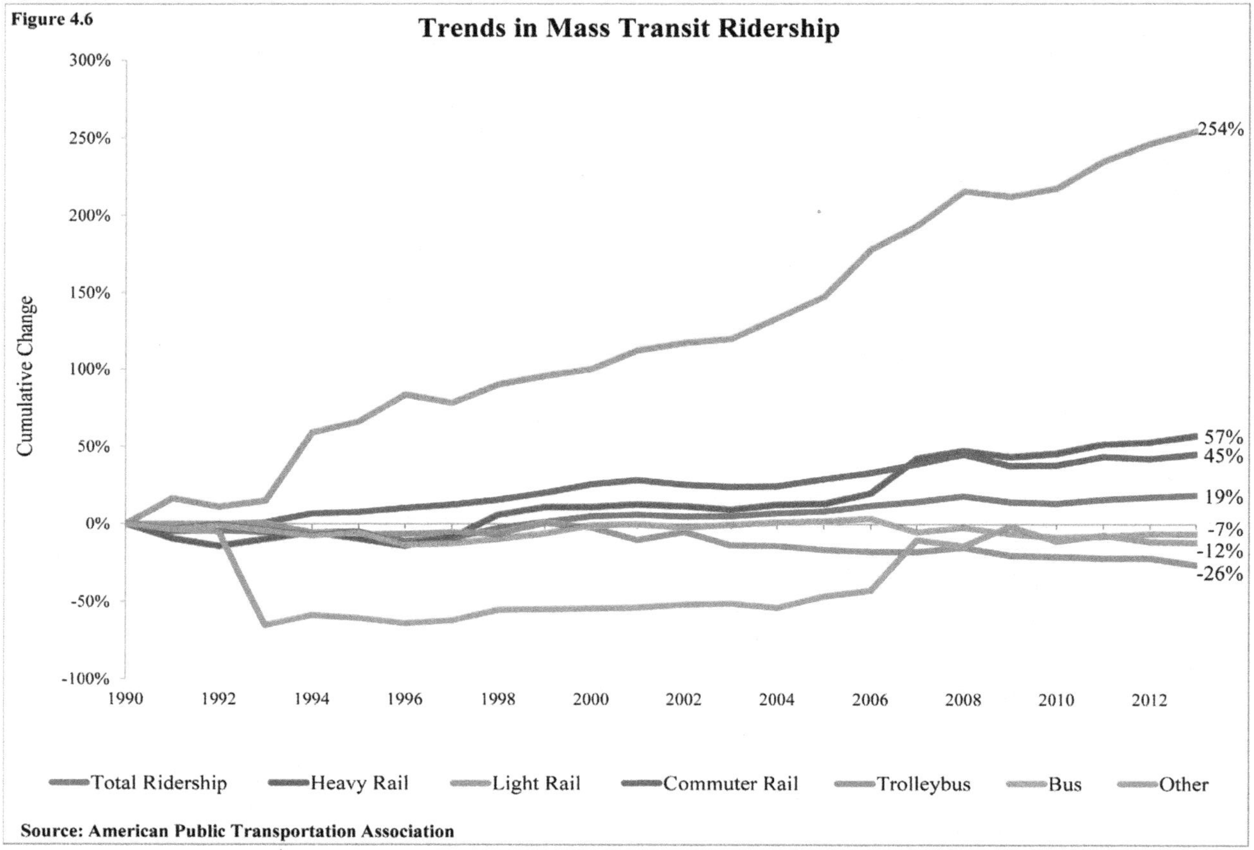

Mass transit systems face problems similar to those confronted by other issuers in the transportation sector, namely the challenges of funding capital expenditures and growing personnel costs dictated by onerous collective bargaining agreements. In the years after the financial crisis, systems like New York MTA raised fees substantially to combat these problems, without attempting to control expenses. Given MTA's and other mass transit systems' monopoly control of public transportation in their respective metro areas, their ability to raise fees without incurring reductions in demand make them strong credits.

Healthcare

The healthcare sector is perceived as being riskier than other sectors in the muni market. The healthcare sector combined with the housing sector is responsible for 73% of bond defaults since 1970; only five general obligation bond issuers have defaulted since that time.[80] The sector has been the subject of regulatory flux since the passage of the Affordable Care Act (ACA) in 2010. Since passage of the act, the ratio of Moody's bond downgrades to upgrades has been 1.3:1.[81]

The ACA has changed the healthcare industry in unforeseen ways and will likely change it for years to come, affecting everything from how healthcare is delivered to how doctors and hospitals are reimbursed for their services.[82] Net-net, the overall impact on hospitals is supposed to be somewhat neutral. While reimbursement rates for services are likely to decline, the number of insured patients will increase, reducing charity care and unprofitable hospital visits.[83] The strongest credits in the healthcare sector are large systems with multiple payers. A diversified revenue mix with both public and private insurance and multiple departments gives hospitals a natural hedge and allows them to address a wide variety of health needs.[84] Those hospitals with low Medicaid and Medicare exposure have higher margins because of the higher reimbursements received from private insurance providers.

The federal government's goal under ACA has been to slow the rise in healthcare costs to below the level of inflation to decrease the healthcare share of the economy. Given these regulatory pressures in the healthcare industry, we expect supply-side costs to continue rising and margins and liquidity to remain low.[85] Well-entrenched hospitals with low amounts of debt in large service areas are likely to fare the best in this environment.[86]

Issuers of revenue debt have faced slow growth since the financial crisis, mimicking the broader economy. Since they are business entities whose operations are distinct from the political process, their risk profiles differ from those of general obligation bonds. Hospital revenues often do not track changes in the broader economy, while state HFA programs function similarly to banks. These issuers are subject to their own idiosyncratic risks. Inclusion in a municipal bond portfolio can diversify this risk and provide a natural hedge for municipal bond investors.

5

Ratings Agencies: The Shadow Regulators of the Municipal Bond Market

Credit ratings agencies (CRAs) occupy a unique position in the lightly regulated United States credit markets. They provide shorthand indications of an obligor's credit quality, allow investors to make quick buy and sell decisions, and set demarcation points for investors, indicating whether or not securities are of investment merit. The role of ratings agencies in the modern financial system has expanded with the rapid growth in capital markets starting in the early 2000s, as financial intermediaries have increasingly looked toward the capital markets as a source of financing. This chapter discusses some of the basics of ratings agencies and their role in the municipal bond market. We also discuss the ratings agency model and how it has changed post-crisis.

Ratings agencies are similar to other associations or services that rate products, yet they are unique because after they rate a bond, they perform continual surveillance on it and adjust their rating based on improvements or declines in the issuer's ability to service its debts. We don't know of other types of ratings services that provide continuing surveillance on the subject being rated. The U.S. Department of Agriculture (USDA) provides quality grades on cuts of meat but doesn't grade the meat continually from the time it is cut until it is served at the dinner table; *Consumer Reports* rates a multitude of products from cars to consumer electronics on a subscriber-pay basis once those products are released, but not after continuing usage; auditing firms provide opinions on the internal controls and accounting practices of corporations on an issuer-pay model, but only once annually, at the end of the year when firms close their books. The continuing surveillance performed by ratings agencies is the way in which they distinguish themselves from these other entities. Ratings agencies are a unique feature of the capital markets.

The ratings agency market is an oligopoly dominated by three firms that rate a variety of issue types within a wide variety of asset classes. Moody's Investors Service and Standard & Poor's each control roughly 40% of the market, and Fitch Ratings controls the remaining 16%.[1] These three major players together command a 96% market share. Other players, such as Egan-Jones and Kroll Bond Rating Agency, are smaller and have been seen as a viable alternative to the business models of the "big three" in the years following the financial crisis. It is argued that because the ratings assigned by Egan-Jones are paid for by investors instead of issuers, the agency is better able to maintain its independence.[2] Kroll's focus on fewer issuers enhances their ability to perform surveillance.

Ratings agencies provide bond ratings to bond issues and bond issuers. A rating on a bond issue will categorically assess the likelihood of repayment based on factors such as that claim's seniority in an issuer's capital structure, project-specific risks, and cash flows; while in the municipal market a bond issuer rating will typically be assigned to an insurance company to assess its claims-paying ability.[3] For example, a municipal bond "wrapped" with a bond insurance policy will typically carry that insurance company's issuer rating because interest and principal payments will ultimately be secured by that company's ability to pay if the insurance policy is drawn upon. This chapter will focus on credit ratings of individual bond issues rather than on ratings assigned to bond insurers, as ratings of the bond issues themselves are more relevant to the discussion of the municipal bond market.

A ratings agency assigns a categorical rating to a bond, indicating the probability of timely repayment of principal and interest by the bond's issuer. The full range of ratings assigned by Moody's, S&P, and Fitch can be found in Figures 5.1, 5.2, and 5.3.

Figure 5.1

Rating	Standard & Poor's Long-Term Issuer Credit Ratings Scale *
AAA	An obligor rated 'AAA' has extremely strong capacity to meet its financial commitments. 'AAA' is the highest issuer credit rating assigned by Standard & Poor's.
AA	An obligor rated 'AA' has very strong capacity to meet its financial commitments. It differs from the highest-rated obligors only to a small degree.
A	An obligor rated 'A' has strong capacity to meet its financial commitments but is somewhat more susceptible to the adverse effects of changes in circumstances and economic conditions than obligors in higher-rated categories.
BBB	An obligor rated 'BBB' has adequate capacity to meet its financial commitments. However, adverse economic conditions or changing circumstances are more likely to lead to a weakened capacity of the obligor to meet its financial commitments.
BB	An obligor rated 'BB' is less vulnerable in the near term than other lower-rated obligors. However, it faces major ongoing uncertainties and exposure to adverse business, financial, or economic conditions which could lead to the obligor's inadequate capacity to meet its financial commitments.
B	An obligor rated 'B' is more vulnerable than the obligors rated 'BB', but the obligor currently has the capacity to meet its financial commitments. Adverse business, financial, or economic conditions will likely impair the obligor's capacity or willingness to meet its financial commitments.
CCC	An obligor rated 'CCC' is currently vulnerable, and is dependent upon favorable business, financial, and economic conditions to meet its financial commitments.
CC	An obligor rated 'CC' is currently highly vulnerable. The 'CC' rating is used when a default has not yet occurred, but Standard & Poor's expects default to be a virtual certainty, regardless of the anticipated time to default.
R	An obligor rated 'R' is under regulatory supervision owing to its financial condition. During the pendency of the regulatory supervision the regulators may have the power to favor one class of obligations over others or pay some obligations and not others.

* The ratings from 'AA' to 'CCC' may be modified by the addition of a plus (+) or minus (-) sign to show relative standing within the major rating categories

Source: Standard & Poor's

Figure 5.2

Rating	Moody's Investors Service Global Long-Term Ratings Scale
Aaa	Obligations rated Aaa are judged to be of the highest quality, subject to the lowest level of credit risk.
Aa	Obligations rated Aa are judged to be of high quality and are subject to very low credit risk.
A	Obligations rated A are judged to be upper-medium grade and are subject to low credit risk.
Baa	Obligations rated Baa are judged to be medium-grade and subject to moderate credit risk and as such may possess certain speculative characteristics.
Ba	Obligations rated Ba are judged to be speculative and are subject to substantial credit risk.
B	Obligations rated B are considered speculative and are subject to high credit risk.
Caa	Obligations rated Caa are judged to be speculative of poor standing and are subject to very high credit risk.
Ca	Obligations rated Ca are highly speculative and are likely in, or very near, default, with some prospect of recovery of principal and interest.
C	Obligations rated C are the lowest rated and are typically in default, with little prospect for recovery of principal or interest.

Source: Moody's Investors Service

Figure 5.3

Rating	Fitch Ratings Long-Term Ratings Scale
AAA	Highest credit quality. 'AAA' ratings denote the lowest expectation of default risk. They are assigned only in cases of exceptionally strong capacity for payment of financial commitments. This capacity is highly unlikely to be adversely affected by foreseeable events.
AA	Very high credit quality. 'AA' ratings denote expectations of very low default risk. They indicate very strong capacity for payment of financial commitments. This capacity is not significantly vulnerable to foreseeable events.
A	High credit quality. 'A' ratings denote expectations of low default risk. The capacity for payment of financial commitments is considered strong. This capacity may, nevertheless, be more vulnerable to adverse business or economic conditions than is the case for higher ratings.
BBB	Good credit quality. 'BBB' ratings indicate that expectations of default risk are currently low. The capacity for payment of financial commitments is considered adequate but adverse business or economic conditions are more likely to impair this capacity.
BB	Speculative. 'BB' ratings indicate an elevated vulnerability to default risk, particularly in the event of adverse changes in business or economic conditions over time; however, business or financial flexibility exists which supports the servicing of financial commitments.
B	Highly speculative. 'B' ratings indicate that material default risk is present, but a limited margin of safety remains. Financial commitments are currently being met; however, capacity for continued payment is vulnerable to deterioration in the business and economic environment.
CCC	Substantial credit risk. Default is a real possibility.
CC	Very high levels of credit risk. Default of some kind appears probable.
C	Exceptionally high levels of credit risk. Default is imminent or inevitable, or the issuer is in standstill. Conditions that are indicative of a 'C' category rating for an issuer include: a) the issuer has entered into a grace or cure period following non-payment of a material financial obligation; b) the issuer has entered into a temporary negotiated waiver or standstill agreement following a payment default on a material financial obligation; or c) Fitch Ratings otherwise believes a condition of 'RD' or 'D' to be imminent or inevitable, including through the formal announcement of a distressed debt exchange.

Source: Fitch Ratings

If a bond is rated higher than BBB-/Baa3 by S&P, Fitch, and Moody's, it is considered "investment-grade," with minimal risk of default to investors.[4] Each agency appends modifiers to its ratings. In the case of Moody's, the numbers 1, 2, and 3 indicate the level of credit quality within a given rating category. For S&P and Fitch, "+" and "-" signs serve the same purpose. For example, Moody's will rate issues Aa1, Aa2, Aa3, indicating the three tiers of credit quality within the Aa category. The S&P and Fitch equivalents are AA+, AA, and AA-.

Bond ratings are qualitative in nature and entail substantial judgment on behalf of ratings agencies. Moody's and S&P state many times in their published methodologies that there are no hard and fast rules or data thresholds dictating which credit ratings should be assigned to a given issuer or bond issue.[5] This judgment, based on experience and industry knowledge, is a key way in which ratings agencies add value, and it is the reason that many investors rely on credit ratings as part of the due diligence process. Over the course of the last 100 years, the ratings agencies have amassed large amounts of data useful for conducting studies and statistical analysis that can aid in investment decision-making. Default studies and annual issuer outlooks published by Moody's, for example, allow investors to gain insights on a sector-wide basis that they might not otherwise glean from holding-level, issuer-based analysis.

Although it is the goal of investors to preempt ratings agency action, the information ratings agencies provide is still valuable. Ratings agencies have access to an issuer's management, which few municipal bond managers have, and are exempt from SEC laws governing material, nonpublic information.[6] The agencies are thus allowed to publish crucial information that would otherwise, by law, go undisclosed—information investors need for informed decision-making.

J. M. Pimbley, in his skilled analysis of bond insurers, titled "Bond Insurers," refers to the ratings agencies as "night watchmen" of "bond insurer strength."[7] We believe the ratings agencies act as "night watchmen" for investors, looking to the safety of their municipal bond holdings, notifying investors in advance of changes in an issuer's circumstances, and enforcing their disclosure requirements.

A wide variety of factors are used in ratings agencies' assessments of an issuer's credit strength. After an initial rating is assigned, it is adjusted up or down based on new information that impacts the credit quality of an issue or issuer. Such information can include changing laws and regulations, lawsuits against an issuer, demographic trends, and business and economic conditions within an issuer's service area. This scrutiny applies not only to public finance issuers, but to any bond issuer who has rated debt outstanding (e.g., S corporations, foreign governments, structured finance transactions, and bond insurance policies).

On January 13, 2012, Standard & Poor's downgraded the issuer credit ratings of Cyprus, Italy, Portugal, and Spain by two notches and lowered their long-term ratings on Austria, France, Malta, Slovakia, and Slovenia by one notch.[8] S&P states this action was taken because of the countries' "collective inability" to "take actions needed to resolve the Eurozone crisis."[9] S&P states in its rationale that the timing of these downgrades signaled that further credit deterioration would likely be in store, as insufficient policy initiatives made repayment less likely in the future.[10]

Markets react to ratings changes based on the extent to which this material information is "baked in" to the price. Figure 5.4 shows that the yields on Italian government debt had been increasing in the weeks leading up to the S&P downgrade from A to BBB+ on January 13, 2012, indicating that market participants sensed a ratings action on the horizon. During this time, the yield increased from roughly 5.9% to a peak of 7.16% on January 9, three days prior to the downgrade. By the time S&P downgraded Italy, the yields had already declined by 52 basis points, indicating first that the market had already priced in a ratings change well before the change actually occurred, and second that the market had priced in a larger ratings change than the double-notch downgrade to BBB+. Regardless of when the market reacts, it is irrefutable that an issuer's credit rating will impact the price of its securities and, by extension, its ability to access the capital markets.

Figure 5.4

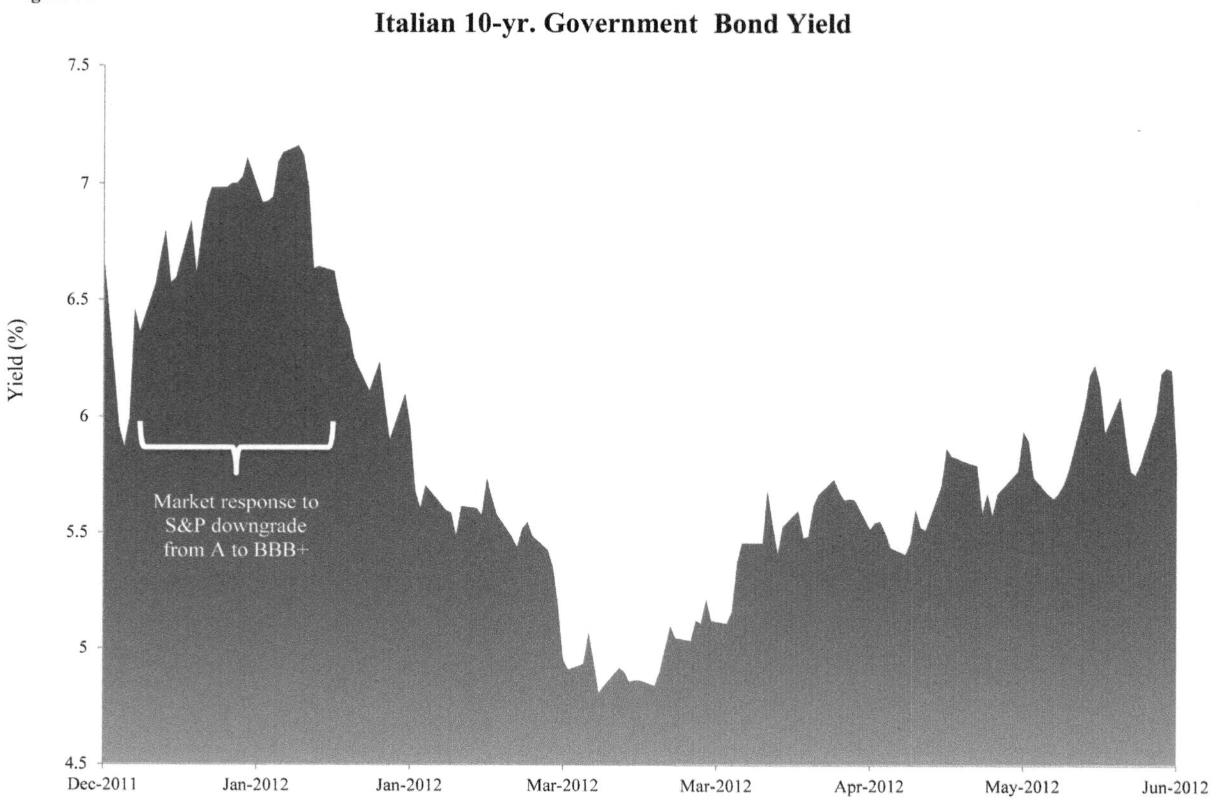

Source: Bloomberg

For various idiosyncratic reasons, most downgrades in the municipal market occur on a smaller scale than sovereign ratings. As an example, on May 1, 2014, Fitch downgraded from A to BBB+ the general obligation, unlimited tax bonds of Beaumont Independent School District (Beaumont ISD) after an FBI embezzlement investigation and confiscation of documents.[11] Fitch states that the district's poor internal controls and supervisory responsibility on behalf of managers signaled ineptitude, reason enough for downgrade despite the issuer's lack of immediate insolvency.[12] There was no noticeable change to the trading value of Beaumont ISD's bonds because of the bonds' guarantees under the Texas Permanent School Fund (PSF). Differing circumstances will determine the extent to which a market will react to ratings changes. Because of the debt's ironclad third-party guarantee from AAA-rated PSF, buyers and sellers placed little value on the change.

Ratings changes can also signify the health of certain sectors within an asset class when we look at them on a collective basis. For example, we see in Figure 5.5 that the number of Moody's upgrades in the tax-backed sector (i.e., general obligation, income, and sales tax bonds) have fallen far short of the number of downgrades since the recession, indicating that it may make sense to underweight that sector.[13]

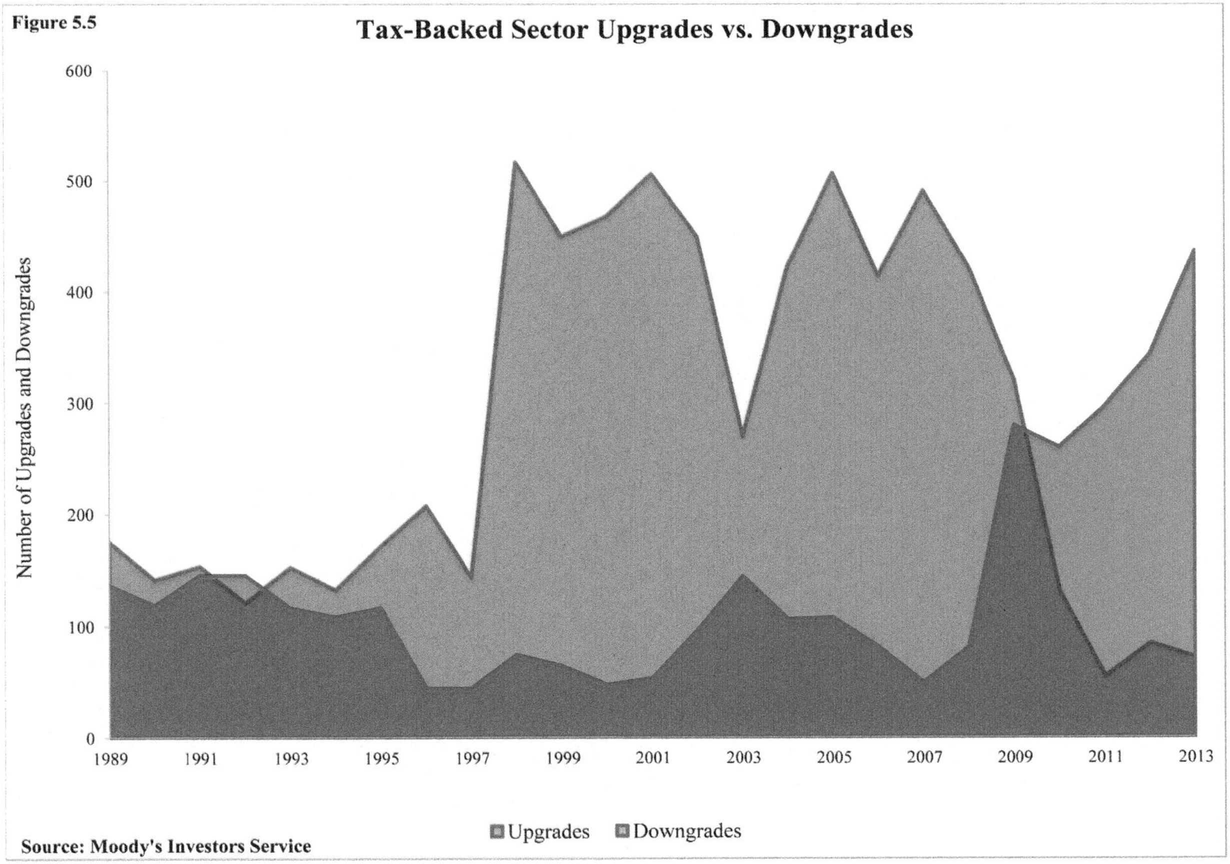

The same holds true for the revenue bond sector in Figure 5.6; however, we note that downgrades have dropped substantially starting in 2012, while upgrades are starting to increase. The prevalence of downgrades in the tax-backed sector is a reflection of slow growth in the economy and tepid recovery in tax revenues, as downgrades have outpaced upgrades every month since 2009. According to Moody's, the sector within the municipal market most impacted by downgrades has been housing, a reflection of the severity of the downturn and overhang of supply, especially in the low-income housing sector.[14]

Figure 5.6

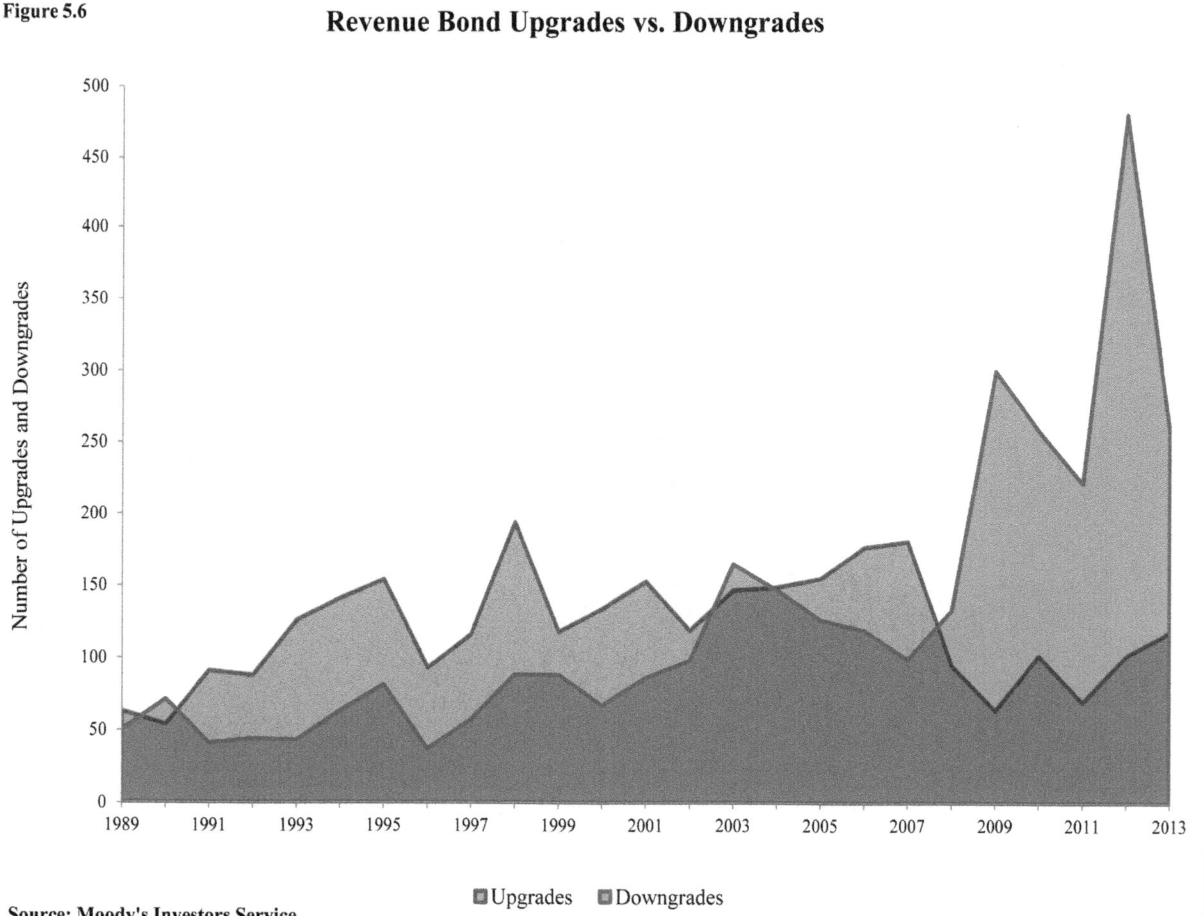

Source: Moody's Investors Service

On a sector-specific basis, it is useful to examine the ratio of downgrades to upgrades. Moody's states that the sector with the highest ratio is housing, followed by the infrastructure sector.[15] We can infer that the credit quality of these sectors may be declining due to broad-based, sector-specific trends. Sectors with a downgrade-to-upgrade ratio of less than one have been improving in credit quality and are likely to outperform, as industry trends are likely favorable. For the revenue-backed sector, although the ratio is less than one, it is increasing. Moody's states that this increase is likely the result of recent higher revenues and successful cost-containment strategies during the recession.[16] In spite of the declining credit quality in some sectors of the municipal market, credit quality within the asset class is still high overall. Of municipal issuers, 94% are rated A or better and are firmly entrenched as monopolistic entities compared to other asset classes.[17]

For example, municipal entities have numerous advantages over corporations: they function as monopolies, can layoff staff when revenues fall, and do not face competition.[18] Credit ratings of the municipal asset class reflect this. As stated in Moody's annual default study, "nearly all municipal issuers have investment-grade ratings, with 93% of issuers rated single-A or higher. By comparison, 21% of global corporate issuers are currently rated single-A or higher."[19]

When ratings agencies decide to take action, the actual reasons for ratings changes vary widely. Enactment of tax cuts have led to downgrades of municipal issuers such as towns and cities, while loan losses and portfolio delinquencies led to the downgrades of European banks in 2011. When new developments occur and their impact on an issuer's rating is uncertain, a "ratings watch" or "outlook change" may be assigned, prior to any change in an issuer's credit rating.[20] Before taking rating action, for example, Moody's, S&P, and Fitch may want to signal to the market that material information has been released.[21] In such cases, a "ratings watch" is assigned, indicating that events have caused the "rating to be placed under special surveillance."[22] Usually ratings watches are triggered by events such as regulatory actions or voter referendums that constitute a deviation from an expected trend or current information.[23] Moody's states that when a ratings agency decides that a change to a credit rating "is likely over the coming six months to two years" due to changes in business or economic circumstances, a "positive outlook" or "negative outlook" will be assigned.[24] A "developing outlook" will be assigned when a rating may be raised or lowered.[25]

Ratings are also used more formally in contractual settings by determining collateral requirements on over-the-counter interest rate swaps and letter of credit agreements. Ratings downgrades in early 2008 because of insurer exposure to subprime mortgage debt created ripple effects throughout the financial markets. Bond insurers were faced with liquidity risk because of provisions in credit default swap contracts requiring them to post collateral in the event that they were downgraded. Outside of the bond insurance industry and munis in general, counterparties to swap transactions were all forced to come up with collateral to back their obligations in the midst of the downgrades of the primary dealers. The downgrade of bond insurance also led to an upheaval in the auction-rate securities market, since downgrades meant that the securities became ineligible investments for money market funds, ultimately forcing issuers to pay penalty rates as high as 12% to underwriters until the bonds could be remarketed. During the financial crisis, ratings downgrades impacted markets in ways that were previously unforeseen.

The Jefferson County bankruptcy occurred because of downgrades of bond insurers XLCA and FGIC. XLCA and FGIC insured hundreds of millions in Jefferson County interest-rate swaps, floating "auction-rate" debt, and variable-rate demand bonds. When both insurers were downgraded to below-investment-grade, Jefferson County was unable to remarket its variable-rate debt, and its swap counterparties were able to demand additional collateral to back the transactions. Given the downgrades, the county would be forced to come up with hundreds of millions of collateral demanded by its counterparties and pay penalty interest rates as high was 10% until it could remarket its short-term debt. Faced with a liquidity crisis, the county entered forbearance agreements with its swap counterparties and ultimately filed for bankruptcy to restructure its debt obligations.

Prior to the financial crisis, credit ratings agencies served as quasi-regulators in the bond market by enforcing timely disclosure policies on behalf of issuers.[26] Ratings are also used by the Federal Deposit Insurance Corporation (FDIC), the Office of the Comptroller of the Currency (OCC), the Federal Reserve, and the Office of Thrift Supervision (OTS) as tools for enforcing federal banking regulations. Ratings are embedded in many federal regulations, mostly dealing with eligibility of investments for banks and pension funds.[27] In Europe, Basel II regulations use public ratings to determine risk weighting for banks and the eligibility of collateral for liquidity-providing operations of the European Central Bank (ECB).[28]

Questions regarding the accuracy of credit ratings in the years leading up to the financial crisis has catalyzed a regulatory response that sought to rein in the practices of ratings agencies and greatly reduce regulators' and banks' reliance on ratings agency data. The Dodd-Frank Act has created the Office of Credit Ratings at the SEC, which has been granted power to examine the ratings agencies on an annual basis, to levy fines for malfeasance, and to revoke Nationally Recognized Statistical Rating Organization (NRSRO) status for providing inaccurate ratings.[29] This last provision of the law is probably the most significant because it gives the SEC blanket authority to prosecute and to significantly regulate the business practices of ratings agencies.

Most significant in the municipal bond arena have been new regulations governing the usage of ratings agency information by commercial banks, which have been the largest net buyers of municipal bonds since the financial crisis.[30] The Dodd-Frank Act has set regulations requiring banks to rely on separate criteria for judging a security's credit quality, apart from Moody's or S&P ratings. Per the law, "the Federal Reserve, OCC, and FDIC issued a notice of proposed rulemaking for implementing ratings alternatives for the computation of risk-based capital for market and portfolio-risk exposures."[31] Specifically, the OCC redefined the term "investment-grade" as it relates to securities in bank portfolios by removing references to credit ratings assigned by nationally recognized ratings agencies. The OCC states that, "Under the revised regulations, to determine whether a security is 'investment-grade,' banks are required to determine that the probability of default by the obligor is low and that full and timely repayment of principal and interest is expected."[32]

Paraphrasing the OCC, in order for banks to meet these new regulations, instead of relying solely on national ratings agencies' due diligence, they must utilize "external ratings" processes and additional analyses that are appropriate for the instrument's "risk profile" and "size and complexity."[33] In other words, a security that is assigned an investment-grade rating by a ratings agency does "not sufficiently satisfy the revised 'investment-grade'" standard by that standard alone; proprietary or external due diligence is required.[34] Further, under the new regulations, banks are required to review their investment portfolios on an ongoing basis to verify that their holdings continue to meet these safety and soundness requirements.

This is a marked change from prior processes. Before the crisis, banks would typically buy a credit based solely on its A or AA rating. The implications of such a drastic change are large. Banks are now somewhat disincentivized to lend to small local governments, which constitute a niche market because of favorable treatment of interest costs used to finance such lending (known as bank-qualified lending). Given banks' newly established position in the municipal bond market as a much greater source of liquidity for smaller local governments than in recent years, red tape and regulatory costs associated with compliance have increased. Much-needed liquidity into the municipal bond market will be compromised.

The new federal regulations governing usage of ratings by regulated entities is a direct response to the practices that ratings agencies engaged in, practices that many market participants have faulted as having "enabled" the financial crisis.[35] We believe the ratings agencies have been unfairly scapegoated to some degree, although some of their actions were cause for concern. In 2007, for example, Moody's downgraded a whopping 83% of $869 billion of securitized mortgages it had rated AAA in 2006.[36] Although it is difficult to predict asset bubbles, in many cases AAA ratings were assigned by ratings agencies to earn fees and secure future ratings business.[37]

In the muni market, there has been a historical discrepancy between ratings given to municipal bonds and those given to corporate bonds based on the differing likelihoods of default between the two asset classes. Prior to 2010, Moody's systematically rated municipal obligations lower than similar corporate obligations, despite historical data suggesting that the credit quality of municipals is higher, on average, and default instances are much lower. Figure 5.7 indicates that from 1970 to 2013, for ratings categories ranging from Aaa to C, the average cumulative default rates on corporate bonds have exceeded those on municipal bonds. For example, from 1970 to 2013, on average, the percentage of municipal issues with an A rating that defaulted over a 10-year period was 0.05%, while for corporates the number was 2.73%, or 55.5 times that amount![38] It should stand to reason that municipal issuers should receive higher credit ratings than their corporate counterparts because of their lower default risk and overall higher quality. Historically, however, this has not been the case, as municipal bond ratings have been biased lower relative to corporates.

Figure 5.7

Cumulative Default Rates, *Average over the Period 1970-2013,* **Municipal vs. Corporate Issuers**

Rating	Year 1	Year 2	Year 3	Year 4	Year 5	Year 6	Year 7	Year 8	Year 9	Year 10
Municipal Issuers										
Rating	**Year 1**	**Year 2**	**Year 3**	**Year 4**	**Year 5**	**Year 6**	**Year 7**	**Year 8**	**Year 9**	**Year 10**
Aaa	0.00%	0.00%	0.00%	0.00%	0.00%	0.00%	0.00%	0.00%	0.00%	0.00%
Aa	0.00%	0.00%	0.00%	0.00%	0.01%	0.01%	0.01%	0.01%	0.01%	0.01%
A	0.00%	0.01%	0.01%	0.02%	0.02%	0.03%	0.03%	0.04%	0.05%	0.05%
Baa	0.01%	0.03%	0.06%	0.09%	0.12%	0.16%	0.20%	0.24%	0.28%	0.32%
Ba	0.16%	0.58%	1.00%	1.50%	1.97%	2.37%	2.79%	3.09%	3.34%	3.53%
B	2.32%	4.56%	6.74%	8.80%	10.72%	12.01%	12.74%	13.42%	14.15%	15.14%
Caa-C	6.67%	9.54%	11.30%	12.29%	12.80%	13.22%	13.69%	14.21%	14.64%	14.64%
Investment-Grade	0.00%	0.01%	0.02%	0.02%	0.03%	0.04%	0.05%	0.06%	0.07%	0.08%
Speculative-Grade	1.06%	1.99%	2.85%	3.67%	4.41%	4.98%	5.46%	5.86%	6.21%	6.54%
All Rated	0.01%	0.03%	0.04%	0.06%	0.07%	0.08%	0.09%	0.11%	0.12%	0.13%
Corporate Issuers										
Rating	**Year 1**	**Year 2**	**Year 3**	**Year 4**	**Year 5**	**Year 6**	**Year 7**	**Year 8**	**Year 9**	**Year 10**
Aaa	0.00%	0.01%	0.01%	0.04%	0.10%	0.17%	0.24%	0.32%	0.40%	0.49%
Aa	0.02%	0.07%	0.14%	0.26%	0.40%	0.53%	0.65%	0.77%	0.87%	0.99%
A	0.06%	0.20%	0.43%	0.67%	0.95%	1.26%	1.61%	1.98%	2.37%	2.73%
Baa	0.17%	0.50%	0.89%	1.36%	1.85%	2.36%	2.86%	3.37%	3.95%	4.61%
Ba	1.11%	3.06%	5.36%	7.81%	10.03%	12.08%	13.86%	15.65%	17.43%	19.27%
B	3.89%	9.23%	14.66%	19.43%	23.79%	27.87%	31.68%	34.91%	37.85%	40.48%
Caa-C	15.78%	26.82%	35.56%	42.55%	48.56%	53.01%	56.63%	60.14%	63.52%	66.02%
Investment-Grade	0.09%	0.27%	0.51%	0.80%	1.10%	1.43%	1.76%	2.11%	2.48%	2.87%
Speculative-Grade	4.43%	9.11%	13.56%	17.48%	20.92%	23.94%	26.58%	28.93%	31.11%	33.14%
All Rated	1.67%	3.39%	4.99%	6.37%	7.55%	8.58%	9.47%	10.27%	11.02%	11.73%

Source: Moody's Investors Service

In 2008, Connecticut Attorney General and soon-to-be U.S. Senator, Richard Blumenthal, filed lawsuits against Moody's, S&P, and Fitch, alleging that they frequently assigned lower credit ratings to Connecticut cities and towns than to corporate issuers despite the historical evidence suggesting that municipalities deserved higher credit ratings.[39] The state alleged that, because of this, these issuers purchased bond insurance and paid debt service costs much higher than they would have paid had the ratings been higher. The three ratings agencies settled with the state for $900,000 in 2011 and were forced to enact reforms.[40] This is oligopolistic behavior.

To penalize municipal issuers by assigning them lower ratings when the performance of the asset class has historically greatly exceeded that of corporate issuers demonstrates blatant inconsistency. Buckling under pressure from state attorneys general, dealers, and investors to correct the disparity, on March 16, 2010, Moody's increased ratings on 18,000 of its 70,000 issuers to bring its municipal rating scale in line with its corporate rating scale.[41] This ratings "recalibration" increased ratings anywhere from 1 to 3 notches, with the most pronounced effects impacting the lowest investment-grade categories.[42] Standard & Poor's has taken similar steps, revising the criteria with which they rate entities, instead of systematically increasing each issuer's ratings to a new scale.

The market's response to Moody's ratings recalibration was significant. Whereas some claimed that pricing changes would not occur, issuers whose ratings changed saw a noticeable decline in their bond yields, especially in borderline-rated credits. Issuers such as the formerly Baa1-rated State of California, which saw its credit rating increase to A3, were able to expand the buyer base of their bonds once their ratings were recalibrated. Institutional investors, whose investment policies forbade the purchase of bonds rated less than A3, piled into this debt, tightening credit spreads, because of its relative "cheapness" versus similarly-rated paper. It is important to stress that the credit quality of such issuers hadn't fundamentally changed post-recalibration, but the change in institutional investor behavior, along with improved perception by retail buyers, lowered bond yields. In the long run, lower-rated issuers were given expanded access to capital, while the credit quality of municipal issuers was reaffirmed.

The recalibration controversy and other disputes relating to the financial crisis have called into question the conflicts of interest inherent in the ratings agencies' business model. We mentioned earlier that, under the "issuer pay" model, an issuer pays for its own credit rating. An issuer can also choose not to have a credit rating or can withdraw an existing rating anytime. "Issuer-pay" credit ratings, it is thought, create an incentive to upwardly bias credit ratings in order to incentivize issuers to pay for them in the first place. The argument has been made that because the credit ratings agencies have an interest in rating as many entities as possible (to increase business volumes), it is likely that they will keep ratings high in order to attract business, to the detriment of regulators and investors, who rely most on this information to make decisions.[43]

The financial crisis demonstrated the conflicted position of credit ratings agencies: on the one hand, they were charged with performing due diligence and understanding the securities they were rating; on the other hand, they were striving to protect and expand the scope and complexity of their businesses.[44] In the years leading up to the financial crisis, ratings agency activity expanded, roughly tracking the increased leverage in banking and capital markets activity during the period.[45] Credit default swap, securitization, and lower capital requirements increased the potential business opportunities available to ratings agencies.[46] By 2008, the revenues generated by rating these complex securities and the derivatives linked to them had expanded significantly, to the point that revenues from these activities alone were greater than aggregate revenues across all their business lines had been in 2001.[47]

Structured finance is exceedingly complex and difficult to evaluate without the help of dealers. That complexity is what sets the ratings process in that arena apart. Dealers and ratings agencies worked together in structuring transactions with levels of subordination and collateralization that would be palatable to institutional investors, utilizing the dealers' proprietary models to model cash flow waterfalls.[48] Given the closeness of this relationship, ratings agencies were incentivized to assign high ratings in order to get the deals placed to earn ratings fees.[49] As a result, the ratings agencies were forced to rely on models that dealers provided to them, models which, it turns out, reflected overly optimistic assumptions about housing prices and economic conditions.[50]

Many have said that the ratings agencies were the enablers of the subprime crisis at each step, from origination to securitization, because of the "investment-grade" ratings assigned to subprime securities. In the absence of investment-grade ratings, demand from institutional investors for these higher-yielding alternatives to "plain vanilla" investment-grade securities would simply not have existed. Artificially high investment-grade ratings ultimately created a flow of investment whereby risk was transferred from originator to end-user (e.g., a bank or insurance company).[51]

During the crisis, regulators concerned with the ratings inflation of these securities suggested that market competition would incentivize greater accuracy on behalf of ratings agencies. But the entrance of Fitch into the subprime ratings market had the effect of increasing ratings inflation instead.[52] S&P and Moody's, seeing the possible threat of new competition, systematically inflated ratings in order to attract new ratings business from underwriters who threatened to go to Fitch for better ratings.[53] This interesting phenomenon is an unintended consequence of a business model that rewards volume of business instead of accuracy.

While there is evidence that the ratings agencies played a role in the crisis, it is inaccurate to scapegoat the agencies as being solely responsible for the entire chain of events that brought the financial system to its knees. Bank regulators were culpable for their lax oversight of primary dealers. The U.S. government (both Congress and the executive branch) pressured lenders to increase loans to lower-income borrowers in order to increase homeownership. Fannie Mae and Freddie Mac increased portfolio leverage to multiples much greater than those of primary dealers, creating a "too-big-to-fail" scenario whereby the government would be forced to bail them out. The financial crisis was triggered by a chain of events made possible by many parties in the process. While that included the ratings agencies, it also included primary dealers, foreign governments, the government-sponsored enterprises (GSEs), commercial banks, and bond insurers.

Frank Partnoy has been a thought leader on the topic of the accuracy of ratings agencies. In his paper "The Siskel and Ebert of Financial Markets: Two Thumbs Down for the Credit Rating Agencies," Partnoy explains that the job of ratings agencies is inherently difficult, and failure almost inevitable.[54] Default risks, financial crises, and accounting scandals are very difficult to uncover, as willingness to pay is highly subjective and very difficult to evaluate.[55] He points out that credit-default swap (CDS) spreads and structural and other mathematical models perform similarly to ratings agencies in predicting defaults.[56] Regulators blamed ratings agencies because downgrades of sovereign entities such as the U.S. government and European countries made it difficult for their banking systems to recapitalize in the aftermath of financial crises. The European Commission even proposed a government-run alternative to the ratings agencies; however, there are conflicts of interest inherent in this model, too.

The common defense put forth by ratings agencies for their mistakes during the financial crisis has been that ratings are opinions and nothing more, and as such are protected under the First Amendment of the U.S. Constitution. But if this is the case, it is difficult to justify NRSRO status conferred on them by regulators. The ratings agencies' business model relies upon this special status since it allows them access to nonpublic information not available to investors. If the agencies' ratings are only opinions, then they carry no more weight than the opinions of other market practitioners such as investors, research analysts, or brokers.

Partnoy discusses the "reputational capital" argument put forth by ratings agencies as for why they are incentivized to provide accurate information.[57] The argument suggests that they are incentivized to provide accurate ratings or risk losing their reputation as accurate providers of information.[18] If they lose their reputation, it is argued, their services will not be valued by the market. This scenario has played out to some degree. Since the financial crisis, ratings agencies have forfeited much reputational capital, as investors have looked to other information sources, including proprietary models, and outside parties for due diligence. As we state above, the OCC has rewritten its regulations governing how banks perform due diligence by eliminating mention of ratings agencies altogether.

Partnoy suggests that regulatory reliance on ratings agencies is the sole reason for their existence and for their firm entrenchment within the bond market; reputational capital is not a consideration.[59] Because ratings agencies provide a "certificate" of a bond's value that can be used to justify a bond purchase to regulators on the grounds that ratings thresholds are written into regulations regarding admissible portfolio investments, institutional investors are highly incentivized and almost required to purchase rated debt in order to defend their investment decisions.[60] Investors pay for certifications by accepting lower yields on these securities. Justifying the purchase of a non-rated security versus an AAA-rated security is difficult and costly in terms of time, continuing surveillance, and regulatory compliance.

Despite criticism of the issuer-pay model, there has been progress toward market or regulatory change governing remuneration of ratings agencies. Egan-Jones has entered the market on a small-scale, subscriber-pay basis, but does not actively rate the vast majority of credit market debt outstanding (especially within municipals). Perhaps vesting of fees over time would incentivize agencies to prioritize the accuracy of ratings; however, this might come at high cost, especially to smaller issuers in the municipal market, where $30K for a bond rating could be an onerous burden. Kroll, as of June 2015, has started to make a footprint in the public finance sector and is gaining traction for its use among institutions and issuers.

There have been suggestions that ratings agencies should be subject to financial liability for losses; however, under U.S. law, financial liability is possible only in instances of fraud; and ratings agencies have not been charged with fraud. In 2013, S&P and Moody's settled with the U.S. Department of Justice over allegations of negligence, however.[61]

With regard to munis in particular, credit ratings agencies act as the gatekeeper for bond insurers by allowing them to write new business.[62] The importance of ratings agency ratings for the monoline insurance companies cannot be overstated. In theory, insurance companies "sell" their credit ratings to low-rated issuers for a premium, in exchange for lowering debt service costs on their outstanding debt.[63] Post-financial crisis, we've found that bond issues rated greater than A/A2 and wrapped with insurance policies do not trade lower in yield as a result of those policies; the policies are therefore not providing meaningful credit enhancement to the market. This was a theme that played out in the years after the financial crisis, as investors grew to distrust the bond insurance industry.

When Assured Guaranty and National Public Finance Guaranty were upgraded in April 2014 by S&P to AA and AA- respectively, bonds wrapped with their policies tightened in spread anywhere from 15 to 50 basis points, depending on the quality of the underlying issuer. Such tightening indicates that municipal bond investors have started to see value in guarantees from bond insurers, and it affirms the insurer's ability to pay claims if needed, an important feature in a market with a historically large retail component. We discuss these in Chapter 6.

Going forward it is expected that the ratings agencies will continue to play a role as information providers and quasi-regulators within the credit markets. Private contracts will continue to be based, to a degree, on credit ratings as a way for counterparties to perform shorthand due diligence on each other, while investors will use ratings as demarcation points to determine which securities are eligible for investment. The bond market is not completely do-it-yourself; ratings perform valuable due diligence and can be counted on in a fast-paced decision-making environment.

Regulators, who themselves were partially to blame for the practices which led to the financial crisis, saw the ratings agencies as useful scapegoats. We note that the ability to predict with certainty an issuer's willingness to repay its debts is an almost impossible task; the ability to predict a financial bubble is even more difficult.[64] Looking back on a financial system built on the ratings-agency model, many have stated that the expectation was perhaps that the ratings agencies should be able to predict bubbles.[65] We believe that credit ratings can serve as useful indicators but should be valued within the context of multiple decision-making criteria and certainly not as a be-all and end-all, as was fairly commonplace in the years leading up to the financial crisis.

6

Bond Insurance: A Comeback in the Cards?

Given there are over 50,000 issuers of municipal debt across 40 different sectors, with an average issue size of less than $10 million, an investor's due diligence process for deciding "which bond to buy," can be quite onerous.[1] Does it make economic sense for individual buyers of municipal debt to perform quarterly on-site visits for issues in their portfolio? In a typically well-diversified portfolio with at least 20 different credits, the answer is probably not. On the flip side, wouldn't it make sense for issuers of municipal debt to actively market their bonds to as many potential buyers as possible in order to lower their borrowing costs? These informational asymmetries have existed in the municipal bond market since its inception and have created the need for third-party expertise to aid in the due diligence process, à la bond insurance.

The importance of bond insurance within the municipal bond sphere cannot be understated. Municipal bond insurers have insured $6 trillion in debt since the start of the industry.[2, 3] The rapid rise of bond insurance from 3% of issuance in 1980 to 60% in 2007 gave rise to commoditization and homogenization in the market that drove acceptance by issuers and investors and increased the ease by which they could access the market as both buyers and sellers.[4] In what is otherwise a fragmented market, bond insurance has enhanced liquidity and shaped the modern municipal bond market as we know it today.

Bond insurance had its start in 1971, when the American Municipal Bond Assurance Corporation, otherwise known as Ambac, insured a bond issued by the town of Greater Juneau, Alaska, to finance the construction of hospital facilities.[5] In this case, buyers of the bonds benefited from the presence of AAA-rated guarantors backing their bonds, without having to delve deeply into the bond's legal structure or the minute details impacting the city's credit quality, while the city benefited from being able to sell bonds to a large buyer base. Following the entrée of Ambac into the municipal bond market and given the ability of companies to insure payment of interest and principal when due on municipal obligations, several other guarantors entered the market.[6]

In 1973, five insurance companies formed the Municipal Bond Insurance Association, or MBIA, to diversify their businesses into municipal bonds.[7] By 1985, four insurers dominated the market, and so the financial guaranty business was born, increasing at its peak to 10 bond insurers by 2007 and insuring $2.5 trillion in debt at that time.[8] As James P. McNichols points out in his paper, "Monoline Insurance & Financial Guaranty Reserving," published by the Casualty Actuarial Society, companies specializing in bond insurance are known as "monolines" because they underwrite only financial guaranty insurance and are unable to enter into other business lines in some jurisdictions.[9] McNichols' insights on the inner-workings of bond insurance have been valuable for the writing of this chapter.

The original intent of bond insurance was to bridge the aforementioned informational gap for municipal bond buyers while lowering the cost of capital for issuers. J. M. Pimbley, who describes the downfall of the bond insurance industry in his in-depth piece titled, "Bond Insurers," which can be found in the *Journal of Applied Finance*, talks about the original economics of bond insurance transactions.[10] We summarize some of his thoughts in the next few paragraphs.

Bond insurers would charge a fee of roughly 0.4% to 0.5% of total debt service for a given deal and limit their business to tax-backed obligations of state and local governments.[11] The primary thesis was that a municipal issuer's taxing authority from an "ad valorem pledge" was available to make bond insurers whole, and any sort of restructuring would limit insurers' loss to the amounts paid on insurance claims during the reorganization process.[12] Given the historical stability of revenues, insurers would be able to recover 100% of the amount owed to them.[13]

McNichols shows that, starting in the 1980s, the monoline bond insurance model changed somewhat, with new entrants coming into the market. The primary flaw of the low-risk underwriting model, with its "zero-loss" expectation, was its unprofitability.[14] As more insurers entered the market, insurance premiums decreased, creating a situation where bond insurers were forced either to expand into riskier business lines or to increase their leverage in order to remain profitable.[15]

The municipal bond insurance business had been profitable up until this time because there had been very little in the way of losses, very few default instances, and limited liquidity requirements.[16] Michael B. McKnight, in his piece "Reserving for Financial Guaranty Products," explains that despite premium compression, the underwriting criteria of the monolines were kept solidly intact for many reasons, not the least of which was the fact that losses, should they occur, could wipe out several years of premium income.[17]

McNichols notes that the first wave of business diversification came in the late 1980s, when insurance companies diversified into insuring the debt of project financings and business-like public instrumentalities such as water and sewer systems, mass transit, and toll roads.[18] Insurers also looked abroad and underwrote similar issuances in previously untapped markets such as South America and Europe. This trend marked a shift in thinking from the "zero-risk," minimal-loss business of public finance to riskier, non-taxpayer-supported projects that were similar to private enterprises.[19] These deals were secured only by cash flows and revenues inherent to their projects and not by a tax-backed pledge. The result was that insurers now had riskier books of business, with uncertain correlations, greater default frequencies, and higher loss-given-default (LGD) characteristics.[20]

J. M. Pimbley shows that in the early 1990s, the insurers embarked on a foray into structured finance, writing policies on senior tranches of asset-backed securities and collateralized debt obligations (CDOs), with the hope that the higher insurance premiums would increase return on equity (ROE) to beyond single-digit levels.[21] In the mid-2000s, the scope of business was expanded into residential mortgage-backed securities (RMBS) and credit default swap markets, exposing the insurers to collateral and liquidity risks they had not been accustomed to in earlier years.[22] The underwriting standards of the insurers dropped significantly with the expansion into non-insurance and exotic products such as synthetic CDOs, CDOs-squared, and trading of credit default swaps.[23] Unbeknownst to insurers at the time, their portfolios increased due to the greater risks inherent in the structured finance market versus the municipal bond market. Defaults in structured finance tended to be more frequent, and losses were much larger.

The aggressive expansion into these markets is what ultimately brought down the majority of bond insurers in 2007. Insurers Ambac and MBIA had net subprime exposures of $30 billion and $22 billion respectively, yet each firm held only $6.5 billion in capital.[24] When these AAA-rated tranches were downgraded to below investment grade, they were forced to post collateral and pay claims on these policies, draining reserves and statutory capital. In 2007, MBIA booked a $1.9 billion loss and was forced to recapitalize.[25] ACA was downgraded to CC from A after its $1 billion loss.[26] Other insurers, FGIC, CIFG, Radian, and XLCA, experienced similar problems. Moody's and S&P responded with downgrades to less than investment grade. The market's opinion of bond insurance changed for the worse, leaving the monoline industry incapacitated and unable to generate new business. Figure 6.1 shows that of the seven bond insurers rated AAA by Moody's and S&P, none of them were able to retain their original ratings during the crisis, while four of them had their ratings stripped due to bankruptcy, liquidation, and new policies, requiring ratings agencies to maintain higher capital levels.

Figure 6.1

Ratings Pre-Crisis			Ratings as of 06/13/2014		
	Moody's	*S&P*		*Moody's*	*S&P*
AGMC	Aaa	AAA	AGMC	A3	AA
MAC	NR	AA+	MAC	NR	AA
BAM	NA	NA	BAM	NR	AA
NPFG	Aaa	AAA	NPFG	A3	AA-
BHAC	Aaa	AAA	BHAC	Aa1	AA+
AMBAC	Aaa	AAA	AMBAC	WR	NR
Syncora (XLCA)	Aaa	AAA	Syncora (XLCA)	WR	NR
FGIC	Aaa	AAA	FGIC	WR	NR
CIFG	Aaa	AAA	CIFG	WR	NR
Radian	Aa3	A	Radian	NR	NR
ACA	NR	A	ACA	NR	NR

Sources: Bloomberg, Raymond James

In the years after the financial crisis, the percentage of municipal bond market issuance that was insured (also known as "market penetration") declined to the low single digits from its peak of 57% in 2005.[27] The percentage of total new issuance sold as insured bottomed at 3% in 2012.[28] The market's distrust of bond insurance was a driver of these lower penetration rates. Figure 6.2 shows the market penetration rates from 2005 to 2014.

Figure 6.2

	2005	2006	2007	2008	2009	2010	2011	2012	2013	2014
Total Issuance	$ 408,282,800	$ 388,838,000	$ 429,893,700	$ 389,631,800	$ 409,688,500	$ 433,268,800	$ 287,718,400	$ 379,608,800	$ 333,476,300	$ 18,870,100
Number of Issues	13,959	12,766	12,659	10,830	11,721	13,828	10,574	13,115	11,428	617
Bond Insurance	$ 232,976,100	$ 191,326,200	$ 201,017,800	$ 72,181,100	$ 35,401,200	$ 26,857,400	$ 15,256,500	$ 13,274,100	$ 12,075,700	$ 740,700
Percent Insured	57%	49%	47%	19%	9%	6%	5%	3%	4%	4%

Sources: The Bond Buyer, Interactive Data Corp

In normally functioning markets, an insured bond will trade as if it were an obligation of the bond insurer itself. Prior to the crisis, an entire subset of the market traded as if the ratings of the bond obligors were those of the insurers. This substitution effect created a commoditized market; bonds traded on spread differentials between the seven dominant AAA-rated bond insurers, not on the credit quality of the underlying issuers. An A-rated entity that had its bonds insured by AAA-rated Ambac, for instance, would be able to sell debt at the lower yields that buyers of Ambac-insured paper would accept, not at the higher yields the issuer would have to offer on its own. The spread differential between the two yields was the "value-add" of bond insurance and also the cost savings to the issuer.[29] As McKnight states, the obligor effectively rents the insurer's rating in return for an upfront payment.[30] The amount of cost savings varies based on the value placed on each insurer by the market.

This "value add" afforded by bond insurance evaporated starting in 2007, when the ratings agencies downgraded insurers, in many cases to levels lower than the ratings on the underlying issuers.[31]

The value of bond insurance is best illustrated by analyzing the divergence in yields that occurred at the end of 2013 and continued into 2014, between uninsured and insured long-term Puerto Rico debt. Figure 6.3 graphs the yields on uninsured PREPA 5% bonds due in 2042 and National Public Finance Guarantee-insured PREPA 5.25% due in 2035. Post-recession, the yields tracked closely without noticeable difference between the two. Investors placed little value on bond insurance because of the power authority's perceived credit strength. When rumors about the island's impending financial difficulties surfaced in the summer of 2013 (catalyzed by a Barron's cover story on the Commonwealth published in late August), yields on uninsured debt started to increase relative to insured debt. A Moody's downgrade of PREPA in late 2013 and new legislation allowing for restructuring of public corporations continued to lift yields on uninsured debt relative to insured debt. The spread between the two increased to 770 basis points, peaking in late June 2014.

Figure 6.3

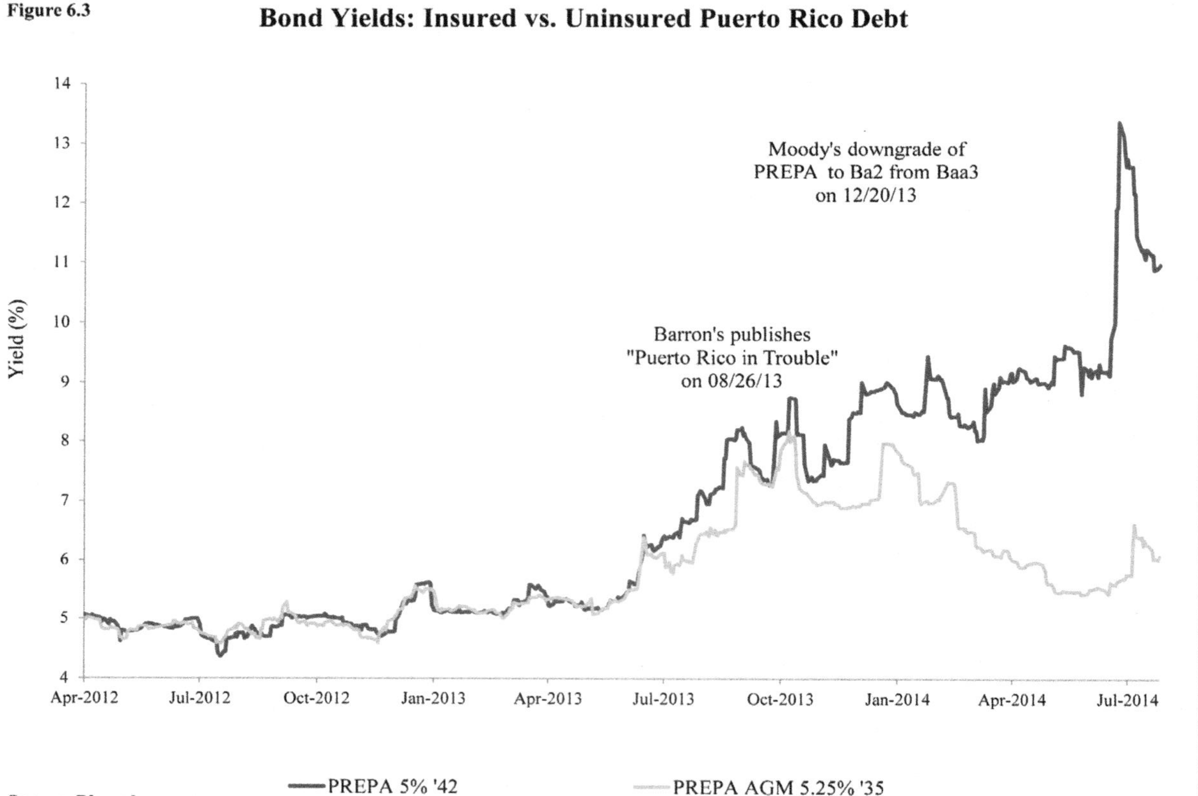

Source: Bloomberg

From the issuer's perspective, such wide divergence between PREPA's insured and uninsured debt allows it to come to market with insured bonds and save substantial amounts of money. The wide divergence in yields indicates investor confidence in insurers and their ability to pay deficiencies in principal and interest. The deteriorating credit quality of PREPA during the time period, depicted by figure 6.3, increased the value placed on insurance.

The value of bond insurance credit substitution increases as the ratings differential between the issuer and the insurer increases. Figure 6.3 shows that the insured PREPA bonds carry ratings of A3/AA-, while the uninsured bonds carry ratings of Caa2/CCC, indicating heightened risk of missed payments and restructuring. Figure 6.4 indicates the synchronized movements in yields on insured and uninsured Los Angeles Department of Water and Power (LADWP) bonds. Since LADWP bonds carry ratings of Aa2/AA+ without insurance and Aa3/AA- with insurance, the insurance policy is of little value to either investors or the issuer. The average spread between the two of roughly 20 basis points in favor of the insured bonds reflects their shorter maturity and call structure, not the value placed on insurance protection.

Figure 6.4

LADWP Bond Yields: Insured vs. Uninsured

Source: Bloomberg

If the spread differential between the issuer's and bond insurer's cost of capital is less than the actual insurance premium, the issuer will not purchase bond insurance. With many insurance companies downgraded to non-investment grade starting in 2007, this scenario unfolded, making it impossible for insurers to write new business. As McNichols states, the most important asset a bond insurer has is its financial strength ratings assigned by the nationally recognized statistical ratings agencies. Bond insurers work with the ratings agencies to set and meet benchmarks in order to preserve high ratings.[32] When their ratings decline, so does the value of what they're selling.[33]

The typical municipal bond insurance policy is paid for by issuers on an upfront basis. The cost of insurance varies based on market conditions and typically ranges between 40 and 50 basis points of total debt service.[34] The cost the issuer pays for insurance must be less than the cost of selling bonds without insurance, so that savings are split between the issuer and the insurer.[35] Typically, higher interest rates portend wider spreads, allowing insurers to charge higher premiums. Bond insurance can also be purchased by investors in the secondary market on a negotiated-premium basis.[36] Investors will sell bonds to the bond insurer and buy them back at a higher price with a new CUSIP identifier and with bond insurance. Unit investment trusts and closed-end funds will "wrap" groups of bonds on a temporary basis for the life of the trust or closed-end fund.[37]

The mechanics of bond insurance are such that it works like most other types of insurance in a buy or sell transaction. For monoline insurance, investors are protected against loss of principal and interest due to nonpayment by the underlying issuer. For all intents and purposes, the bond insurer is the ultimate source of payment on the debt, so the bond's credit rating will reflect that of the insurance company and not the issuer. In the normal course of business, the value of the bonds may decline due to downgrades and interest rate changes; bond insurance policies will not cover such losses and can be canceled only because of fraud or factual misstatements on behalf of the issuer (as with any other contract); the bond insurance policy attaches to each individual bond regardless of owner.[38]

Another important function of bond insurance receives less attention, namely the ability of bond insurers to negotiate with distressed issuers when a default occurs.[395] Analyst David Veno of S&P states that as bond insurers are truly in the "bond insurance game" for the long haul, they have more tools at their disposal and are better able than investors to negotiate settlements when a default occurs.[40] Whereas an investor can sell out of its exposure to any single issuer if the need arises, insurers cannot. They will, in fact, seek to maintain their business relationships with issuers in order to write business in the future.[41] Issuers will seek similar arrangements with insurers to lower their capital costs on future bond issues. Their interdependence means that insurers are more likely to get favorable treatment in distressed scenarios.[42]

The large size of insurers' exposures makes it easier for them to participate directly in restructuring plans and negotiations, given that, in certain cases, they have majority control above set thresholds.[43] As a result, the recovery rates insurers are able to achieve tend to be higher than those achieved by investors who own uninsured bonds.[44] Owners of insured bonds would not experience disruptions in expected payments when a policy kicks in, and insurance companies have many resources at their disposal that are not available to individual and professional investors.

Because of the large typical size of their exposure in a given insurance transaction, insurers are much more able to negotiate with bond trustees, bond counsel, and other parties to avoid defaults before they occur. By uncovering these problems through monitoring, insurers can deal with covenant violations and other early warning signs of credit deterioration before these escalate into larger problems.[45]

J. M. Pimbley points out the inherent flaws in the insurer model. When premiums are shrinking, how is it possible to profitably insure against ultra-low-probability events such as municipal bond defaults?[46] Pimbley states that the probability of municipal bond defaults historically has been close to zero (0.06% of Baa-rated issuers), and the loss-given-default experience has been low relative to the default rate of similarly-rated corporates(close to 80% versus 30% for senior unsecured debt).[47] With multiple entrants into the bond insurance business in the 2000s, premiums compressed and insurers were actively encouraged by ratings agencies to diversify into higher-premium businesses like structured finance in order to maintain their ratings.[48] This inherent problem of insuring ultra-low-probability events for low premiums requires the use of leverage in order to get adequate returns on equity (with leverage defined as insured par to statutory capital).[49] In the years leading up to the crisis, insurers increased the size of their insured books by more than 100 times their capital base. Statutory leverage limits for monolines under New York Insurance Law are 300:1, as regulators consider default risk to be sufficiently low to justify these limited capital requirements. Even the ratings agencies considered leverage of 100:1 to be "sufficiently low" to justify AAA ratings.[50] Thus, bond insurers are highly leveraged enterprises vulnerable to widespread credit deterioration.[51]

Pimbley also discusses the issue of market efficiency.[52] If the market is valuing credit risk between insured and uninsured bonds at 50 basis points, how is it that insurers are adequately compensated by charging premiums at less than these amounts? The insurers argue that the answer lies in market inefficiency. Large numbers of relatively illiquid, small issues make arbitrage difficult in the muni market. Therefore, market inefficiencies persist so that insurers are able to capitalize while continuing to insure to a zero-loss standard.[53]

During the financial crisis, bond insurers teetered on the brink of collapse, crippled in part by the ratings agencies' downgrades. Since that time, there have been a series of settlements between insurers and banks whereby the insurers have settled claims accusing banks of misleading them regarding the quality of mortgages in various insured transactions. In May 2013, for example, Bank of America settled with MBIA for $1.6 billion in cash, $500 million in loans, and the surrender of $130 million in insurance policies.[54] Immediately following the settlement, MBIA was upgraded by S&P to AA- and was able to resume writing new insurance business for the first time since the crisis.

The credit quality of other insurers has improved since the crisis as well. As of early 2015, there are three active insurers: Assured Guaranty, Build America Mutual, and National Public Finance Guarantee. Most large exposures have been either reinsured or divested. One could say that the industry is poised for a comeback, hinging on ratings upgrades, renewed investor confidence, and higher interest rates.

Bond insurers are heavily regulated in the states where they conduct business. These regulators set risk limits on their portfolios, establish required statutory capital levels, and regulate the types of policies that are underwritten. New York Insurance Law happens to be the governing law for most insurers and limits the amount of obligations insured by a single entity and backed by a single revenue source.[55] Most regulations compare the insured par amount standing, or average annual debt service for a single entity, to policyholders' surplus and contingency reserves in order to determine an insurer's risk level.[56]

Pimbley states that the most important aspect of monoline regulation, however, is the prohibition on guaranteeing obligations that accelerate in the event of default.[57] As previously mentioned, bond insurance policies guarantee the payment of principal and interest *when due*.[58] When a default occurs, bond insurers will start to pay principal and interest to bondholders but will accelerate the required payment of principal and interest from debtors. Put another way, this means they can collect accelerated payments but are prohibited from making accelerated payments in case of default. This simple rule is the enabler of the monoline insurance business model.[59] It allows insurers the possibility of making money even when an insurance claim occurs.[60] For example, assuming an entity misses a payment, the bond insurer will accelerate payment of principal and interest that is due, receiving an upfront payment in the short run. The insurer will then be able to invest this amount, along with the premium, for the duration of the bond's life, thereby realizing a present value gain between the upfront payment and the amounts paid out to bondholders. Thus, a missed payment by an issuer may be profitable for the insurer.

Because investors cannot demand immediate repayment but must wait until the bond matures, insurers are not forced to come up with liquidity to cover large losses on short notice. Given the amount of leverage inherent in the insurer business model, they are simply not "made" to cover unexpected draws on liquidity.[61] Instead, insurers pay claims over time out of income generated by their investment portfolios.

Capital adequacy is the primary metric by which both investors and ratings agencies judge the health of insurance companies. In simple terms, capital adequacy is the amount of cash and securities on hand relative to a company's insured exposure. Regulators set broad-based limits on capital within each asset class, usually setting broad measures such as leverage ratios. Ratings agencies set more stringent capital adequacy guidelines based on risk-weighted loss expectations.[62] They assign credit ratings reflecting a number of inputs such as default rates, amount of par exposures, and concentrations of risk.[63] The role of ratings agencies as de facto regulators incentivizes insurers to adhere to high standards in order to retain investment-grade ratings.

The common methodology utilized by ratings agencies involves conducting "stress tests" of portfolio exposures under depression-like scenarios. As an example, Moody's will estimate losses using a Monte Carlo simulation, which will output losses and probabilities associated with those losses.[64] If the ratio of capital to probability-weighted losses is greater than one, the insurer's capital meets the test of adequacy. Moody's will index ratings based on the amounts by which an insurer's capital exceeds these potential losses.[65]

There are many ways to measure an insurer's amount of capital and reserves. Generally speaking, an insurer will set aside reserves adequate to cover expected losses based on historical loss experience within a given asset class. Historical data shows that during the last 40 years, 0.1% of investment-grade municipals have defaulted.[66] It follows that insurers are required by ratings agencies to insure only investment-grade bonds (in order to retain investment-grade ratings). They should set aside reserve amounts consistent with this loss experience. Thus, for every $100 in debt service insured, insurers will maintain $0.20 to $0.40 cents in loss reserves.[67] This amount may seem paltry but is consistent with the low-risk nature of bond insurance within the municipal asset class. Typically, statutory capital is defined for regulatory purposes as policyholder surplus, or cash and reserves on hand to pay bondholders.[68]

In the years following the financial crisis, however, losses due to depression-like scenarios have posed a less immediate threat for bond insurers than have exposures to single obligors. Since 2009, there have been several high-profile municipal bankruptcies, the largest of which have been the City of Detroit, with $22 billion in outstanding debt, and Jefferson County, Alabama, with $4.2 billion. In addition, the Commonwealth of Puerto Rico's ability to service its $20 billion in public corporation debt remains an open question and a serious concern. In the years following the crisis, both active insurers had exposures to these issuers and made payments to bondholders when due. Assured Guaranty insured a portion of post-bankruptcy bond issues that allowed Jefferson County and the City of Detroit to pay off existing creditors as part of their reorganization plans.

As of June 2015, the current capital levels of the market's two largest insurers suggest that their resources are sufficient to pay on these claims. For one, as we've seen with the Jefferson County reorganization plan, the insurer remains an important component of post-bankruptcy financing.

Given the insurer's active role and that these entities depend heavily on capital-markets access and bond insurance, it is unlikely the insurers will get "stiffed" by large write-downs of principal value. Recent experience suggests that for this reason, insurers still writing business are likely to get better treatment than will defunct insurers with bankruptcy claims.

With investors not longer paying a premium for bond insurance in the years following the crisis, it has been difficult for insurers to attract new business. The incremental impact of quantitative easing and financial repression by the Fed has moved interest rates to generational lows, decreasing spreads to the point that writing new business is not profitable. Many pundits have suggested that large-scale bankruptcies and investor panic will increase spreads and the demand for bond insurance, as occurred in the aftermath of the Detroit bankruptcy. We have also witnessed this phenomenon in the aftermath of Puerto Rico's passing legislation to allow its public corporations to restructure. This "bankruptcy legislation" sent shock waves through the market for uninsured PREPA debt, which traded as low as 11%. Insured debt was not as adversely impacted and widened out from 6.5% to 7%. Such wide spread differentials illustrate the bond insurance's attractiveness and demand.

As of June 2015, it looks as though bond insurance activity will pick up slightly but not return to its pre-crisis levels in the near term. Insurance penetration was 4% in 2013 and is expected to increase to no more than 8% in 2015, a far cry from the 57% of new issuance that was insured in 2005.[69] This trend reflects two dynamics. First, investors will not sacrifice yield for credit enhancement when interest rates are very low.[70] Second, mistrust spiked as a result of widespread reputational damage to the majority of insurers in the wake of the financial crisis.

A mainstay, however, has been the need to insure bond deals issued by less well-known issuers. Build America Mutual stepped into the market in 2012 to fill this void, but on a much smaller scale than firms with larger books of business such as NPFG and Assured Guaranty. At the industry's inception, insurers focused on this part of the market because of its stability and predictability. The entrance of new insurers drove down premiums, making this niche less profitable. We suspect that adherence to this model of low-risk underwriting will be essential for a return of bond insurance to a solid footing in the municipal bond market.

7

Municipalities in Recession

In this chapter, we will discuss the plight of cities during and after the Great Recession. Local governments have undoubtedly been one of the hardest hit sectors within the municipal bond market. As a sector that depends on property taxes as its primary revenue source, local governments were forced to make very difficult decisions to shore up their budgets in response to large-scale declines in home values. Five years after the recession, cities like Chicago, San Bernardino, and Stockton are still struggling to bounce back.

The term "local governments" has a broad definition and includes a wide range of entities including cities, towns, villages, school districts, and some special districts. (See Chapter 2, "A Profile of the Municipal Bond Market," for an explanation of the types and functions of local governments.) Local governments are crucial because they are closest to citizens and impact them on a daily basis more so than do states, counties, and the federal government. When a local government becomes insolvent, road paving, park maintenance, local police and fire protection, and K-12 education are scaled back. Unlike states, local governments couldn't simply cut "soft" transfers of revenues to other entities during Great Recession; instead, they had to deal with sticky costs, which are much more difficult to cut, like essential personnel, pension benefits, and salaries. How does a government scale back such services as police and fire protection? Higher taxes, debt financing, renegotiation of contractual agreements, and headcount reductions were all options used to fix state budgets. However, the inability to dial 911 for the fire department impacts citizens more than federal government shutdowns.

Some local governments are highly dependent on states for transfers specified in revenue-sharing agreements and for school district aid. Others rely very little on states and generate revenues primarily from their tax base. After the recession, states were forced to come up with revenues to pay for ongoing policy priorities such as education and the rising costs of Medicaid and unemployment insurance, with lower amounts of state aid. Discretionary outlays to local governments, an easy target for states, were cut; those local governments most heavily dependent on state transfers, especially for K-12 education funding, were hurt the most.[1]

Figure 7.1 shows the breakdown of local government revenues by source at the end of 2013.

Figure 7.1

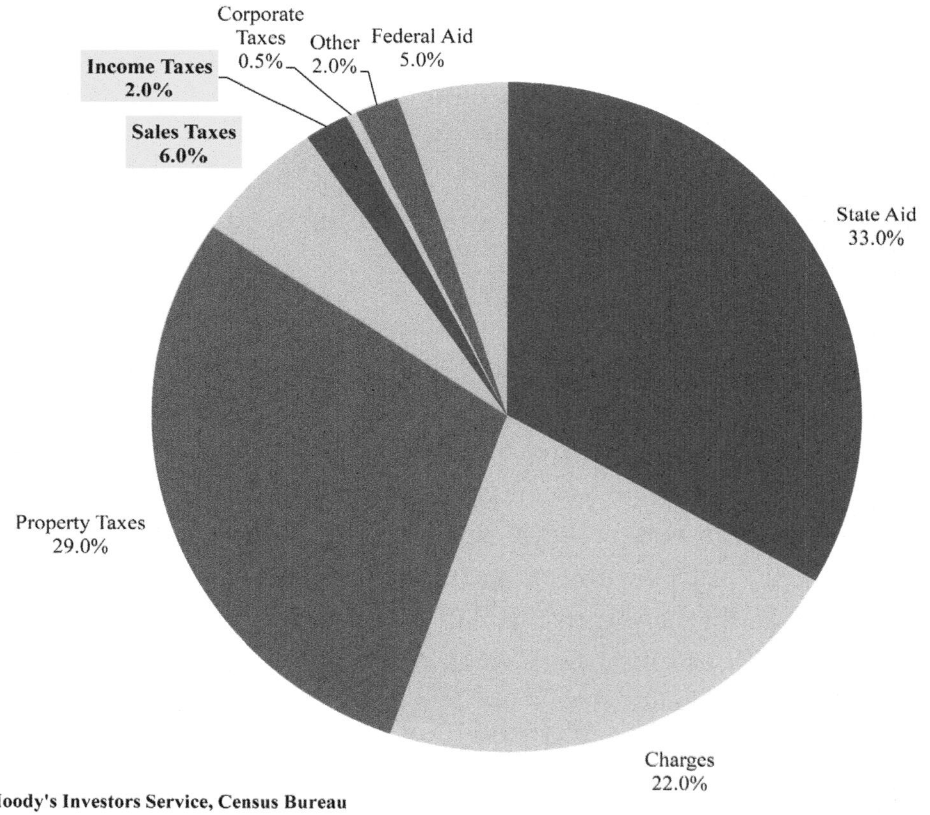

Sources: Moody's Investors Service, Census Bureau

Historically, property taxes have been a very stable revenue source; local officials set a budgetary amount they would like to raise and then determine the millage needed to raise that amount.[2] Transaction-based taxes are not like this. They are determined based on the number of sales, or the amount of income generated within a given area, and are much more volatile. Figure 7.1 shows that sales and income taxes make up approximately 8% of local government revenues.

Figure 7.2 shows the stability of the property tax base historically.[3] We see that even during the worst housing downturn since the Great Depression, with real estate values declining up to 40% in areas like Phoenix, Atlanta, and Orlando, property taxes leveled out but did not decline.[4]

Figure 7.2

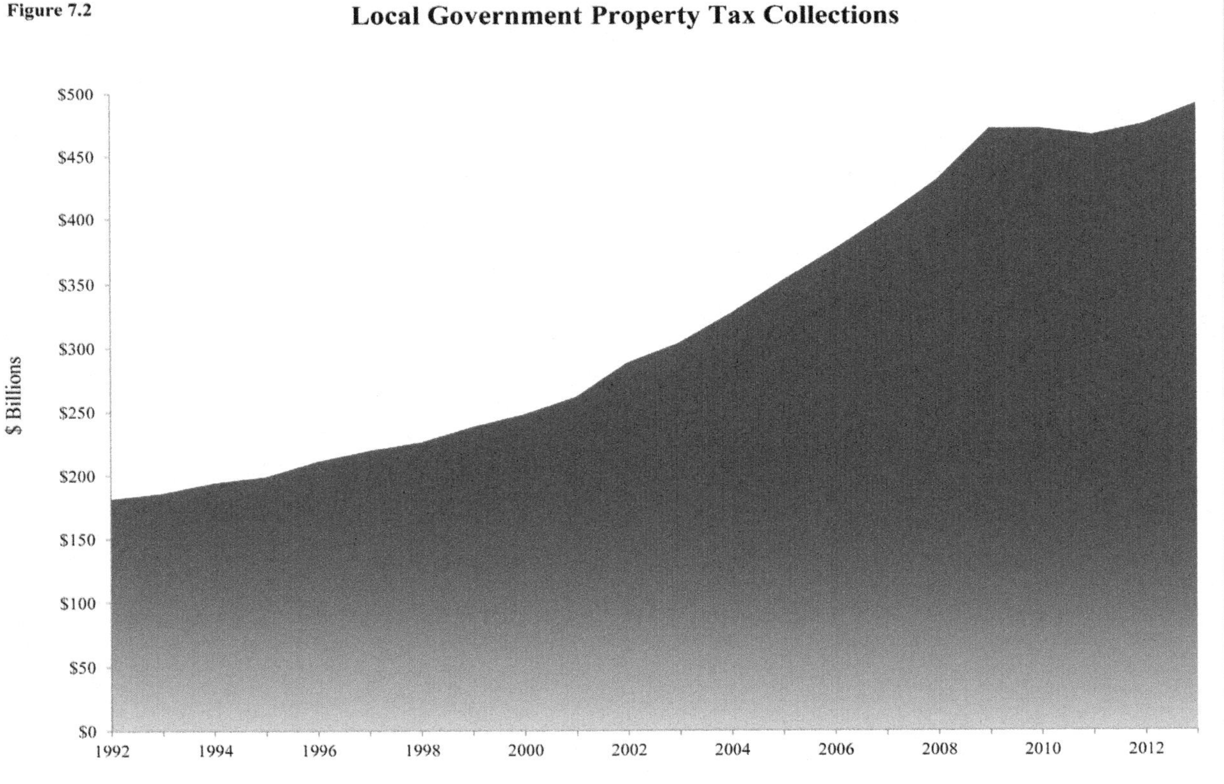

Source: Census Bureau

Historically, the presence of property taxes as a stable funding source for important services in most areas has allowed municipalities to continue providing those services. Leading up to the crisis, the volatility of local government revenues increased as municipalities turned to sales tax revenues for new financing needs.[5] The growth in sales tax revenues, driven by cash-out equity withdrawals from peoples' homes, presented an untapped revenue source for state and local governments. When the real estate market collapsed from 2007 to 2008, this revenue source evaporated.[6]

State funding to local governments also declined for two reasons: first, states cut discretionary funding to local governments in order to free funds to pay for non-discretionary expenditures such as means-tested welfare. Second, since the cuts to funding for local governments were more politically palatable than direct cuts to other programs, such cutbacks were used as a budget-balancing tool. It turns out that cuts to transfers from state governments to other governments don't result in equal cuts to the services provided by those local governments. A $1 cut in state K-12 education funding, for example, will likely not result in a $1 expenditure reduction on the local level. Local governments will likely find other funding sources to make up the deficiency, either through higher charges for services or through fees. Census Bureau data show that to deal with budgetary problems, 39% of states cut state aid, 37% cut state-shared revenues (mostly sales taxes collected by states and remitted back to the municipality), and 18% cut transfer programs.[7]

Figure 7.3 shows federal transfers to states and local governments from 2001 to 2012. During that time, such transfers increased by 41%, but they dropped in 2009 and 2014.[8] In 2010 and 2011, such transfers were bolstered by the American Recovery and Reinvestment Act. Since then transfers have started to decline and are no longer a growing source of funding for local governments.

Figure 7.3

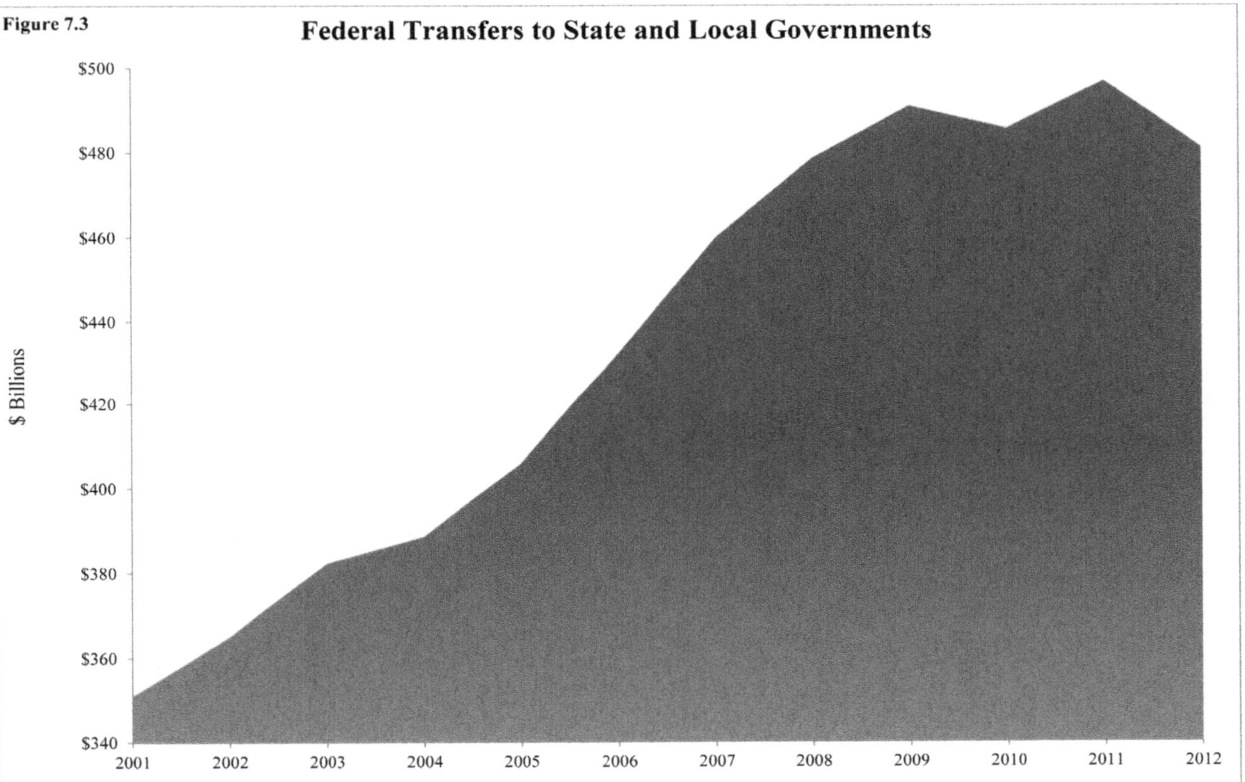

Source: Census Bureau

Because of their subordination to mandatory entitlement spending, transfers to local governments are also subject to leveraging effects. After funding mandatory entitlements, states transfer remaining revenues to local governments. If entitlements are 30% of a state's budget, a 25% decline in tax revenues will result in a 36% decline in revenues to local government because the state must make mandatory outlays for programs such as Medicaid and unemployment insurance.

The goal of all local governments has been to balance the needs of different constituents by raising revenues to pay for programs while reducing total spending.[9] During and after the recession, raising sales tax and user fees has been the alternative deemed politically preferable to renegotiating onerous labor contracts that govern pay increases and benefits under collective bargaining agreements.

Such actions, however, serve merely as stopgap measures, delaying the cuts that will inevitably be required. Although the needs served by local governments have not declined since the recession, the essential services local governments provide need to be reduced or their costs restructured.[10]

As Moody's states in its 2014 outlook for U.S. local governments, there are limits to the amount of taxation that a taxable base can bear without driving out businesses and citizens to lower-cost jurisdictions.[11] While the general obligation pledge is open-ended and requires that a local government commit all revenue-producing powers to pay debt service, many times local governments opt to favor collective bargaining agreements over bondholders in distressed scenarios.[12] This is a political, not a strictly choice. The City of Stockton filed for bankruptcy during the summer of 2012 without any attempts to negotiate with creditors. The filing sought to keep collective bargaining agreements intact while forcing haircuts on bondholders. In the emergency budget passed by the city prior to the bankruptcy process, the city failed to reduce its payments to CalPERS, the state-affiliated sponsor of California's pension plan, while all-but repudiating its payments to creditor Franklin Resources, Inc.

Since the recession, escalating personnel costs under collective bargaining agreements have been the biggest challenge facing local governments and will continue to be in the foreseeable future. The roots of these problems date back to the mid-1990s, when politicians promised retirement benefits for previous, current, and future employees at levels that would later prove to be unsustainable. This next section will discuss these benefits, which have been a growing burden for local governments. Such benefits include annual pension payments at some multiple of final-year salary for city or county officials and health benefits for spouses and family members (also known as other post-employment benefits, or OPEB).

As the working-age population has started to decline and the population grays, the annual burden placed on municipalities to fund these benefits has increased, creating budgetary strains. Chronic underfunding of these plans, especially during difficult economic times, has forced local governments to allocate an increasing share of their current revenues to fund benefits. A Pew Charitable Trusts' study titled "A Widening Gap in Cities" examines the plight of 61 major cities post-recession. The study shows that local pension plans were 70% funded and OPEB obligations were only 6% funded at the end of 2009.[13]

Pew states that the soundness of a local government's pension system is both a driver and a reflection of its overall financial health.[14] Escalating costs under collective-bargaining agreements have been driven largely by higher pension-funding requirements.

In an ideal world, a pension fund set up for the benefit of a local government's employees would be funded at 100%. This means that a defined-benefit pension plan that pays out benefits to retirees on an annual or monthly basis will have assets adequate to cover these expenses without contributions needed from the fund's sponsor (in this case, the local government). By "funded" we are referring to the ratio of the plan's assets to its liabilities. In the current economic environment, a plan funded at 80% can be considered healthy and well-funded (as is the case, for example, in the State of Georgia), whereas those falling significantly below this percentage would be considered underfunded.[15] The State of Illinois' pension system, the most underfunded state system in the United States, was funded at only 39% the end of 2013.

Figure 7.4 shows the average funded ratio of the 19 local pension plans included in the Public Plans Database compiled by the Center for Retirement Research at Boston College.[16] According to the chart, the average funded ratio of the 19 plans has declined from roughly 90% in 2001 to 83% in 2009.[17] The 83% funded level cited for these 19 plans understates the funding problems seen by many local governments not included within this group. For example, the City of Atlanta's public employee pension plan was only 60% funded at the end of 2011.[18] Other cities such as Boston, Wilmington, and Little Rock also had plans funded at 60% or less.[19]

Figure 7.4

Local Pension Plan Funding Levels: 2001-2009

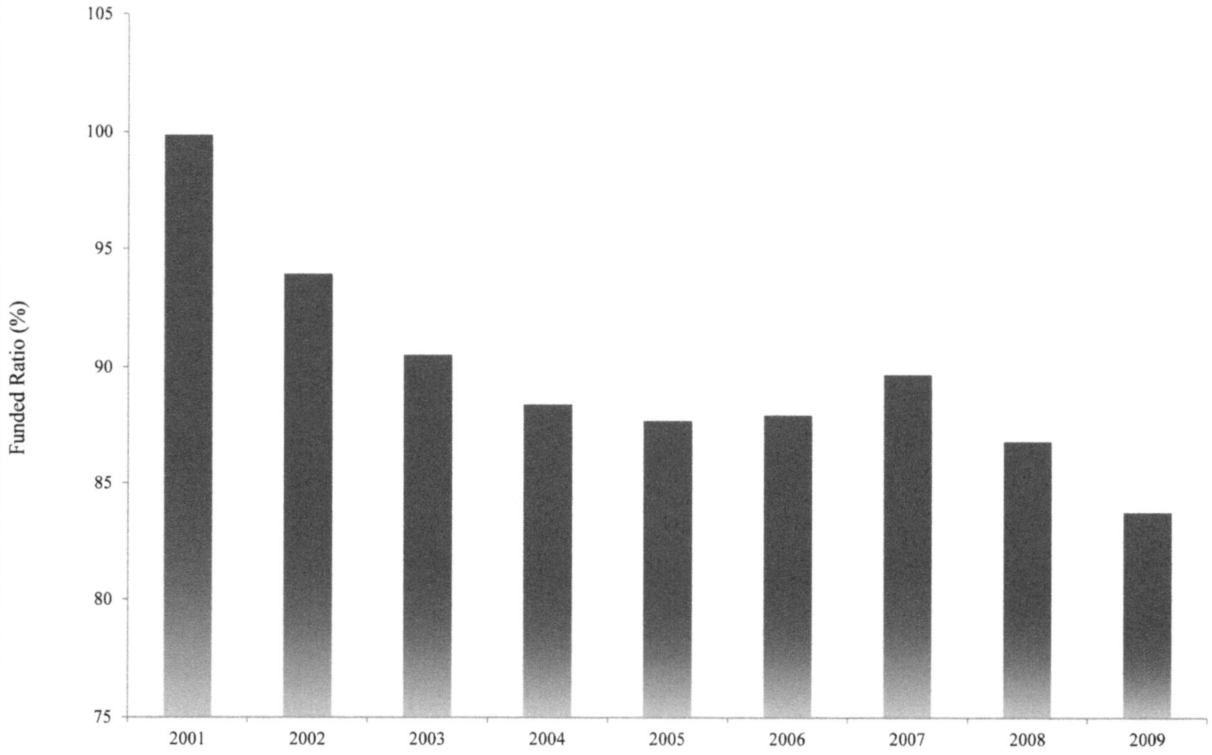

Sources: Cumberland Advisors, Public Plans Database compiled by the Center for Retirement Research at Boston College

Chronic underfunding of a local government's pension plan leads to a drain in taxpayer dollars down the road, amplifying the plan's liability and increasing on an exponential basis the payments required in future years.[20] A $100 pension payment reduces a pension plan's unfunded liability more, percentage-wise, if the payment is made now rather than a year from now.[21] By not making fully required payments into their plans on an annual basis during the Great Recession, local governments increased their burdens manifold down the road. This was a tactic used by local governments in the 2009 and 2010 budget cycles, when the availability of funding for pension payments reached multi-decade lows due to steep declines in revenues.[22]

The concept of a "required pension payment" has a direct bearing on the health of a local government's pension plan.[23] There are many assumptions and moving parts that determine what a local government "should" contribute to its plan annually if that plan is not 100% funded.[24] This "required" payment, known as an annually required contribution (ARC), is the amount needed to fully amortize the pension fund's unfunded liability on a 30-year schedule. Put another way, it is the amount that must be paid annually over the course of 30 years to bring the plan's funded ratio to 100%. The ARC changes annually based on a multitude of factors that affect a plan's funded ratio.

For example, multiple years of missed ARC payments or payments falling short of the ARC, will increase the ARC in future years and reduce the plan's funded ratio. This has been the case with many municipalities that have chronically underfunded their plans and increased plan liabilities. Poor stock market performance will increase ARCs. When plan assets decline in value relative to liabilities, additional assets must make up the difference. Lower interest rates will increase the plan's unfunded liability and the amount of fixed income assets needed in order to pay out benefits to plan beneficiaries.

For all of the above reasons, increasingly high ARCs have plagued cities in the years during and after the financial crisis. Pew states that local governments that chose to skip or make reduced payments got short-term relief at the expense of higher costs down the road, not unlike the consumer who makes a past-due credit card payment.[25] As pension and retiree healthcare payments must come out of the same pool of tax dollars, local governments were forced to raise taxes, cut services, or issue debt to finance their contributions.[26] In many cases, funding higher pension costs came at the expense of job cuts. For example, when the City of Los Angeles' ARC increased by 25% in 2009 as a result of investment declines in 2008 and 2009, budgetary strain and other factors led to the elimination of 2,500 positions in its 2010 budget season.[27]

The best gauge of the impact of pensions on a city's budget is the size of its ARC in relation to its total payroll.[28] Pew shows that larger cities under budgetary stress, such as Chicago, typically have an ARC equal to 30% of payroll, whereas better-funded cities such as Charlotte, Seattle, and San Francisco pay less than 10%.[29]

There is also the question of social equity. Unfunded liabilities pass the bill for retirees' benefits to future generations.[30] In other words, required contributions are payments that current taxpayers are making for services provided in the past.[31] To put this into perspective, consider the City of Boston. With its pension plan 60% funded, $81 million of its $108 million ARC in 2009 was used to pay current benefits to retirees, while only $26 million was used to contribute to the plan on behalf of current employees.[32] In the City of Providence, whose pension plan was only 42% funded in 2009, 51% of all property taxes went to make payments to pensions and retiree healthcare, crowding out other services and forcing tax increases.[33] Pew explains that the problem is compounded by the fact that when cities are unable to invest in long-term securities with higher potential returns because of greater liquidity needs, returns on portfolio assets suffer from cash drag or lower returns.[34]

Many states, notably New Jersey and Illinois, borrowed large sums of money to make payments into their pension systems. These borrowings are almost always doomed to fail because of their unfortunate timing. New Jersey issued bonds in 1997 to make pension payments into its system, only to see the money evaporate during the tech sell-off in 2001.[35] In June 2003, Illinois issued $10 billion in general obligation bonds, the largest municipal bond deal ever, to make payments into its pension system. Ten years later, the system is one of the worst-funded state systems in the country. Some local governments have resorted to borrowing as well.

Differing plans' discounting assumptions across municipalities often distort the actual size of a given plan's pension liability. Plan discount rates are utilized to discount the plan's future payments in order to arrive at a value for the pension plan's liability.[36] These discount rates are supposed to reflect risks and the long-term return on a plan's assets. Most states utilize an 8% rate; in reality, the average return on a plan for the past five years has been roughly 6%.[37] An artificially high 8% rate has the effect of understating the size of a plan's liability. Predictably, lowering the discount rate can increase debt burdens on municipalities by increasing plan liabilities. Pew cites New York City as an example. Lowering the city plan's discount rate from 8% to 7% would increase the city's required annual contribution by $1.8 billion,[38] roughly 4% of annual tax revenues.

Even though markets improved in 2009, 2010, and 2011, funding levels continued to decline in spite of higher contribution levels as a result of "smoothing," an accounting technique that allows issuers to realize changes in funding levels over the course of multiple years instead of a single year.[39] Pew also states, that as a result of this "smoothing," many plans have not yet fully felt the losses incurred because of stock market declines in 2008, pushing the problem into future years.[40] Pew has found that local governments with higher benefits do not necessarily have funding problems in future years; however, those local governments that do not set aside enough money to pay for those higher benefits end up having financial difficulties down the road.[41]

Pension benefits have long been subject to abuse by employees who have sought to "game" their plans into paying higher benefits.[42] Such tactics have created drains on the assets of municipalities and pension plans.[43] The Los Angeles Times has published reports on the subject as it pertains to California municipalities.

Annual pension benefit payments are calculated using formulas that consider length of employment, hours worked, sick leave, and compensation in the year or years immediately preceding retirement. Prior to widespread passage of reforms enacted in the years following the financial crisis, employees manipulated their final years' salary numbers by cashing out unused vacation pay, grants given for graduate degrees, and extra benefits.[44] This practice is known as "pension spiking." Such "spiking" was banned by CalPERS and other pension systems in the early '90s because of widespread abuse, but it is still practiced by beneficiaries to some degree.[45]

For example, the LA Times reports that one Ventura County undersheriff was able to add $92,600 in unused vacation to his final year's pay to increase his benefit payments to roughly $258,000 annually, or 20% more than he earned while working for the county.[46] The Ventura County chief executive was able to increase her final year's salary (upon which her benefits were based) to $272,000 annually by adding the following items to her salary: $34,000 in unused vacation pay, $11,000 for earning a graduate degree, and $24,000 for extra benefits owed by the county.[47] The Ventura County pension system is notoriously generous, with 84% of retirees receiving more than $100,000 per year in benefits.[49]

In spite of such abuses, pension plans are extremely difficult to reform for legal reasons, and attempts to implement reform can be politically damaging to politicians. Orange County, California, attempted to reform its pension plan, but its efforts were thwarted by the California Supreme Court, which ruled that pension benefits are property of beneficiaries and cannot be taken away.[49] San Bernardino has included reduced payments to CalPERS as part of its bankruptcy reorganization plan; however, this provision has been litigated heavily and it is not certain that these reforms will pass. The State of Illinois has passed pension reforms that are also being litigated in the Illinois Supreme Court. The City of Chicago is in a similar bind.

Typically, reforms passed on both the state and local levels have sought to end pension spiking by changing benefit calculation formulas, while slowing the rise in benefits.[50] To avoid litigation, some cities have attempted to restructure costs without addressing pension benefits; however, those cities continue to deal with the cost pressures of higher benefit payments.[51] We saw this in California with the City of Vallejo, which entered bankruptcy in 2008 and emerged in 2011 without addressing its rising pension costs. In 2014, many speculated that the city would be forced to reenter bankruptcy in order to restructure its pension costs. Vallejo shows that local officials seeking to get reelected will reform pension benefits only after all other potential areas of cost savings have been targeted.

Reforms such as lowering cost-of-living adjustments, increasing employee plan contributions, shifting employees to defined contribution plans, or raising the retirement age have been used to some extent; however, they are not a panacea.[52] Continued funding of ARCs, even on a 100% basis, can still result in underfunding. This occurred in San Francisco when its funding ratio decline from 100% to 97% in 2009.[53] In 2011, San Francisco voters overwhelmingly voted to increase employee contributions and limit cost-of-living adjustments to deal with the problem.[54]

Another tactic has been to limit benefits for employees hired after a specified date; however, this modest approach has had limited success and is just a first step toward more widespread reforms. The State of Illinois attempted this strategy in 2010 only to be faced with the necessity of making further reforms down the road.

The difficulty with local government administration of pension plans is that, in bad economic times, the earnings of pension plans are reduced even as revenues of local governments are falling. State-level legislation granting cities permission to skip payments in order to alleviate budgetary stresses has only worsened the problem.[55] States such as New Jersey and Pennsylvania passed these short-term measures only to see the pension-funding requirements of their local governments increase sharply afterwards.[56]

More alarming than pension underfunding has been the underfunding of other post-employment benefit (OPEB) obligations, namely healthcare benefits. Whereas local pensions were 60% funded after the financial crisis, OPEB obligations were just 6% funded.[57] Cities like Chicago fund these expenses on a pay-as-you-go basis: Current payments into the system pay only current benefits, and there are no assets in the plan securing these benefit payments.[58] Many cities have chosen to abandon their OPEB plans altogether due to increasing healthcare costs. Shifting employees to Medicare once they turn 65 is also an attractive option.[59] In the future, OPEB obligations will be easier to reform, as they are not considered "protected rights" under state constitutions.[60] If not addressed, the absence of needed reforms will mean that OPEB obligations will continue to crowd out other areas of local government budgets.

Local governments have faced formidable challenges since the Great Recession, and for the most part they have been able to overcome these difficulties. Incidences of distress have been comparatively rare and are usually the result of poor management compounded over the course of decades. Defaults in California cities, Detroit, and Harrisburg have been one-off events. General obligation bondholders recovered an average of 70% to 80% of principal versus the 60% average in the corporate market. The credit quality of local government issuers as a whole remains very high. In this chapter, we explore some of the transitory factors that impacted issuers during and after the Great Recession; however, we are not suggesting that local governments will be unable to service debt obligations going forward. Local government defaults remain rare: The total number of annual bankruptcy filings in the municipal bond market is in the mid-to-high single digits, compared to roughly 10,000 annually for corporate bankruptcies. As an added benefit, local governments have the ability to cut spending without reductions to revenues; and if need be, they have adequate margin to increase taxes during difficult economic times.

Sometimes the political process can subvert rational decision-making. Attempts to rein in pensions in some cities were met with political resistance from labor unions with firmly entrenched interests. Many officials have chosen to punt the issues only to see these obligations escalate in later years. For the most part, however, local governments have done the dirty work of shoring up their budgets to regain solvency, much to the dismay of these special interest groups. In later chapters, we discuss those few issuers who have not successfully done this. Chapter 8 discusses bankruptcy, the last resort of insolvent issuers, while Chapter 9 presents well-known case studies of municipal distress in the years following the Great Recession. In the end, we find that solutions to fiscal problems are gradual, to be successfully effectuated over the course of many years. Unfortunately, they are always painful.

8

An Overview of Municipal Bankruptcy

In this chapter we will discuss municipal bankruptcy under Chapter 9 of the Bankruptcy Code, the primary means by which municipalities can adjust their debts and seek relief from creditors. Chapter 9 is much different from traditional bankruptcies and is not understood well by the municipal market because, historically, instances of extreme financial distress have been very rare.[1] It was not until 2009 that we started to see Chapter 9 filings pop up in places like California due to the lingering effects of the financial crisis and municipalities' unwillingness to negotiate with creditors out of court.

This chapter is devoted to the Chapter 9 Bankruptcy process because of its complexity and relatively recent entrance into the municipal bond market conversation. We will discuss the causes of fiscal distress that ultimately lead to bankruptcy, the legality of municipal bankruptcy to begin with, and whether it is needed as a tool to adjust debts. A study of case law shows, perhaps surprisingly, that Chapter 9 Bankruptcy is typically used to seek relief from non-debt liabilities such as legal judgments, and pension or healthcare liabilities.[2] Only in the aftermath of the Great Recession have we seen high-profile cases, such as Detroit and Jefferson County, file to get out from under the burden of indebtedness.

Municipal default data indicate that municipal distress, in general, is extremely rare. In Moody's' historical default study, comparing munis to corporates during the period from 1970 to 2013, we see that 0% of AAA-rated municipal issuers defaulted over a rolling 10-year period, while 0.5% of AAA-rated corporate issuers defaulted.[3] For investment-grade bonds, the default rate for corporates over this period was 40 times that of municipals.[4] For municipals and corporates overall (not just investment-grade), the default rate of corporates was 98 times the default rate of municipals.[5] Historical data confirms that municipal bonds are relatively safe compared to other asset classes. Bankruptcy, while rare, is not a major risk in the asset class.

In the United States, there are approximately 10,000 to 11,000 Chapter 11 corporate reorganization filings every year, whereas there have been only 645 Chapter 9 filings since 1937 (the year that modern municipal bankruptcy legislation as we now know it was passed).[6] Attempted Chapter 9 filings are typically blocked by states or thrown out by federal judges when they are not done in good faith. The dearth of case law has made federal Chapter 9 statutes subject to wide interpretation, which has led to a broad array of outcomes in Chapter 9 proceedings.[7]

Bankruptcy benefits municipalities because it stays lawsuits against them and allows them to effectively adjust debt and contractual obligations by ceding control to a bankruptcy judge.[8] The Detroit bankruptcy, for example, was seen by many as a necessity because negotiations with unions were futile: The haircuts on health and pension benefits needed in order to restore the city's financial condition were too great. Soon after appointment of the emergency manager, lawsuits began to pile up and numbered in the hundreds. The only way to efficiently address the needs of all stakeholders in a cost-effective way was to file for Chapter 9 Bankruptcy.

The road to bankruptcy is littered with failed negotiations, expensive lawsuits, and lack of compromise.[9] In most cases, bankruptcy is not needed to shore up finances, as efforts to reduce costs and increase revenues can typically be undertaken on an out-of-court basis. This was the case with New York City's fiscal distress that occurred in the mid-1970s. Unlike other forms of bankruptcy, a missed bond payment does not automatically trigger a Chapter 9 proceeding.[10] Chapter 9 proceedings are voluntary on the part of the municipality.[11] Natalie Cohen, a thought leader on the subject, states that Chapter 9 proceedings are typically started only when various classes of creditors, contract holders, and pension beneficiaries initiate lawsuits and the cost of fighting those lawsuits becomes cost-prohibitive.[12]

So what are the causes of fiscal distress that ultimately lead to a bankruptcy filing? Moody's has distilled the cases of bankruptcy to two root causes: Structural insolvency precipitated by broad-based macroeconomic conditions, and idiosyncratic events typically associated with project financings.[13] These problems are often compounded by poor management, corruption, and fraud. Often the root cause of a bankruptcy will be poor management, but the catalyst that sets it in motion will be the onset of difficult macroeconomic conditions.

James Spiotto of Chapman Strategic Advisors has made important contributions to the market's collective knowledge of Chapter 9 Bankruptcy. In this chapter, we draw on his work in his contributing chapter to *The Handbook of Municipal Bonds*. Poor management often results in fraud designed to enrich managers at the expense of other stakeholders or to hide poor financial performance. For example, Larry Langford, president of the Jefferson County Commission from 2002 until 2006, was convicted on "60 counts of bribery, money laundering, and mail and wire fraud" for accepting payments, jewelry, and other valuables in exchange for steering underwriting business to JP Morgan.[14] As Langford continued to profit from sending business to JP Morgan, the frequency of such underwriting transactions intensified, increasing the indebtedness of the Jefferson County Commission. In November 2011, the county filed for bankruptcy due to its over overwhelming debt and inability to make good on derivative swap agreements tied to these transactions.

The City of Detroit, after 50 years of secular decline, filed a petition to enter Chapter 9 Bankruptcy following a long series of failed negotiations for the city's $20 billion in outstanding liabilities. Given its degree of insolvency and stagnation, with accumulated annual deficits of $237 million, bankruptcy was the only option that would allow the city to impose the large-scale haircuts on creditors needed in order for the city to continue its operations.[15] Detroit's nearly 100,000 creditors and 130 creditor classes meant that it would be difficult to simultaneously perform good faith negotiations with all parties without inadvertently benefiting certain creditors at the expense of others.[16] The process involved a series of bilateral agreements whereby creditors would sue Detroit and reach settlements one after another until the city's resources were drained.[17] The creditors who sued first were prioritized while those who waited to act were inadvertently disadvantaged.[18]

When the governor of Michigan declared a state of emergency for the city in March 2013, various stakeholders rushed in to sue the city, hoping to front-run a potential bankruptcy filing whereby a bankruptcy judge would "flatten" their claims and impose large haircuts.[19] The legal costs of such a process are very high. The city used its already strained resources to hire legal staff to address such claims either in court or out of court to reach some sort of settlement. The bankruptcy ended these lawsuits and handed control over to a bankruptcy judge.

The Great Recession was the straw that broke the back of other cities, such as San Bernardino, which filed for bankruptcy in July 2012. The already poor city faced a significant decline in housing prices and high personnel costs driven by the increasing costs associated with servicing its public employee pension plan. In the years leading to the recession, the city's population grew substantially and housing values increased. Figure 8.1 shows the escalation and subsequent drop in home values for the Riverside-San Bernardino-Ontario Metropolitan Statistical Area utilizing the Freddie Mac House Price Index for the area. Figure 8.1 also shows the sharp increase in home prices until 2006, followed by a decline of 53% from peak to trough until 2009.[20] Such large swings in home values impact consumer spending trends and employment, which have follow-through impacts on local governments.

Figure 8.1

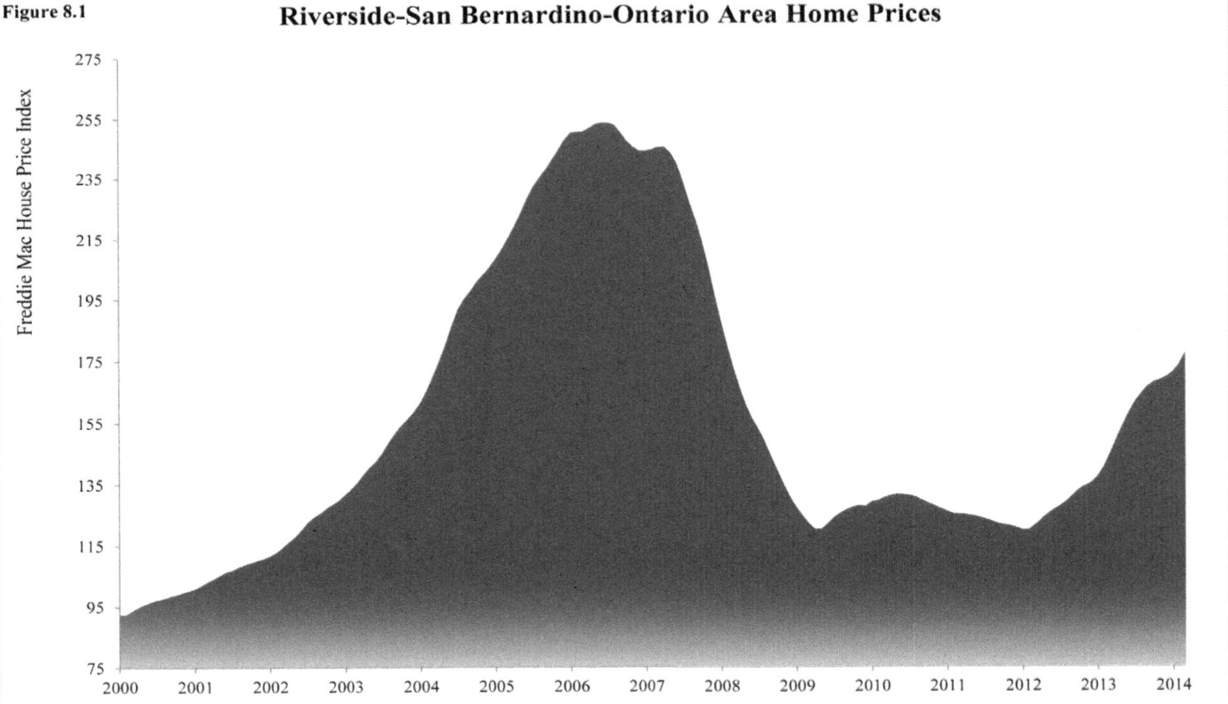

Sources: Bloomberg, Freddie Mac

In San Bernardino, as in other cities in the Inland Empire, population growth fueled heavier demands for city services, requiring increasing numbers of city employees and raising expenses.[21] During this time, the city negotiated overly generous benefits for its public employees under collective bargaining agreements with its seven employee unions.[22] Provisions included retirement ages ranging from 50 to 55 years, contributions for employees' share of pension payments to CalPERS, and full cost-of-living adjustments.[23]

What city officials did not know was that San Bernadino was already effectively insolvent. It was not until after the city's finance director stepped down in December 2011 that San Bernardino's true financial situation was discovered in July of the following year. The city's finance director, James Simpson, published a report with recommendations in July 2012 on how to shore up the city's finances.[24] Instead of adhering to the report's recommendations, the city council declared a fiscal emergency that authorized the city to declare bankruptcy.[25]

With proper management, the city might have been able to avoid filing for Chapter 9. Several other cities in the Inland Empire region facing difficult economic headwinds chose to enter mediation instead of immediately filing for bankruptcy. San Bernardino's unwillingness to negotiate out of court brings into question its willingness to reduce operating expenses in addition to making payments on its bonds. The Chapter 9 Bankruptcy requirement that cities must first attempt good faith negotiations with creditors in order to be eligible for bankruptcy seems not to have been met here.

The case of San Bernardino illustrates a common theme in the years after the financial crisis. Instances of financial fraud increased as governmental entities sought to hide poor financial performance to stay in compliance with bond covenants and prevent ratings downgrades. A typical sign of poorly managed cities is the lack of multi-year budgetary planning: Cities that plan to balance their budgets over a two to three year horizon are likely to address issues proactively.[26] It is clear that the macro economy worsened San Bernardino's financial situation to some degree, but the city's blurred financial picture, a result of poor financial controls, also led to major cash-flow problems and a bankruptcy filing.

Harrisburg, Pennsylvania, demonstrated a similar unwillingness to make difficult decisions, opting to file for Chapter 9 as the "first choice" to deal with its insolvency, instead of the "last choice."[27] John Buntin, Staff Writer at *Governing the States and Localities*, does a good job of telling Harrisburg's story in his November 2011 piece titled "Harrisburg's Failed Infrastructure Project." Buntin relates the story from the perspective of the city's mayor, Stephen Reed, and its city council, which, it appears, over the course of 28 years took the city to the brink of collapse.[28] In 2010, newly elected mayor Linda Thompson attempted to reverse course and correct Reed's and the city council's previous wrongs by seeking "distressed city" status, giving the city access to revenues from the state's nonresident wage tax and enacting an out-of-court plan of adjustment paid for with Act 47 moneys.[29]

The city council vetoed three separate out-of-court recovery plans proposed between 2010 and 2011, but opted to file for bankruptcy, as a way to avoid implementing these plans. Given the alternatives, (1) raising taxes and cutting services to city residents but continuing to pay debt service or (2) not paying debt service but continuing with services without imposing tax increases, the city chose the latter.[30] When the city council filed a bankruptcy petition without mayoral or state approval in 2011, the state swiftly stepped in, declared a fiscal state of emergency, and appointed an emergency receiver to devise and implement a fiscal recovery plan. The plan—which raised taxes, leased city assets, and asked creditors to extend debt schedules—was filed in August 2013 and consummated in December 2013.[31] Since the plan satisfied various creditor groups and determined "who gets what," it successfully proceeded in line with projections.[32]

As in the case of Harrisburg, a bankruptcy process starts with the municipality's filing for some sort of relief (conditional on a fiscal plan of action) or an intercept of state funds; in Pennsylvania, it was access to nonresident wage tax revenues to alleviate budgetary pressures.[33] For most municipalities, this relief is sufficient to improve finances. If these actions are not sufficient, the municipality will hire an outside, independent manager to run the city's operations and engage an outside consultant who will generate a plan with recommendations on how best to achieve budget stabilization.[34] This process occurs on an out-of-court basis and is carried out by the state-appointed manager. The emergency manager will attempt to implement this plan, which often involves higher taxes, asset sales, and cuts to various creditor groups. If creditor groups do not agree to the plan on an out-of-court basis, or if the plan is in danger of failing due to lower-than-expected proceeds from asset sales, the emergency manager will weigh the costs of bankruptcy against those of continuing litigation in state court.[35] If a bankruptcy is the preferred path, the manager will seek state permission to file, and the case will be taken up in federal district court. The process of state authorization is a requirement for municipalities in 24 of the 50 states.[36]

The 2008 recession impacted Harrisburg's finances somewhat, but decades of debt accumulation as a result of spending on unneeded "pet projects" ultimately reached a point where existing revenues were insufficient to pay debt service on accumulating debt obligations.[37] Chapter 9 Bankruptcy was attempted but doomed from the outset as the city failed to satisfy the requirement of "good faith" negotiations with creditors prior to filing. The city council's intent was simply to stiff creditors without having to make politically unpopular decisions like raising taxes. A bankruptcy filing was abused as a way to get protection from state intervention instead of breathing room from creditors. After appointment of the state receiver, who would design a state-run bankruptcy alternative, Chapter 9 was to be pursued only if the state receiver's alternative plan failed. In this case the costs of a messy series of lawsuits and attempted negotiations would ultimately outweigh the costs of bankruptcy, as happened in Detroit, and the city would file.

The Commonwealth of Pennsylvania was authorized to appoint a receiver under the powers granted to it in the 10th Amendment of the U.S. Constitution, which allows states to control the affairs of their local governments. However, a critical question remains unresolved: Is the state legally allowed to intervene in a bankruptcy procedure when the power to enact laws governing bankruptcies is reserved exclusively for the federal government (and not states) under Article I, Section 8, Clause 4 of the U.S. Constitution?

Many states act as gatekeepers by setting parameters that determine whether or not a municipality can legally file for bankruptcy. The sovereignty of states versus the powers of the federal government is the issue. The 10th Amendment, which has been interpreted as granting states those powers not enumerated Article I of the Constitution, is the most commonly cited legal reference for states' rights regarding municipal bankruptcies. Article 10 is also cited as the legal ground for the argument that bankruptcy court should not be able to abrogate state and local collective bargaining agreements. Yet, the supremacy clause under Article 6 of the U.S. Constitution makes federal statute the law of the land.[38]

Just because the power to break contracts is given to the federal government does not mean that federal statutes on Chapter 9 municipal bankruptcy are constitutional. James Spiotto, an authority on the subject of Chapter 9, has written a great deal on the history of the statute.[39] On numerous occasions since its passage in 1937, Chapter 9 municipal bankruptcy law has been challenged and found to be unconstitutional on the grounds that it violates states' rights.[40] The paucity of case law has made Chapter 9 open to many interpretations since that time.[41] Subsequent rulings by the Supreme Court have overturned various provisions of Chapter 9, and amendments passed by Congress have transformed the law into what it is today.[42]

Article I of the Constitution gives Congress power to enact bankruptcy laws to create the legal apparatus by which people can adjust their debts.[43] Under the U.S. Constitution, municipalities (unlike corporations and humans) are not regarded as people. For this reason, the federal government cannot extend its powers to infringe on the sovereign powers of municipalities under the 10th Amendment.[44] It is precisely because the law does not define state and local governments as people that Chapter 9 exists as a separate chapter from Chapters 7 and 11 in the U.S. Bankruptcy Code. This conclusion derives from a landmark Supreme Court decision in 1936 in the case of Ashton v. Cameron County Water Improvement Dist. No. 1.[45]

Chapter 9 is a far different animal from Chapter 7 and Chapter 11, which govern how corporations may adjust their debts. In a Chapter 9 case, there is substantial limitation of the jurisdiction and legal powers of the court and creditors.[46] This is a major distinction between municipal and other forms of bankruptcy because a Chapter 9 case ensures that the bankrupt entity maintains its sovereignty under the 10th Amendment.[47] Creditors cannot force a municipality into bankruptcy the way they can force a corporation or an individual into a Chapter 11 Bankruptcy, nor can the assets of a municipal entity be liquidated. The municipality is never considered to be a "debtor-in-possession"; the court simply acts as a facilitator of the process by which the judge approves or rejects the bankruptcy petition and oversees the enactment of a plan of adjustment that will allow the municipality to return to solvency.[48] If the plan of adjustment is approved, the municipality will be released from its original obligations under the terms of the plan and emerge from bankruptcy.[49]

A petition for Chapter 9 Bankruptcy protection is completely voluntary on behalf of the municipality and is approved by a judge only once it is found that the municipality has attempted to negotiate with creditors in good faith.[50] The "good faith negotiations" test is important and can weigh more heavily than insolvency in a judge's decision to accept or reject a bankruptcy petition.[51] This provision is intended to discourage municipalities from using bankruptcy as a "strategic tool" instead of regarding it as a last resort when all attempted negotiations have failed. In the years following the financial crisis, when the politically unpalatable choices were raising taxes on already fiscally strapped residents, laying off workers and cutting services, or defaulting on debts, the correct political choice (from the perspective of an elected official seeking to get reelected) was to default on debts. The correct economic choice, in order to preserve access to capital markets and avoid stigmatization, would be to negotiate with bondholders. Harrisburg's City Council attempted this strategy. Warren Buffett cited Harrisburg's action as his reason for exiting the bond insurance business. As political willingness to repay debts declined, bankruptcy and defaulting on payments looked to be an increasingly attractive option.

The bankruptcy process is costly and can take years, as has been the case with cities such as Stockton and San Bernardino. After filing a petition with the local circuit judge, the municipality must present a prepetition plan of adjustment (or "workout" in Chapter 11 parlance), with a proposal for how it intends to emerge from bankruptcy.[52] This plan will likely include increases in revenues, such as higher taxes and service fees, and reductions to fixed costs in the form of bond principal reduction on outstanding debts, cuts to personnel, and renegotiation of collective bargaining agreements. This plan is unlikely to be approved by the judge in its original form, but it provides a starting point from which the judge will launch negotiations with creditors in order to formulate a final and binding "post-petition" plan of adjustment.[53] The plan is likely to require litigation and the hiring of lawyers, accountants, investment bankers, and consultants to work on behalf of the municipality. In order for the post-petition plan to pass and be agreed upon by all parties, it must meet the "fair and equitable" criteria that are spelled out in Chapter 11 statutes and incorporated by reference in Chapter 9 of the Bankruptcy Code.[54]

The "fair and equitable" requirement in Chapter 9 Bankruptcy is one of its distinguishing characteristics. In Chapter 11, it is taken to mean that a workout plan cannot benefit one party at the expense of another (i.e., an entity's shareholders and creditors). Municipalities do not have shareholders, so the judicial interpretation of this provision has been that a municipality's residents are its shareholders.[55] There is little in the way of Chapter 9 case law establishing precedent as how best to interpret this statute, but the case law that does exist suggests that a bankruptcy plan must take reasonable steps to balance the needs of residents and creditors since they find themselves on opposite sides of the negotiating table.[56] Creditors favor raising tax revenues and cutting costs over principal reductions, while residents favor debt restructuring over increasing taxes and layoffs, and cutting to city services.

A plan of adjustment typically will pursue both strategies by looking for inefficiencies and savings, terminating burdensome labor contracts, modifying collective bargaining agreements and retiree benefits, selling or leasing municipal assets, privatizing assets, consolidating services with other municipalities, and securing grants and other support from state and/or federal programs.[57]

To fairly accommodate opposing interests, the judge must decide how much to reduce a municipality's operating costs by shrinking city services (to the benefit of bondholders) and how much to reduce principal and interest payments on debt (for the relief of residents at the expense of bondholders). Under a Chapter 9 proceeding, in contrast to a Chapter 11 proceeding, a municipality's assets cannot be liquidated because of its full sovereignty as guaranteed under the 10th Amendment.[58] Quoting from Subchapter 1, Section 904 of Chapter 9, "the court many not...interfere with—(1) any of the political or governmental powers of the debtor; (2) any of the property or revenues of the debtor; or (3) the debtor's use or enjoyment of any income-producing property."[59] The role of creditors in determining this outcome is much more limited in Chapter 9 than in Chapter 11. The municipality must be able to continue its operations (which include new debt financing) as the provider of essential services such as water, sewer, fire, police protection, and education for the benefit of its citizens. This is required even if the cost of providing those services is the reason for the municipality's insolvency.[60]

The high implicit and explicit costs of bankruptcy suggest that it is usually the least desirable alternative for a municipality seeking to reduce its debts. Out-of-court settlements with creditors or state intervention are typically more cost-effective. A municipality's missed debt service payments do not trigger an initiation of bankruptcy proceedings as would be the case for Chapter 11, and simply filing for bankruptcy does not relieve a municipality of servicing its obligations. There is a place in municipal finance for bankruptcy; however, its usage should be limited to extreme circumstances where an entity's finances must be "reset" and the wrongs of years of poor leadership must be undone. The high costs of bankruptcy are borne by municipalities over many years, and once-bankrupt issuers pay higher yields on their debt for years to come. Out-of-court settlements and state intermediation are usually the preferred outcomes.

History offers a number of cases of fiscally distressed municipalities that stood at the brink of collapse, chosen not to file, and instead resolved fiscal problems out of federal court.

Between 1929 and 1937—prior to the enactment of modern municipal bankruptcy law—there were 4,700 defaults by governmental issuers.[61] The majority occurred following the Great Depression without court intervention.[62] The 1975 New York City fiscal crisis plan put forth by the State of New York and the federal government was effectively a state-run bankruptcy. The State of New York appointed a receiver, broke collective bargaining agreements, and reduced payments to creditors—the same actions likely to have been implemented in a federal bankruptcy plan of reorganization, should it have occurred instead.[63] This was done for reasons of cost, as the implicit and explicit costs of a state-administered plan are much less than those incurred in a federal bankruptcy filing. In a federal case, state involvement is limited. The municipality's creditors and residents end up bearing the administrative cost of hiring the financial advisors, bankruptcy lawyers, and accountants required for the city to defend itself.

The City of Detroit's bankruptcy cost $126 million during its first 13 months, which is approximately 0.7% of its outstanding contractual liabilities.[64] New York City's fiscal recovery plan in 1975, for its $16 billion in outstanding contractual obligations was complex, and much larger in today's dollars (roughly $70 billion) than Detroit's; yet, it was administered by the state.[65] The city didn't file for bankruptcy and the cost was lower. The fact that Detroit's debt burden was smaller in real terms than New York City's should dispel notions that bankruptcy is the better alternative for large, complex cases. Given bankruptcy's high cost, ultimately borne by both taxpayers and creditors, the question arises as to whether it is worth the expenditure. As James Spiotto has put it, "a recourse for adjudication of claims has been proven throughout history to be a necessity for a fair and just society."[66] Attempts to use bankruptcy as a strategic tool to stiff bondholders almost always fail under the supervision of a federal judge or in the presence of state oversight. We advocate the use of Chapter 9 Bankruptcy as a "reset" button only in important cases where a municipality's level of insolvency is so great that a near eradication of debts will have to occur.

9

Case Studies of Distressed Local Governments

Prior to the financial crisis, fiscal stress was an issue not germane to the municipal market. It was simply not something that happened frequently enough to warrant research efforts. The historically low rate of municipal bankruptcy and missed payments by municipal bond issuers stemmed from the monopolistic taxing power and stable revenue streams of state and local governments and the high credit quality of the asset class. Because of their inherent stability and flexibility in cutting expenses without sacrificing revenues, issuers rarely missed payments on outstanding debt. Usually, missed payments occurred because of idiosyncratic risks associated with inherently speculative financings, project-specific risks, or even clerical errors. It wasn't until the financial crisis occurred that pockets of distress among multiple issuers started to occur as a result of systemic, economy-wide factors. The financial crisis changed the rules of the game.

In the previous chapter we distilled the causes of fiscal distress down to two root situations: (1) structural insolvency resulting from broad-based macroeconomic conditions, and (2) idiosyncratic events typically associated with project financings.[1] In this chapter, we will discuss on a case-by-case basis the major attention-grabbing distressed situations that have occurred since the financial crisis began. There have been five such major pockets of municipal fiscal distress: Detroit, Harrisburg, Jefferson County, a handful of California cities, and Puerto Rico. (We will address Puerto Rico in Chapter 12, "The Puerto Rico Conundrum.")

Detroit, Michigan

We start with the poster child of fiscal distress, Detroit. Detroit's fiscal crisis is the upshot of a half-century of deterioration resulting from the decline of American auto manufacturing and related industries. The financial crisis brought with it economic stagnation that resembled scenarios other municipalities experienced during the Great Depression. The city's 25% unemployment rate (13% higher than the national average) and the plummeting of home prices to an average transaction price of roughly $7,500 in 2011 were symptoms of the extreme economic blight eroding the city's tax base.[2] Widespread corruption spanning decades exacerbated the problem; misappropriations of funds and debt transactions that were intended to enrich public officials accelerated the city's path toward insolvency. Moody's and S&P rated the city's debt as speculative-grade, or "junk," starting in the early '90s. In July 2013, the city officially filed for bankruptcy protection from creditors after missing an interest payment on outstanding general obligation debt in June of the same year. The municipal bond market viewed a Detroit bankruptcy or distressed intervention as almost inevitable.

Figure 9.1

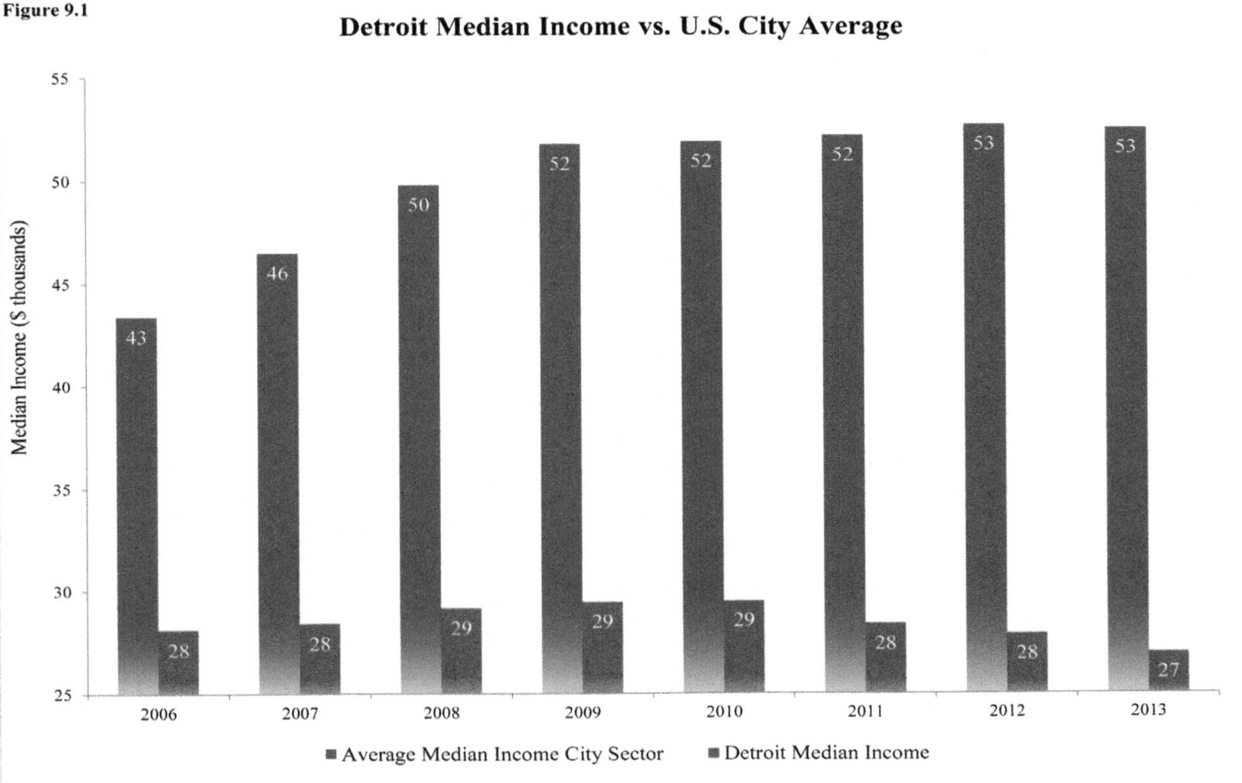

Sources: Census Bureau, Investortools

To get a better sense of the city's abject state of affairs, consider Figures 9.1 and 9.2, which show the city's median incomes and housing values versus nationwide city medians. Incomes are only 50% of the sector-wide median and have declined 4% since 2006.[3] Median housing values, which are just 30% of city medians, have declined 33% since 2006.[4]

Figure 9.2

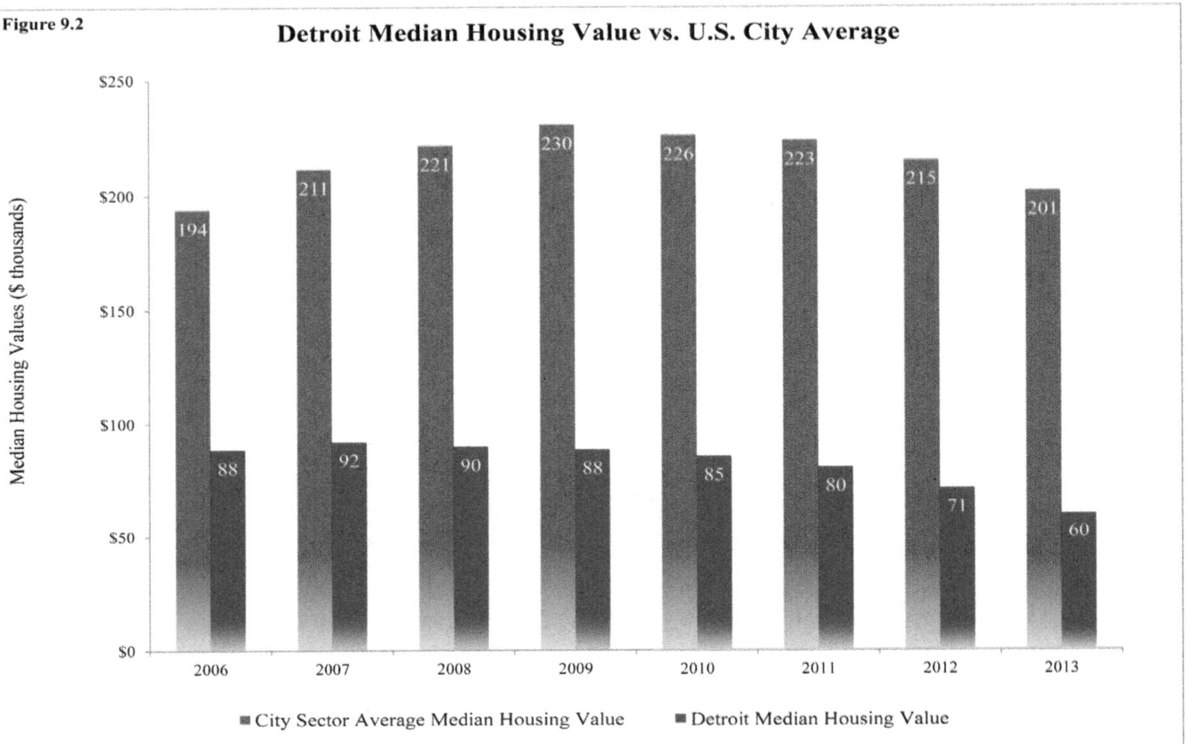

Sources: Investortools, Census Bureau

The poor regional economy has had follow-through effects on the city's ability to generate tax revenues. In 2013, when the city was no longer able to buy time with debt-financings, the city's declining revenue base and rising expenses meant that there were few options left on the table for shoring up its finances. Given a poor and diminished population base, new revenues were largely unavailable. Further cuts to city services were also not feasible—services had already been cut in prior years to pay the city's ballooning retirement and debt-servicing costs.[5]

Bankruptcy was the inevitable outcome and was seen as the only way to transform the city into a viable place once more.[6] The State of Michigan's appointment of Detroit Emergency Manager Kevyn Orr, a former bankruptcy attorney, in early 2013 was seen as an initial step toward a possible bankruptcy filing. In June, Mr. Orr filed a reorganization plan prior to filing for bankruptcy.

The filing was met by lawsuits from the city's hundreds of creditors. These lawsuits ultimately became the catalyst for the city's voluntary filing.[7] Orr's reorganization plan shocked municipal market participants because of the severity of losses imposed on both creditors and pension beneficiaries and the low recovery rates for secured claims that had traditionally been viewed by the marketplace as sacrosanct.

The original restructuring proposal put forth by the emergency manager put GO bondholders and pension beneficiaries on equal footing. This move was seen as an extreme measure: At that time, the general obligation pledge was still considered a secured claim and "sacrosanct"—senior to all other claims against a debtor, requiring the debtor to raise taxes to repay bondholders. The emergency manager's decision to treat a general obligation pledge as unsecured, and his initial offer of 20 cents on the dollar for Detroit's general obligation bondholders (while water and sewer bonds were left mostly intact), "flipped" the municipal market's standard perception of an issuer's capital structure upside down. As a result, the market penalized treatment of local GO debt, particularly Michigan local GO debt, with an added risk premium of 30 to 40 basis points. After negotiation with holders of GO debt, the recovery amount increased to 76 cents on the dollar.

Coincidental with the plan of adjustment, Orr filed a lawsuit in U.S. Bankruptcy Court against two service corporations the city used to issue debt in order to fund payments to its pension system. The complaint alleged that the sole purpose of these corporations was to engage in illegal debt transactions designed to circumvent the state's statutory debt limitations. Since the transactions were illegal, their claims were void and unenforceable by the court.

The emergency manager's lawsuit against pension certificate of participation (COP) holders was a legal maneuver to force acceptance of the reorganization plan. The Detroit emergency manager's claim questioning the legality of such financing structures was somewhat naïve, yet it raised questions about how holders of COP debt will be treated in distressed situations. Since COPs are in fact contractual obligations similar to leases, the bankruptcy judge is given the power under a Chapter 9 proceeding to reject them and not cure them at all. Holders of the COP debt eventually settled with the city for roughly 12 cents on the dollar.[8]

Jefferson County, Alabama

Strong parallels can be drawn between the bankruptcies of Detroit and Jefferson County, Alabama. They both were the result of a decade-long history of corruption and poor management. In the mid-'90s, Jefferson County was charged by the EPA to retrofit and make capital improvements to its outdated sewer system to meet federal clean water standards.[9] The county entered into complex financial transactions and $3.27 billion in floating-rate debt to finance the upgrade.[10] The complexity of these transactions and the amount of outstanding indebtedness sparked a liquidity crisis in the summer of 2008, bringing the county to its knees. At the time of Jefferson County's bankruptcy in 2011 on $3.1 billion in outstanding debt, it was the largest municipal bankruptcy in history.[11]

Instead of issuing level, fixed-rate debt, as is typical in municipal bond transactions, Jefferson County's advisors, who sought to benefit from the amount and type of debt issued, advised the county to issue floating-rate debt and "swap" it into fixed-rate debt by entering into derivative transactions. These transactions were much more lucrative for the investment banks underwriting them, which is why Jefferson County was guided to enter into them heavily. The total size of the capital improvement program, $2.4 billion, was paid for with $3.27 billion in debt and $4.3 billion in interest-rate-swap derivative transactions, for a total of $7.5 billion in obligations.[12]

Figure 9.3 shows Jefferson County's capital structure. The left-hand side shows the warrants issued by Jefferson County (technically, Jefferson County issued "warrants" instead of "bonds," although both are very similar in substance) to finance aforementioned capital improvements and the county's general operations. The transactions ranged from $13 million to $600 million.[13] The right-hand side of Figure 9.3 lists the swaps that were issued against these transactions in order to synthetically convert them into floating or fixed-rate instruments. Under normal scenarios, to eliminate basis risk, the notional amount of the outstanding swaps will equal that of outstanding debt instruments; however, in this case, the total amount of outstanding swaps was $5.48 billion versus $4.5 billion of outstanding debt.[14]

Figure 9.3

Jefferson County's Complex Capital Structure

Outstanding Warrants

Business-Type Activities	
Series 1997 - A Warrants	$ 57,030
Series 2001 - A Warrants	$ 13,740
Series 2002 - A Warrants	$ 101,465
Series 2002 - C Warrants	$ 806,738
Series 2003 - A Warrants	$ 25,220
Series 2003 - B Warrants	$ 1,137,025
Series 2003 - C Warrants	$ 1,052,025
	$ 3,193,243
Governmental Activities	
Series 2001 - A GO Warrants	$ 28,185
Series 2001 - B GO Warrants	$ 120,000
Series 2003 - A GO Warrants	$ 56,310
Series 2004 - A GO Warrants	$ 51,020
Series 2004 - A LO Warrants	$ 607,115
Series 2005 - A&B LO Warrant	$ 318,500
Series 2006 - Lease Warrants	$ 85,755
	$ 1,266,885
	$ 4,460,128

Outstanding Swaps

Issue and Counterparty	**Original Notional Amount**
Business-Type Activities	
Series 2002 - A Warrants:	
JPMorgan Chase Bank	$ 110,000
Bear Stearns	$ 110,000
Series 2002 - C Warrants:	
JPMorgan Chase Bank	$ 539,446
Bank of America	$ 110,000
Lehman Brothers	$ 190,054
Bear Stearns	$ 824,700
Series 2003 - B Warrants:	
JPMorgan Chase Bank	$ 1,035,800
Bear Stearns	$ 633,078
Bank of America	$ 379,847
Series 2003 - C Warrants:	
JPMorgan Chase Bank	$ 789,019
Bank of America	$ 263,006
Series 1997 - A, 2001 - A, 2002 - C:	
JPMorgan Chase Bank	$ 200,000
Series 1997 - A, 2002 - C, 2003 - B:	
JPMorgan Chase Bank	$ 175,000
	$ 5,359,950
Governmental Activities	
Series 2001 - B Warrants:	
JPMorgan Chase Bank	$ 120,000
	$ 5,479,950

Sources: Jefferson County Commission Audited Financial Statements September 30, 2009

When bond insurers MBIA, Ambac, and XLCA were downgraded in 2008, the city was forced to post hundreds of millions in cash to back its obligations on the swap contracts and pay punitive interest rates after failed remarketing of its short-term debt.[15] The city filed for bankruptcy protection in November of 2011 and emerged two years later. Bondholders recovered 60% of par value, paid for with the proceeds of a $2.1 billion bond issue.[16] The recovery under Jefferson County's bankruptcy plan was much higher than under Detroit's because of the lower magnitude of insolvency and the inclusion of new revenues in addition to haircuts on debt.

Jefferson County's distress and ensuing bankruptcy were the municipal bond market's wake-up call and the beginning of uncertainty in a world without bond insurance. As this was the first major bankruptcy stemming from events linked to the financial crisis, it brought a renewed focus on distress and the treatment of various classes of creditors in Chapter 9 Bankruptcy proceedings. Prior to the financial crisis, investors would not have considered state laws and the legality of their claims. For example, Alabama law does not recognize the general obligation pledge as having a statutory lien; it is therefore considered an unsecured pledge.[17] Thus, instead of receiving full payouts on their claims, general obligation bondholders were forced to negotiate alongside other creditors in the bankruptcy.[18] Jefferson County sewer warrant creditors, on the other hand, were treated as "secured," given their statutory lien on sewer revenues.[19] School warrants, payable from dedicated sales taxes, were also considered secured because of their lien on a separate sales tax.[20]

This thinking began to create questions about the value of the general obligation pledge. Revenue bonds started to trade at a premium to general obligation bonds because of their dedicated nature and backing from a stable stream of essential revenues. The Jefferson County bankruptcy had far-reaching implications for the rest of the market and prompted a focus on underlying revenue streams rather than on the quality of the bond insurer.

In the wake of Jefferson County, news headlines circulated about municipal defaults and pockets of stress. The financial crisis and ensuing, deeply protracted recession reduced revenues to all municipal issuers to some degree as a result of tax base declines. Pension underfunding and escalating personnel costs under burdensome collective bargaining agreements created additional pressures for local governments. The market was in limbo at this point. Was Jefferson County a one-off idiosyncratic event, or was it the precursor to systemic weakness and strategic use of bankruptcy in the municipal market? Were local governments willing to repay burdensome debt and pension obligations in good faith, or would they use Chapter 9 Bankruptcy as an "easy out?" In years prior, local governments made draconian cuts to services as stopgap measures. To shore up local government budgets, the politically palatable choice was to cut payments to creditors instead of imposing further cuts to services. In California, strict limitations on property tax increases and the state's home rule policy of nonintervention made bankruptcy an attractive option for those local governments severely weakened by the recession.

In addition to declines in home values, high unemployment, and low income growth, pension obligations to California's $299.4 billion state-run employee pension fund, CalPERS, have crippled California's local governments.[21] Rising pension payments after the recession reduced funds to pay for basic infrastructure needs, teacher salaries, and fire and police protection. Local governments, crushed under the burden of rising obligations, have opted to file for bankruptcy. Can a federal bankruptcy judge impair contractual relationships between a state and a local government, or does this process violate the 10th Amendment of the U.S. Constitution, which preserves state sovereignty? This question was heavily litigated in the Stockton bankruptcy. CalPERS' lawyers argued that because CalPERS is an arm of the state, impairment would be a violation of the 10th Amendment of the U.S. Constitution. In approving the city's plan of adjustment, Judge Christopher Klein ruled that the federal government did have the power to break these contracts under the "Contracts Clause" in Article 1 of the U.S. Constitution, which gives the federal government exclusive power to modify contracts.

The paragraphs that follow present case studies of local California governments that experienced distress in the years leading up to 2008. The tie that binds all of them is the widespread declines in home values that catalyzed the financial distress they experienced in the years following the Great Recession.

Atwater, California

Atwater is a typical, small, agricultural community with a population of 28,000 located in California's San Joaquin Valley. It declared a fiscal emergency in October 2012 as a result of financial uncertainty and distress that built up between 2009 and 2012.[22] The city had roughly $82 million in debt outstanding across government and business-type activities, and its general fund was on the hook for all of it.[23] Declining property taxes resulting from lower home values, a new wastewater treatment plant, and an unwillingness to reduce personnel costs created structural imbalances in the city's budget that significantly reduced municipal cash flow and undermined the city's ability to remain solvent.[24]

Figure 9.4 shows the city's general fund balance, which was negative for five of the six years prior to its declaring a financial emergency.[25]

Figure 9.4

City of Atwater: Revenues vs. Expenditures

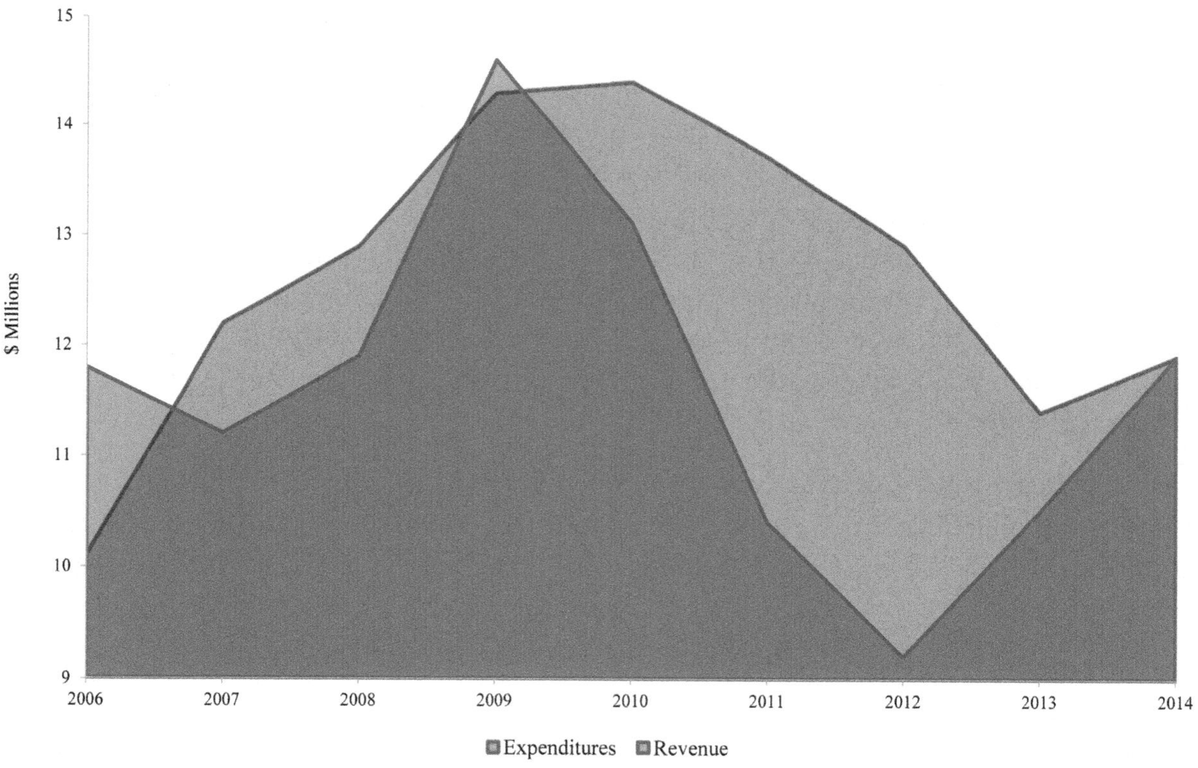

Source: City of Atwater, 2013 Comprehensive Annual Financial Report

As a result, the city was forced to increase debt issuance to fund deficits, transfer restricted funds from its water and sewer entities to pay debt service on general obligation bonds, and increase rates on city-provided services to levels higher than those in surrounding communities.[26] The city's ability to pay debt service was reduced to barely sum-sufficient levels.[27] The declaration of fiscal emergency was an inevitable step toward some sort of restructuring because of the city's lack of leadership in controlling its finances and protecting bondholders. Fortunately for bondholders, the declaration allowed the city to lay off personnel, restructure labor contracts, and reduce benefits without having to reduce payments to bondholders. In January 2013, with voter-approved increases in sales taxes and higher fees as part of its 2014 budget, the city was able to avoid bankruptcy.[28] We consider this to be a success story in that consensus was achieved without the use of bankruptcy, which would have cost the city millions in legal fees and heightened debt service costs for many years to come.

Vallejo, California

In the spring of 2008, Vallejo, California, showed the first sign of distress among California cities and filed for Chapter 9 protection on $53 million of general obligation debt.[29] Vallejo is extremely important in our analysis because it set the precedent. Before Vallejo, the need for Chapter 9 relief usually arose from one-time, idiosyncratic events, such as legal judgments (think Mammoth Lakes; see below).[30] Vallejo was the first major city to file for bankruptcy because it had become structurally insolvent due to systemic factors such as the combined impacts of the housing, economic, and banking crises. The city's structural insolvency came as a result of its unsustainable expenses and stalled revenues that reduced reserves. Vallejo's experience highlighted the mostly negative aspects of bankruptcy. The city paid $13 million in legal fees to CalPERS. Those fees could have gone toward bondholder recoveries or payments. The one positive was that Vallejo was able to restructure labor and debt contracts deemed otherwise unsustainable, to the tune of over $100 million.[31] On the other hand, the bankruptcy was very expensive, largely because of its long duration and continued litigation from impaired classes of creditors.

Since early 2015, the city has been in danger of relapsing into bankruptcy for failing to deal with its escalating pension costs as part of its bankruptcy plan.[32] Pension costs, which hit $14 million in 2014, were 40% higher than in 2012, crowding out government services.[33]

Mammoth Lakes, California

Mammoth Lakes, California, filed for bankruptcy on July 2, 2012, to seek protection against a legal judgment equal to 2.1 times its annual operating budget.[34] This bankruptcy filing was a "one-off" and more congruous with municipal bankruptcy filings that occurred prior to the recession, which were usually a result of judgments and other idiosyncratic risks. Mammoth Lakes highlights the inherent fragility of smaller municipalities in dealing with financial problems.

Located 300 miles north of Los Angeles, the city of 8,200 residents had $2.678 million in certificates of participation outstanding.[35] In 1997, the town entered a development agreement that required real estate developer Terrance Ballas to construct retail and residential buildings near the Mammoth Yosemite Airport.[36] In return, Ballas would receive rights to develop a $400 million hotel project on 25 acres of airport land and an option to buy the land.[37] The town backed out of the deal because it wanted to use the land to extend the airport's runway to accommodate larger jets. In 2006, the developer, through its closely held company Mammoth Lakes Land Acquisition, sued the town for breach of contract and was awarded a $30 million judgment.[38] The judgment accrued interest at 7% and grew to $43 million until August 2013 when the city settled out of court with the developer.[39] The town's bankruptcy plan did not allow restructuring lease payments on its $2.678 million in outstanding debt, which amounted to 1.2% of its general-fund expenditures.[40] As of early 2015, the city was able to settle with the developer and the issue has been resolved.

The Mammoth Lakes case illustrates a separate type of bankruptcy filing, typical of what would have occurred in the absence of the broader macro-economic declines on the national level that impacted the other California case studies we present.

San Bernardino, California

An important tenet of any bankruptcy is that it is a remedy to be used only when all attempts to renegotiate debts fail. San Bernardino's "first resort" use of Chapter 9 Bankruptcy is an exception and illustrates how politics can cloud rational, economic decision-making. Since the early 2000s, the city's personnel expenses for public safety increased 350%.[41] Reserves in the general fund were depleted by the middle of the decade, and the city entered into debt transactions and labor agreements that severely strained its finances.[42] The city reached a breaking point in June 2012 when the city council realized that the resources on hand were insufficient to make August debt service and other contractual obligations—this after a decade of fiscal mismanagement and structural budget imbalances. California Law AB 506 allows debtors to bypass private 30-day negotiations with creditors if it is determined that the city will be insolvent before the 30 days has elapsed. To remedy that issue, it was more convenient for the city to declare, eventually allowing it to pass an emergency budget (after a month of wrangling) that included no general-fund payments toward its $50 million POBs (pension obligation bonds) out of a total $233 million in outstanding debt.[43] The San Bernardino bankruptcy is still in court, primarily because of the city's impairment to CalPERS in its plan of adjustment.

Stockton, California

Stockton, California's bankruptcy plan of adjustment is noteworthy because it did not impair investors, but bond insurers who own the city's debt. Bond insurers who recovered less principal as a result of CalPERS' non-impairment, fought Stockton's plan in court. The result was a long, drawn-out battle between Stockton and its creditors.

The city's dire financial situation was the result of its fundamentally weak economy. Figure 9.5 shows the city's unemployment rate versus the national average. Stockton's unemployment rate increased to 20% in 2011 versus 9.1% nationally.[44] It has since declined to 15.6%, but is elevated relative to the national rate of 7.9% as of the end of 2013.[45]

Figure 9.5

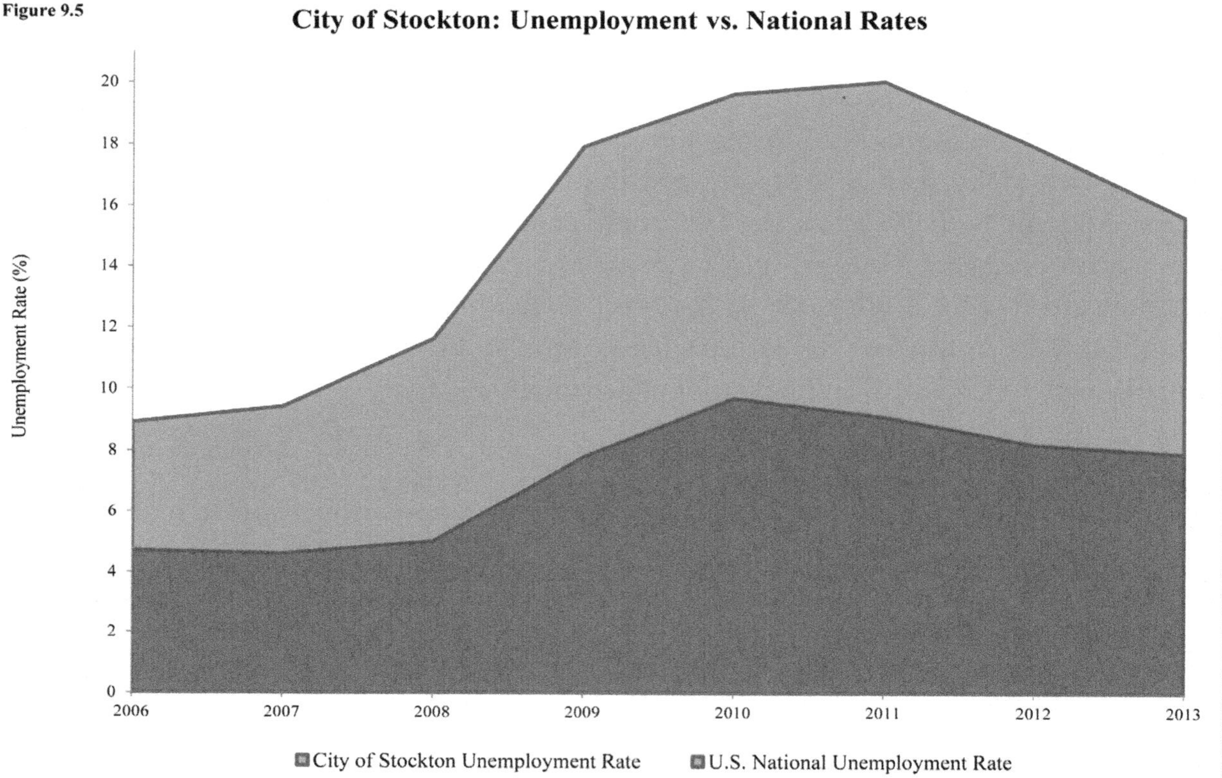

Sources: Census Bureau, Investortools

Stockton filed for bankruptcy on June 28, 2012, after AB 506 negotiations with its creditors broke down, having failed to achieve a negotiated settlement that would allow the city to adopt a balanced budget for FY12-13, as required by law. A pendency plan submitted by the city during the mediation process—essentially a budget for the city after Chapter 9 protection—did not include payments for debt service on $350 million out of its $702 million of debt and reduced costs for labor, retirees, and long-term healthcare obligations.[46] Stockton's bankruptcy plan was approved by the judge as of early 2015, and bondholders recovered 12 cents on the dollar. The city's unwillingness to impair its pensions while bondholders recovered pennies thwarted the process. Institutional holders of the city's debt have appealed this decision; however, the low recovery for bondholders will lengthen the progress toward emerging from bankruptcy.

California law factored into the distress faced by California cities and their ensuing bankruptcies. Many states, such as Michigan, New Jersey, and Pennsylvania, require state approval or a state intervention before a filing. State intervention is a way to forestall bankruptcy's spillover effects to other entities geographically close to bankrupt municipalities.[47] During the Detroit bankruptcy, local Michigan governments paid, on average, 0.3% to 0.4% higher debt service costs as a result of flight from local Michigan bonds by retail investors. State intervention into the operations of Harrisburg, Pennsylvania, through the appointment of a receiver, prevented a bankruptcy that would have spilled over to local Pennsylvania governments. The intervention into the affairs of Harrisburg's divided local government provided a swift and low-cost resolution that put the city back onto solid financial footing.

Harrisburg, Pennsylvania

Earlier in the chapter, we noted that there are two causes of bankruptcy and distress: (1) broad-based macro themes and (2) idiosyncratic risks associated with project financings.[48] Harrisburg falls into the latter category. The city's bankruptcy had its roots in debt transactions and financings that occurred in the 1970s. During then mayor Stephen Reed's close to 30-year tenure, the city engaged in bond financings to build projects of little economic value to the city.[49] The straw that would eventually break Harrisburg's back were $282 million in debt guarantees the city entered into from 2003 until 2005, on bonds issued by the Harrisburg Authority to retrofit a waste-to-energy facility (incinerator).[50]

The incinerator, built in 1972 as an alternative to oil-based energy sources in response to OPEC supply shortages, went through multiple phases of construction that were complicated by faulty building practices and several facility failures.[51] We credit journalist John Luciew of Harrisburg's Patriot-News for his chronicle of the facility, which we refer to extensively in this section. The facility was supposed to bring revenues to the city by selling facility usage to trash haulers operating in Dauphin County and the City of Harrisburg.[52] In 2003, the majority of the Harrisburg Authority's city-guaranteed debt was issued to retrofit and improve the facility.[53] Dauphin County entered into an agreement with the Authority to direct its trash there in exchange for control over rate increases. The retrofitting was not completed on time and ran over budget, resulting in the need for additional debt issuance to fund repairs and pay debt service.[54] Yes, that is correct. Debt was issued for the sole purpose of making interest payments on existing debt. This desperate measure bought the Authority some time; eventually, it had to raise fees to pay the increased debt-servicing costs anyway.[55]

In late 2008, the Authority requested a $100-per-ton rate increase, which was turned down by an arbitrator.[56] Debt service payments reduced liquidity; the Authority's operating deficit increased as revenues from operations were barely able to pay operating and maintenance expenses, let alone debt-service costs; and the authority defaulted on its debt in 2008.[57] The city had not made the payments on its guaranteed debt, as its financial situation continued to worsen.[58] In 2012, the city missed payment on its general obligation debt, setting into motion a process by which a state-appointed receiver would devise and implement a plan to return the city to solvency.

The case of Harrisburg highlights the role a state can play in governing the process by which a municipality enters bankruptcy. State statutes govern the actions of their local governments. In Chapter 9 Bankruptcy, the way bankruptcy will play out depends on a complex interplay between explicit and implied powers spelled out under the Constitution and each state's laws. Regardless of state, however, the one constant is that federal law gives states legislative authority to govern their municipalities, which includes governing the ability of states to file for bankruptcy. States often serve as "gatekeepers" in this process.[59]

In the years since the Harrisburg incinerator default, the city attempted bankruptcy filings to force a default on debt without having to layoff public employees. These attempted filings, the result of a broken political system in the city, did not succeed, resulting in a state takeover. The case was resolved swiftly by the state-appointed receiver through asset sales that generated recoveries of 60% to 70% for general obligation bondholders and 66% for incinerator bondholders.[60]

Conclusion

Historically, the number of municipal defaults has been only a small fraction of the number of defaults in the corporate bond market, and bankruptcy law governing municipal bankruptcies has been tested few times relative to the law governing corporates. It took a once-in-a-century financial crisis to test the finances of local governments, a testament to their overall flexibility and willingness to make required budgetary decisions. There are always a few bad apples. In these cases, a difficult economy, often accompanied by corruption and poor management over decades, are the key ingredients that foment municipal distress, defaults, and bankruptcies.

10

Build America Bonds to the Rescue

The Build America Bond (BAB) program was a temporary, two-year municipal market stimulus program introduced as part of the American Recovery and Reinvestment Act in February 2009. The program's intent was to stimulate investment in infrastructure and create jobs by allowing municipalities to issue new-money, taxable bonds whose 35% subsidy from the federal government was a cheaper alternative to tax-exempt bonds. The program was a huge success from multiple standpoints. During its two-year span, state and local governments used the program to finance $188 billion in new infrastructure projects at very low cost and create thousands of construction jobs while strengthening and improving the nation's infrastructure.[1] The program also had measurable impacts on credit markets. BABs, as they have come to be called, were typically issued as high-quality, long-duration instruments and provided a diversification alternative to corporate bonds for liability-matching institutions such as banks and pension funds. BABs also took long-term supply out of the tax-exempt market, driving down interest rates for municipal issuers. This reopened the spigots for low-cost issuance following a period of constrained access to capital markets.

Research firm Municipal Market Analytics (MMA) explains the market dynamics that led to the creation of BABs.[2] It was 2008, and levered bondholders such as hedge funds and tender-option bond programs were forced to sell their long-term bonds because they could not roll over short-term indebtedness. Money market funds did not want to purchase this short-term paper because they distrusted the credit quality of bond insurers. Retail investors, who are typically last to the party, sold bond positions and mutual fund shares, creating a domino effect and a spike in yields that was exacerbated by poor liquidity.[3] With all of these entities selling at the same time, volatility increased. A financing alternative was needed for state and local governments. Build America Bonds came to the rescue.

Figure 10.1 shows the municipal bond market hemorrhaging that occurred before and during the financial crisis. The ratio of the 30-year muni yield to the 30-year Treasury yield measures the muni market's dysfunction relative to the Treasury market, the benchmark for all asset classes.

Figure 10.1

30-yr. Muni/Treasury Yield Ratio

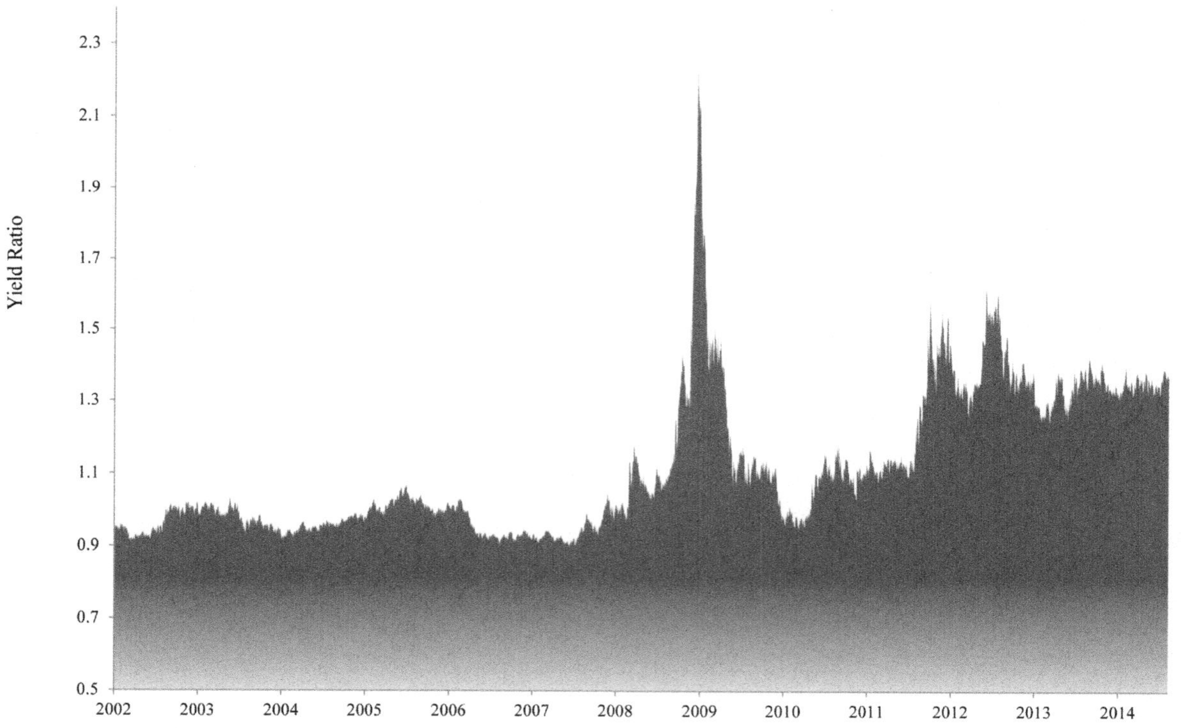

Sources: Bloomberg, Municipal Market Advisors

From 2000 until the financial crisis, this ratio's historical average was 0.96 (i.e., tax-exempt municipal bond yields have traded at 96% of Treasury yields). Panic selling out of municipal bonds and into Treasury bonds throughout 2008 and into 2009 increased the ratio from an already elevated 1.14 to 2.32 in December 2008, a roughly 2-standard-deviation move (see Figure10.1).[4] The standard deviation increased from low single-digits to approximately 25% by December 2008, making it nearly impossible for issuers to access capital. Virtually "riskless" issuers such as the State of Ohio or the New York City Municipal Water Finance Authority paid rates as high as 5.5% and 6.35% respectively, to issue long-term debt at the height of the crisis. This, at a time when long-term Treasury yields were at 30-year lows of close to 4%.[5]

By the end of 2008, with long-term municipal bond issuance coming to a standstill, action needed to be taken. If not, the stagnation would eventually funnel into the economy and trigger an adverse feedback loop of major declines in real economic activity and further financial market declines. Washington would do everything in its power to prevent this.

BABs were the government's solution to the illiquidity and inefficiency of the muni market. The program had many synergies. By issuing taxable, subsidized bonds into the much larger and more efficient corporate bond market, state and local governments could circumvent the muni market and continue to get financing. Issuers were given a more stable platform of institutional buyers to whom to market their debt. And buyers of bonds were given a diversification alternative of much higher credit quality than typical corporate issuance.

After the start of the program, the market started to cure itself. In a market with less supply, muni yields relative to Treasuries started to decline, creating a better funding environment for local governments to invest in new projects.

BABs were introduced to the market on April 15, 2009. In the months that followed, tax-exempt buyers returned to the market, particularly in the longer maturities, and yields plummeted.[6] High-grade yields rallied 35 basis points within the first week of the program.[7] Yields on taxable BABs declined as well, posting significant gains as the instruments became accepted as an important component of investment portfolios for all types of buyers.[8] The fact that issuers could count on direct payment of subsidy incentivized new, low-cost investment in infrastructure and unlocked a fountain of new issuance for projects from 2009 through 2010 to front-run the program's sunset.[9] Looking at the relative health of the municipal bond market during the Build America Bond program (see Figure10.2), the intended goal was reached: Municipal bond yields declined in secular fashion from mid-2009 to the end of 2010.

Figure 10.2

Muni Yields: 2009-2010

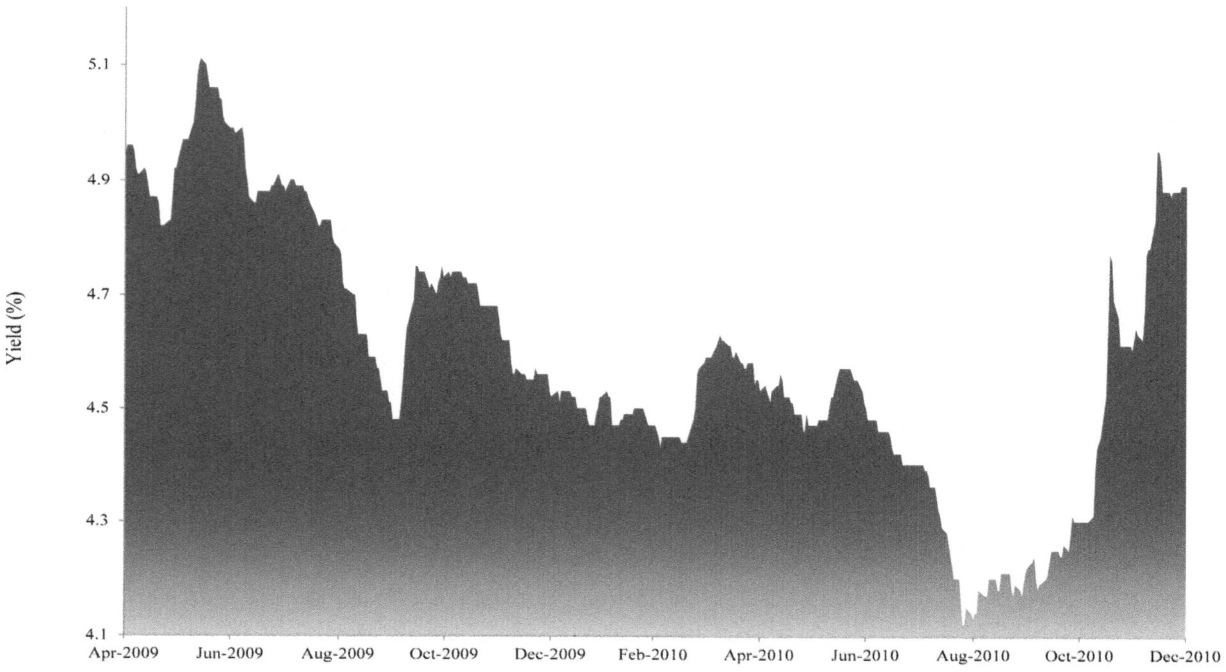

Sources: Bloomberg, Municipal Market Advisors

The entrance of BABs into the marketplace has reignited a debate over the most efficient delivery mechanism for government subsidy: Whether it is direct payment from the federal government or the interest cost savings of issuing tax-exempt bonds versus taxable bonds. Many saw the program as being a more efficient way of providing government subsidy to tax-exempt issuers not subject to the vagaries of supply and demand and the various technical factors impacting tax-exempt and Treasury yields.[10] Since the introduction of direct-payment bonds from the federal government in the 1980s, academics and politicians have studied the efficiency of the municipal bond market and delivery of subsidy.[11] The BABs program compares well to alternatives.

The Congressional Budget Office (CBO) and the Joint Committee on Taxation (JCT) have done in-depth research on the subject of subsidy delivery under tax-exemption versus direct-pay. The following paragraphs will detail their work. We encourage interested readers to check out the report published in October 2009, titled *Subsidizing Infrastructure Investment with Tax-Preferred Bonds.* [12]

Since the financial crisis, tax-exempt financing has not been an efficient way of delivering a subsidy: Borrowers receive only a portion of the revenues the federal government forgoes by not taxing the bonds.[13] For this reason, the federal government would like to end tax-exemption on municipal bonds and replace it with direct issuer subsidies. The CBO states that, in addition, tax-exempt financing is regressive, as forgone revenues "accrue to investors in higher income tax brackets that receive greater savings through the exemption as yields on tax-exempt debt increase."[14] This amount lost by the federal government in the form of foregone tax revenues is estimated to be roughly $26 billion annually.[15]

Tax credit bonds such as Build America Bonds, on the other hand, do not have those disadvantages.

As tax-exempt bond rates increase relative to taxable rates, the subsidy cost to the federal government stays constant, but the actual subsidy decreases.[16] The cost to Treasury increases because the marginal buyer of the taxable bond switches to purchasing a tax-exempt bond and the Treasury forgoes additional revenue.[17]

The issuer's tax-exempt subsidy changes with market rates.

When an issuer issues taxable BABs, the subsidy rate is 35% of the coupon paid to the issuer by the federal government. When the issuer issues tax-exempt debt, the subsidy rate in percentage terms is calculated as:

Taxable debt yield - tax-exempt debt yield ÷ taxable debt yield.[18]

The CBO's illustration explains the logic behind the value of the subsidy.[19] If the taxable market yield is 6% and tax-exempt yield is 4.5% and a buyer with marginal tax rate of 25% purchases the tax-exempt bond, then the subsidy and cost to the federal government are equal, as follows:

Subsidy to the issuer = 6% - 4.5% = 1.5%
Cost to federal government = forgone tax revenue = 0.25 x 6% = 1.5%

The subsidy to the tax-exempt issuer from the federal government is simply the interest it saves versus issuing taxable debt. At this point, the buyer in the 25% marginal tax rate faces a tossup between buying the taxable or the tax-exempt bond. The cost of the subsidy to the government is equal to the actual subsidy.

The CBO states that if the tax-exempt rates increase to 5%, the cost of the subsidy to the federal government increases, while the actual subsidy remains unchanged:

Subsidy to the issuer = 6% - 5% = 1%
Cost to federal government = 0.25 x 6% = 1.5%

As the tax-exempt yield rises, the attractiveness of tax-exempt bonds increases to the marginal buyer who will forgo buying taxables. As the tax-exempt yield continues to increase, buyers with ever lower marginal tax rates purchase the tax-exempt bond, further increasing the cost to Treasury. It makes sense for anyone whose marginal tax rate is higher than the market-implied tax rate to purchase tax-exempt bonds. The purchaser of a tax-exempt bond demands a return equal to or greater than the after-tax yield on a taxable bond. Thus, if the investor's marginal tax-rate is higher, it does not take as high a yield on the tax-exempt bonds to entice him into purchasing them.

The revenues forgone through tax-exempt debt are a type of financial support from the federal government known as tax-expenditure, similar to the mortgage interest deduction.[20] A direct payment to the issuer, as opposed to a direct subsidy, is more easily controlled by the federal government and not subject to changes in tax rates or changes in the relationships between the taxable and tax-exempt market. That is why they are also the mode of subsidy preferred by the current administration.[21] Historically, the implied subsidy has been between 20% and 30%, while the cost to Treasury has been roughly 33%.[22] However, this tax rate may be understated. The average issuing denomination of munis is much lower than that of corporates. If the tax-exempt market yield is higher than the yield afforded by taxable corporates due to a liquidity premium, then the inefficiency of the tax-exempt subsidy is overstated. We can also make the case that the muni market yield is lower because of greater credit quality, as is evidenced by historical studies that show the default rate on corporates to be much higher than the default rate on municipals.[23]

Notwithstanding these assumptions or statements about efficiency, the U.S. tax-exempt municipal bond market has historically been a very stable and reliable way for state and local governments to access the capital markets. The Build America Bond program complemented the tax-exempt market at a time of dysfunction and primed the pump for a continued functioning of the market.

Figure 10.3

BABs Yields vs. Similar Corporates

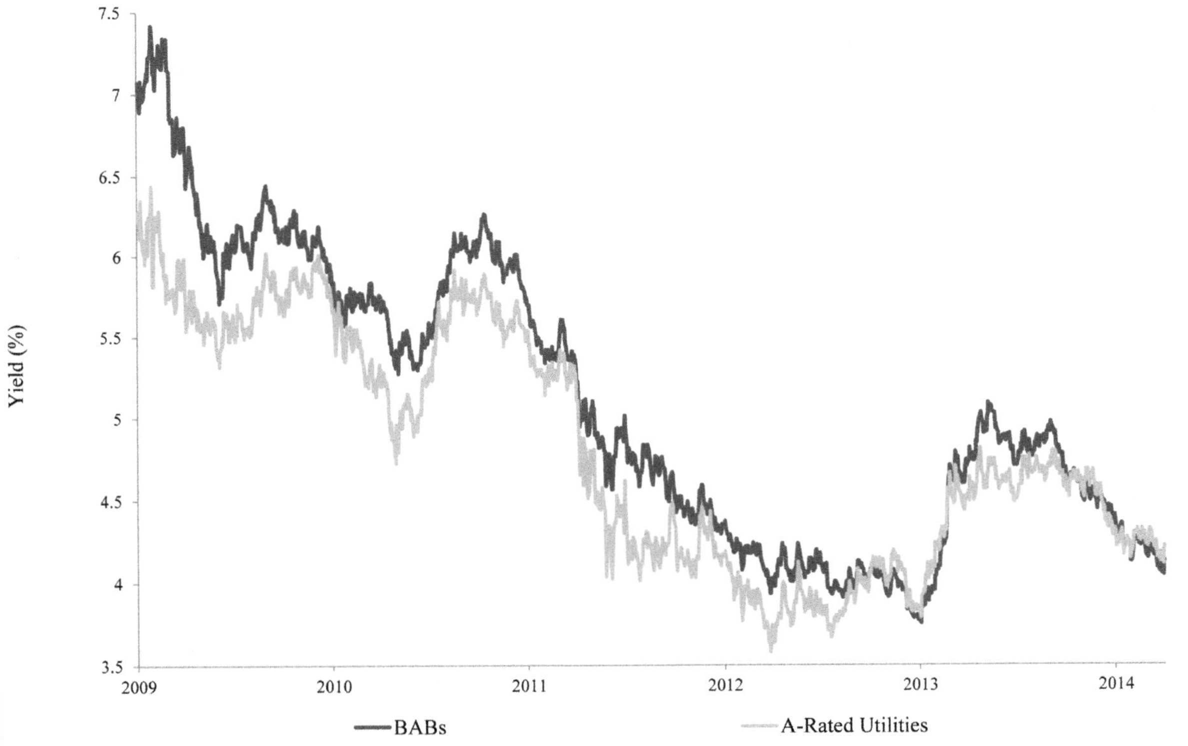

Sources: Bloomberg, Merrill Lynch Indices

BABs continue to be a great buy for investors. They are a high-credit-quality, non-correlated portfolio diversifier with significant yield concession over typical corporate securities. Figure 10.3 shows that on average, since program inception, the yields on BABs have exceeded those of their corporate counterparts. Figure 10.4 shows the yields on BABs versus tax-exempt bonds, which did not track quite as closely together and in fact reversed in mid-2013 when tax-frees traded at higher yields than BABs.[24] This reversal occurred because of cracks that emerged in the tax-exempt market as a result of the Detroit bankruptcy. That the BABs market did not react illustrates the different buyer bases of BABS versus tax-exempt bonds.

Figure 10.4

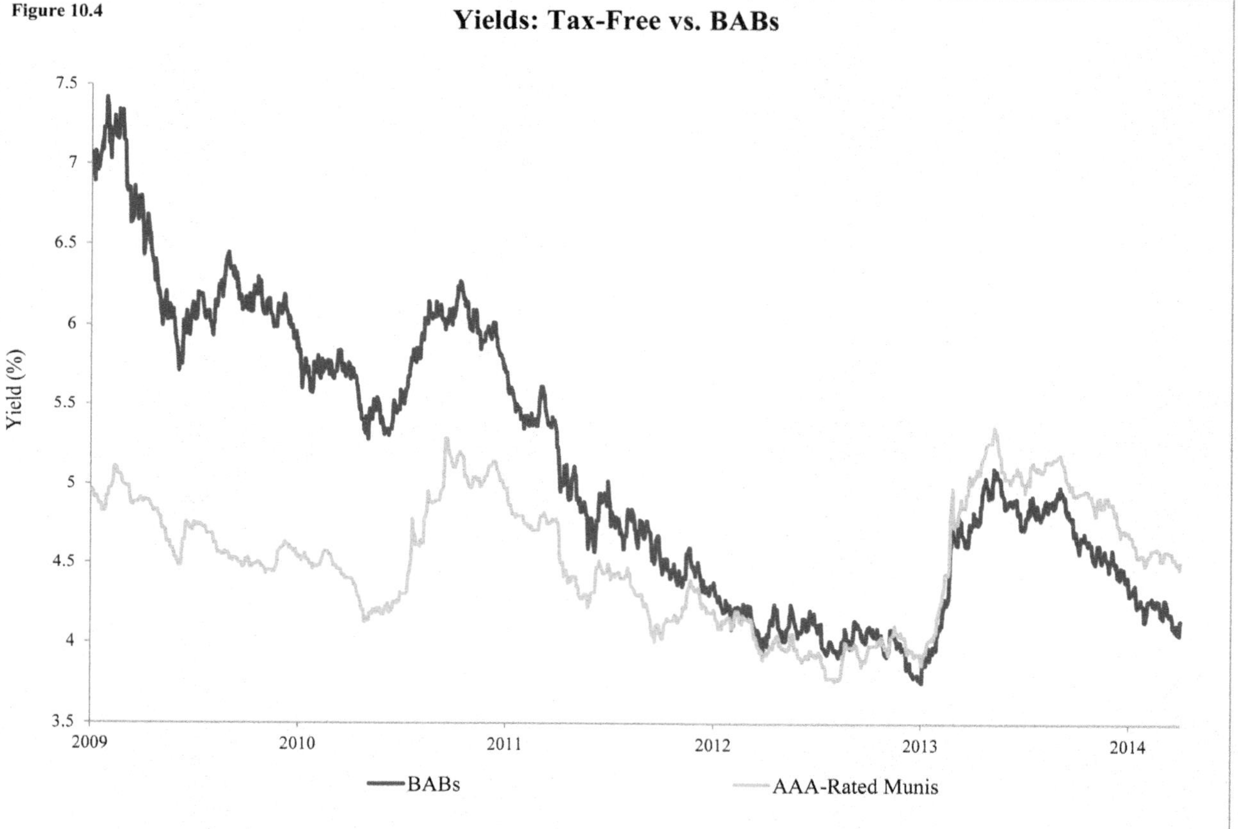

Sources: Bloomberg, Merrill Lynch Indices, Municipal Market Advisors

The Build America Bond program came to an end in 2010 under the original terms of the legislation and was not reauthorized by Congress. Concerns over the program's high cost to the government and its incentives toward debt issuance were not palatable to political decision-makers at the time. In our view, the arguments regarding cost are somewhat misguided. As we point out, the direct cost of BABs to the federal government is lower than the cost of tax-exempt issuance, and the delivery of the subsidy is more efficient and not subject to market vagaries between tax-exempt and taxable issuance.

The program springboarded infrastructure investment that will serve the United States for years to come. Since the sunset of the program, we have seen various bills introduced containing BABs, none of which have passed. Nonetheless, Build America Bonds' popularity with institutional investors and issuers made them an effective tool in curing the municipal bond market post-financial crisis and enhancing investors' bond portfolios.

11

Headline Risk in the Municipal Bond Market

The headline risk that has dominated the municipal bond market in the past five years is not new. There have been a number of "event risk" headlines that caused municipal bond market liquidity to diminish, or yields to rise, or both. These illiquidity drop-offs are by no means limited to municipal credit. They can be driven by legislative events, natural disasters, and investors' fear of inflation.

A good example of legislative events causing headline risk occurred in March 1986, when Congress was searching for new sources of revenue. Bob Packwood, former U.S. Senator and chairman of the Senate Committee on Finance from 1985 to 1987, started to publicly mull over the idea of taxing municipal bonds. His musings got sufficient airplay with the press, creating downward pressure on bond prices as the market ground to a halt. Bids, if any, were essentially constructed as if the tax-free municipal bonds were taxable. The message finally got to Senator Packwood that he was causing a total disruption in the municipal capital markets. The market soon returned to normal. Of course, "normal" during the 1980s meant that municipal bond yields traded decently below Treasury yields, reflecting demand for tax-exempt income and a world much less concerned with credit risks such as pension funding, escalating labor costs, and falling home values.

The legislative headline-risk monster also raised its head in the beginning of 1995, following the 1994 mid-term elections, which saw a Republican majority take over the House of Representatives led by Representative Newt Gingrich of Georgia. One of the tenets of the Republican platform, also known as the "Contract with America," was the elimination of federal tax on interest income with the goal of boosting a savings rate that had become very low. While not taxing municipal bonds per se, this provision of the "Contract with America" would have had the effect of placing municipal bonds on the same playing field as U.S. Treasuries, agencies, mortgages, and corporate bonds. Neither dealers nor investors knew exactly what the fate of this legislative proposal would be, so the easiest course was for dealers to bid municipal bonds as if the bonds were taxable. Once again, the municipal bond market ground to a halt—and then soon cured itself.

Temporary pockets of stress have impacted municipal bond issuers located in areas affected by natural disasters. In the last 30 years, both the San Francisco Bay Area earthquake of 1989 and Hurricane Andrew in Miami-Dade County, Florida in 1992 occasioned a temporary halt in liquidity as damage assessments were made. Illiquid markets ensued over a number of days, not weeks, and soon rebounded.

The impact of Hurricane Katrina on the greater New Orleans area in 2005 caused a temporary halt in the trading of bonds issued by local municipal entities located in Louisiana and Mississippi near the Gulf of Mexico. The illiquidity also spread to the Gulf Coast of Texas and the Florida Panhandle. The "hurricane risk premium," an artifact of hurricane Katrina, is still present in the hardest hit areas of Louisiana and Mississippi eight and a half years later. It was highest in September and October of 2005—roughly 75 to 100 basis points. It has since declined to between 25 and 35 basis points.

On the pure municipal credit side, there are a number of examples—pre-financial crisis—of headline risk.

New York City: 1975

In 1975, New York City was nearing bankruptcy, with nearly $5 billion in debt and an over-reliance on short-term note funding that had to constantly be "rolled over."

The temporary nonpayment of New York City notes in 1975 sent shock waves through the municipal bond market. The city asked the federal government for help. The response from the Ford Administration was "no," prompting the famous New York Daily News headline, "Ford to City: Drop Dead." Yields rose on all New York credits. The State of New York responded with the creation of the Municipal Assistance Corporation (MAC), an authority created by then-Governor Hugh Carey that would oversee the city's finances by receiving tax revenues and managing the city's other loans. The MAC brought about a change in New York City's financial situation, which the city is still benefitting from today. At the time, however, the authority's actions stressed the secondary market for New York City and related bonds. In the mid 1970s, it was hard to find a good bid on a New York City bond, including bonds backed by dedicated revenues, such as the Triborough Bridge and Tunnel Authority or the Port Authority of New York and New Jersey.

In time, the MAC had done it, bankers lent money to the cit, and the city recovered. But it was easily 10 years before New York City debt started to trade closer to the general market.

The Washington Public Power Supply System (WPPSS) Default ("Whoops")

WPPSS was a consortium of hydroelectric and nuclear power plants in the Pacific Northwest, which in the 1970s, embarked on a project to build five nuclear power plants. Cost overruns on the plants and a decline in electricity usage well below forecasted loads led to a cancellation of two WPPSS plants and a construction halt on two others. In 1983, WPPSS defaulted on over $2 billion of municipal bonds, which at the time was the largest municipal default in U.S. history. Though not all of the projects defaulted, the penalty in terms of additional yield paid by all Washington issuers continued for at least another 10 years while the WPPSS case worked its way through the court system. The WPPSS default highlights the regional nature of headline risk. Credits like Seattle Water, or even the State of Washington, paid much higher bond yields because of WPPSS. This lingering bias regarding bonds in the State of Washington and the Pacific Northwest also impacted issuers with little or no linkage to WPPSS, such as school districts and hospitals.

The Texas Oil Drop: 1986 to 1987

In the late 1980s, headline risk in the municipal market attached itself to a commodity—oil. The late 1970s and early 1980s had seen a large spike in the price of oil, partly because of U.S. inflation, but also because of the turmoil (then and now) in the Middle East, which was heightened at the time by the Iran hostage crisis.

The price of oil declined 70% from $35 to $10 per barrel in the three years from 1983 to late 1986, as shown in Figure 11.1. Municipal bonds of all types from revenue to general obligation—even bonds insured by the Texas Permanent School Fund (PSF), which were then, as now, rated

AAA—dropped in price, and yields soared. Bonds of Texas issuers were 50 to 75 basis points higher in yield than similarly rated bonds in the general market.

Of course, this disparity proved an opportunity. Oil eventually worked its way back into an upward price pattern and bond markets in Texas returned to normalcy.

In early 2015, there was a breathtaking drop in the price of crude oil from approximately $100 per barrel in early June 2014 to $50 per barrel. Six months later, the oil's price plunge had not affected the price of Texas bonds. It was still too early to tell whether the markets would see the drop in price as temporary or permanent. If the oil market remains depressed, there is a good chance that the drop will be factored into economic projections, and impact municipal bond issues from oil-dependent states such as the Lone Star State and Alaska.

Figure 11.1

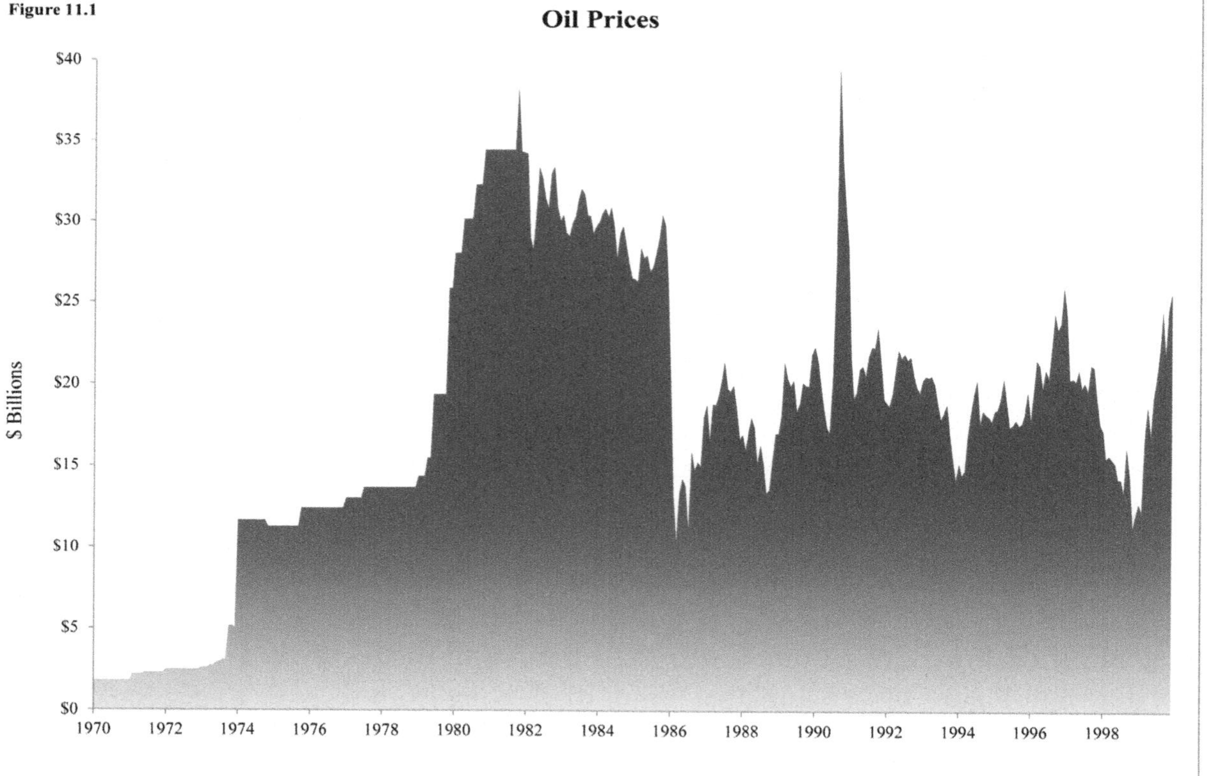

Source: Bloomberg

Orange County, California: 1994

In December 1994, Orange County, California, one of the wealthiest counties in the United States, filed for bankruptcy. The culprit was its treasurer, who made derivative bets in the short-term market by funding a trading strategy with short-term debt and investing in higher yielding longer-term bonds. This strategy backfired as the Federal Reserve hiked short-term interest rates throughout 1994. The losses on the derivative investments caused Orange County to run out of cash in early December. This crisis not only impacted the county, but also many local municipalities in California that had co-invested with Orange County in their investment portfolios to enjoy economies of scale. In many cases, other issuers in the county borrowed to invest with Orange County, in essence using leverage to invest with leverage. Proposition 13 in California, which limits increases in property taxes, was partly to blame. Municipalities were looking for almost anything that would provide additional revenues in a world where their power to raise property taxes was extremely limited.

Orange County's bankruptcy shook the municipal bond market in general, but it particularly hurt the market for California bonds. The market asked "what if?" about other local government bonds. The California local GO market came to a halt with bids few and far between. This catalyst caused the municipal market at large to slump severely. Figure 11.2 shows long-term, AA-rated muni bond yields in 1994.

Figure 11.2

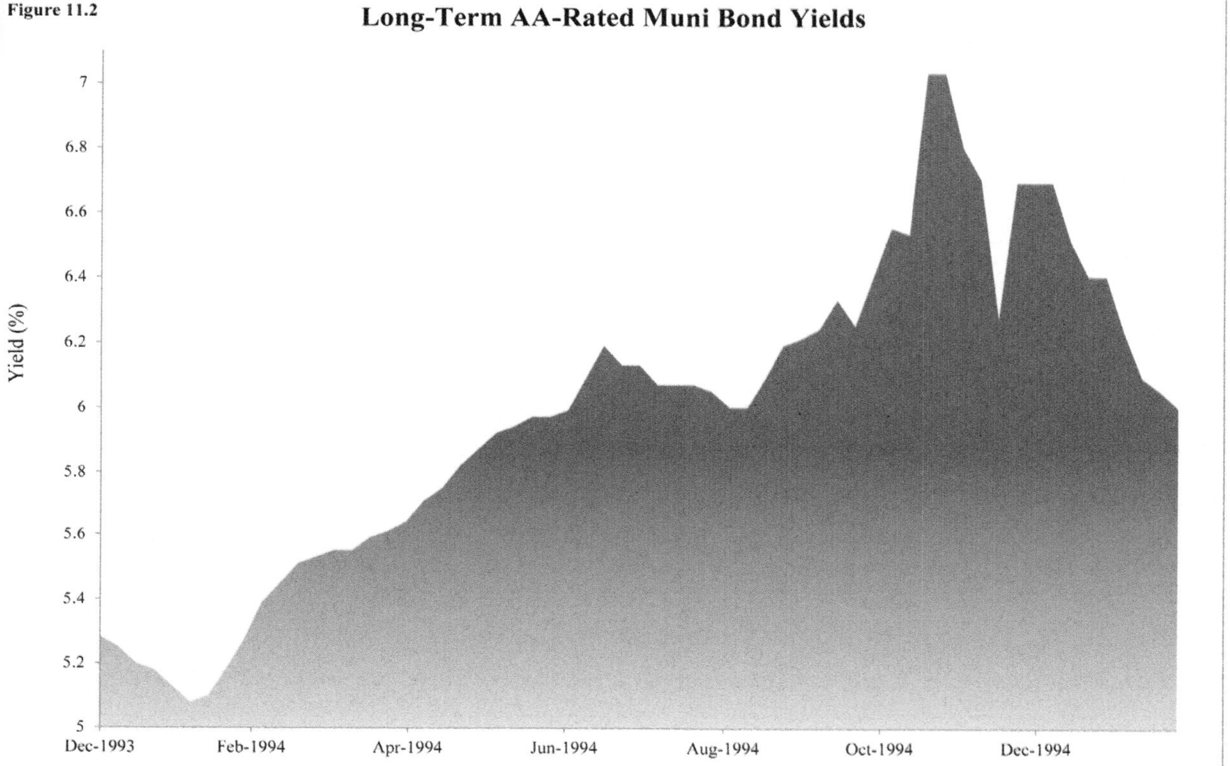

Source: Bloomberg, Moody's Investors Service

The situation was resolved when former California State Treasurer Thomas Hayes was called in to manage the county's finances. The saving grace was that Orange County was one of the country's wealthiest.

The county eventually issued new debt to refinance the short-term debt that had not been paid, and bankruptcy ended a year and a half after it was declared. Nonetheless, market-wide headline risk persisted throughout December 1994.

Credit Scare of 2010-2011

This is an example of headline risk that was not caused by a municipality or an outside event but by a retail market that panicked in the winter of 2010–2011. Meredith Whitney, a respected bank analyst who gained significant notoriety in 2007 for predicting the financial crisis, announced in December 2010 on CBS's *60 Minutes* (and in the press prior to this time) that 2011 would see "hundreds of billions of dollars" of municipal defaults.

The effect on munis was swift and immediate. Retail investors sold out of municipal bond funds. When bond funds are overburdened with redemptions instead of inflows, they have no recourse but to sell bonds to meet those redemptions. Since the sell-off happened to many bond funds at once, liquidity disappeared fast and bond yields increased. Once again headlines—not fundamentals—were driving market illiquidity. Figure 11.3 shows the bond fund redemptions (negative investor flows) in late 2010 and into 2011.

Figure 11.3

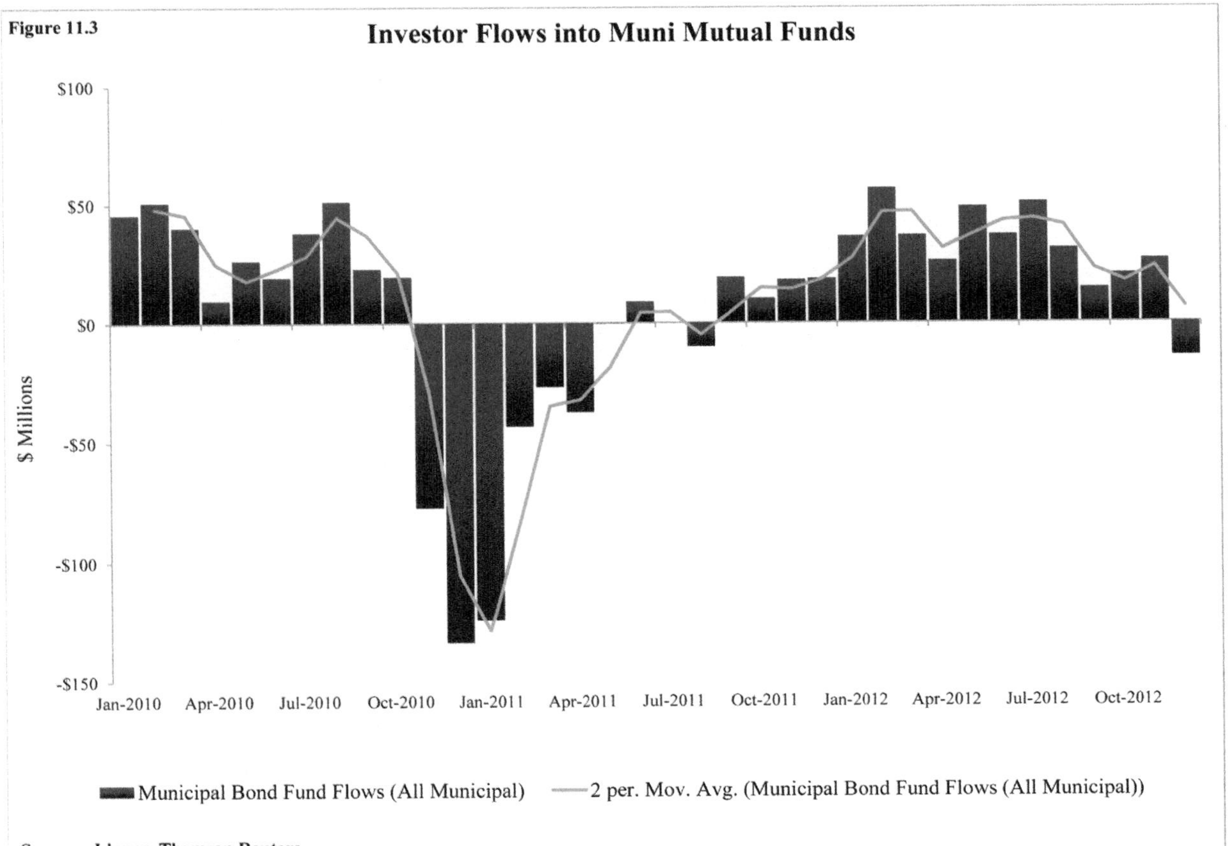

Sources: Lipper, Thomson Reuters

This process tends to self-correct over time as yields rise to a level that is attractive for investors to re-enter the market. When this occurs, outflows cease and the market returns to normal.

Figure 11.4

Negative Headlines and Rising Yields

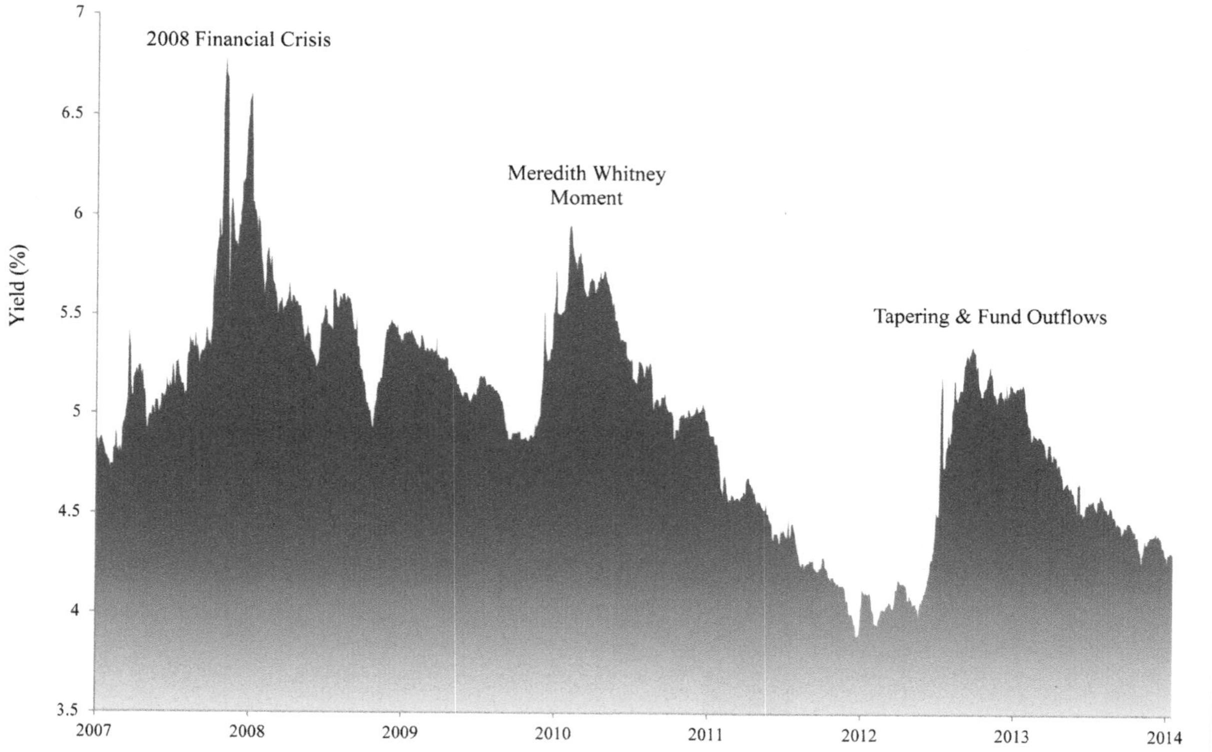

Source: Bloomberg, Cumberland Advisors

During this meltdown, retail investors were fleeing bond funds mostly due to their fear of what was forecast on various media outlets. The truth was that municipal credit was the healthiest it had ever been and had already started to improve from the depths of the Great Recession. Municipal tax receipts started to increase as 2010 progressed. By January 2015, the increase accelerated. Due to the nature of bond funds, which pay dividends, most investors own intermediate-to-longer term bonds unless their expressed goal is to own shorter maturities. If credit, as opposed to headline risk, were the reason for the market sell-off, shorter maturities would also have sold off, but they did not. Credit events tend to flatten yield curves. Figure 11.5 shows that five-year muni yields did not change very much compared to the hemorrhaging that occurred in longer-term bond yields.

The Meredith Whitney headline event began to cure itself in mid-2011 when investors realized that a long-maturity, tax-free municipal bond yield near 6% looked absurd compared to a 4.25% 30-year U.S. Treasury yield.

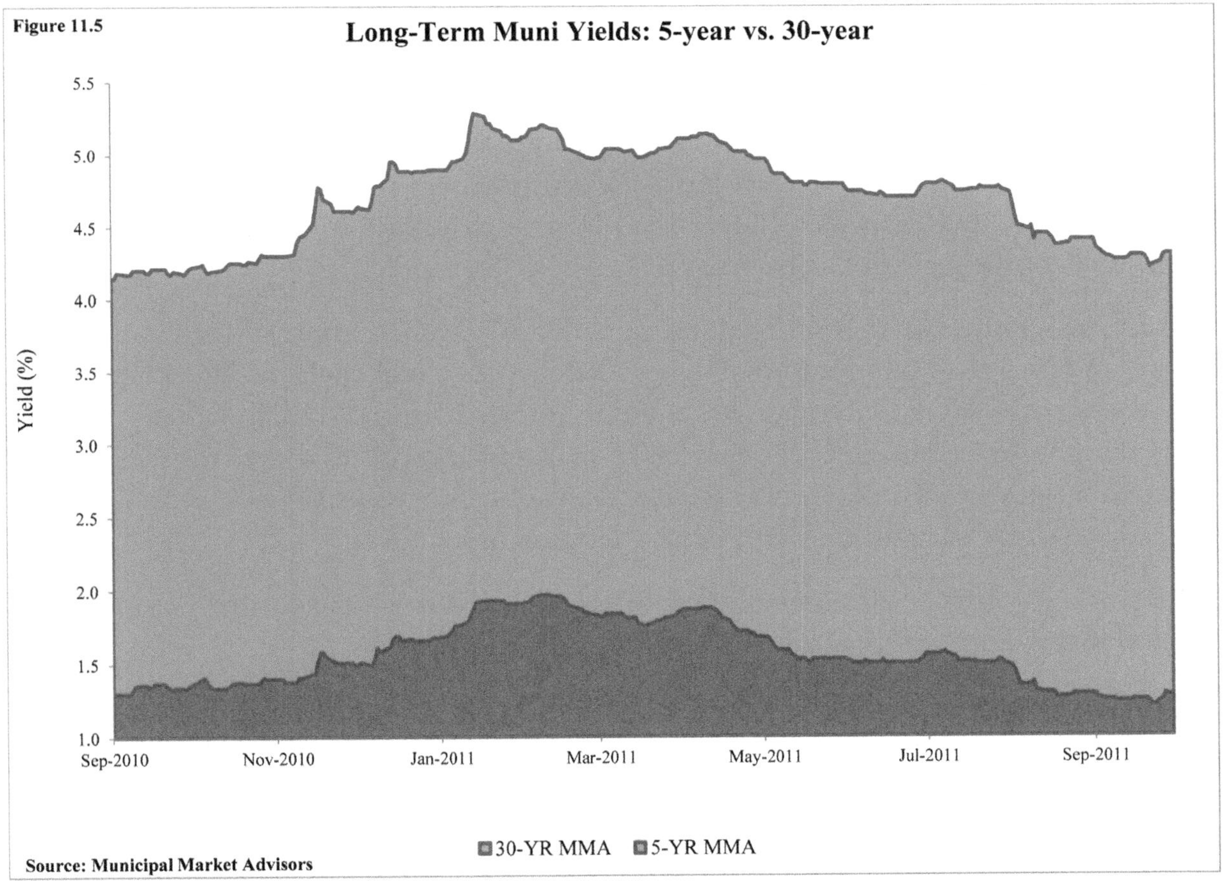

Puerto Rico

The years 2013 and 2014 were very rocky for owners of Puerto Rico municipal bonds. The Commonwealth's economic climate had been eroding for a number of years. The process started with a loss of tax benefits for corporations doing business in Puerto Rico. Jobs disappeared from the island. Many working-age citizens left the island in the 2000s in search of better employment opportunities on the U.S. mainland, exacerbating the problem. As the recession deepened, pension liabilities began to soar, and the process fed on itself and created a negative feedback loop.

Debt of the Commonwealth and its agencies has traded cheap to the market for a number of years. However, since interest on Puerto Rico debt is exempt from state taxes in all 50 states, it had a place in over three quarters of all municipal bond funds. Over the years, Puerto Rico debt had been a "filler" for a number of bond funds—especially single-state bond funds that invested only in bonds of, say, Massachusetts or New Jersey. When portfolio managers could not find enough bonds from in-state, they turned to Puerto Rico to satisfy their investing needs. Bond funds had as much as 25% of their portfolios invested in Puerto Rico paper.

The market began to turn in the spring and summer of 2013 as a number of the Commonwealth's agencies began to see their bond ratings downgraded by the ratings agencies. The Puerto Rico debt market had seen a fall-off in December 2012, but it quickly bounced back in January as the deluge of January coupon payments and redemptions of matured and called bonds was reinvested by retail investors, supporting the market for Puerto Rico debt. Indeed, many of the brokerage houses had clients invested in various types of Puerto Rico instruments.

But it was not until August 2013, when *Barron's* published a cover page titled "Troubling Winds from Puerto Rico," that headline risk entered the picture.

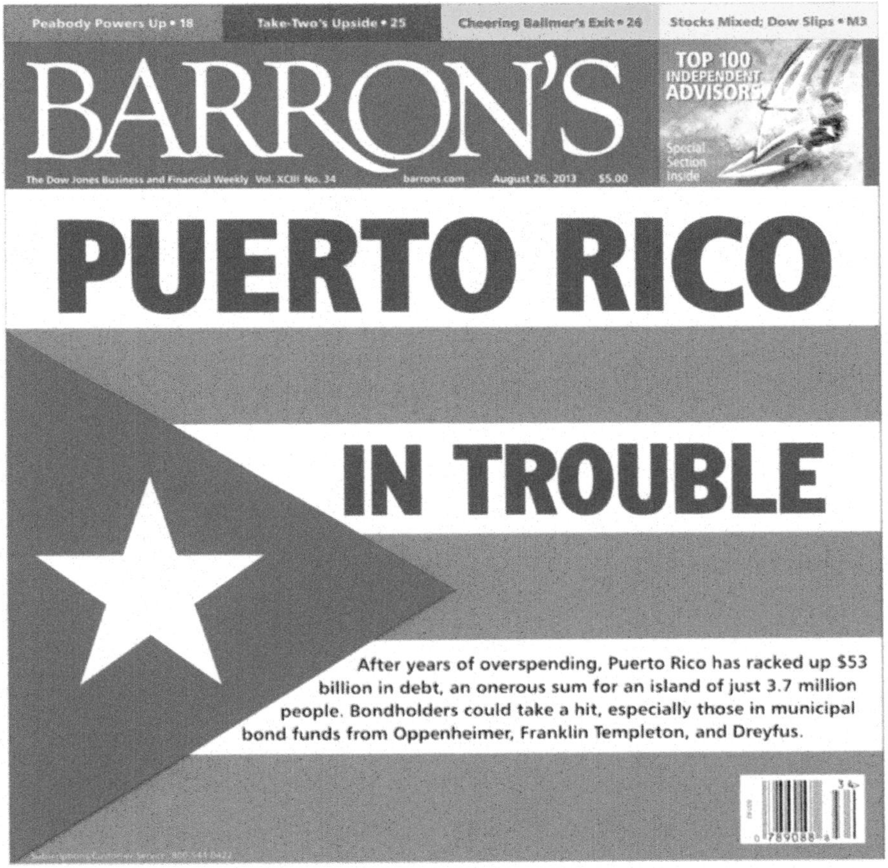
Peabody Powers Up • 18
Take-Two's Upside • 25
Cheering Ballmer's Exit • 26
Stocks Mixed; Dow Slips • M3
BARRON'S
The Dow Jones Business and Financial Weekly Vol. XCIII No. 34 barrons.com August 26, 2013 $5.00
TOP 100 INDEPENDENT ADVISORS
Special Section Inside
PUERTO RICO
IN TROUBLE
After years of overspending, Puerto Rico has racked up $53 billion in debt, an onerous sum for an island of just 3.7 million people. Bondholders could take a hit, especially those in municipal bond funds from Oppenheimer, Franklin Templeton, and Dreyfus.

This match lit the fuse that began to blow up the Puerto Rico market. Again, headlines caused liquidity issues to become much more consequential than they would have been otherwise. It was not as if Puerto Rico's financial woes were not known—they were. *Barron's*, however, fanned the flames of investors' concerns. Suddenly funds were hit with redemptions as clients took the *Barron's* article to heart and sold out for fear of a municipal market meltdown. The fund redemptions spilled over to individual managed accounts and, within weeks, the rout was on. Uninsured Puerto Rico bonds were soon trading at 9% to 10% yields, which was 300 basis points higher than before. Bonds insured by active insurers, like Assured Guaranty, were trading at 6% to 7% yields, 200 basis points higher than prior to the *Barron's* article. Figure 11.6 shows the timeline of Puerto Rico yields.

Figure 11.6

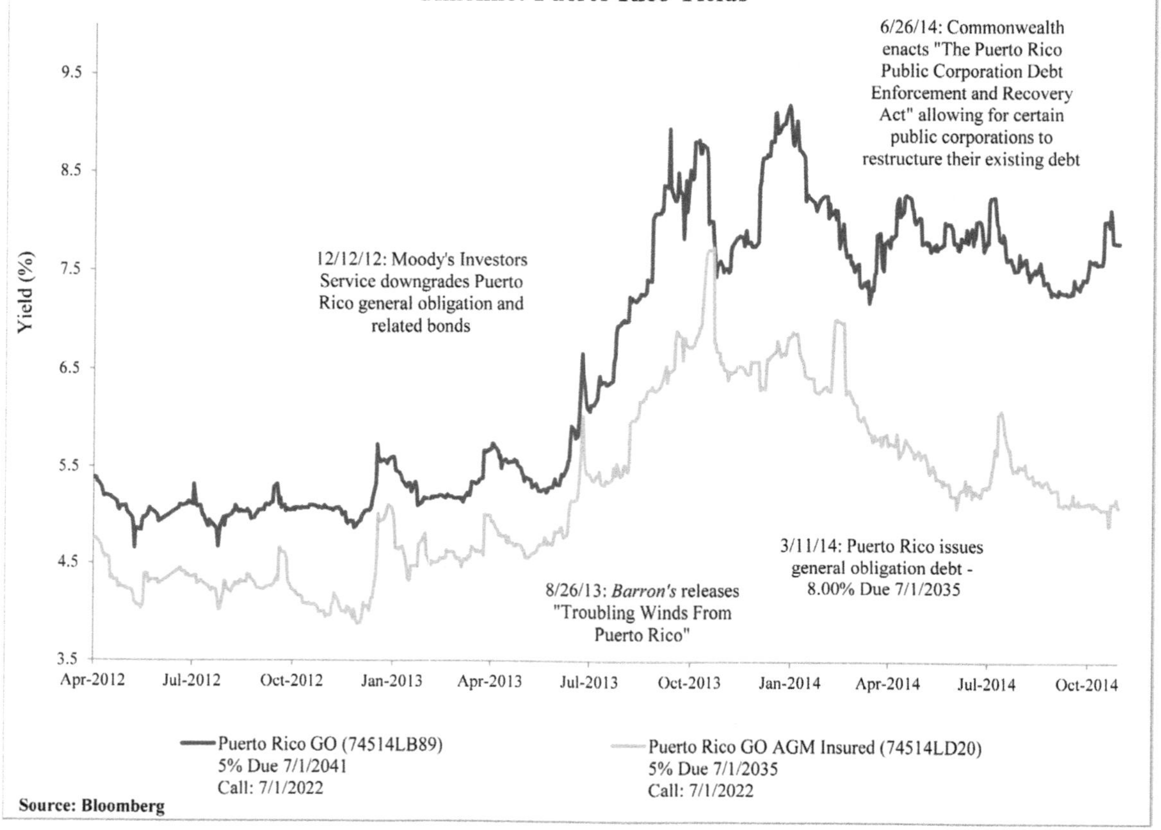

Once brokerage firms started to prevent retail clients from buying Puerto Rico paper, an important "leg" supporting the Puerto Rico municipal bond market had been kicked away. We can see the effects of headline risk, considering that bonds from insurers such as Assured Guaranty and MBIA—who still have at least AA ratings—also traded off significantly, but not nearly as badly as their uninsured brethren.

Another anomaly of headline risk is shown in Figure 11.7, which compares an insured Puerto Rico bond with an insured bond issued by Guam, another United States territory. The Guam issue has a slightly better underlying rating, but not good enough to warrant the yield gap. We can attribute this to the headline risk that is dominating the market for Puerto Rico bonds.

In the wake of the *Barron's* article and the clampdown by brokerage firms no longer allowing the purchase of Puerto Rico debt, retail investors had to abandon the market. The same can be said of the bond funds that are much more sensitive to the quantity of their Puerto Rico holdings now than they were a few years ago. Both retail investors and funds do not feel as constrained by Guam bonds. This reality shows in the yield spreads.

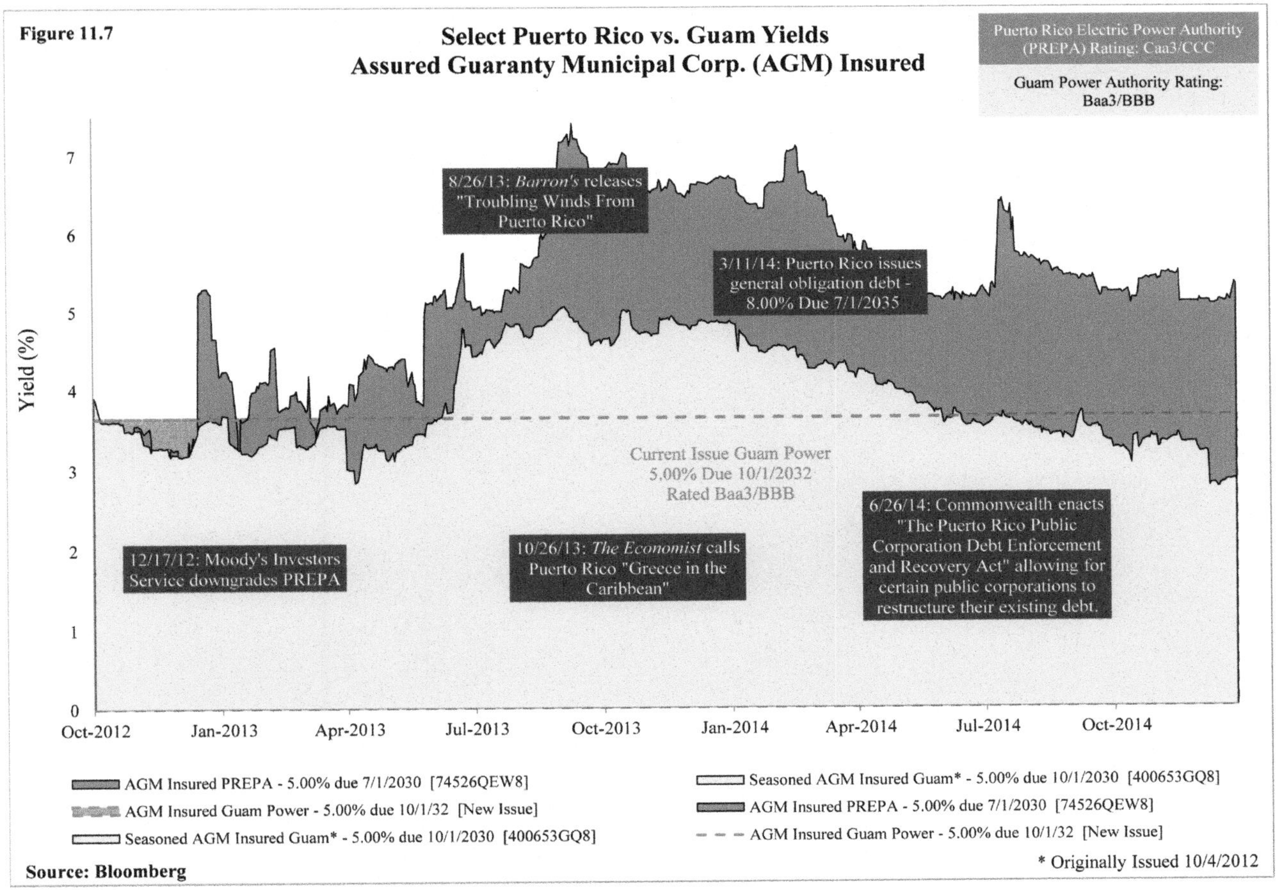

Our discussion highlights a few of the many headline risk examples that show how news can punish liquidity in the markets. In all of these cases (with Puerto Rico still a developing story as this book goes to press in July 2015), the backup in yields prompted by liquidity issues proved to be transitory. That is the nature of the municipal bond market. Most issues have a monopolistic-type claim on their service areas. It is true that outright calamitous conditions can provide a backdrop where there is interruption of debt service. With selective judgment, however, these headline risk cases have proven to be buying opportunities for investors willing to see beyond the headlines.

12

The Puerto Rico Conundrum

"Puerto Rico matters because it is large enough to be disruptive, especially to the municipal markets," Tom Tzitzouris, Director at Strategas Investment Research Partners, explained to an audience at the opening of the January 2014 Global Interdependence Center (GIC) conference on Puerto Rico. The situation looked darkest, Tzitzouris explained, in August 2013 when the "taper tantrum" was rocking the markets, Treasury yields were surging, spreads were widening, and the bankruptcy of Detroit and the Chicago downgrade were spawning front-page headlines. Had Puerto Rico's debt woes sunk the Commonwealth into the vortex of a full-blown debt crisis in those uncertain days, that crisis would have exacted what Tzitzouris characterizes as "maximum carnage" in the municipal markets and posed a significant threat to a fragile U. S. recovery. Fortunately, Puerto Rico's worst-case scenarios did not materialize during that window of maximum vulnerability. Measures that bought time for Puerto Rico also bought time for the world to buffer itself against the prospect of a Puerto Rico default.

After averting a near crisis, Puerto Rico still matters to municipal markets. For that reason, we dedicate this chapter to the Commonwealth's challenges and prospects. This section draws upon the presentations given at the January 2014 conference, co-sponsored by GIC and Strategas who have graciously permitted us to include this material in our book.[1] As became clear at the conference, over the long haul, challenges for Puerto Rico remain daunting. After a discussion of the Commonwealth's current challenges, we will provide a discussion of history leading up to this point, followed by our near-term outlook.

According to Don Rissmiller, founding partner of Strategas and GIC board member, The Commonwealth of Puerto Rico's status as a territory of the United States confers upon it a unique status in U.S. law that entails both benefits and liabilities. The island boasts an inviting climate and is advantageously situated as a trade location. Its residents enjoy the benefits of American citizenship, and the United States provides for the Commonwealth's defense. For tax purposes though, Puerto Rico is treated as a foreign country. Residents don't pay federal or state taxes. Historically, tax law has created advantages for companies that establish production in Puerto Rico, notably pharmaceutical companies. Rissmiller points out that the problem for Puerto Rico comes when decisions made in Washington, D.C. are not tailored to local challenges. Monetary policy set by the Fed can have profound effects on money flows on a small island, as can changes in tax law. In 2006, tax policy changes removed certain incentives for businesses to locate production in the Commonwealth. Assessing their options, companies began to relocate, taking jobs with them. Since 2006, Puerto Rico's labor force participation rate has declined dramatically. That decline began well before the 2008 financial crisis as production moved elsewhere and has persisted despite the ongoing recovery in the banking sector.

The employment picture in Puerto Rico is dramatically weaker than it is among the states and the continental U.S. as a whole. The participation rate in the U.S. is approximately 63%—about the same level as it was 25 years ago—compared to Puerto Rico's current 41%. The participation rate is critical to the question of whether any government can pay its debts: It tells us how many people can contribute to paying off debt by paying taxes. The higher the labor participation rate, the more tax revenues there are; conversely, the lower the participation rate, the more people are dependent on government transfer programs. Figure 12.1 shows the Puerto Rican labor force participation rate. Changes in the labor participation rate tend to be "hard to reverse quickly" through policy tools. "This is more like turning a supertanker than a speedboat," Don Rissmiller observes.[2]

Puerto Rico Labor Force Participation Rate

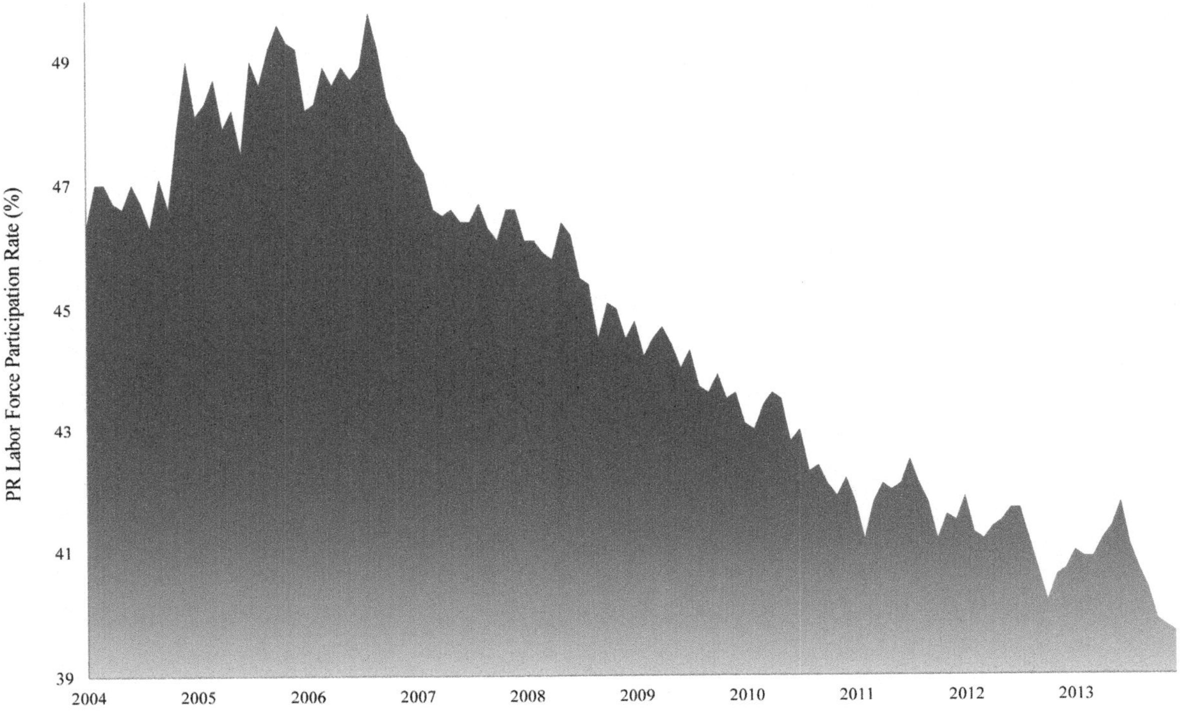

Sources: "Puerto Rico: The Island's Economics" presentation by D. Rismiller (Strategas), Puerto Rico Government Development Bank

Puerto Rico's status means that it does not have monetary policy control at the Commonwealth level, so it can't print money, or change the currency, or the terms of trade. Its central bank is the U.S. Fed. Though the Fed provided easy money in response to the financial crisis, that hasn't been enough monetary easing to turn the headlines around in Puerto Rico, and tapering is well underway.

The Commonwealth has only its fiscal policy tools to address its debt troubles. Its economic fortunes depend in part on tax policy decisions made in Washington, not at home on this island of three million people, saddled with a debt of $73 billion. As Puerto Rico, with a GDP of about $100 billion, struggles to address a problematic debt-to-GDP ratio, its shrinking population and weak labor participation remain hurdles that will be difficult to overcome, Rissmiller concludes.

A further challenge takes the form of Puerto Rico's pension system's unfunded liabilities. Wells Fargo's Natalie Cohen notes that Puerto Rico has one of the most underfunded pension systems among jurisdictional subdivisions of the U.S., with shortfalls amounting to approximately $35 billion, depending on how they are estimated.[3] That is a calculation using a conservative discounting rate, applied to the pension liabilities as they are presently known and in the law. Remaining assets represent less than 7% of the actual accrued liability.[4] Among those assets are loans to participants in various forms including home mortgages, education loans, and personal loans. In other words, the bulk of the assets that remain in Puerto Rico's pension system are booked as assets, but are actually loans to the very folks to whom the pensions are promised or provided. We have to ask how the structure of those loans should be examined under these circumstances.

In the event of a Puerto Rico debt crisis and failure to pay, what would be the plow-back provisions regarding those loans? How could anyone expect pensioners to pay back money that they borrowed against their pension benefit when the pension benefit itself is threatening to be eroded by a debt restructuring or default? Until July 28, 2014, the date on which the Puerto Rico Debt Enforcement and Recovery Act (or "Recovery Act") was signed, there was no direct legal guidance for Puerto Rico to resolve this situation and no resolution mechanism in the event that it was to occur.

This law was an attempt to create a statutory framework for the Commonwealth's public corporations to restructure their debt and contractual obligations, analogous to U.S. Chapter 9 Bankruptcy laws. It dispelled prior notions held by market participants that the Commonwealth would come to the rescue and bail out its public corporations. In years past, the demarcation points between what constituted GO vs. agency debt was blurred. With this legislation, no longer would these corporations be treated as within-arms-length conduits acting on behalf of the Commonwealth; instead, they would function as independent enterprises, with more autonomy. From the Commonwealth's perspective, this structure would allow the enterprises to restructure their debts without impacting the Commonwealth's finances. But in February 2015, this law was overturned.

As a result, the outlook for the net funded capability of Puerto Rico's post-retirement benefit package and direct pension benefit is fraught with great uncertainty. The ability to fund and further develop the pension system also faces that uncertainty. There are extraordinary circumstances surrounding the retirement systems of Puerto Rico at a time when the entire debt structure of the Commonwealth is seriously questioned.

Whether in the City of Detroit or the State of Illinois, California cities or the Commonwealth of Puerto Rico, we are discovering that unfunded pension liabilities pit pensioners against debtholders when governments' debts overwhelm their resources and beleaguered taxpayers are left to hold the bag.

And in the United States, as elsewhere, the population is aging. The ratio of active workers to retirees has declined to 1.7:1.[5] In Puerto Rico, Natalie Cohen notes, this ratio is now approaching 1:1. The result is not a very sanguine outlook for pensioners and those who depend on this system to provide benefits. Essentially, Puerto Rico has nearly exhausted all of the program's assets. Any benefit payments would have to be derived from a collective "pay-as-you-go" system that would drain the coffers of this governmental entity.

On a positive note, there have been pension reform legislation initiatives at work in Puerto Rico. Some of them have passed into law. Several of these are currently being litigated. We might expect that it will take about 20 years for this system to restore itself to some sort of balance. The outlook for the Puerto Rico pension system is highly questionable. As indicated in Figure 12.2, the Commonwealth's pension plan is only 11% funded, considerably lower than any U.S. state.[6]

Figure 12.2

Pension Funding Ratios by State

Wisconsin	99.9%	Missouri	76.9%	West Virginia	64.0%
Washington	98.1%	Utah	76.5%	Montana	63.9%
North Carolina	93.9%	California	76.0%	Pennsylvania	63.9%
South Dakota	92.6%	Minnesota	75.0%	New Mexico	63.0%
Tennessee	92.1%	Arizona	74.3%	Alaska	59.2%
New York	90.5%	Arkansas	71.4%	Colorado	59.2%
Delaware	88.3%	Nevada	71.0%	Hawaii	59.2%
Florida	86.4%	Virginia	69.5%	Indiana	58.4%
Idaho	84.4%	Vermont	68.4%	Rhode Island	58.2%
Oregon	82.0%	Massachusetts	66.4%	Mississippi	58.0%
Texas	82.0%	Michigan	66.4%	Kansas	56.4%
Georgia	81.9%	North Dakota	66.3%	New Hampshire	56.2%
Wyoming	79.6%	Alabama	66.2%	Louisiana	55.5%
Iowa	79.5%	New Jersey	65.4%	Connecticut	49.1%
Nebraska	78.5%	South Carolina	65.4%	Kentucky	46.8%
Maine	77.2%	Oklahoma	65.3%	Illinois	40.4%
Ohio	77.2%	Maryland	64.4%	**Puerto Rico**	**11.2%**

Sources: Cumberland Advisors, Morning Star

Given the structural challenges Puerto Rico faces in managing its debt troubles, it is logical to ask whether the United States is likely or able to step in to help the Commonwealth. There are two separate issues, according to Joseph Engelhard, Senior Vice President at Capital Alpha Partners: what the policy options are and what is, politically speaking, likely to happen.[7]

The second question may be the more crucial one, at least for the time being. As of the beginning of 2015, political winds in Washington currently do not seem to favor support for supplying direct help to Puerto Rico. Engelhard sums up the situation this way:

In our view, while the U.S. could, if it wants to, distinguish Puerto Rico from other municipalities both legally and politically due to its status as a commonwealth, we view the range of additional direct support the Puerto Rico government could receive as very limited, at least for the near term. And this is partly due to the lack of a sense of urgency in Washington, DC, and also partly due to the administration's public stance…that Puerto Rico is fine; they don't need a lot of assistance.

The White House has thus taken the position that Puerto Rico will pay its debt and does not need the help. Some analysts suggest that the White House is adopting that stance because it does not have any other choice: It would not be able to win congressional approval for a direct bailout of Puerto Rico.

How, after all, can the U.S. Congress vote direct aid for Puerto Rico when it does not vote aid for Detroit, Harrisburg, or Stockton? Why should a governing body that has incurred chronic deficits over a long period of years be bailed out by the federal budget?

Though direct aid looks unlikely in the near term, Washington is already helping Puerto Rico in many ways, Engelhard points out. Federal funds are transferred through various transmission mechanisms from Washington, D.C. to Puerto Rico, to the tune of 21% of the Commonwealth's $100 billion economy in 2012. There are also various payment systems for welfare, health benefits, and other benefits that go to residents of Puerto Rico via federal programs. Puerto Rico's residents are eligible for Social Security benefits, disability, Medicare and Medicaid, and more (though they are not eligible, in all instances, for the same level of benefits), and about a third of Puerto Rico's residents receive food stamps and other nutritional assistance.

Significant federal support comes in the form of tax legislation, as Engelhard details. Figure 12.3 shows the breakdown of Puerto Rico's revenues, 58% of which are derived from grants and contributions from other entities, primarily the U.S. government.

Figure 12.3

Breakdown of Puerto Rico Revenues

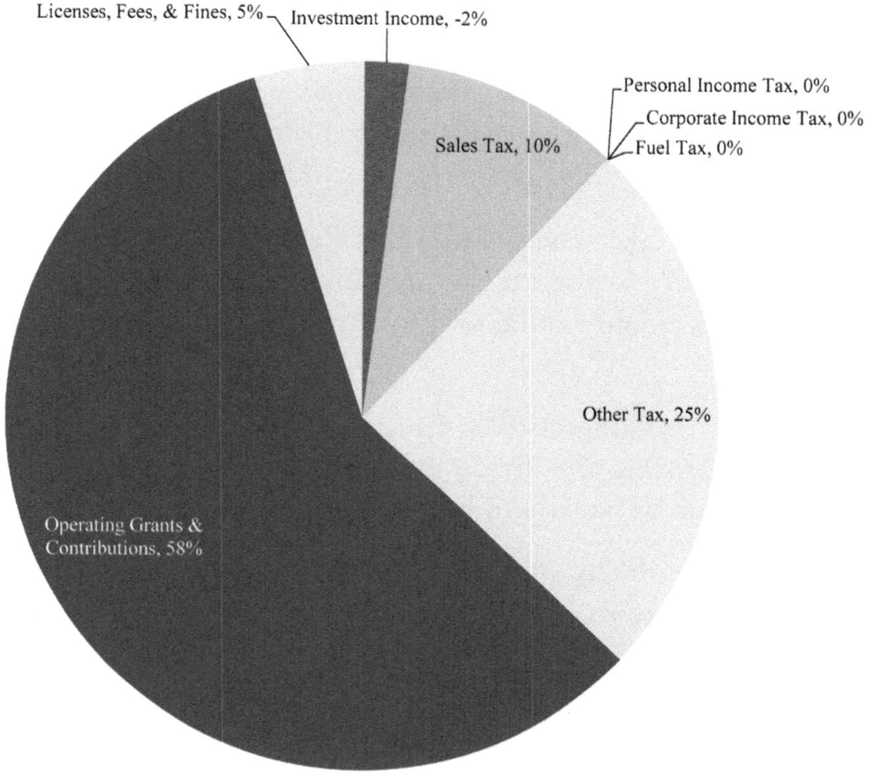

Sources: Investortools, Puerto Rico Fiscal Year 2013 Financial Statements

The U.S. rum excise tax cover-over program sends all but 25 cents of the per-gallon tariff on rum to the Puerto Rican government. Puerto Rico's excise tax for manufacturing companies, enacted in 2010, is used by companies as a U.S. tax credit, a practice the U.S. Treasury and the IRS have not challenged. Thus, tax payments that would otherwise have gone to the U.S. Treasury are paid as an excise tax to Puerto Rico in what amounts to roundabout support of the Commonwealth's economy via an interpretation of U.S. tax law.

Beyond that, a White House task force created in November 2013 is working with Puerto Rico's government to find additional ways for Puerto Rico to take advantage of existing federal programs. The United States might help most readily, Engelhard suggests, by extending a higher rum tax that has now returned to lower levels and by refraining from disallowing a U.S. tax credit for the excise taxes that companies pay to Puerto Rico. Changes in tax law affecting the Commonwealth have considerable capacity to affect the Puerto Rico economy for good or ill.

In the event that Puerto Rico fails to make payments on its debt, however, the question of assistance from Washington becomes more serious and pressing. Any direct help from Washington, D.C. is highly unlikely before a default. What might happen to the financial markets following a default is a separate question. A significant meltdown might be enough to induce both parties in Washington to change their position.

Engelhard concludes by saying,

> *Finally, the most effective help may actually come from the advice of the White House Puerto Rico Task Force, which is advising Puerto Rico on how to solidify their fiscal situation and successfully implement structural reform.*
>
> *Ultimately, it will be up to the leadership of the Puerto Rico government and their ability to pass structural reform and implement their economic growth agenda. To the extent the U.S. sees that happening, it will be easier for additional U.S. support to follow.*

Not only is Puerto Rico regularly affected by decisions made in Washington; but as John Mousseau points out, it is also vulnerable to market reactions spurred by news headlines.[8]

News reports move markets and change the pricing of securities, including tax-free municipal bonds. Events and news have historically driven bond pricing. Puerto Rico is a particularly large issuer of municipal bonds and is a prominent name in many portfolios. Therefore, news generated around Puerto Rico as its credit has deteriorated and as it was recently downgraded to "junk bond" status elevated headline risk generally and headline risk concerning Puerto Rico debt specifically, as noted in Chapter 11.[9]

Figure 12.4 shows the movements in some Puerto Rico securities from 2012 until the end of 2013 as a result of headline risk. Yields on securities increased on multiple occasions in response to headlines. When *Barron's* published its cover story titled "Puerto Rico in Trouble" on August 26, 2013, yields on subordinated Puerto Rico Sales Tax Financing Corporation (COFINA) debt increased to 9% within a few weeks after trading at less than 5% only a few months earlier.

Figure 12.4

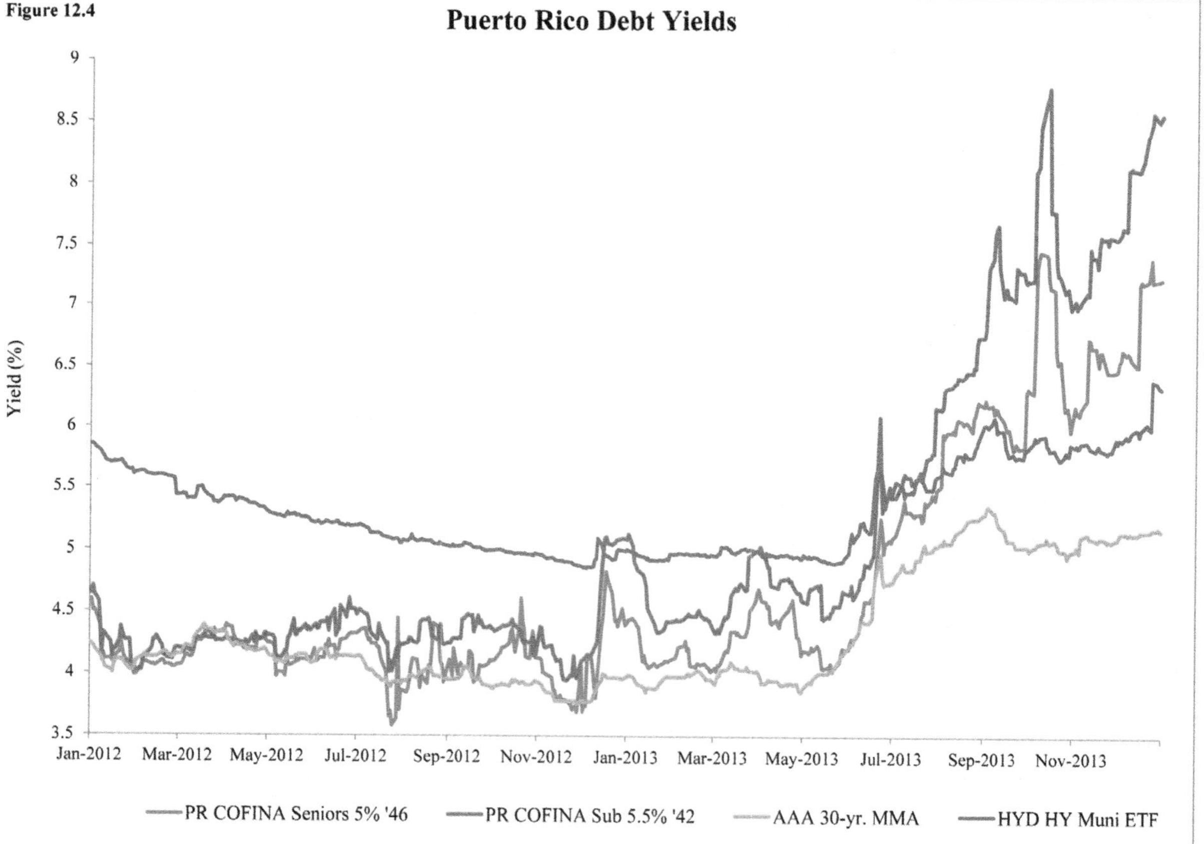

Sources: Bloomberg, Cumberland Advisors

At the time of the GIC conference in January 2014, Puerto Rico still had the lowest of investment-grade ratings. Robert Kurtter, Managing Director of U.S. State and Regional Ratings at Moody's Investment Service, and David Hitchcock, Senior Director at Standard & Poor's

Public Finance Ratings, discussed ratings agencies' views and issued warnings about negative watches for Puerto Rico debt and the possibility that downgrades could be forthcoming.[10] Since the conference, Standard & Poor's, Moody's, and Fitch have downgraded Puerto Rico to below investment-grade, otherwise known as "junk bond," status.

Ratings agencies' views are important. They determine institutional qualifications for certain holdings and impose on certain institutions rule-based decision-making that could influence whether or not those institutions buy, sell, or hold. In this particular case, Puerto Rico has been a deteriorating credit for some time. The presentations at the conference were generally not surprising to the participants, though the subsequent downgrades that took place were expected by some and not others. The views articulated on January 15, 2014, are now validated by actions that have taken place since the conference.

An issue that was alluded to at the January 2014 GIC conference, but not discussed in full, had to do with the way disputes or defaults in Puerto Rico debt might be resolved. Current law provides for disputes regarding debt issued by Puerto Rico and its various divisions to be adjudicated in Puerto Rico courts. Some market participants are no longer certain that Puerto Rico courts would hear competing claims without a bias in favor of the Commonwealth. In the conversations taking place with underwriters who might potentially help Puerto Rico access the bond market, negotiations as to jurisdiction for resolution of future disputes are underway. We note that the Commonwealth has sought to circumvent adjudication of claims for its public corporations with its passage of the Puerto Rico Public Corporation Debt Enforcement and Recovery Act in June 2014, as discussed in Chapter 11.

Some of this discussion has to do with an agreement in a bond indenture stipulating that the bond issuers would agree to adjudicate disputes in New York courts. Two theories underlie this. The first is that if agreements take place between the bond issuer and the bond purchaser at the time of a new issue, those agreements can be binding on both parties. The second is that New York is an appropriate jurisdiction if all agree to it because it is the financial center of North America, and underwriting and financial transactions would be processed or administered in New York.

The structure of debt would then be different in Puerto Rico. Earlier debt issues would operate under Puerto Rico law, but a new issue might be structured and operate under New York law. It is possible, some analysts suggest, that a GO bond issued by Puerto Rico under New York law could have a senior claim because of the structure by which disputes are adjudicated, compared to a GO pledge issued under Puerto Rico law. The Commonwealth would be making the pledge in both cases. However, the way in which a nonpayment dispute would be resolved could be different. The idea is that the New York legal system would create a super-senior GO pledge. Therefore, it would enable Puerto Rico to access debt markets by means of that structure.

On March 11, 2014, the Commonwealth of Puerto Rico did just that and successfully sold $3.5 billion in a GO bond issue brought under New York law instead of Puerto Rico law. The bond issue had been in preparation for months, as the legislature in Puerto Rico had to pass an enabling law so that the bonds could be issued in this format. This was done at the request of Puerto Rico's bond underwriters and financial advisors. The ultimate cost to the Commonwealth was nearly 9%. The ratings on the bond issue were all below investment-grade with no insurance or credit enhancement.

The official statement governing the terms of this bond issue runs approximately 250 pages. We will not incorporate it into this book, but we include the link in the endnotes to this chapter.[11] The agent that handled this bond offering for the Commonwealth of Puerto Rico is the Government Development Bank.

We do not know how litigation would proceed in the event of a default. In the disclosure made in order to complete the bond issue, the Commonwealth of Puerto Rico offered the following explanation and description of the litigation risk:[12]

> *In accordance with the Act, the Secretary of the Treasury has provided in the Bond Resolution, and the Secretary of Justice has approved, that the laws of the State of New York shall apply to any action or proceeding arising out of the Bonds or the Bond Resolution. The Commonwealth has not previously issued general obligation bonds that are governed by the laws of any jurisdiction other than the Commonwealth. Accordingly, there can be no assurance given as to how a court would apply New York law to a claim brought for the enforcement of the Commonwealth's obligations under the Bonds.*
>
> *Even if the bondholders were to obtain a judgment from a New York court or U.S. federal court located in New York, there is no assurance that the issuing court will have the power to enforce the terms of the judgment against the Commonwealth.*

For example, if a judgment is issued by a New York court against the Secretary of the Treasury directing the Secretary to apply available Commonwealth revenues, as described above under "Bondholders may face delays enforcing their remedies under the Bonds, and the availability of some remedies is not certain," and the Secretary of the Treasury does not honor the judgment within any time limits set by the issuing court, the bondholders will likely be required to bring a subsequent lawsuit in Puerto Rico seeking to have the Puerto Rico court to order the Secretary of the Treasury to comply with the terms of the other court's judgment.

Although a judgment from a New York court should be given effect in Puerto Rico pursuant to the full faith and credit clause of the U.S. Constitution, such a judgment must meet certain minimum requirements before a Puerto Rico court will give it effect. There can be no assurance that any judgment from a New York court will satisfy the requirements for a Puerto Rico court to give effect to such judgment.

On the basis of the foregoing and in light of the fact that there is no precedent for the inclusion in general obligation bonds of the submission by the Commonwealth to both the governing law of the State of New York and the jurisdiction of its courts sitting in Manhattan (or the federal courts sitting in Manhattan) in connection with such bonds, as well as the fact that a court has considerable discretion in the exercise of its powers, there is no assurance that the inclusion of the choice of law and jurisdiction provisions contained in the Bond Resolution and in the Bonds will provide any benefit to, or alternatively, will not work to the detriment of, the holders of the Bonds.

There is an evolution underway in Puerto Rico: A new, unique financing of a GO bond. There is no precedent to indicate probable outcomes in case we have adjudication of disputes. Only time will tell whether Puerto Rico defaults on this bond or other bonds and whether any claims will be asserted in the courts of New York.

A timeline of events starting in 2010 has called into question the Commonwealth's ability to service its debts and those of its closely held public companies, which rely heavily on the Commonwealth for operating grants and subsidies. We view Puerto Rico as an economy stuck at an unhappy crossroads: Both as a sovereign government resembling a Caribbean or Central American economy and an entity resembling a U.S. state.[13] It is difficult to superimpose American laws, policy, and culture on what is fundamentally a Latin American country.[14] This is a major reason for the Commonwealth's awkward status as a territory acting under somewhat false pretenses as a U.S. state.[15]

Puerto Rico's distressed finances are the manifestation of an economy that has been on the decline for almost two decades.[16] Puerto Rico is financially insolvent. Our conversations with experts and market practitioners have cited multiple symptoms: Escalating pension costs, a declining population, the expiration of tax incentives for U.S. companies, and low tax collections, to name a few. The main driver for this insolvency has been the Commonwealth's structurally imbalanced economy that is over-reliant on capital-intensive manufacturing instead of technologically sophisticated, knowledge-based industries.[17]

In countries with low labor costs, such as China or the nations of Central America, this imbalance would ordinarily not be a problem; however, Puerto Rico's high labor costs (and high costs of doing business) make it fundamentally uncompetitive.[18] Over the last 80 years, these high costs have largely been negated by subsidies from the U.S. federal government, primarily through tax incentives for U.S. corporations to relocate to Puerto Rico.[19] When these incentives were phased out and the Commonwealth was taken off of life support in 2006, the Puerto Rican economy plunged into recession.[20]

American companies being heavily incentivized to establish offshore production in Puerto Rico was a major boon to the economy.[21] American companies benefited from Puerto Rico's low labor costs compared with those in the U.S. mainland, while Puerto Rico was able to develop from a small exporter of sugar cane to a large industrial producer of petrochemicals and textiles.[22] This arrangement was almost a case of "too much of a good thing." Over time, Puerto Rico became complacent: It was not forced to continually reinvent itself under the capitalist forces of creative destruction as had other advanced economies.[23] Instead, it was staying the course as an industrial producer similar to the United States during the 1950s and '60s.[24]

Since 1921, American companies have received some sort of incentive from the U.S. federal government to relocate subsidiary operations to the Commonwealth.[25] Under the Revenue Act of 1921, U.S. companies were given tax credits on income derived from subsidiary operations.[26] Passage of Internal Revenue Code Section 936 under FDR continued this tax credit, equal to 100% of income generated from subsidiaries operating in Puerto Rico. Puerto Rico's access to American markets as a U.S. dollar-based exporter and as a source of cheap labor gave it huge cost advantages over other countries, both in North America and abroad, incentivizing American manufacturers to relocate there.[27]

The benefits of the tax incentives had their greatest impact during the 1950s.

Under a series of laws known as "Operation Bootstrap," passed in 1948 by both the U.S. federal government and the Commonwealth, tax incentives were broadened substantially.[28] Puerto Rican exporters were given preferential access to U.S. markets; and American companies were given up to 90% deductibility on Puerto Rican source income against their Puerto Rican tax liabilities, reducing their effective tax rates to 4.5% from 35%. The economic impacts of these incentives were extraordinary.[29] From 1950 to 1970, real GNP growth averaged 6% annually versus 3.7% for the mainland; the agricultural sector shrank while manufacturing employment roughly tripled.[30] An industrial renaissance occurred, transforming Puerto Rico from an agrarian-based exporter of sugar cane to a large manufacturer of petrochemicals and textiles.[31]

The intended industrialization of the Commonwealth declined by the 1980s as the pace of economic growth subsided.[32] Despite the creation of manufacturing jobs from what were formerly agrarian jobs, employment growth slowed to a standstill. Many companies, instead of reinvesting profits back into the Commonwealth to build new plants and factories, repatriated their money back to the United States for better growth opportunities.[33] Demand for labor remained stagnant as those companies with operations in Puerto Rico kept their more labor-intensive operations in the United States while expanding capital-intensive operations in Puerto Rico. By the end of the 1980s, it was clear that the costs of Section 936 tax incentives to the U.S. government were increasingly unjustified when measured in terms of the economic benefits to both the Commonwealth and the United States, making the incentives a prime target for deficit reduction under Bill Clinton's balanced-budget proposals.[34] From fiscal years 1996 through 2006, Section 936 was gradually phased out and the ability of Puerto Rico to attract new business development was handicapped substantially.[35]

Further dampening Puerto Rico's edge over other competitors was the emergence of lower-cost exporters as trade partners of the United States, namely Mexico, under the North American Free Trade Agreement (NAFTA); Latin American economies; and China, upon its entry into the World Trade Organization (WTO) in 2000.[36] Puerto Rican companies were no longer competitive in industries where labor costs made up the majority of expenses; wages were low relative to the United States, but high relative to other countries.[37] Whereas Puerto Rican companies were forced to pay factory employees roughly $6 per hour versus $11 on the U.S. mainland, Chinese companies could pay workers $1 per hour. Puerto Rico's lack of technological and knowledge-based industries also hampered its ability to attract rapidly growing software and other tech companies.[38]

At present, Puerto Rico's economy is overly concentrated in the manufacturing sector, where it is uncompetitive due to its cost disadvantages, namely, the high cost of labor and electricity. Figure 12.5 breaks down Puerto Rico GDP by industry as of the end of 2011. The chart shows that manufacturing makes up a disproportionate share of output, close to 50%.[39]

Figure 12.5

Puerto Rico GDP by Industry

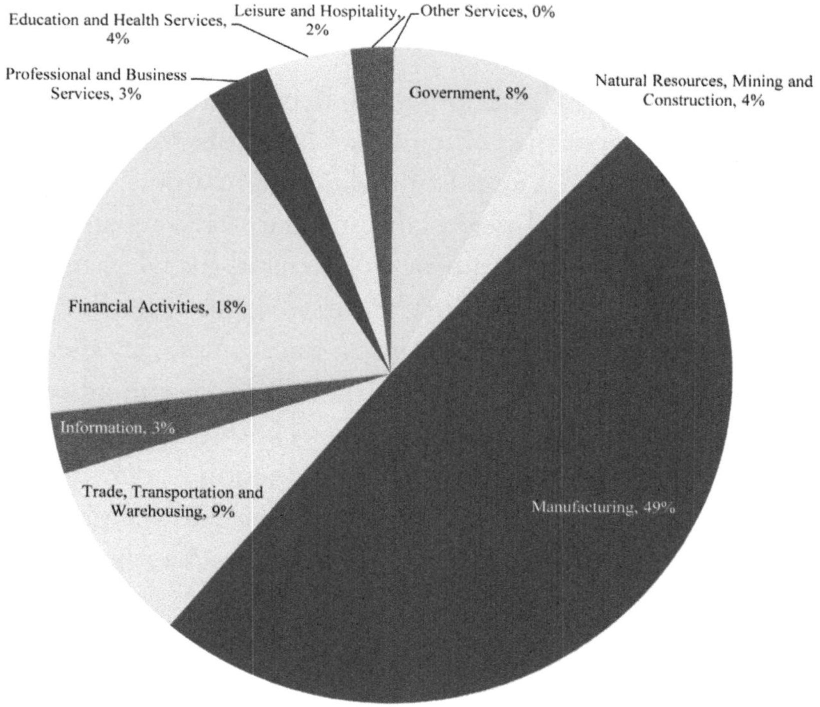

Sources: Puerto Rico Planning Board, U.S. Department of Labor, Wells Fargo Securities

While the long-term effects of NAFTA and China's entrance into the WTO have been especially damaging as the playing field has leveled, energy costs on the island are more than double what they are on the U.S. mainland; and labor costs are high because of high taxes and welfare costs. A typical country with its own free-floating currency would be able to devalue its way out of recession by stimulating exports and lowering the cost of its goods in terms of its trading partners' currencies, thereby creating jobs.[40] That Puerto Rico cannot do this creates another hurdle for ending its economic stagnation and chronically high structural unemployment.

The only two fiscal means by which the Commonwealth could grow its manufacturing sector would be through the reinstitution of tax incentives or the devaluation of its currency.[41] Because these options are not on the table, it must instead reorient itself to higher-growth industries such as biotech or software development to stimulate employment and increase real incomes. The current administration is more or less attempting to do this by offering tax incentives and institutional reforms that reduce administrative red tape. However, there are no short-term fixes.[42] Structurally transforming an entire economy requires time and the educating of an entire workforce, which would likely need to occur over the course of an entire generation.[43]

The Commonwealth's attempts to solve its structural problems through Keynesian public sector involvement have had minimal positive effects.[44] The Puerto Rican government's share of the economy is substantial, which is partially the reason for its insolvency. The economy is reliant on government subsidies and ownership of public utilities and corporations to extend those subsidies.[45] Unfortunately, the government runs these enterprises to fulfill its political objectives instead of treating them as business enterprises.[46] As a result, the Commonwealth's energy costs are extremely high, contributing to its lack of competitiveness.

Since 2000, Puerto Rico has relied on deficit financing to plug its budgetary holes.[47] Figure 12.6 shows that the Commonwealth's change in net assets, a measurement similar to net income for corporations, has been negative for 11 out of the last 12 years. It appears as though the recession exacerbated the downward trajectory, as change in net assets declined from positive $620 million in 2008 to negative $5.3 billion in 2013.[48]

Figure 12.6

Puerto Rico: Negative Operating Results

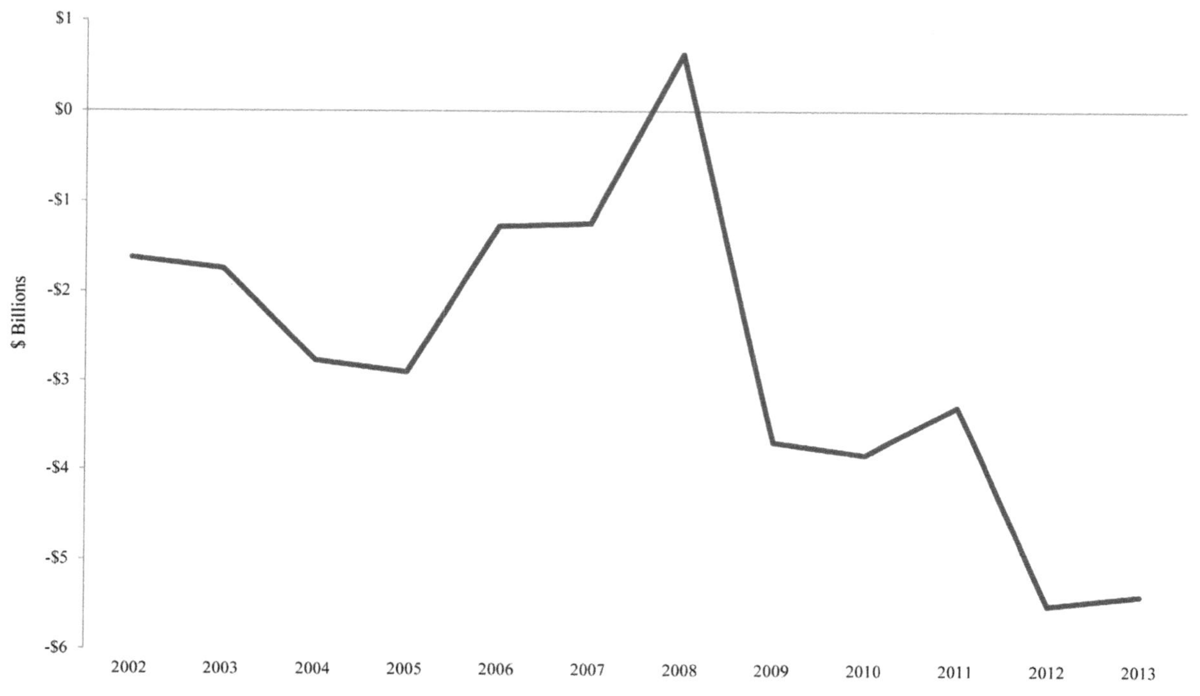

Sources: Investortools, Puerto Rico Fiscal Year 2013 Financial Statements

The Commonwealth is at a point where it is utilizing debt issuance to pay interest on existing indebtedness. This is a major problem. That the economy has contracted every year since 2006 (nine years prior to this writing) indicates the seriousness of its problems and what will likely be a continued struggle to grow its tax base organically. As the economy contracts, its debt burden continues to increase. With an ever-higher portion of the economy dedicated to servicing existing indebtedness instead of new investment, the economy will likely continue to struggle. Failure of the Commonwealth to service its existing debts would create shock waves through the municipal market that would impact all issuers of municipal debt.

Structural problems that have been fomenting over the course of an entire century must now be addressed. Whether the path forward will entail continued involvement with the United States, or whether Puerto Rico should wend instead toward economic and currency independence, will be a crucial question for the Commonwealth to answer in establishing its identity. Regardless of the outcome, which will be determined in part by both politics and circumstances, the Commonwealth must make important changes if it is to thrive and grow in the 21st century.

13

Pension Problems and the Land of Lincoln

In the years after the financial crisis, financial troubles catapulted the State of Illinois to the forefront of the financial market discussion regarding management of public finances. Illinois has become the poster child for state budget problems and a classic example of the role politics can play in clouding rational budgetary decision-making. Though the state's troubles were two decades in the making, it was the 2008 financial crisis that shoved Illinois over the edge: Tax revenues declined by 20% over the next two years, and demand increased for social welfare programs as a result of higher unemployment and lower incomes, squeezing the state's budget.[1] In "Report of the State Budget Crisis Task Force: Illinois Report," Richard Ravitch and Paul Volcker summarize the state's problems. They show that prior to 2008, Governor Rod Blagojevich expanded eligibility for social welfare programs even as he pledged not to raise taxes to pay for them.[2] This fiscally irresponsible course crippled the state's ability to weather even the slightest of revenue declines. The recession tipped revenues and expenses further out of balance and drained the state's reserves.

Many states solved such cyclical problems by using various stopgap measures such as long-term debt, inter-fund borrowing, and payment deferrals of current expenses. The long-term secular growth of the state's unfunded pension liability meant that Illinois used these tactics on a much larger scale. Stock market performance during the 1990s had reduced the need for large general fund contributions to the state's pension funds because of the increasing asset funding levels. In the wake of the 2008 crisis, though, the sharp decline in asset prices and ensuing low-interest-rate policy worsened the plight of an already underfunded system: They not only reduced the state's funds with which to make pension contributions, but also the value of the plan's assets while increasing its liabilities.

The state's pension funding practices have been a continuous drain on its finances since the early 1990s. The state's pension system refers to five plans collectively, which have $66 billion in assets and $165 billion in liabilities as of mid-2013.[3] Figure 13.1 shows the funded status of each of the five plans.[4] Collectively, the Illinois state pension systems are 40% funded; however, the funding levels range from 16% for the General Assembly Retirement System to 42.5% for the Teachers' Retirement System.[5]

Figure 13.1

	Market Value of Assets	Pension Benefit Obligation	Funded Ratio
Teachers' Retirement System	$ 39,858,768,000	$ 93,886,988,000	0.42
State Employees Retirement System	$ 11,877,428,896	$ 34,720,764,557	0.34
Judges Retirement System	$ 610,195,584	$ 2,156,804,991	0.28
General Assembly Retirement System	$ 51,849,558	$ 320,461,498	0.16
State Universities' Retirement System	$ 14,262,621,179	$ 34,373,104,000	0.41

Source: State of Illinois Comprehensive Annual Financial Report Fiscal 2013

To understand Illinois' path to its current state of fiscal problems, we start with the Pension Funding Act of 1994. We paraphrase from disclosures the state made for a $3.7 billion bond issue in November 2011.[6] The Pension Funding Act of 1994 was a flawed piece of legislation that would govern the state's approach to addressing—inadequately even then—its pension funding shortfalls.[7] From that period forward, budgetary mismanagement would compound fiscal problems over more than two decades. The state, unwilling to effectively address problems when they first presented themselves, saw its liabilities escalate over 20 years until present day. When the Illinois General Assembly passed the Pension Funding Act in 1994, the legislation specified the annual payment schedule required over the span of 50 years for the state to achieve 90% funding by the end of fiscal year 2045 for its five state-sponsored retirement systems.[8] In each fiscal year beyond 2045, the Pension Funding Act required annual contributions necessary to maintain the 90%-funded ratio for each system.[9] The offering document states "the funding plan consisted of two parts, a ramp-up period of increasing state contributions" from 1996 to 2010 and then payments necessary to bring funding to 90%.[10]

The law sounded viable, but the devil lurked in the details. An actuarially determined funding schedule that adheres to government accounting standards would have required contributions adequate to fully fund the program in 30 years, but the legislation instead stipulated a 50-year funding schedule.[11] Consequently, the state's annual payments fell short of the annual amounts needed to achieve full funding, ranging from 30% to 50% of required levels.[12]

Figure 13.2 shows the state's annual funding history of its pension plans starting in 2003. With the exception of 2004 (when the state issued $10 billion in bonds to make a one-time contribution), the state never paid the full amounts needed to fund the plans.[13] Insufficient contributions resulted in chronic underfunding from 1996 to 2002, and the plan's unfunded liability continued to grow.[14] Yes, the state acted in compliance with its own law and was able to balance its budget by making these artificially low payments, but legislators ignored the growth in the unfunded liability, lulled into complacency by strong stock market performance at the time and a political unwillingness to knuckle down and address the problem.

Figure 13.2

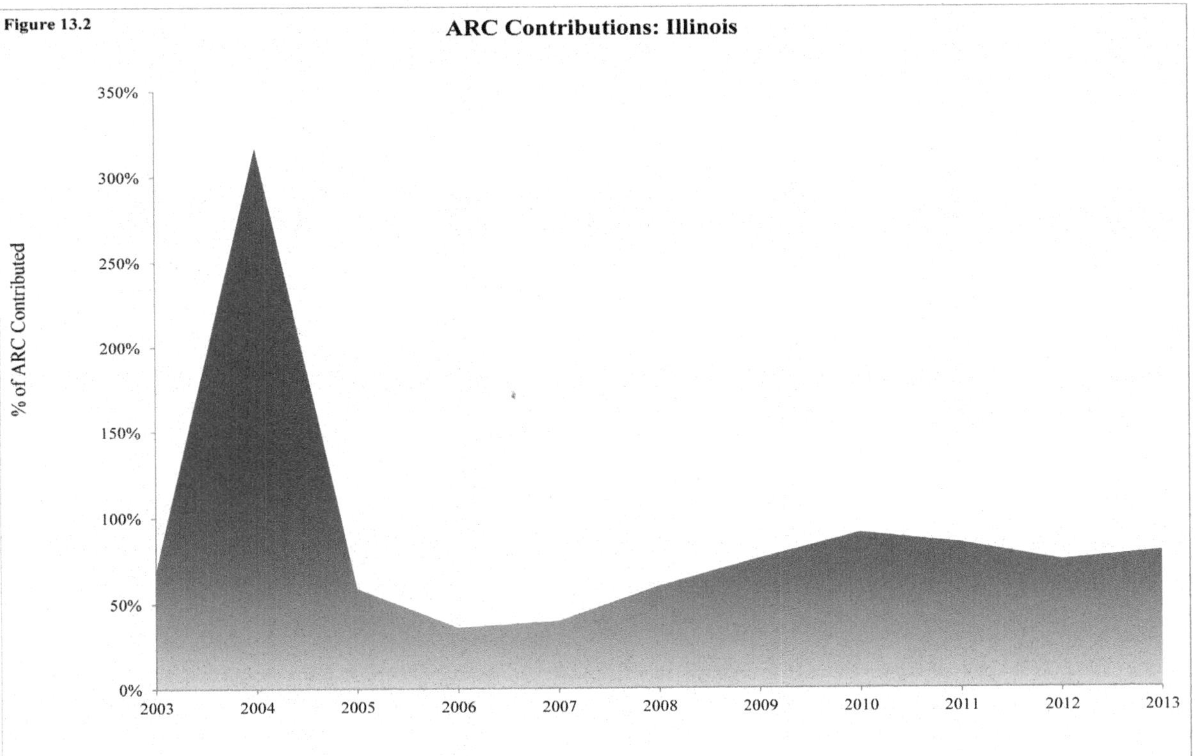

Sources: Investortools, State of Illinois Comprehensive Annual Financial Report Fiscal Year 2013

By underfunding the plan prior to 2010 (thereby increasing its unfunded liability) and specifying that payments starting in 2010 should then be sufficient to bring plan assets to 90% funding by 2045, the state set itself up for balloon payments beginning in 2010.[15] Payments were back-end loaded, not because doing so made any sort of fiscal sense, but for the sake of political expediency.[16]

Separately from its pension troubles from 2002 to 2013, the state and its component units have run annual operating deficits.[17] This practice was acceptable in the early 2000s because the state's debt burden was still moderate at the time. In 2002, the state's total outstanding long-term debt was $29.1 billion, a far cry from today's $73 billion (60% of which has been used to make contributions to the pension system).[18] At the time, the pension system's 75% funding ratio and recent strong stock market performance during the tech boom led many to believe that the state's pension problems would solve themselves. When the state's funding ratio declined rapidly from 75% to 63% in 2003, it was clear that the pension system's underfunding was indeed serious and needed to be addressed.[19] How it would be addressed, whether through one-time fixes or long-term, sustainable reforms, was an important question.

The state's initial solution was debt financing out of its general fund to increase plan assets. This didn't work or address the underlying problem of cost growth. It wasn't until 2011 that the state enacted benefit reductions to reduce the pension liability.[20]

In 2003, under the Pension Bond Act, the state issued $10 billion in pension obligation bonds, the largest-ever municipal bond deal.[21] The state's bond offering documents state that of the $10 billion, $7.3 billion was used to fund a portion of the state's unfunded pension liability; $300 million was used to "reimburse" the general fund for 25% of its 2003 annual contribution; and $1.86 billion was used to reimburse the state for its 2004 contribution.[22] This was done as an alternative to raising taxes, which Blagojevich had promised not to do in his election campaign.[23] The $7.3 billion contribution under the Pension Bond Act reduced both the state's unfunded liability in the short-term and the "future required statutory contributions" by the annual amount of "debt service paid on the 2003 bonds."[24] Nonetheless, the bond issue was still a short-term palliative that did not address the underlying problems.

Ravitch and Volcker state that, "At the time of the financing, it was assumed that the investment returns on assets from bond proceeds would be greater than debt service on the 2003 bonds," decreasing its unfunded liability.[25] History (e.g., Orange County, California, and the State of New Jersey) shows that these inherently speculative, leveraged transactions fail. Ravitch and Volcker go on to show that, "In actuality, the significant investment losses experienced by retirement systems in 2008 and 2009, combined with the reductions in the required annual contributions from debt service payments on the bonds, created an even greater increase in the pension system's unfunded liability."[26] For example, in 2005, the state made the required annual payment, reduced by an amount equal to debt service on the 2003 bonds, yet the liability continued to increase.[27] In 2006 and 2007, under statutory pension holidays, the state contributed 44% and 55% of the statutory amounts, respectively.[28] The state made the full contributions in 2008 and 2009, less the amount paid in debt service on the bonds.

By 2010, the actuarially required contribution amount increased by 50% from 2005. Given the severity of the national downturn and a drastic decline in sales and income-tax revenues, the state again relied on long-term debt to fund its pension system, this time issuing $3.5 billion in general obligation pension bonds to fund part of the state's $3.6 billion contribution.[29] The remainder of the payment came from the state's general fund, a substantial amount, but still not 100% of its required annual contribution. The pension payment in 2010 was approximately equal to the state's net deficit that year and more than the state spent on public safety.[30]

Issuing debt to fund contributions to the state's pension system was nothing more than a short-term fix. The legislature never addressed the structural problems burdening the pension system, namely, the generous salary increases and benefits.[31] By investing the entire principal amount of the issuance into the assets of the system instead of putting it into productive use, the state increased the hurdle rate it needed to surpass in order to remain solvent. Investments in income-bearing assets such as infrastructure or mass transit would have offset some of the interest burden with a revenue stream. In this case, the debt only increased the state's future interest costs by between $100 to $150 million and turned a contractual obligation that could have been restructured via legislation into an indebtedness that could not.[31] This continues to be the major pitfall of debt-financed pension fund contributions.

After much hand-wringing during a time of political paralysis, the state legislature and governor both agreed to modest pension reforms in 2011; this was, of course, after issuing an additional

$4.1 billion of general obligation bonds to make the 2011 annual pension contribution.[33] The pension reform legislation passed in 2011 created a two-tier pension system, one for employees hired after 2011 and one for those hired before that time, leaving the benefits of pre-2011 employees intact while reducing benefit payments and growth in those benefits for those hired after 2011. The reform achieved these reductions by increasing the minimum age at which employees could begin receiving benefits; by lowering cost-of-living-adjustments, or COLAs, as they are known; by creating salary caps on payments; and by modifying the salary formula from which benefits are calculated.[34] These reforms were intended to increase the five retirement systems' funding levels to 90% by 2045.[35] Two years into the reforms, as a result of low interest rates and a large number of retirees, the unfunded ratio decreased from 43% to 40%.[36] It was clear at this point that more needed to be done. After more paralysis, more significant reforms were passed by the legislature in December 2013, this time with reforms applying to all employees.

Under the new reforms, which are currently under review by the state's supreme court, more cost adjustments will be made to benefit payments, and the contribution schedule will bring the funding ratio to 100% by 2039, or 25 years from the enactment of the reforms. Whether or not these reforms will withstand litigation remains to be seen, as the rights of pension beneficiaries are protected in the state constitution.[37] Implementation of the reforms may be delayed during litigation. Until reforms are implemented, unsustainable benefits will continue to accrue to beneficiaries.

The following is an excerpt from a Moody's ratings report on Illinois, noting concerns:

> *Factors contributing to the rating change included the substantial deficit accumulated in the last two fiscal years, expected to take several years to reverse, and the state's enlarged debt commitments of recent years. Finances remain vulnerable, as is evident in revenue short falls and increased social service spending needs which prompted the passage in January of the emergency budget act which authorized $500 million cash flow borrowing in February. A key factor in maintaining credit quality will be the scope of efforts to reduce the accumulated deficit and restore balanced financial operations, as embodied in the coming year's budget.*[38]

It may shock readers to learn that this ratings report was authored in September 1991. Even in the early '90s, Illinois' finances were tenuous. However, the state's low tax rates and debt burden gave it maneuvering room to increase cash flows in emergency situations, options that are currently not on the table.[39] The 1991 excerpt reads much like recently published research detailing the state's problems. That Illinois' credit rating was still Aaa in 1991 is a testament to its ability to shore up its finances with these short-term fixes—at least for a while.

The state muddled along this path, avoiding a real financial reckoning during the following two decades, until it was fiscally overwhelmed. Looking at change in net assets for the State of Illinois since 2002, revenues consistently fell short of expenditures.[40] The worst fiscal year for Illinois during that time period was 2010, which saw revenues fall short of expenditures by $8.4 billion, more than double the loss from two years prior.[41]

Figure 13.3

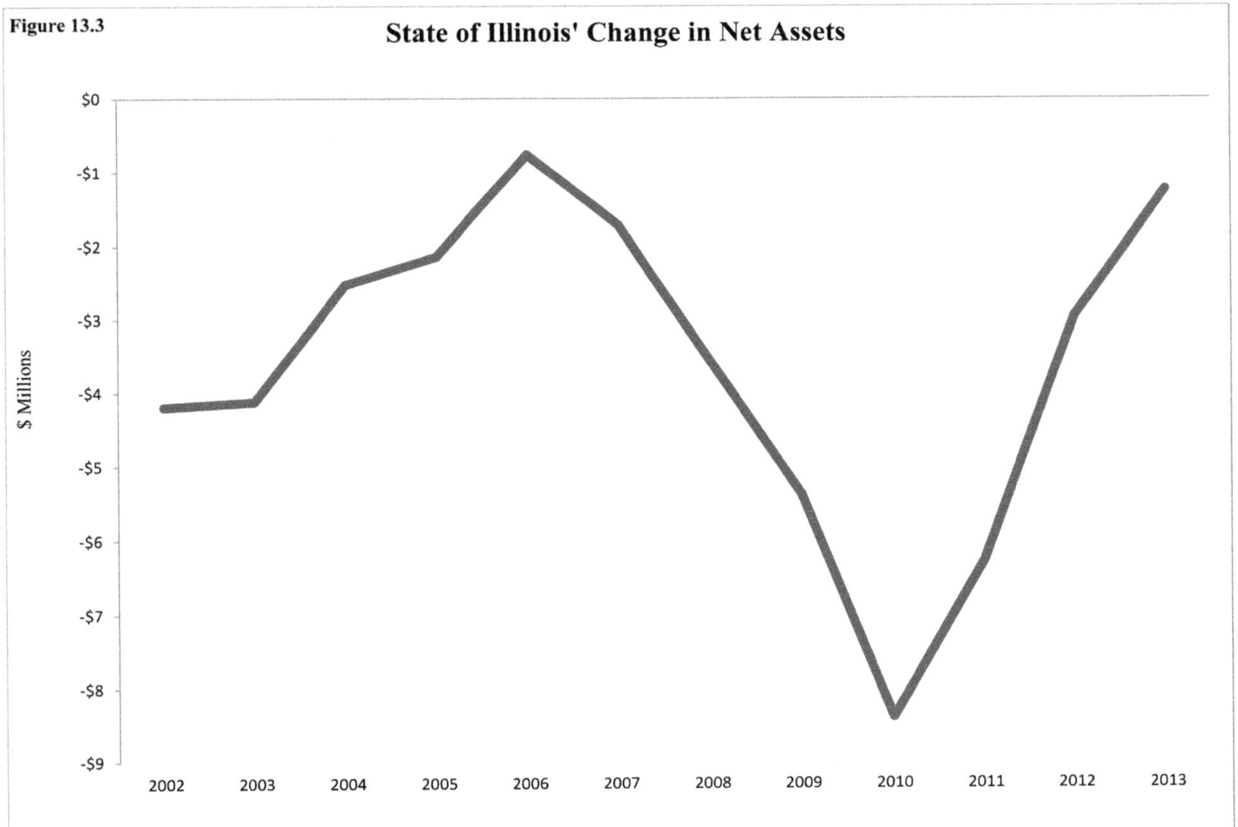

Sources: Investortools, State of Illinois Comprehensive Annual Financial Report Fiscal Year 2013

Ravitch and Volcker explain that the election of Rod Blagojevich in 2002 later proved to be a tipping point. Blagojevich ran on a platform advocating for the creation and expansion of social welfare programs for children, seniors, and the poor—without raising taxes.[42] They state that "during his two terms as governor, new programs were created and expanded, such as free health insurance for children, preschool, free public transportation, and prescription drugs for Illinois seniors," without new revenues to pay for them.[43] Ravitch and Volcker go on to point out that with the expansion of these programs and the budgetary strains that went with them, "Illinois' fiscal condition was poor going into the recession."[44] The recession-induced 20% decline in tax revenues coupled with greater demand for services made the situation much worse, swelling the state's backlog of unpaid bills to $10 billion and its net deficit (all funds on accrual basis) from $3.6 billion to $10 billion.[45] Rod Blagojevich's investigation and impeachment created an atmosphere of paralysis and dysfunction that would plague the Land of Lincoln for years to come.[46]

Governor Pat Quinn's assumption of office in 2009 and subsequent election in 2010 brought a much-needed change in leadership to fix Illinois' insolvent budget. To deal with the state's $8 billion backlog of bills, the legislature temporarily increased the state's individual income tax rate from 3% to 5% and its corporate income tax rate from 4.8% to 7%, with both rates set to decrease gradually starting in 2015.[47] These measures greatly improved the state's revenue situation: Income tax revenues jumped by 40% from fiscal years 2011 to 2012, reducing Illinois' reliance on payment deferrals and interfund transfers.[48]

As Ravitch and Volcker also point out, a focus on Illinois' general fund by itself is somewhat misplaced. Illinois utilizes over 600 special funds apart from the general fund (such as special state funds, federal trust funds, and grant funds) to account for flows of incoming resources and outgoing expenditures.[49] The general fund accounts for less than half of all spending.[50] Whereas assessing the financial health of other states with more transparent accounting practices is somewhat more straightforward, saying that Illinois' general fund is "balanced" ignores most of the state's revenues and expenditures. The state's practice of moving expenses and revenues between funds also serves to obfuscate its true financial picture, making its finances difficult to understand.

During the 2013 and 2014 fiscal years (from July 2012 to the end of June 2014), the state took major strides in addressing its fiscal imbalances by making difficult cuts to education, Medicaid, and other welfare programs. In 2013, for the first time, the state addressed its backlog of unpaid bills, paying roughly $2.5 billion out of the $8 billion due.[52] The governor also signed into law significant pension reforms that significantly reduced the pension system's unfunded liability.

Enactment of these reforms will be an important part of a comprehensive solution that fixes the state's finances. Governor Quinn's proposed 2015 budget is a step in the right direction as well, permanently extending the corporate and individual income tax rates established in 2011, while enacting targeted cuts to pensions. Whereas prior to 2013, it was difficult to get some members of the Illinois General Assembly to even acknowledge the problems, now the state is able to work toward long-term budgetary sustainability. Illinois' financial problems were compounded over the course of decades. The solutions to these problems will need to be implemented over the course of decades.

14

The State of State Infrastructure Spending

We have discussed the role of state and local governments in funding infrastructure in Chapter 4, discussing revenue bonds. In the years immediately following the recession, headlines regarding funding for the Highway Trust Fund and an ongoing debate over what to do about America's "crumbling" bridges, streets, and airports brought the issue of America's aging infrastructure to the forefront. The secular decline in motor vehicle fuel taxes and lower vehicle miles traveled created a "funding gap" for the construction, renovation, and rehabilitation of highways, airports, and mass transit systems, raising policy questions about the role of government and its ongoing commitment to infrastructure investment.[1]

These issues have been addressed by pundits from both sides of the aisle. Democrats and Republicans have argued from the vantage point of "Keynesian multiplier effects," i.e., a dollar invested in public infrastructure will increase output by more than one dollar because of economy-wide productivity gains.[2] This chapter will discuss the current state of public infrastructure in the U.S. while dispelling some common myths about the often discussed "infrastructure gap" and the Highway Trust Fund. The case can be made that, on a cyclical basis, American investment in highways, streets, and surface and air transportation is the highest it has ever been and has remained a stable component of GDP since the 1980s. In real terms, however, infrastructure spending is down.

To be sure, public infrastructure investment is paid for primarily by state and local governments. Spending amounts to roughly $260 billion annually, a small amount compared to the roughly $700 billion or so spent annually by private sector entities on construction (mostly on housing).[3]

The federal government contributes only 15% of these costs.[4] Figure 14.1 shows the breakdown in U.S. public infrastructure spending type. About 60% of public infrastructure spending in a given year is used for three primary purposes: highways and streets, transportation (mass transit and airports), and schools (both K-12 and postsecondary). The balance is spent on things like sewage and waste disposal, public power, and water supply.

Figure 14.1

Total Public Construction *as of 2Q2014 (in $millions)*	**$**	**264,699**
Residential	$	5,423
Nonresidential	$	259,276
Office	$	7,910
Commercial	$	1,700
Health care	$	10,241
Educational	$	59,662
Public safety	$	9,144
Amusement and recreation	$	9,174
Transportation	$	30,780
Power	$	12,208
Highway and street	$	75,274
Sewage and waste disposal	$	21,693
Water supply	$	12,155
Conservation and development	$	7,992

Source: Census Bureau Value of Construction Put in Place

Outlays for highways and transportation, often characterized as having been curtailed since the financial crisis, are actually at or near 2010 peaks, currently running at about $30 billion for transportation and $80 billion for highways and streets.[5] Figure 14.2 illustrates this point.

Figure 14.2

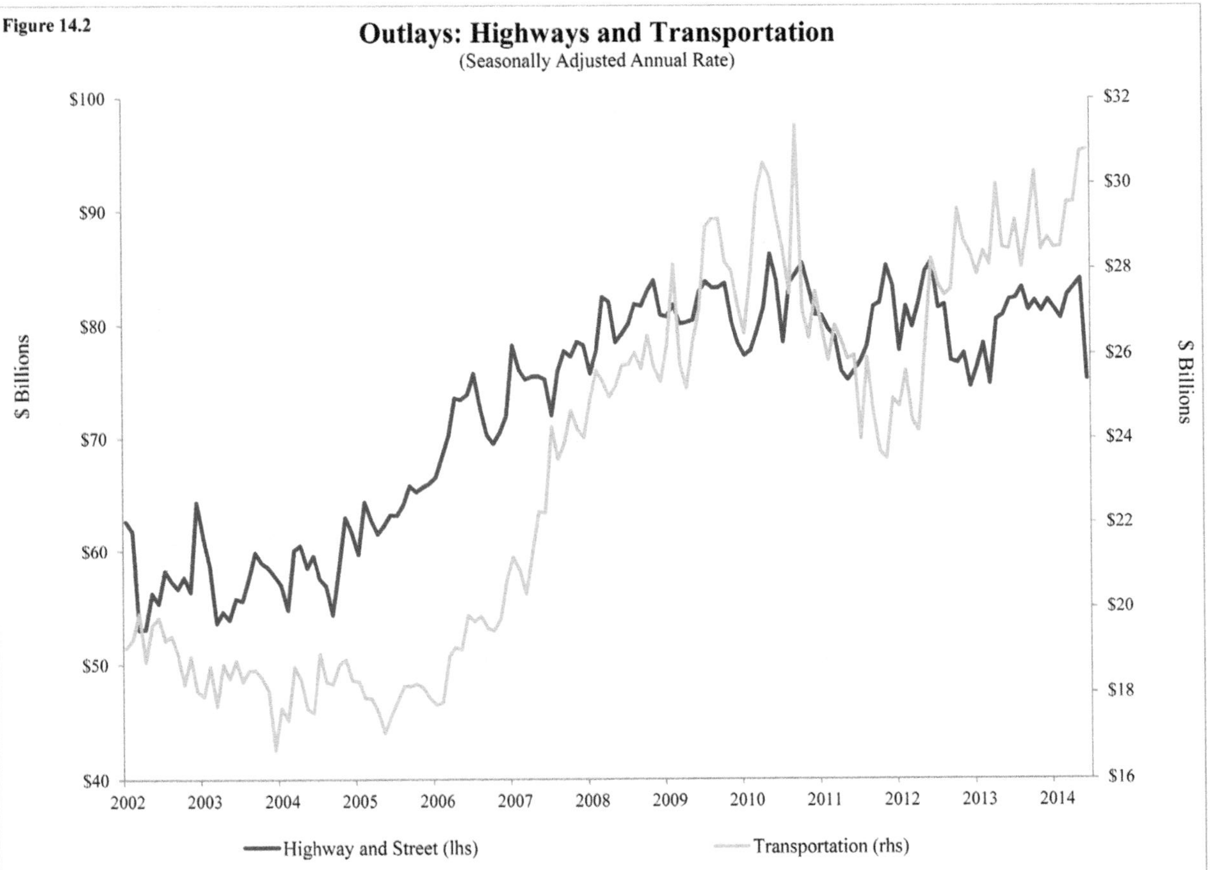

Source: Census Bureau

There have not been secular declines in spending for these components of public infrastructure; yet, from Figure 14.3 we can see that total public construction from all tiers of government has declined from its $320 billion peak reached in 2009 to about $280 billion annually as of April 2014.[6]

Figure 14.3

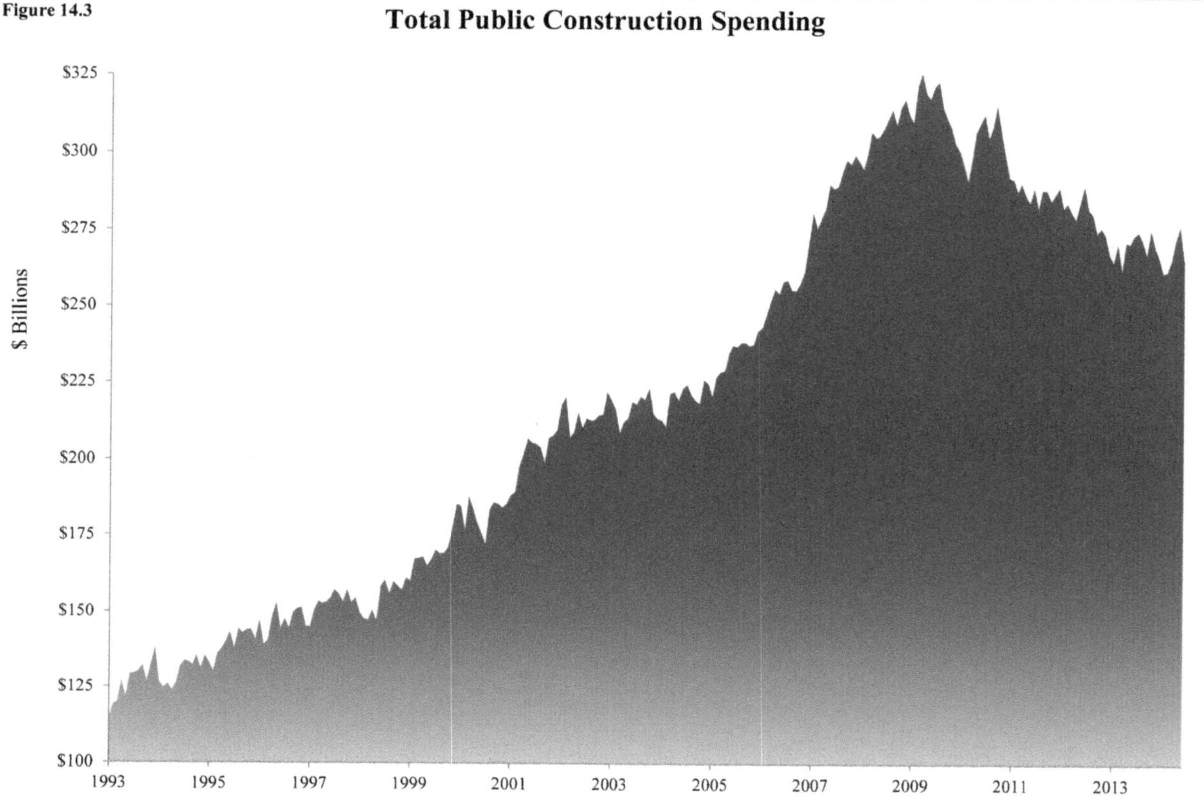

Sources: Census Bureau, Federal Reserve Bank of St. Louis FRED database

So to clarify our earlier statements on public infrastructure investment, there has definitely been a shortfall in total public infrastructure investment since the financial crisis, but that shortfall does not occur because of reduced spending on highways and transportation. Figure 14.4 shows that the decline has resulted primarily from falling education infrastructure expenditures for the construction, renovation, and rehabilitation of pre-K schools, community colleges, and universities. Infrastructure investment in education is currently running at $60 billion annually, down from $90 billion annually at its peak in 2009, accounting for 50% of the decline in public construction spending from 2009 to the present.[7] When pundits discuss "crumbling infrastructure," it is not the nation's highways and bridges that have seen cuts in funding, but primary and secondary schools, community colleges, and universities instead.

Figure 14.4

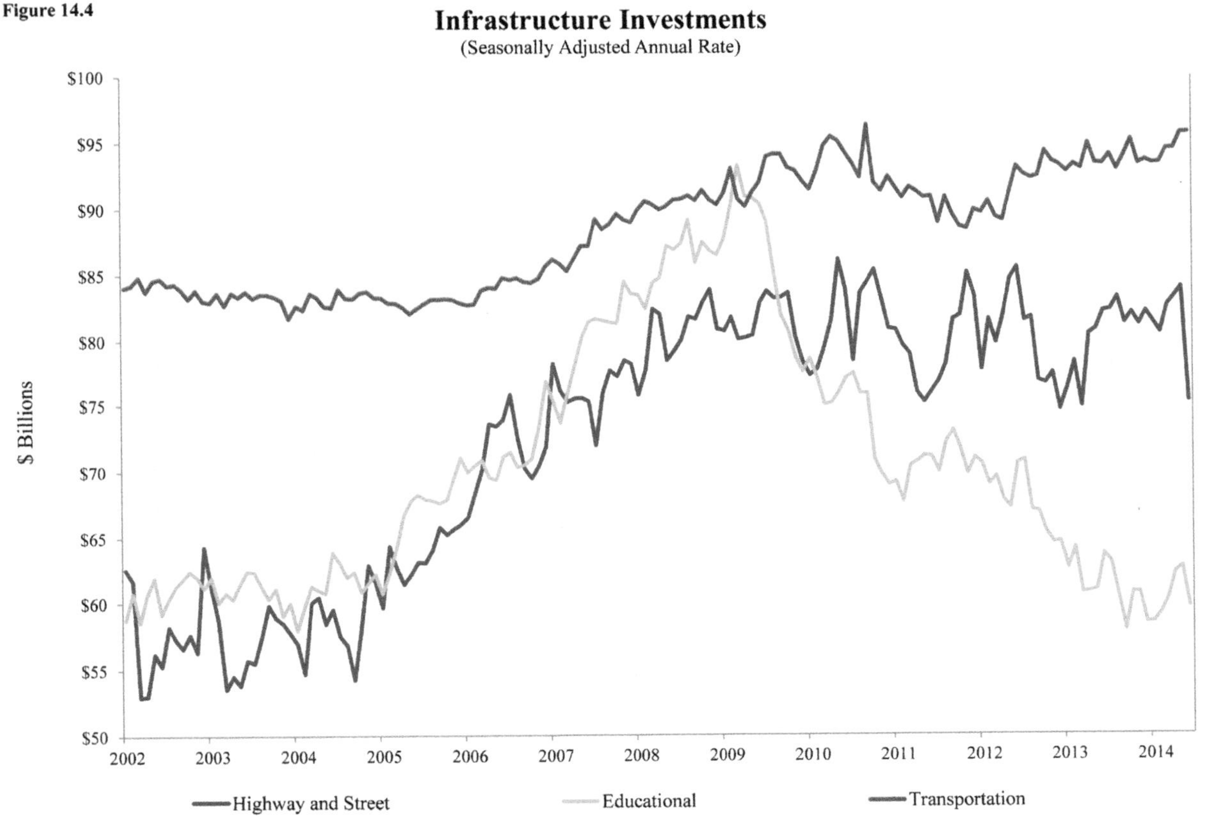

Sources: Census Bureau, Federal Reserve Bank of St. Louis FRED database

Demos.org, a website that tracks higher education expenditures, shows that from 2008 to 2012, outlays for higher education from the five states with the largest 2010 budget gaps declined by 30.6%, with the largest cuts coming in the State of Arizona, which cut funding by 51%.[8] K-12 education has also been a target for state and local governments looking for cost savings.

A report published in May 2014 by the Center on Budget and Policy Priorities (CBPP) shows that, in real terms, 48 states are funding K-12 education at levels lower than they did prior to the recession.[9] For example, Oklahoma's funding is down 22.8% since 2008, and Alabama's K-12 education spending is down 20%.[10] While these cuts are not direct cuts to infrastructure spending, the linkages are clear. Given a choice between cutting payrolls or delaying construction or expansion, renovation, or rehabilitation projects, those who craft state, local, district, and institutional budgets are quick to cut new investments, an alternative justifiably preferred to laying off essential personnel. Notwithstanding, state and local governments have laid off approximately 300,000 teachers since the recession. These layoffs prove that expenditure cuts have also hit payrolls.[11]

On both the state and local levels, education has suffered much greater reductions in funding than transportation infrastructure because of differences in their funding mechanisms. Revenues for schools come from general state and local tax revenues (mostly property sales and income taxes), which declined substantially in the years after the financial crisis (collectively, the 50 states faced a $190 billion shortfall in 2010).[12] Funding for surface, water, air transportation infrastructure, water distribution, and sewage treatment are all payable out of dedicated revenue streams, such as user fees, tolls, and even sales taxes, that match the useful lives of the projects being financed. Because they constitute essential infrastructure, they are much less sensitive to broad-based declines in employment, falling housing prices, and other macro factors.

In addition to revenue pressures, escalating costs from teacher, police, and firefighter salaries and public employee retirement benefits have pressured outlays. Since the recession, these costs have grown dramatically to the point that, in some places, legacy retirement costs eat up 30% of total payroll expenses and up to 50% of total property tax revenues (as in the cases of Chicago and Providence, RI, respectively).[13] To the extent that these costs, which are mandatory and not subject to the appropriations process, continue to increase, education infrastructure investment will continue to be crowded out.

From a different angle, there are several arguments made as to why the United States needs new infrastructure. Most of these arguments ignore cyclical effects and suggest that the absolute level of infrastructure spending since the 1980s has been too low. Infrastructure spending in the post-war era peaked at 3.5% of GDP during the 1960s, when the interstate highway system was being completed and the government spent heavily on public universities under the GI bill.[14] Figure 14.5 shows the current level of construction spending as a percentage of GDP since the mid-1990s. The graph shows that spending follows swings in the business cycle. During the most recent decade, construction spending topped out at 2.2% in 2009 and has since declined to 1.6%.[15]

Figure 14.5

Construction Spending Follows Swings in the Business Cycle

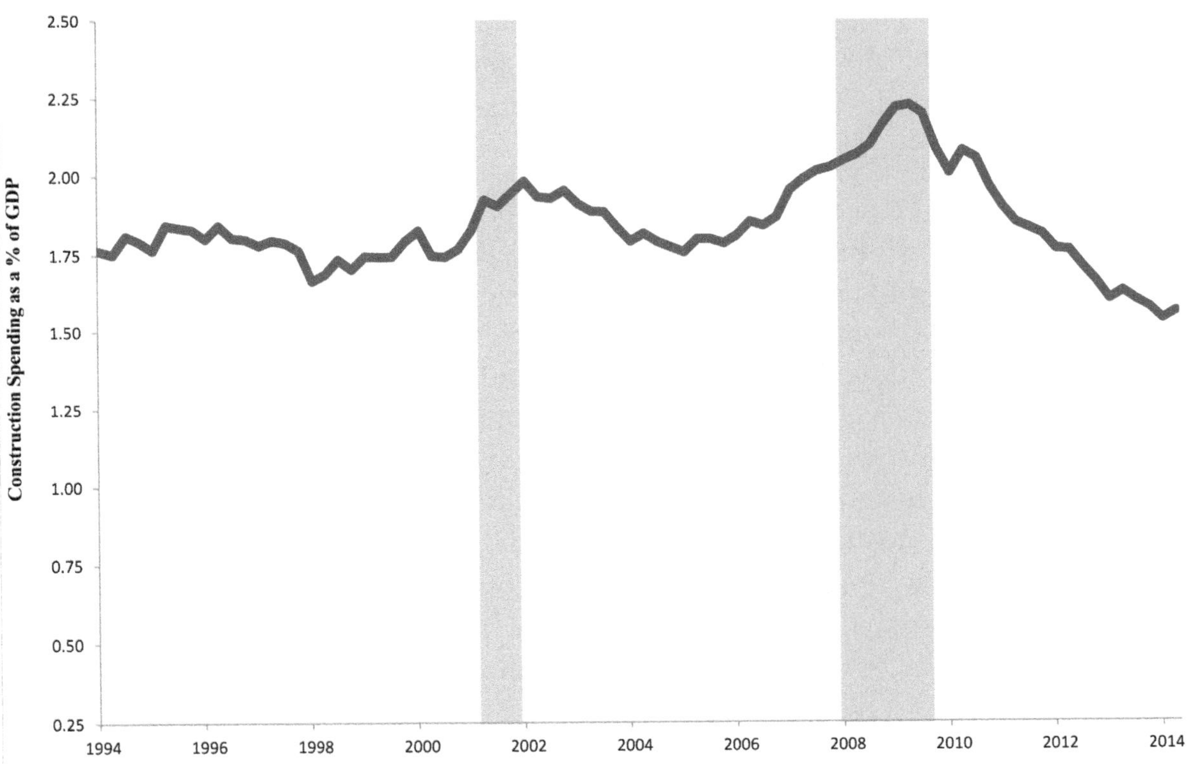

Sources: Bureau of Economic Analysis, Census Bureau, Federal Reserve Bank of St. Louis FRED database

There is no shortage of academic and independent literature on the "correct" amount of infrastructure spending needed. The most well-known studies have come from the "Infrastructure Report Card," published annually by the American Society of Civil Engineers (ASCE), which has stated that \$3.6 trillion in new infrastructure spending is needed by 2020 in order to upgrade existing infrastructure to an acceptable level.[16] McKinsey & Company, the gold standard for reports on infrastructure investment, has stated that an incremental \$150 billion annually will be needed to lift U.S. GDP annually by 1% through increases in potential GDP from productivity gains.[17] The World Economic Forum's Infrastructure Index ranks the United States number 14 in the world in terms of the quality of the nation's infrastructure.[18]

Although it is not possible to pinpoint the "right" or "correct" amount of infrastructure spending, we can discuss some of the problems in the American approach to infrastructure spending. Critics of the U.S. system state that the inefficiencies in U.S. infrastructure finance stem from adherence to the public-sector model of financing. Resource allocation to projects is based on politics and referenda within the various levels of government, not based on risk-return profiles, as it would be in the private sector.[19]

Several groups have argued that the most efficient delivery mechanism for new infrastructure is the private sector. Chris Edwards in his piece "Infrastructure Investment," published by The Cato Institute, a libertarian think tank, has argued that "infrastructure spending should be allocated to the highest-valued projects and constructed in the most cost-effective manner" to maximize the benefits afforded by improved infrastructure.[20] The basic premise of Edwards' argument is that most of America's infrastructure investment, to the tune of about $950 billion spent annually, is provided by the private sector.[21] Problems associated with heavy government spending on infrastructure, on the other hand, include a history of pork barrel politics and cost overruns more typical in government projects than in private projects. Edwards states that "many types of infrastructure currently owned by governments" were once "owned by the private sector" and that, prior to the 20th century, 2,000 turnpike companies in the United States built more than 10,000 toll roads still in existence.[22] "Until the mid-20th century, most urban rail and bus services were private,"[23] he says.

According to the Organisation for Economic Co-operation and Development (OECD), since 1990, OECD countries have sold or "privatized" about $900 billion in state-owned assets, about 63% of which have been infrastructure assets.[24] Many countries have stopped short of full privatization and opted instead for what are known as "public-private partnerships" (PPPs). These government-private sector partnerships contract various functions out to private entities.[25] According to Edwards, "most commonly" these entities will bid on various elements of "project financing, management, maintenance, and operations, shifting risks from government to the private sector."[26] In the years since the financial crisis, given historically low interest rates and far from robust issuance of long-term bonds, PPPs have been in high demand among long-term investors such as pension funds.[27]

The OECD states PPPs and privatization offer two primary advantages over government-run infrastructure: The allocation mechanism to high-return investments and "the more stable funding stream from debt and equity markets versus the volatile and politically charged budgetary cycle."[28] Edwards points out that the private sector systematically searches for high-return investments based on risk-reward profiles. The public sector, on the other hand, allocates based on budgetary authorization, which is an inherently political process.[29]

PPPs work in the United States as follows: A public entity—let's consider a toll road as an example—will sell a stream of revenues associated with the operation of that toll road to a private entity, for a certain period of time, in exchange for an upfront payment. In this concession agreement, the private entity will be able to set rates and fares to maximize its revenues during the length of the transaction.[30] The payment sum received by the public-sector entity can be used at its discretion. The benefits of PPPs are manifold: Toll roads and mass transit systems are no longer run with general fund support, but are run instead as self-sustaining enterprises; service and routine maintenance usually improves; and new building projects are typically not delayed during the grant-approval process.[31] PPPs are used much more heavily in Europe than in the United States, but they are a growing source of budgetary relief given current funding pressures.

There have also been calls in the United States for privatization of infrastructure assets via outright asset sales. In the years following the crisis, many local governments—the city of Philadelphia, for example—sold its natural gas transmission business to shore up its finances. Such sales serve to skirt the issues of poor maintenance of assets and pave the way for more efficient use of resources.

The alternative to greater private sector involvement has been the specter of greater federal government involvement, which has been pitched regularly by the Obama Administration through the creation of a national infrastructure bank. Although such proposals have been met with resistance from Congress, existing programs such as the Transportation Infrastructure Finance and Innovation Act (TIFIA), have been expanded.[32] The TIFIA program plays on the notion of a national infrastructure bank by granting the Federal Highway Administration (FHA) the ability to loan out 10 to 30 times its appropriations from Congress for qualified infrastructure projects. TIFIA effectively turns FHWA into a Fannie Mae or Freddie Mac.[33]

The problem with an expanded federal government role is that states, local governments, and private companies are better at assessing the infrastructure needs because they make decisions locally. Also, state and local governments finance themselves at tax-exempt rates, with a cost of capital at or lower than the cost the federal government incurs.[34]

Last, we turn to a discussion of the infrastructure budgeting process, mainly on the state level. This discussion will focus primarily on research from the National Association of State Budget Officers (NASBO), which periodically explores topics involved in state budgeting.

A funding challenge for state and local governments is paying for ongoing project expenses, repairs, and replacements of crucial infrastructure. After the new bridge, road, or school is built, it is often very poorly maintained.[35] This is undoubtedly due to the fact that infrastructure is typically partially funded with grants from outside entities, either states or the federal government.[36] Grants heavily incentivize building of infrastructure, but do not pay for ongoing expenses.[37] Thus, many politically popular new projects are embarked upon, but do not receive annual funding for ongoing maintenance from the state and local governments that built them.[38] Investing in infrastructure, much like the purchase of a new home, requires commitments over time, carries risks due to the vagaries in budgeting and government spending, and requires intensive financial planning.[39]

A large portion of public infrastructure, roughly 85%, is paid for by state and local governments. Capital grants from the federal government subsidize 15% of these costs in a given year.[40] Recently, through Build America Bonds, the federal government's role in infrastructure spending has increased; however, the secular trend since FDR and the World War II era has been a declining federal government role.[41] Since then, infrastructure spending has declined from 3.5% to 2.5% of GDP. As states are currently facing capital constraints, state budgets have held back capital spending in the years following the crisis. The economic contraction and a greater demand for entitlements have been primary reasons for the lower spending. Welfare spending is often a more urgent expenditure, and states have deferred maintenance projects because of it. Budgetary planning requires a consideration of costs and benefits both now and in the future.

According to NASBO, budgeting for infrastructure investments is, more than anything else, an estimate of its cost or a "road map" of the revenues generated by the asset being constructed, along with the outlays required for renovation and maintenance.[42] There are several unknowns involved, but the purpose of any planning is to understand the impact of projects on future operating budgets.[43] Usually states will forecast revenues and expenses utilizing 5 to 10 year projections.[44] NASBO shows that in 33 states, this planning is done by centralized public works agencies that coordinate and oversee projects done statewide.[45] Of the 50 states, 26 enact annual budgets solely for capital expenditures; 25 states have a joint legislative and gubernatorial review of such projects.[46] New Hampshire is unique in that it requires its state agencies to submit estimated return-on-investment figures when seeking approvals for projects.[47]

Typically, the demand for new projects and capital spending will exceed available resources, and priorities are often set by looking at urgency of need and the extent of repairs and replacements.[48] Some projects are financed entirely through debt or revolving funds with subsidies from taxpayer funds.[49]

The topic of reauthorization of the BABs program has come up as a way to increase infrastructure spending. In 2009 and 2010, state and local governments issued $185 billion in debt to finance building, expansion, and renovation of projects with BABs. These are seen as a more efficient and cheaper mode of financing because the federal government is better able to recover its subsidy costs through BABs than through the issuance of tax-exempt bonds. Although there have been questions about the program's efficacy because of federal budget tightening under sequestration, it was an effective catalyst for new investments. There has been talk of bringing the program back, but nothing has developed beyond preliminary discussions. For a comprehensive discussion of BABs, see Chapter 10.

As we close this chapter, we would like to dispel a few myths regarding a topic that has garnered constant news attention since late 2014, and that is the lack of available funding for the federal Highway Trust Fund (HTF). We stated previously that the total value of public and private infrastructure spending put in place as of April 2014 is close to $950 billion on a seasonally adjusted annual rate. The amount spent by federal, state, and local governments is $260 billion, $81 billion of which comprises state and local government expenditures for building new highways and expanding, renovating, and rehabilitating existing ones.[50] Outlays from the HTF during the next three years will constitute a very small percentage of this total amount—only $2.67 billion annually, or roughly 3% of all spending on highway construction and 1% of public construction.[51]

This conclusion is based on the methodology used by the Congressional Budget Office in its publication titled "The Highway Trust Fund and the Treatment of Surface Transportation Programs in the Federal Budget," published in June 2014.[52] At the end of 2013, HTF's highway account, which accounts for 86% of the trust fund's outlays (the other is the transit account), had a $4 billion balance, an additional $66 billion in contract authority (the ability to enter into a contract, not considered an outlay), and $28 billion available to states but not yet spent, for a total of $94 billion.[53] The CBO points out that tax receipts are expected to be $34 billion annually until 2017, or $102 billion, which means that net new spending out of HTF over three years are $8 billion, or $2.67 billion annually.[54] For the mass transit account, the situation is similar.[55] Appropriations from the federal government's general fund to top-up HTF totaled $6 billion in 2013 and were budgeted to be $10 billion in 2014, slightly larger than $2.67 billion.[56] The reason for the discrepancy lies in differences between budgetary authorization and outlays, which is beyond the scope of this book. Even if funding for outlays from HTF does not get reauthorized, the amount is small in the grand scheme of things. Assuming that Congress decides not to top-up the trust fund during the next three years, the impact on infrastructure investment will be quite small, relatively speaking, since infrastructure expenditures are, for all intents and purposes, state and local functions.

There have been many suggestions regarding how best to fix the system of funding the highway trust fund. The most recent increase in excise taxes for funding HTF occurred 20 years prior to the writing of this chapter.[57] The CBO's analysis of the impacts of higher taxes on funding suggests that higher taxes won't come close to fixing the problem.[58] Paraphrasing from the CBO, a one-cent tax increase will raise $1.5 billion annually.[59] In order to meet obligations by revenue increases alone, gas taxes would have to increase 10 to 15 cents per gallon. The question of affordability comes into play. Most Americans can afford to pay a little more, but only because of our country's vast energy resources, which lead to reduced costs. The average family spends 3% of average household income on energy.[60] Higher energy costs detract from discretionary spending. There is a rule of thumb that a penny increase in gasoline prices reduces non-energy consumer spending by $1.4 billion.[61]

The CBO has stated that a possible solution to the problem of adequately funding the HTF programs might take the form of a "mileage-based user fee to raise revenues" instead of a tax on gasoline consumption.[62] Any usage-based fee is preferable to continued general fund transfers that serve as a short-term plug, but fail to incentivize efficiencies in the system or to promote cost-benefit allocation of resources.

Public infrastructure investment is important because it lays the groundwork for the transacting of everyday business that contributes to economic prosperity. Political commentary in years following the financial crisis has obscured the hard evidence, pointing to a mounting fiscal cliff for the Highway Trust Fund. In a challenging political environment where infrastructure investment is a low policy priority, as is the case with HTF, Public Private Partnerships can be an effective fix. In the coming years, infrastructure spending will remain a major component of economic output, but with a varying mix of both private and public funding.

15

A Tale of Broken Promises: Trouble in the Garden State

All states faced problems during and after the recession. Higher unemployment increased demand for state welfare programs, but also reduced sales and income tax revenues to pay for them. New Jersey's finances, like Illinois', were overextended before the recession hit. In the fall of 2008, the state's budget deficit was $400 million; by spring of that year it increased to $7 billion.[1] In their working paper, "Institutions Matter: Can New Jersey Reverse Course?," Eileen Norcross and Frederic Sautet show that the state's pension system was "under-funded by $34 billion, and outstanding debt total[ed] $45 billion," with most of that debt accruing during the 15 years prior to the crisis.[2]

The election of Chris Christie in 2009 marked a sea change in how the state would manage its financial problems. Governor Chris Christie, who ran on a mandate of lower taxes and fiscal responsibility, was elected as a reaction to the overspending and expansion of social welfare programs undertaken by the Jon Corzine Administration during the prior four years.

Figure 15.1

New Jersey Revenues vs. Expenditures

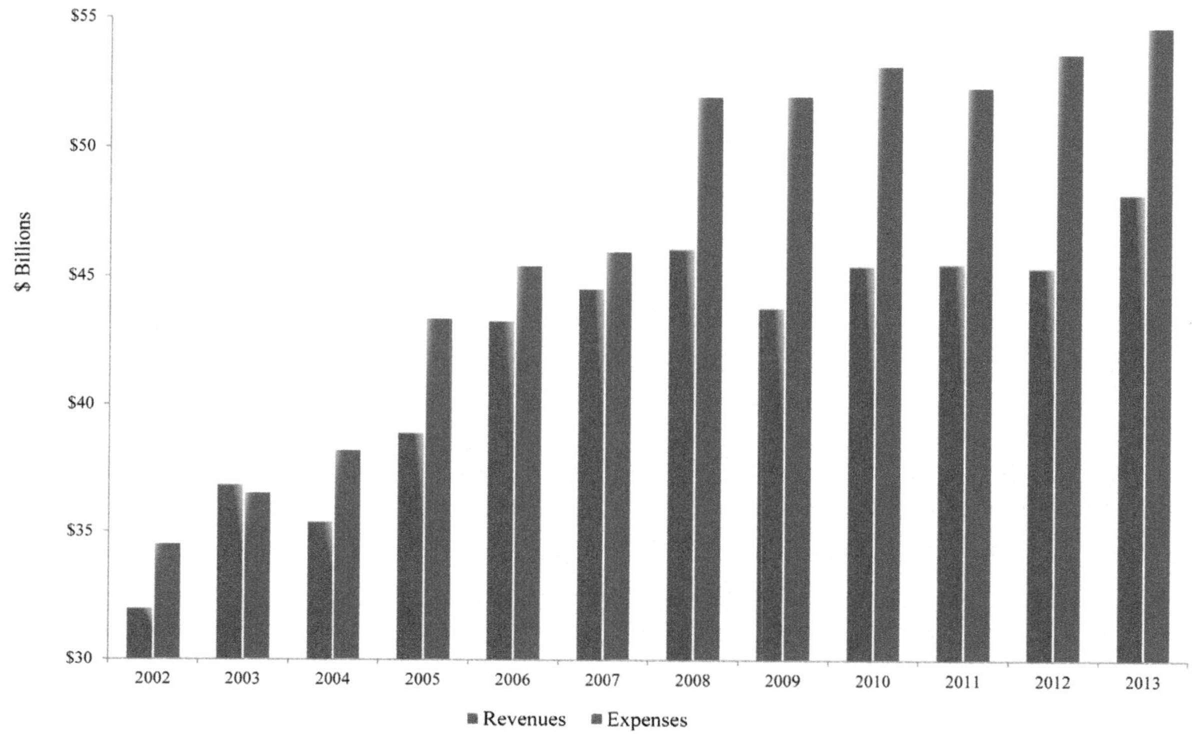

Sources: Investortools, State of New Jersey Annual Financials

There has been a structural mismatch between the state's outlays and its ability to pay its bills. The state skipped payments to its pension system, increased taxes, and issued debt to balance its budget over the course of 20 years. Figure 15.1 shows the state's revenues versus expenditures during the 12 years from 2002 to 2013. In only one year, 2003, the state's revenues were greater than its expenses.

The irony is that New Jersey's general fund budget has been "balanced" every year since 1947, the year the balanced budget requirement was passed.[3] (The term "balanced budget" has a narrow legal definition, and the governor and legislature circumvent it regularly.) Figure 15.1 depicts this trend, with expenses rising to a much greater extent than the revenues used to pay for them.[4]

The state's current financial distress results from three factors: a highly progressive and volatile revenue structure, the result of tax increases on the state's wealthiest residents over time; expenditures on schools and Medicaid that are difficult to rein in; and involvement in extraneous and non-profitable enterprises, such as gambling and high-risk insurance pools.

The state's biggest problem is its school funding structure. Norcross and Sautet note that school spending in New Jersey is protected by strict constitutional requirements guaranteeing ever-increasing transfers to disadvantaged communities.[5] The state spends 35% of its budget on its public school system via transfers to local governments and school construction in poor communities.[6] This is typical in state budgets, but constitutional protections limit changes in the funding structure.

In 1985, the New Jersey Supreme Court ruled in the landmark case of *Abbott versus Burke*, that the funding structure for education did not "meet the state's constitutional requirement of a 'thorough and efficient' education system."[7] Property taxes in wealthy communities were greater than those in poor communities, leaving poor school districts relatively underfunded. Since that time, the state has been forced to transfer funds to these districts with funding deficiencies, known as "Abbott Districts," to equalize funding on a per pupil basis.[8] These lawsuits have been initiated on behalf of disadvantaged students by the New Jersey Education Law Center (ELC), a private foundation whose stated goal is to act as "advocates for equal educational opportunity."[9]

In many years, as was the case in 2009, the New Jersey ELC has sued the state for not meeting requirements under the Abbott District program.[10] The New Jersey Supreme Court has ruled in favor of both sides in recent history. When rulings have been in favor of the ELC, the state has been forced to come to market and issue bonds to meet the constitutional funding requirement, plunging the state further into debt.

The most recent judgment occurred in 2009, with passage of New Jersey's 2010 fiscal year school budget. Funding levels based on established formulas were upheld by the Supreme Court after a challenge by the ELC in the prior fiscal year. However, midway through the 2010 school year, the state's finances deteriorated, with revenues coming in $2.2 billion lower than previously expected.[11]

Because of the state's balanced budget requirement, Governor Christie made midyear cuts to education to bring expenses in line with revenues.[12] Rajashri Chakrabarti and Sarah Sutherland, writing for the Federal Reserve Bank of New York in their piece "New Jersey's Abbott Districts: Education Finances during the Great Recession," note that the midyear cuts were challenged by the Education Law Center, and in March 2011, the state was ordered by the New Jersey Supreme Court to "make a payment of $500 million to Abbott Districts."[13] The majority of New Jersey school districts did not receive any portion of this appropriation, only the 31 Abbott Districts.[14]

Of the total amount of state aid going toward education, the 31 Abbott Districts received approximately 50% of this amount[15] and 92% of the state's preschool aid.[16]

The program presents another conundrum for the state: How to meet its constitutional balanced budget requirement in light of Abbott District rulings. Should constitutional education funding requirements trump constitutional balanced budget requirements? The balanced budget requirement in the New Jersey State Constitution reads as follows:[17, 18]

> *The Legislature shall not, in any manner, create in any fiscal year a debt or debts, liability or liabilities of the State, which together with any previous debts or liabilities shall exceed at any time one per centum of the total amount appropriated by the general appropriation law for that fiscal year, unless the same shall be authorized by a law for some single object or work distinctly specified therein.*

This section limits annual long-term debt issuance to less than 1% of total appropriations. The state has used a legal maneuver to enable it to continue issuing debt in excess of these constitutional limits to pay for education. In Detroit's bankruptcy, Emergency Manager Kevyn Orr filed suit against holders of debt that was structured to avoid statutory limits, claiming that such issuances were illegal. New Jersey's similar use of debt can be construed in the same way. We have to wonder how the New Jersey Supreme Court can turn a blind eye to the state's circumvention of one law to comply with another. If the two laws are mutually exclusive, one should be ruled unconstitutional.

The loophole to the balanced budget requirement has been structured as follows: By creating various authorities as special-purpose vehicles to issue debt, the state can appropriate moneys in the form of lease payments to the special-purpose vehicles whose sole purpose is to pay debt service.

Because lease payments are legally considered appropriations and not interest on debt, the state satisfies its constitutional debt restrictions. Many special vehicles have been created for this purpose: The New Jersey Economic Development Authority, New Jersey Transportation Trust Fund, and the New Jersey Education Facilities Authority, to name a few.

The state has been so dependent on this financing structure that its lease and contract debt has tripled between 2003 and 2013, while the "actual" general obligation debt on its balance sheet has not. Figure 15.2 shows the tripling in New Jersey's lease and contract debt issued by these authorities from 2003 to 2013.[19]

Norcross and Sautet show that, historically, both Democratic and Republican governors have buckled to the pressure of funding Abbot Districts. Since 1992, $11 billion in debt has been issued to make these payments: Roughly 35% of the state's current outstanding long-term debt.[20] They state that "In 2000, the Whitman Administration issued $8.6 billion in school construction bonds" to upgrade school buildings in Abbott Districts, but two-thirds of the planned schools were never built.[21] In 2004, Jim McGreevey borrowed $1 billion against tobacco settlement proceeds and another $900 million against motor vehicle surcharges to pay for school construction. In 2008, prior to voter referendum, "Jon Corzine issued $3.9 billion in school construction bonds" that were used in part to meet court-mandated Abbott decisions.[22]

Most of the debt issued took the form of lease and contract debt, which is technically considered to be a legislative appropriation rather than debt. It was only in 2008 that the state passed a limitation on debt issued by a state or state authority, subject to appropriation, which is why there is somewhat of a leveling off starting in the FY10 budget (enacted in 2009).[23] Norcross and Sautet write that the state has reached a point where reform is needed, not just because of the high costs of the education-funding requirement, but also because of statistical evidence suggesting that funding hasn't improved educational outcomes.[24]

Figure 15.2

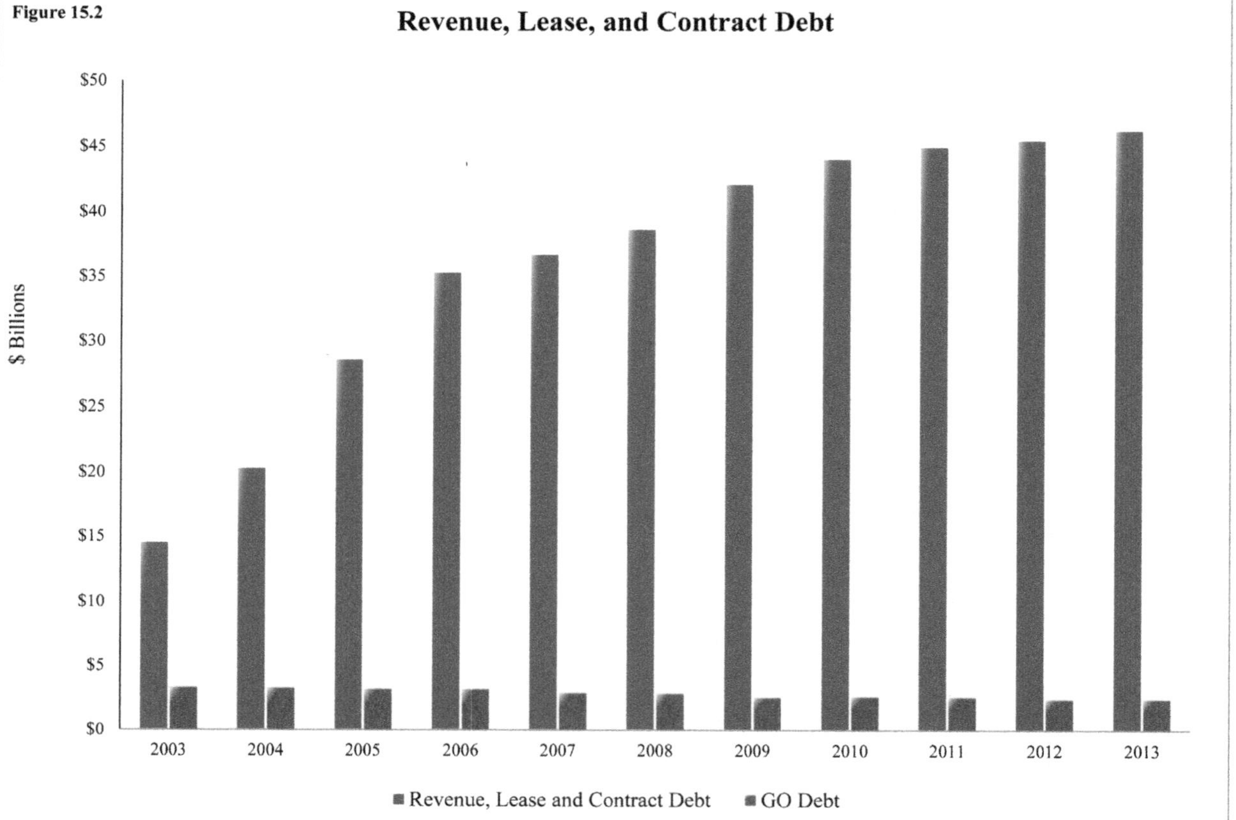

Sources: Investortools, State of New Jersey Annual Financials

Debt issued to pay for welfare expenditures has crowded out core expenditures, including those for key infrastructure like transportation. Figure 15.3 shows the increase in debt service as a percentage of expenditures from 2006 to 2013. In 2002, debt service was 1.5% of expenditures. It is now 5.5%.[25] Expenditures on transportation infrastructure have actually declined by 30%. Social welfare programs, such as Medicaid, Temporary Assistance for Needy Families, and unemployment insurance increased by 20%.[26]

Figure 15.3 **Rising Debt Service: Consuming NJ's Budget**

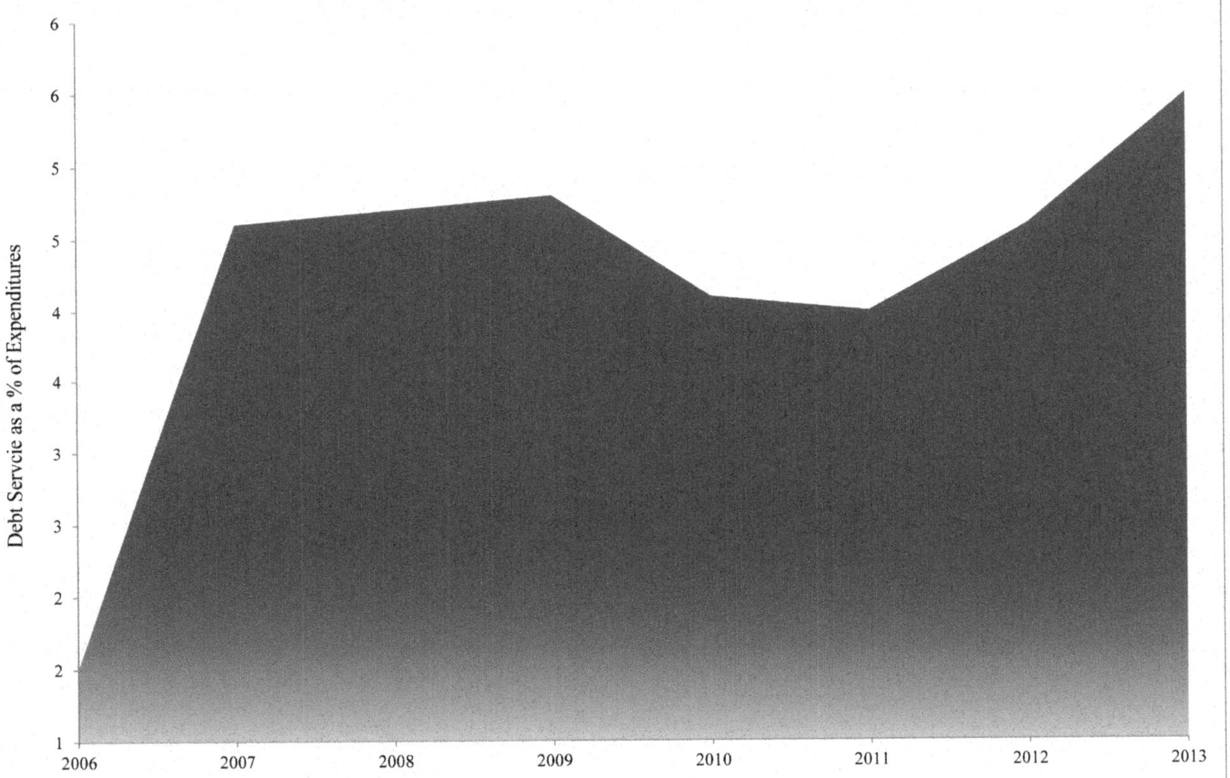

Sources: Investortools, New Jersey Annual Financials

Ravitch and Volcker in their "Report of the State Budget Crisis Task Force: New Jersey Report," point out the problem Medicaid funding has been for the state's finances. Since New Jersey's Children's Health Insurance Program (CHIP) was expanded in 1997, the state's Medicaid program has had high income-eligibility thresholds and a generous benefits scheme.[27] Given high levels of healthcare inflation and coverage expansion during the 1990s, Medicaid spending "doubled from $1.8 billion in 1996 to $3.34 billion in 2007" and rose as high as $5 billion in 2010.[28] Increasing expenditures for Medicaid have forced the state to choose one of three options: Cut Medicaid, raise taxes, or reduce funding for other programs.[29]

Medicaid expansion is a cause for growing concern. As Norcross and Sautet show, it is highly incentivized by the federal government and extremely difficult (both politically and practically) to cut.[30] If New Jersey reduces its own Medicaid expenditures by $1, for instance, Medicaid spending is reduced by $1.50 because of the state's federal Medicaid matching rate of 50%. Because federal matching money is treated by politicians as "free money" in the state's budget, cuts to Medicaid or any other federally subsidized program are politically difficult.[31]

The American Recovery and Reinvestment Act (ARRA) of 2009 served to subsidize the state's Medicaid spending without addressing the state's underlying problems.[32] The state received $17.5 billion in federal dollars from the program, one-third of which went toward Medicaid as part of Federal Medical Assistance Percentage (FMAP), dwarfing the $650 million invested in highways and infrastructure and the $600 million allocated toward education.[33] As Norcross and Sautet observe, the ARRA exacerbated the state's overspending.[34]

Ancillary programs have drained the state's budget as well. For example, in the early 2000s, the state used deficit financing to create a high-risk insurance pool for residents who lacked auto insurance.[35] The NJ Personal Automobile Insurance Plan is part of the New Jersey Automobile Insurance Guaranty Fund, which receives loans from the state to shore up its unfunded liability. New Jersey's 2013 budget summary shows that "in 2013, the fund received a $1.3 billion loan from the New Jersey Property-Liability Insurance Guaranty Association" equal to approximately 4% of the state's revenues.[36] Other ongoing state projects include investments in transportation, corrections, and sports and exposition facilities.[37]

The New Jersey Sports and Exposition Authority (NJSEA), the conduit that issues debt for non-core-entity operations, was originally created to operate various sports venues and betting facilities around the state, such as MetLife Stadium, the Meadowlands, and Monmouth Park Racetrack. NJSEA has issued debt for its own operations and for the state of New Jersey as a conduit. In 2003, NJSEA embarked on the construction of the Xanadu Meadowlands Complex, a facility with multiple uses, including an indoor ski slope, concert hall, and water park. The authority provided hundreds of millions in tax incentives such as forgone sales-tax revenues and authorization for tax-exempt bond financing.[38] Renamed The American Dream Meadowlands, the project has dragged on and has yet to open.

The State of New Jersey has high wealth levels, allowing the state to sustain high levels of per capita spending and debt. Prior to 2008, financing this spending was tenable because of the state's moderate debt relative to personal income and low debt service as a percentage of expenditures. As indicated in Figure 15.4, however, over time the state's debt growth outpaced growth in personal income. From 2002 until 2013, personal income increased by 44%, while the state's debt burden increased by 153%.[39] Such outsized debt increases tax an ever-larger share of taxpayers' incomes.[40] Reduced after-tax incomes have the ancillary effects of reducing discretionary spending and sales tax revenues, further reducing revenues to the state government.

Figure 15.4

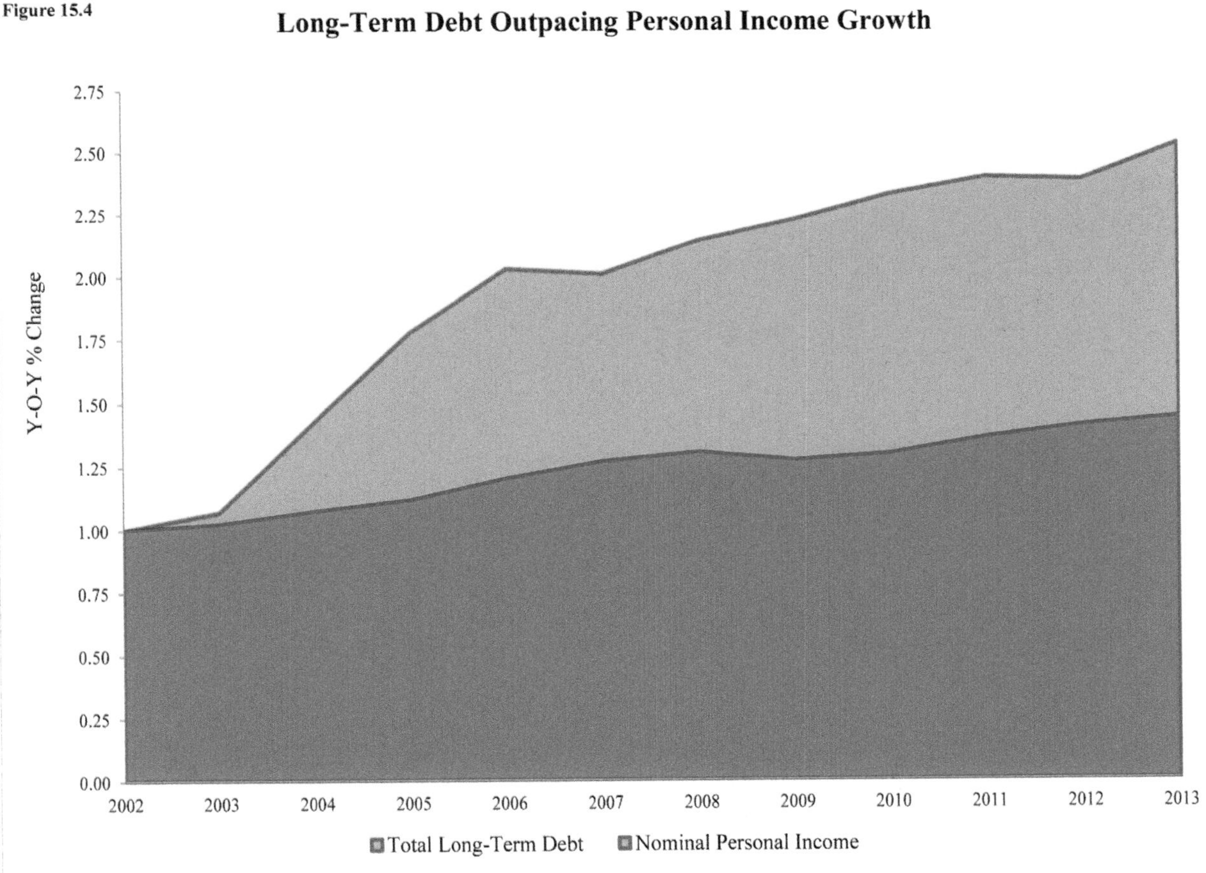

Sources: Investortools, New Jersey Annual Financials

Norcross and Sautet speak to the level of taxation in the state versus the level of services actually provided.[41] The residents of New Jersey, in theory, voted for a desired level of taxation, services, and social programs payable out of their tax dollars. However, the government circumvented its accountability to the voters by using budget gimmickry and debt issuance to pay for services, obscuring the true cost of New Jersey's actual spending and thus creating, in Norcross and Sautet's words, a "fiscal illusion."[42] Debt proceeds are not revenue, but the state legislature treated them as such. One way this was done was through evasion of the state's debt limits.[43]

Since the 1990s, the state's budget has been artificially balanced by skipping pension and OPEB payments. OPEB has been payable on a pay-as-you-go basis, meaning current workers are merely paying the health benefits of current retirees instead of funding the plan with assets.

Figure 15.5 shows actual payments as a percentage of required payments over time for the state's six pension funds.[44] Since 1998, the state has not paid the full amount required into any of its plans, and in most years it paid less than half the required amounts.[45] In 1999, the Teachers' Pension and Annuity Fund liability increased by 90% when the state extended benefit payments to surviving spouses.[46]

Figure 15.5	JRS	CPFPF	PFRS	PERS	SPRS	TPAF
Actuarially Accrued Liability as of 12/31/12	$ 585,700,787	$ 9,179,981	$ 3,926,525,679	$ 18,290,829,021	$ 2,581,950,846	$ 51,406,540,290
1998	92.0%		87.4%	0.0%	0.0%	82.2%
1999	0.0%		25.3%	0.0%	0.0%	0.0%
2000	0.0%		61.1%	0.0%	0.0%	0.0%
2001	0.0%		0.0%	0.0%	0.0%	0.0%
2002	0.0%	92.0%	0.0%	0.0%	0.0%	0.0%
2003	50.1%	76.4%	0.0%	0.0%	0.0%	0.0%
2004	17.9%	36.6%	18.8%	1.0%	0.0%	0.0%
2005	27.4%	49.2%	30.6%	0.4%	0.5%	0.0%
2006	34.3%	46.2%	36.6%	0.4%	27.4%	8.0%
2007	53.1%	21.1%	58.8%	56.8%	52.9%	49.7%
2008	15.2%	14.0%	14.9%	16.1%	14.8%	14.0%
2009	1.7%	0.0%	2.0%	3.6%	1.9%	1.4%
2010	3.2%	0.0%	2.1%	4.1%	1.1%	1.8%
2011	5.7%	68.8%	7.3%	7.9%	6.5%	6.0%
2012	47.5%	21.9%	52.8%	42.1%	46.3%	44.8%

Sources: State of New Jersey Annual Financials, State of New Jersey Division of Investment Comprehensive Annual Financial Report Fiscal Year 2013

Unfunded pension obligations resemble debt in that they require a future outflow of resources. The obligations grow when the state misses payments. Figure 15.6 illustrates the New Jersey's 200% growth of debt, OPEB, and pension liabilities as a percentage of personal income from 2003 to 2013.[47]

In some years, as in 2000, federal law enabled the state could skip payments because its pension plans were fully funded.[48] However, changes in plan valuation levels allowed the state to make lower payments, and "pension holidays" were granted to the state and local governments during the recession. As a result, funding levels have dropped.[49] Pension deferrals compounded the shortfall by allowing governments to dedicate revenues needed for the pension system to other programs. Given the difficulty of cutting programs, governments were unable to pay full amounts. Instead, governments required contribution "phase-ins" that allowed them to repay full amounts gradually.[50]

Like the State of Illinois, New Jersey has issued debt to fund its pension system. In 1997, the Whitman Administration and the legislature issued $3.4 billion in pension bonds to plug the state's unfunded pension liability. The funds would be invested in the stock market, the ultimate goal being to reduce the state's contributions by $625 million over the next 15 months.[51] The net effect on the state's debt burden was a wash. The debt sale converted the state's contractual obligation, which could more easily have been restructured, into debt. According to Moody's, in order for the transaction to reduce the plan's unfunded liability, returns on bond proceeds would have had to exceed interest payments over time.[52] The state's indebtedness increased and the plan's funded ratio…until the collapse of the tech bubble.

The Christie Administration has also underfunded the state's pension system. In 2014, $693 million of the required $1.58 billion was paid. In 2015, $680 million of $2.25 billion was budgeted to be paid into the system.[53] These fractional payments, upheld by the New Jersey Supreme Court, resulted in lower funding levels and growth in the unfunded liability. Figure 15.6 shows that the state's unfunded pension liability tripled from 2007 to 2013, while OPEB increased by 6.35 times. The system's funded ratio declined from 75% to 54% during this period.[54] With such funding shortfalls, it is hard to imagine going down the same path without reforms to plan benefits and eligibility.

Figure 15.6

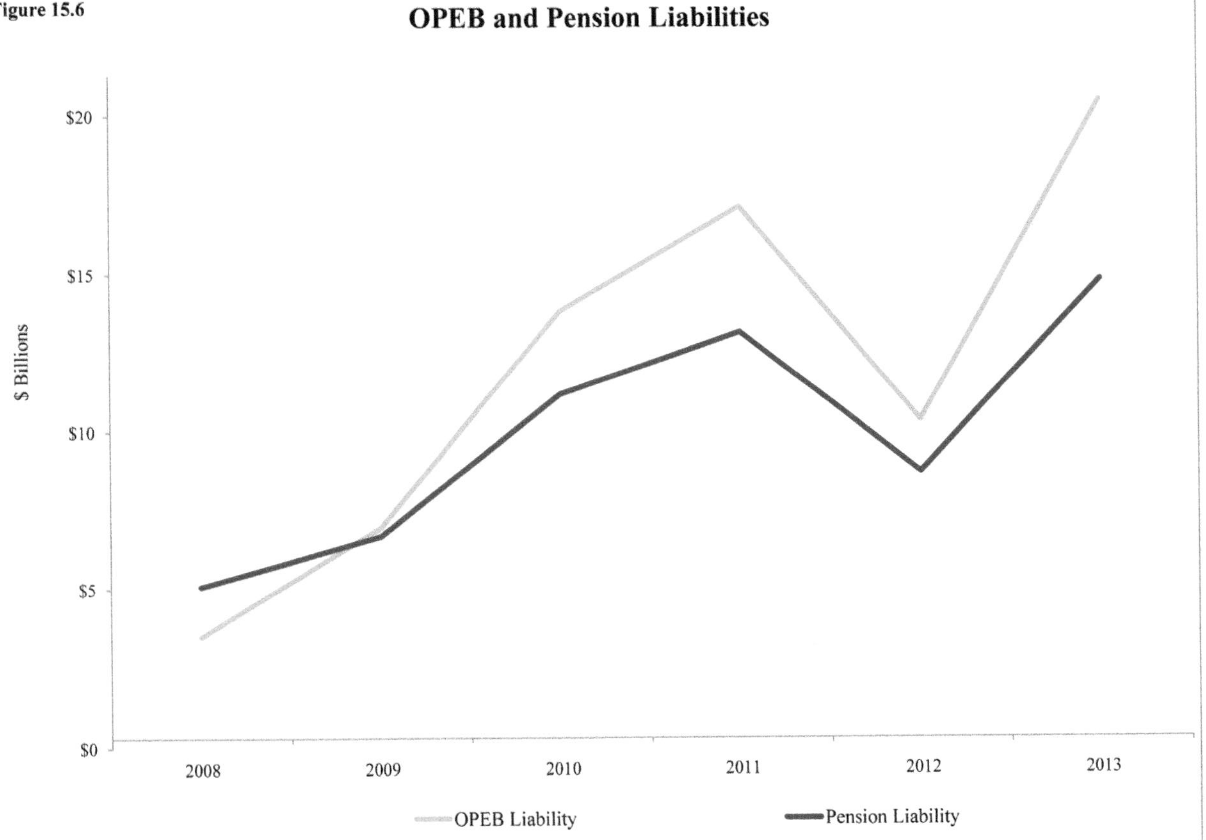

Sources: Investortools, State of New Jersey Annual Financials

History shows that fiscal problem-solving takes time and is fraught with legal battles and political paralysis. New Jersey has gone through a difficult period of deleveraging its balance sheet during the last few years, with limited debt issuance and spending restraints. All the while, the state's unfunded liabilities and its commitments to Abbott Districts continue to grow. We believe that still more has to be done to effectively address the state's pension underfunding. A difficult balancing act will have to be performed in providing services and payment of OPEB and required pension contributions. The choice of how to balance these needs is a political one to be decided by voters.

Problems of funding public schools, Medicaid, and pensions were built up over decades and will be solved over decades. Constitutional limitations severely constrain the ability to cut expenditures, and the New Jersey Supreme Court has proven a barrier to fixing the state's budgetary problems.

Section I
Conclusion

Muniland is a much different place now than it was a few years ago. As we continue in this post-recession, uneven-growth environment, there are many unanswered questions and unforeseen risks to state and local governments. The answers to these questions will impact investment decisions for market practitioners and the lives of all Americans.

The upshot of the financial crisis is that governments have been forced to do more with less. Tax revenues are now more volatile. Economic growth is slower, yet entitlement spending is growing. The role of government in the lives of citizens is changing. In the midst of the struggle, the vast majority of rational officials have chosen the prudent path of preserving payments to bondholders in order to maintain continued access to affordable financing and provide services. However, sometimes the political process can subvert rational decision-making. It took a once-in-a-century financial crisis to test the finances of local governments. Their response is a testament to their overall flexibility and willingness to make required budgetary decisions. Problems built up over decades will likely be solved over decades.

Issuers of all types of municipal debt have faced slow growth since the financial crisis, mimicking the broader economy. Changing federal oversight, industry risks, and broader macro factors will all impact credit quality in coming years. Inclusion of the various credit types in a municipal bond portfolio can diversify this risk and provide a natural hedge for municipal bond investors. Most issuers have a monopolistic claim on their service areas; and while it is true that calamitous conditions can lead to an interruption of debt service, selectively, these headline-risk cases have proven to be buying opportunities for investors willing to see beyond the headlines.

Despite hearsay talk about the demise of ratings agencies, they will continue to play a role as information providers and quasi-regulators within the credit markets. As we are getting ready to publish in July 2015, we still have not seen a viable alternative to the credit ratings assigned by the nationally recognized statistical ratings organizations. The same goes for insurers. To predict with certainty an issuer's *willingness* to repay its debts is an almost impossible task, and to predict a financial bubble is even more difficult.[1]

Mistrust in bond insurers is still prevalent as a result of widespread reputational damage growing out of the Great Recession.[2] The insurers' mainstay has been the need to insure bond deals issued by less well-known issuers. Build America Mutual stepped into the market in 2012 to fill this void, but on a much smaller scale than firms with larger books of business, such as National Public Finance Guarantee and Assured Guaranty. We suspect that adherence to the model of low-risk underwriting will be essential for a return of bond insurance to a solid footing in the municipal bond market. The notion that a bond is "AAA-rated and insured" and therefore "I don't need to know any more than that" is outdated.

As we progress beyond the period of austerity and into the second half of the 2010s, new problems present themselves. The near 60% drop in crude oil prices, from the peak of $107 in June 2014 to $44.45 in January 2015, has called into question the ability of oil-producing states to manage revenue declines. The rapidity and extent of this decline was unanticipated by most state budget officers.[3] Those states whose operating budgets are most dependent on oil tax revenues will likely feel the most pain.[4]

Rising entitlements and pension obligations have created a divergence between the states that have effectively dealt with such problems and those that have not.[5] States that have not, such as Illinois and New Jersey, continue to see their finances deteriorate. Market participants and concerned citizens are monitoring reforms as they make their way through legislatures and the courts. Hopefully, our discussion of how we navigated these volatile waters has provided insight into the market's current functioning and given readers confidence in investing in this very important market segment.

Section II

Munis in Real Time—

Lessons on How We Successfully Navigated the Financial Crisis

In Section II of this book, we will discuss the period of 2008 to 2015 through the lens of market commentaries published by professionals at Cumberland Advisors at the time these market events occurred. The purpose is twofold: To describe market impacts in response to these catalysts, rather than just the catalysts themselves; and to provide a view that contrasts with our attempts to "Monday morning quarterback," the market, which we did in Section I. This period marked a sea change in how people view and participate in the municipal bond market. Our goal is to illustrate these transitions by presenting the collective mindset of the marketplace in real-time.

We start in the weeks immediately following the Lehman Brothers bankruptcy with the decline in liquidity that ensued. The closing of bond desks at various dealer firms coupled with selling from hedge funds created a spike in relative yields that has yet to return to normalcy as of the date of this book's publication. From there, we segue into Build America Bonds and the corrective impacts stemming therefrom, starting in April 2009. That Build America Bonds repaired the tax-exempt municipal market from 2009 until 2010 was a major theme that temporarily drove relative muni yields to levels comparable with Treasuries.

Disruptive events occurred along the way: The Gulf oil spill of 2010, Jefferson County, and Puerto Rico headline risk all created confusion and the need for proactive; and in some cases, contrarian decision-making. History rhymes rather than repeats itself, and past is prologue. This section is meant to serve as a guide to readers in their future investment decisions.

16

Municipal Madness Again

John R. Mousseau
October 2, 2008

The municipal bond market has witnessed one of its most dramatic sell-offs in the past three weeks—most of this in the wake of the Lehman Brothers bankruptcy. This has happened as all non-treasury markets have seized up. The capital markets are awaiting the potential bailout plan from Congress, but the municipal (as well as other markets) have backpedaled at breathtaking speed, with yields higher by 75-80 basis points in the past two weeks alone, which translates into price declines of 8-10% this month. Many AA or better rated bonds are trading at 5.75% to 5.85% yields. This is almost 140% of the U.S. Treasury yield, unprecedented in the market, and in the long run unsustainable, in our view. To put the backoff this month in perspective, the Lehman Brothers Long Bond Municipal Index is down 9.9% year-to-date; 8% of this was in the month of September.

The dramatic fall-off can be seen in the chart on page 264. This shows the difference in yields between the Bond Buyer 40, an index of longer, higher-rated, investment-grade, tax-free bonds, published by The Bond Buyer newspaper, and yields on the 30-year U.S. Treasury bond, over the past three years. The normal state of affairs is for tax-free bonds to yield less than Treasury bonds (red area) because of their tax-free nature. That has been turned on its head in a historical proportion. The green area on the graph—with munis yielding more than Treasuries—shows how aggravated this has become this year, and in the last month particularly.

There are a number of reasons for this:

- A LACK OF LIQUIDITY ON WALL STREET. The Lehman bankruptcy sent shock waves through an already fragile credit market, creating much higher short-term yields as well as intermediate to long-term yields. This year has seen the closing of bond departments at Bear Stearns, UBS, and Lehman Brothers (returning as an arm of Barclays), with further reductions by virtue of the merger of Merrill Lynch with Bank of America and Wachovia with Citicorp. This has left retail as the major buyer (though they have started buying).
- HEDGE FUND SELLING. We witnessed this in February, when hedge funds (who buy tax-free bonds with funding based on short-term muni rates) sold non-stop for five days on the heels of the freeze-up in the auction-rate market. We have seen much more of this in the wake of the Lehman bankruptcy as short-term rates have skyrocketed. Thus bonds have been sold into a market with no bid.
- THE DOWNGRADES OF MOST OF THE BOND INSURERS. This has been by Moody's and Standard and Poor's in response to the insurers' insuring of mortgage-backed pools that have fallen in value. Because there have been some defaults in these pools, many of the insurers have not put up the capital that Moody's and S&P have requested; some of the insurers, FGIC and CIFG, were downgraded to below investment-grade; and Ambac and MBIA, the stalwarts of municipal bond insurance, were downgraded in June, losing their AAA status and being put on watch for further downgrades. This has made the market look at only underlying ratings.
- THE BANKS ARE NOT HOLDERS OF MUNIS BECAUSE OF THE TAX CODE. The tax economics keep them from buying anything that isn't bank qualified, so they don't have inventories of munis to use as collateral pledges with the Fed. Hence the muni market is a degree removed from other debt markets when it comes to the Fed's liquidity provision. Therefore it is not getting any help from the Fed's policies

We believe the tax-free bond market is at the cheapest level it has been since early 2000. On a relative basis it is the cheapest it has ever been. Intermediate and longer tax-free bond yields have moved above their averages for the past 20 years. We feel it is the most OVERSOLD it has been in a generation and represents incredible value.

What are some of the factors that will bring the main market into a degree of normalcy over time?

- DIRECT RETAIL BUYING. This has been picking up speed, and we expect it to continue to accelerate.
- CROSSOVER BUYING. This is purchasing by nontraditional municipal bond buyers such as pension plans, charitable foundations, and state and local governments. They realize that muni safety is second only to Treasuries and that in short-term paper there are yields HIGHER than they can buy in the taxable markets, while in the longer end the tremendous RELATIVE value offered by tax-free bonds will show good performance as the two markets eventually return to a normal relationship.
- FUTURE INCOME TAX INCREASES. With the financing of the bailout plan and a lowering revenue stream to the U.S. Government, whoever is elected President is most likely faced with raising the marginal federal income tax rate. Right now, with many longer yields above 5.5%, this translates into roughly 8.5% on a taxable equivalent basis. And in higher-tax states this taxable equivalent approaches 9% when state taxes are taken into effect. This certainly approaches long-term equity returns
- CASH HITTING the MARKET. Many firms are settling with clients who have had funds invested in short-term, closed-end, preferred auction-rate securities, which froze up last February. This amount could be in the $30-40 billion dollar range and will be available over the next month or two. With interest rates presumably higher by 75 to 85 basis points in only a few weeks, this will attract investment.

At Cumberland we are using this extraordinary opportunity to improve call protection on portfolios, achieve some tax-loss swapping now, and lock up yields which we have not seen in many years.

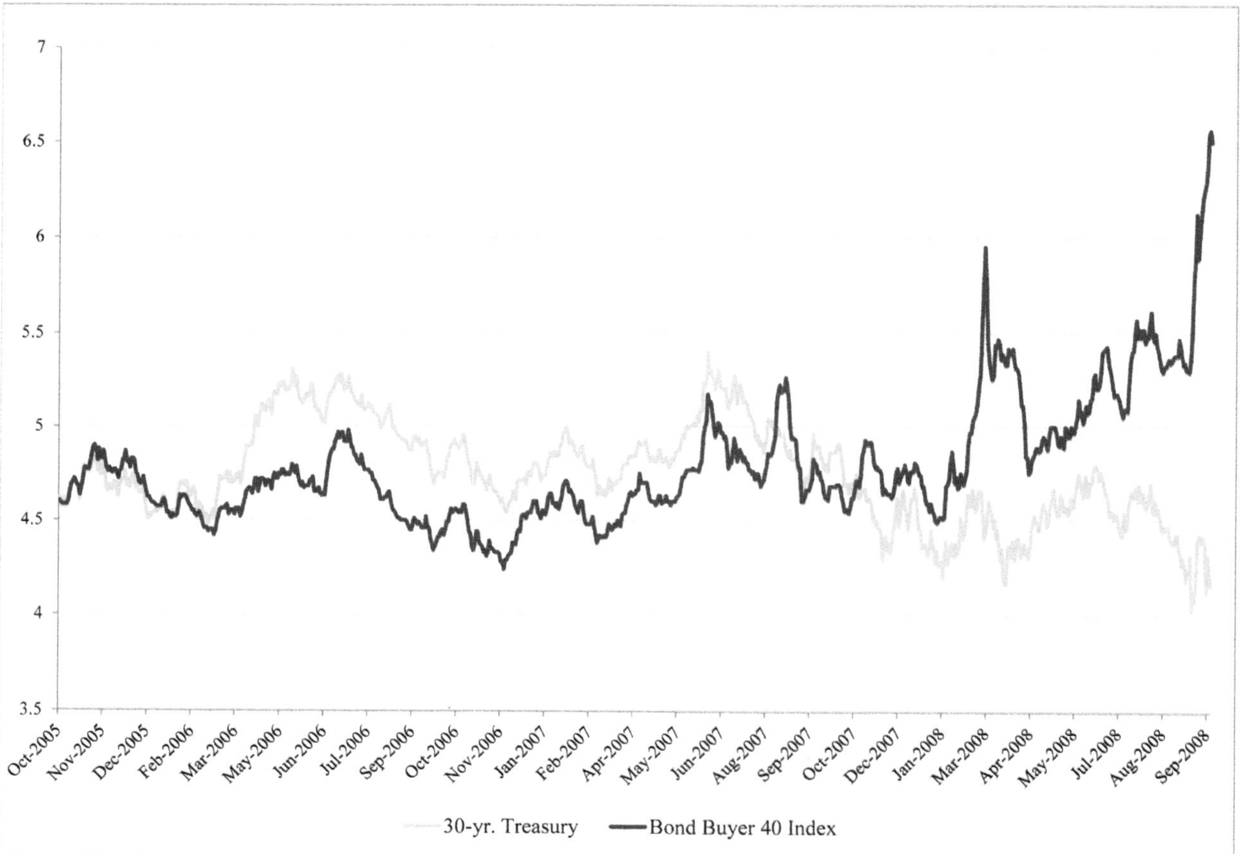

Source: Bloomberg

17

Big Changes in Muniland

David R. Kotok
April 19, 2009

Big changes are coming in Muniland. This commentary is the first in a series about them.

It used to be that all investors had to think about when they considered municipal bonds was whether they were AAA-insured and whether or not they were traditional tax-free or subject to the Alternative Minimum Tax (AMT). Those good old days are long gone.

AAA bond insurance has been severely discredited. Investors now realize that they were buying into an unsecured creditor status on an opaque structure. That realization and the subsequent losses they experienced first led them to be averse to most municipal risk; hence, there was a flight from all munis. Subsequently, as they have returned to Muniland, they realize that they need more than casual help. For firms like Cumberland this has been a huge boost to our value-added business proposition.

Other changes in Muniland are already affecting pricing and terms of new muni issues. Banks have received a benefit through recent legislation and now may own up to 2% of assets in non-bank-qualified municipal bonds. Previously banks were essentially restricted to bank-qualified bonds (BQ) only. These are small Issues which are customarily placed with banks by local government units. Banks are allowed to own BQ debt because of an exception to an interest-rate penalty in the tax law that was originally passed in 1986. The 2009 law change has had the effect of encouraging some banks to expand their portfolios of tax-free municipal bonds. Cumberland has developed a service designed for banks that seek to optimize their profits using this new law.

Another important and dramatic change is in the Build America bond program. Here the federal government is agreeing to pay 35% of the interest cost on a municipal bond, under certain conditions. The issuer pays the other 65%, and the bond is subject to federal income taxation.

This means new issuers of bonds must consider both taxable and tax-free structures. We are seeing the first Build America bond issues come to market. So far the economic tests have encouraged the use of taxable Build America municipal debt under this program as a substitute for what would previously have been tax-free municipal debt. We expect this program to precipitate a huge change in the $2.7 trillion municipal bond market.

Build America program bonds also operate as a boost to Cumberland. We have used taxable municipal bonds for years as a form of fixed-income management. Peter Demirali has capably led that sector in the firm, while John Mousseau has been the point person on the tax-free municipal bond side. They get the credit for the successes; my job is to be responsible for the errors.

Build America now means we are busier than ever in both categories. We have to examine this program and the options for both taxable fixed-income and tax-free fixed-income clients. And the tax bracket of each individual affects the decision since the Build America federally mandated arbitrage rate is 35%, while the taxpayer's marginal rate is variable.

Build America structures are different than traditional tax-free ones. One example is in debt service (DS) reserve funding. Taxable Build America bonds fund their DS reserves under tax-free rules. Traditional tax-free municipal bonds are allowed to fund DS with borrowed moneys but are subject to complex arbitrage rebate rules. Bonds with DS are sometimes viewed as more secure than those without them. This trade-off needs to be examined issue-by-issue.

Retention of a state income tax-free nature while being taxed at the federal level is another issue for Cumberland to examine. In many cases a Build America bond can be exempted from state income tax even as the federal tax is imposed. This nuance is sometimes material in choosing one form of bond over the other.

There are many more details about the new Muniland. We will be explaining them to readers over the next few months.

Suffice it to say that the landscape of the municipal bond arena is rapidly changing. Valuation of bonds and credit review requires much attention these days. The lazy days when investors could make decisions on AAA-insured tax-free bonds with no homework needed are over. Municipal bonds have morphed into an asset class that requires a full effort.

Anyone who thought bonds were boring is being proven wrong. It has become an exciting time in Muniland.

18

Moody's, Munis, and Cousin BABs

David R. Kotok
August 16, 2009

In their August 13 "Special Comment" Moody's outlined the current condition of the state budgets and of the various revenue sectors like airports, toll roads, higher education facilities, and hospitals. Nearly two years into a recession, the report is not pleasant reading.

Expenditure budgets are being cut. Tax receipts continue to arrive below projections, which necessitates further budget cuts. A downward spiral seems to be underway. The muni sector appears to be in a depression.

In part, the damage to state and local budgets has been blunted by huge federal stimulus. This is viewed as temporary by government finance officers, since they must attempt to balance their budgets and may only count on federal assistance that is funded. The term "funded" means that they have the money in hand or will definitely receive it so that they can pay the bills. Thus unfunded items do not count even though they may be anticipated.

Forward-looking projections for municipal bond issuers are truly bleak. They show reduced revenues based on the most current projections of economic weakness. Tax receipts are forecast at extreme recession levels. These budgets do not include any unfunded federal help. Projections are based on all federal programs expiring as determined by present law. Credit ratings by Moody's and other agencies are based on these worst case scenarios, which is why so many issuers are on credit watch or have been downgraded.

Direct payments are one form of help from the feds to the states and locals. Indirect forms are another. Build America Bonds (BAB) are an example of the indirect form. When certain qualifications are met, the federal government will reimburse the state or local issuer 35% of the interest cost on BABs issued in 2009 and 2010. The current law that authorized BABs expires after 2010. No one knows if Congress will extend it; hence, local government savings from using BABs is not projected after 2010.

In 2009, between $60 billion and $80 billion of BABs will be issued as taxable fixed-income securities; these are substitute issues for what would normally be tax-free munis. Buyers of these new instruments include tax-deferred accounts like pensions or IRAs in the U.S. and various foreign investors who find the yields on BABs attractive. Neither of these bond-investor groups would be interested in lower-yielding tax-free munis, since they are not paying taxes to the U.S. government. But they are seizing the opportunity to own BABs.

A secondary effect of BABs is to put downward pressure on tax-free yields in the seasoned bond market as well as in the new-issue Muni markets. Tax-free munis have to compete against BABs. Issuers make the choice between the two based on the net cost to them. Since the BABs subsidy is 35% of the interest cost, the downward pressure of this "tax arbitrage" has pushed tax-free muni yields substantially lower than what they were only 6 months ago.

In the shorter-term maturities, tax-free muni yields are now about 65% of the taxable reference. In other words, this section of the muni market has been fully corrected. The tax arbitrage is 100% returned. There has been a full compression of the extraordinary spreads that were reached at the pinnacle of the financial crisis.

Readers may remember the collapse period of municipal finance when the weekly floating-rate resetting instrument issued by the Port of NY and NJ had a failed auction, which spiked the yield to 20%. That's right 20%, tax-free federally and in NJ and NY. That probably marked the absolute extreme of tax-free muni market dysfunction. Today, similar paper yields a fraction of 1%.

While very short-term munis are back to normal at about 65% of Treasury yields, intermediate-term munis are rapidly restoring their more traditional spreads that are based on the tax arbitrage. They are down to the 70% to 80% of Treasury yields depending on the state and maturity.

At the longer end of the muni curve (30 years) the tax arbitrage is still not restored, although it has been correcting from the extremes reached last year. Many very high-grade muni issues are available at yields above 100% of the referenced U.S. Treasury security. It the pinnacle these munis were yielding as much as 150% of Treasury reference yields.

In the case of some issues this unusually high yield is due to the questions about creditworthiness. But credit quality is not the only reason for this mispricing. Hence, opportunity exists in the good credits which are also mispriced for other than credit worthiness reasons.

We can make this statement and back it up because we are still seeing federally backed housing agency tax-free bonds trading at tax-free yields above their Treasury yield reference. In this muni sub-sector case we are comparing a taxable U.S. Treasury bond with a tax-free state housing agency bond that has federal backing. The credit support is the same government of the United States and is dependent on the U.S. government's ability to pay. Since the U.S. has unlimited capacity to pay U.S. dollars because it can finance them with the assistance of the Federal Reserve, the markets deem U.S. obligations as riskless when it comes to default.

So why shouldn't the tax-free rate be substantially lower than the taxable rate? There are several contributing factors to this anomaly. Those factors help explain why this is a great opportunity for investors.

First, only the 20 million or so high-bracket American taxpayers are the typical buyers of tax-free munis. They have other investment options like stocks, real estate, gold, foreign currencies, etc. Since the financial crisis, many of them have large capital loss carry-forwards; that means they can obtain capital gains on future investments without federal income taxation. Tax-free munis have a competitor when cap gains are untaxed. At Cumberland we are structuring some specific hedged muni accounts designed to seize this opportunity that the market is currently providing.

Secondly, many of those same Americans were hurt in the market crash period and are insecure about any investment. That is why the cash hoards are huge by traditional standards.

Thirdly, the tax-free muni sector was not a direct recipient of any of the special tools that the Federal Reserve used to restore credit-market functionality. The Fed is focused on the banking system. The banks have restrictions when it comes to tax-free muni holdings, so the Fed's liquidity injections did not reach to the tax-free muni world as easily as they have to other sectors like commercial paper or Fannie Mae mortgages.

Lastly, traditional retail muni conduits like closed-end funds were discredited by the payment problems associated with the adjustable-rate preferreds. Many investors were hurt, and this sector is still in the process of a longer-term workout. Litigation over the disclosures surrounding the preferreds is underway. The result is that buyer support for closed-end muni funds evaporated during the crisis.

Other forms of tax-free muni mutual funds have costs associated with them and are not conducive to large, separately managed accounts, in our view. Bond ETFs also have characteristics which we, and other skilled managers, find unattractive. The bottom line is that the major source of funds for the longer-term tax-free muni market remains the very wealthy or high-tax-bracket American taxpayers who are allocating money to this sector. That is why long-term tax-free munis are still cheap.

Cumberland has been a total-return muni manager for decades. John Mousseau, an owner-manager, heads that section of the firm. We also have a long-term history of using taxable municipal bonds. It was established years before BABs existed. Peter Demirali, an owner-manager, leads that taxable muni effort. Both asset classes are growing rapidly.

The financial crisis, which harmed other sectors of markets, spurred record growth for Cumberland. Our tax-free and taxable separately managed account business has reached all-time records in assets under management, numbers of clients, and institutional consulting portfolios under review. Cumberland's employment is at a record level. Our firm is expanding.

In sum, market cycles over the last decade featured the tech stock bubble and NASDAQ correction of a few years ago, followed by a bull stock market that peaked in October, 2007. The subsequent collapse of markets and the crash after the Lehman Brothers failure has damaged financial markets and the economy. Years of recovery time will be required to correct them.

During this crisis period, tax-free and taxable municipal bonds suffered terrible damage that had no precedent in the post-World War II period. They reached astronomical yields at the extreme. They are still cheap for reasons outlined above. So we are very active and look forward to more growth. It has been and will continue to be a very busy time.

I thank my friend and client of many years, Michael K, for prodding me to write this commentary.

19

The MAGI Returns to Muniland

David R. Kotok
March 6, 2010

There are mixed forces impacting the valuation of municipal bonds. Some are muni-favorable; they get little respect these days. Some are muni-bad; they engender fear in bond buyers. One of the bad ones (MAGI) is obscure but poses a risk down the road.

Muni-favorable forces include the fact that higher income tax rates are destined to occur. Taxes are certainly not going to go down. Huge deficit spending implies they will be up. The math is easy. The higher the tax rates go in the future, the more desirable tax-free municipal bonds are to high income-tax-bracket investors.

Polling among the 25 to 30 million wealthy Americans whose incomes are high enough to justify the ownership of tax-free bonds confirms this view. Almost all of them believe that income-tax rates will be higher two years from now than they are today. Virtually none believe they will be lower. There are only a few who think tax rates will be unchanged.

If any of the political proposals about taxes come to pass, the top income-tax rates in the United States will become the highest in most Americans' experience. Some proposals take those tax rates up substantially; others take them up in lesser amounts. Under nearly every scenario the highest U.S. marginal-rate brackets will be above 50%, second only to Denmark and about equal to Sweden. Remember that the Alternative Minimum Tax (AMT) raises the marginal rates above the maximum stated in the code because it removes the deductibility of state income taxes and blocks other deductions. Thus the marginal rate goes higher. We believe the income-tax hikes coming to the United States make the strongest case in decades for owning tax-free municipal bonds.

The Build America Bonds (BAB) program acts to compress interest rates on tax-free bonds. The program is a confirmed success. It is in its second year of operation. There are proposals in the Congress to extend it and make it permanent. Under the current BAB program, bonds are issued by state and local government units for certain types of projects. 35% of the interest payment of the local issuer is reimbursed by the federal government, so the net interest cost to the issuer is 65% of the taxable bond interest rate.

Most of the new-issue BAB underwritings are now done on a negotiated dual-track scale in which the underwriters compare the taxable fixed-income market with the tax-free fixed income market; they do this at each maturity in the new-issue scale. They then elect the choices that are the least costly to the issuer. The procedures for these new bond issuances are now well established. Well over $100 billion of BABs will be issued in 2010.

The impact is to take that $100 billion away from issuance in the tax-free municipal bond market and move it to the taxable market via the BABs. For the issuer of municipal bonds that opens up a whole new set of bond buyers, including pension funds and eleemosynary institutions. For the high-tax-bracket individual investor, that means there is a developing and growing scarcity of tax-free bonds. The scarcity can cause tax-free bond interest rates to fall relative to taxable ones. We see that spread-tightening trade continuing all year.

Relatively fewer tax-free municipal bonds mean lower interest rates and higher prices for them, since the set of bond buyers remains unchanged. So BAB helps compress and lower tax-free interest rates. The evidence overwhelmingly supports that conclusion.

Muni-bad forces come from two areas.

The first is concern about their creditworthiness. Bond insurers have been downgraded or eliminated from the game, rating agencies and their ratings of municipal bonds are suspect, and the typical bond buyer has now experienced both of those negatives. In the old days and for decades, municipal bond buyers thought they only needed to know that a bond was triple-A rated and insured. Beyond that, they paid very little attention to the underlying credit qualities of the issuer. Most investors actually ignored the issue itself.

Those days are gone. Clearly, a lot more research work has to be done on munis. At the same time, the underwriters and the distributors of municipal bonds have been injured by the difficulties established in some of the closed-end mutual funds and by the lack of capital in the system. That combination has made munis very, very cheap. In the crisis period tax-free municipal bond interest rates were well over 100% of their corresponding taxable U.S. Treasury interest-rate references.

In the intermediate end of the yield curve, that is no longer the case. At the ten-year maturity, that percentage test is now in the high 80s or 90s, and varies with market conditions. It has been gradually restoring to normalcy. We expect that to continue and to see the percentage reach the high 70s to low 80s. Those are the established standards in which tax-free high-grade municipal bonds would trade at interest rates well below 100% of taxable federal government debt rates and consistent with a tax arbitrage of the income-tax brackets.

In the very long end of the yield curve, the resumption to normalcy is still underway but has far to go. Recent high investment-grade tax-free municipal bond issuance is still being priced above 100% of the corresponding Treasuries. This has spawned a management style in which those who fear a forthcoming rise in all interest rates are able to hedge their tax-free bonds with derivative-structured exchange-traded funds (ETFs). They give up a portion of the income but protect themselves from parallel interest-rate shifts in the yield curve. There's a trade-off involved—less income for more safety—and some larger and more sophisticated investors are electing to take that trade-off. At Cumberland, we now have tens of millions in this type of separate account structure.

Notwithstanding the desirability of tax-free munis, the public fear-mongering about defaults continues to keep tax-free municipal bond interest rates higher than they would otherwise be. This creates a distortion in the market and has many observers, bond buyers, and investment-oriented agents painting tax-free municipal bonds with a very broad brush. So it is common now to see fear-mongering headlines that essentially say all state and local government bonds are bad, all of them are going to default, and that the financial crisis and the deficits are destroying all public budgets.

Such a drastic, sweeping conclusion is a mistake. It clearly violates any understanding of state and local government finance and budgeting. There's a vast difference between an incinerator in Harrisburg that may have been poorly contemplated and the water company in Cleveland or the turnpike in New Jersey. There are tens of thousands of state and local government credits in the United States; the total asset class is approximately $2.8 trillion dollars. The one thing we know with certainty is that we are not going to have $2.8 trillion dollars of state and local government bonds, issued by 60,000 different governmental entities, all default. Simply put: it ain't gonna happen. Fear-mongering is making the buying opportunity in tax-free munis available to those investors smart enough to seize it.

The forthcoming California General Obligation tax-free bond issue is a good example of how fear-mongering has impacted pricing to an extreme. The CA issue is expected to come at a 6% tax-free interest rate for the long maturity. For a taxpaying individual that is worth 9.23% if you are in 35% bracket, 9.93% if you are pushed into the 39.6% bracket contemplated under present law, and above 10% if you are in a high CA state tax bracket and over 11% if you are in the worst case as a CA taxpayer and also in the AMT.

Compare this with the experience in Greece where the latest euro denominated Greek bond yields a little over 6%. Note that Greece and California have similar credit ratings. CA is a baa1 by one rating service and an A by another.

The last issue, which is a negative for tax-free bonds, comes through the development of an insidious change in the tax code. Here we come to the term "MAGI." We have examined a case study with one of our clients who called this to our attention. MAGI is the acronym for "modified adjusted gross income." Many are familiar with term "adjusted gross income." It's a concept they see and utilize every year as they prepare their income taxes. They understand how their accountants derive an adjusted gross income to be used with the IRS.

MAGI is the technique the federal government is now using in the pricing of Medicare Part B (medical insurance) premiums. Using MAGI to determine what an individual's Medicare premium will be enables the government to alter the premium with means testing. This is an indirect form of taxation. Part of the calculation of MAGI is to add back tax-free municipal bond interest to the taxpayer's other income in order to determine what their Medicare Part B premium will be.

At the present time, the submission of information on tax-free income is voluntary and on the honor system. Reporting systems are not fully in place yet, so that 1099s revealing tax-free interest received are not set up to convey this detail to the Internal Revenue Service and other agencies.

We expect that to change and a reporting system to eventually be in place so that all interest from tax-free municipal bonds will be reported and used by the government in the calculation of various means-tested facilities and government services. That is the first step towards raising the prices of those services so that individuals who have very large tax-free bond portfolios will find themselves having to add back the tax-free interest in order to determine how much they have to pay, or how much the federal government will charge them for a particular health insurance service. Imagination can quickly take this to where it may lead as an indirect form of taxation on the higher-taxed individual American taxpayer.

The long-term implication is an attack on tax-free bond interest, and the politics of that attack by populist governments who develop such rhetoric are obvious. The indications, though, are that the present ownership of tax-free municipal bonds, if they are attacked, would be grandfathered. That, too, could add to a scarcity premium in the future and make them even more valuable.

We realize that this last item is speculative on our part. The Obama Administration and Congress have not indicated that they are going to remove the tax-free municipal bond from the American security environment. There hasn't been a discussion of elimination of the tax-free municipal bond for years. But the introduction of Build America Bonds, which compresses municipal interest rates, and the development of the concept of MAGI both suggest that some future political pressure could be applied in ways that would reduce or eliminate the issuance of tax-free municipal bonds in some future period of time.

For now, the composition, pricing, and desirability of tax-free municipal bonds are paramount and well-established for those who are in higher federal income-tax brackets, and for those who are in states whose income taxes play a major role in the economics of the state. Tax-free municipal bonds are currently cheap. Taxable BABs are, too. Both represent very good values in the bond market. The returns on them are still not restored to the valuations that were in place before the financial crisis ensued.

Additionally, the electronic credit-reporting system that is now in place for state and local governments, and the lack of municipal bond insurance, have added to the creditworthiness of existing and new-issue municipal bonds, because successful new issues and offerings have been scrutinized in much greater detail by bond buyers and by their investment professionals. The old days of depending on the rating agencies and the bond insurers are gone. That's good for the bond buyer who understands the level of professionalism needed in this asset sector.

And this is also good for the managed tax-free municipal bond account where the homework has been done on the credits. For Cumberland these developments have meant back-to-back record growth years, an expanded staff, record assets under management, and an enlarged institutional consultation business.

It took a financial crisis, rating agency failure, bond insurer demise, and Lehman's bankruptcy to get the sleepy, boring tax-free municipal bond out from under the Rodney Dangerfield syndrome. We made it. Tax-free munis and BABs now get some respect.

20

The Oil Spill and the Municipal Bond Market

John R. Mousseau
August 12, 2010

It has been over three months since the beginning of the oil spill in the Gulf of Mexico. Since then it has cost billions of dollars in terms of lost jobs, tourism, and the battering that local fishing industries have had to endure.

At Cumberland Advisors, we have written about the impact in the Gulf region and on the country as a whole in our "Oil Slickonomics" series.

We have also written about the potential impact of the oil spill as it relates to the municipal bond market. We have concerns on a long-term basis regarding debt-service coverage on already issued bonds that depend on tourism-derived sales taxes or usage taxes from bridges or roads leading to the affected areas. We also had concerns in regard to the potential damage that the oil spill could cause to drinking water and aquifers near affected areas, especially if the oil spill and its movement were to be exacerbated by tropical storms. To this list of concerns, we would now add the current moratorium on well drilling, an economic hammer that will inflict even more damage on already beleaguered Gulf Coast economies.

We took a proactive stance on this. Cumberland Advisors selectively sold about 40 different issues of bonds that we thought might face negative repercussions from the Gulf disaster. The reason for this action was simple. Where good market bids could be achieved, we could take the proceeds of these sales and invest in similarly structured bonds and diversify away from the POTENTIAL risk without an impact on yield to portfolios. Since then we have watched the gushing well that has just been capped, the expanding slick of oil across the Gulf, and a municipal bond market that has not changed greatly vis-à-vis the oil slick. Clearly this will be an evolving story that will depend on cleanup efforts, nature's recuperative powers, tropical storm formation for the balance of the hurricane season, and consumer confidence as it relates to tourism and the seafood industry.

Cumberland is joining the Global Interdependence Center this week in a conference in Baton Rouge, Louisiana, focused on the oil spill and its effects on fishing, tourism, state and local governments, and present and future environmental concerns. We will use this event as a launching point for a renewed look at the Gulf region, the impact on the municipal bond market in general, and the Gulf municipal credits in particular.

21

The Harrisburg Mess—Second Inning

John R. Mousseau
September 14, 2010

The city of Harrisburg received a "Hail Mary" pass this weekend when the Commonwealth of Pennsylvania stepped in to prevent the city from defaulting on its general obligation bonds, on which $3.3 million of payments is due September 15th.

The commonwealth is "fast-tracking" payments to Harrisburg, which include payments for fire protection as well as pensions. The payments also include funds that will allow the city to hire a Chicago-based consulting firm that will help the city reduce its debt. City council members discussed the possibility of declaring bankruptcy earlier this month. That step is very rare in municipal finance in the United States.

We believe this proactive approach by the state, though slow in developing, was correct. The ramifications of missing payments on general obligation debt by an issuer of Harrisburg's size would stretch beyond just the city. They would impact central Pennsylvania towns and cities in general, and indeed, a case can be made that all issuers in Pennsylvania—including the commonwealth itself—would be hurt by paying higher interest rates on their own debt in the municipal bond market. There are certainly precedents for this in the bond market; e.g., New York issuers paid higher interest rates after New York City missed payments on some its notes in the mid-1970s, and municipalities in the state of Washington paid higher than normal interest rates for years after the fiasco of the Washington Public Power Supply System (WPPSS) in the mid-1980s.

The city came to this crossroads by building an incinerator plant, which ended up way over budget, saddling the city with $280 million in debt. The city stopped making payments on the incinerator debt earlier this year. Much of this debt is now being paid by bond insurers and by Dauphin County. This week Assured Guaranty, one of the bond insurers, and Dauphin County have asked in court to have a receiver appointed to collect the payments for the incinerator and also to get a court order forcing Harrisburg to levy taxes sufficient to pay the incinerator debt.

We have no doubt that if Harrisburg were to miss payments on their general obligation debt, Ambac insurance, which insures parts of the city's general obligation debt, would seek relief in the courts to compel Harrisburg to raise taxes and sell assets to pay their debt. Indeed, the consultant that the city is hiring can be expected to propose the sale or lease of municipal assets in Harrisburg to cover their general obligation debt service. This could include parking facilities and utilities. We may witness the privatization of municipal services under duress. Most municipal services are priced in a "political" pricing system. Privatized municipal assets will be priced in a more efficient "economic" pricing system.

Clearly, this is just the beginning, but the commonwealth's efforts certainly should be seen in a positive light. The focus will now shift to the political turmoil between Mayor Linda Thompson of Harrisburg and the city council, which has, so far, balked at raising taxes. The council is still one member short of a quorum that it needs to legally act on the present situation.

Cumberland Advisors has steered clear of Harrisburg's debt, but we are monitoring this situation. From a trading perspective, we believe it does have implications for central Pennsylvania credits.

22

The Spike in Muni Yields—An Opportunity

John R. Mousseau
November 16, 2010

The tax-free bond market has been hit with a spike in long-maturity yields, bringing yields to their highest level of the year. Long-maturity tax-free yields have risen 40-50 basis points and many longer high-quality bonds are now yielding more than 5%. And this has all happened in less than two weeks. How did it happen?

In a perfect storm of events, long tax-free bond yields have been pushed higher by three factors:

1. Higher long-term Treasury yields. The thirty-year U.S. Treasury bond moved from 3.98% to 4.40% yesterday (November 15th). Most of this was related to the Federal Reserve's plan for Quantitative Easing and the proposed makeup of the Fed buying. Most purchases would be in the intermediate area and not in the long maturities. Since then, long Treasury yields have skyrocketed and long tax-free yields have followed along.

2. Build America Bonds (BABs) have NOT been authorized beyond year-end. There has been a Senate proposal to extend BABs authorization through the end of 2011, albeit with a lower subsidy rate of 32% instead of the current 35%. If the lame duck session of Congress does not pass extension, this will have to wait

to be addressed by the new Congress, which may or may not pass extension. The newly elected Republican majority in the House of Representatives lowers the odds of BABs extension, in the eyes of the market. Thus, BABs supply has increased greatly as issuers try to beat the year-end deadline. Higher BABs yields means LESS downward pressure on tax-free yields since the after-subsidy cost (yield) for BABs issuers is lower than for tax-free yields.

3. Higher tax-free supply. Tax-free issuers who have issues that are not BABs-eligible (refunding bonds, general-purpose bonds) have moved up their issuance to the present instead of first quarter 2011. Their reasoning is that without BABS there will be a big shift back to tax-exempt supply; therefore, they are moving up their issues. The effect has been self-fulfilling, as the supply has overwhelmed the market, forcing yields higher. The chart below shows tax-free visible supply, which was trending downward the entire year up to the last two months—it has been clearly affected by the BABs effect.

There are four reasons why we think this is a terrific opportunity:

1. This has not been credit-driven. This is long-maturity bonds following Treasury yields higher, and driven by the confluence of uncertainty regarding BABs legislation and the resulting supply bulge. This is not inflation-driven. Twelve-month trailing inflation is 1.1%.

2. In a world where a thirty-year Treasury is 4.35 to 4.40%, a long, high-quality tax-free bond yielding 5% is a taxable-equivalent yield of almost 7.7%. It is much higher when state taxes are also figured in. And many high-quality issues are trading cheaper than 5%.

3. The normal December and January demand from reinvestment and maturing and called bonds could be in the $35-40 billion area. That is in front of us. A lot of first-quarter supply is being pushed into this quarter. That will be behind us. And there is certainly a chance that Congress does extend BABs, albeit at a lower subsidy rate.

4. If longer Treasury yields continue to climb and tax-free yields eventually return to some degree of normalcy versus Treasuries (as happened in April of this year), there is the chance for many 5.50 to 6.50% coupons to be pre-refunded by their issuers. Cushion bonds have been beat up in this market, as well, and offer very compelling values. We believe this is the best opportunity in over a year for long maturity tax-free bonds, and are acting accordingly.

In summary, this is the cheapest that tax-free bonds have been in over a year. This is driven by factors that are unrelated to normal bond market movements such as inflation, employment, etc. We believe this is the best opportunity in over a year and are acting accordingly.

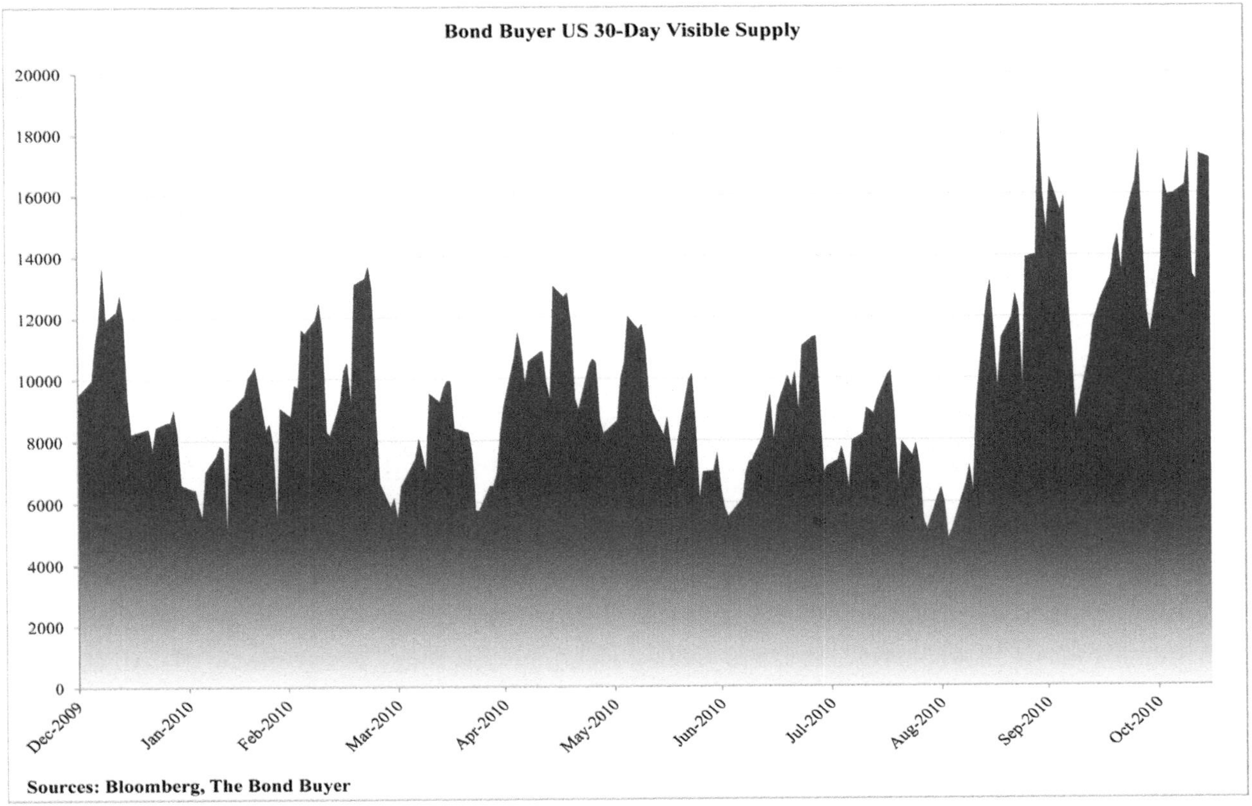

23

Muni Defaults—Whitney and Roubini

David R. Kotok
March 26, 2011

The rule on staying alive as a forecaster is to give 'em a number or give 'em a date, but never give 'em both at once.

—Jane Bryant Quinn
Reader's Digest, 1 Dec. 1980

Meredith Whitney broke the rule. This now haunts her to the point that she declined to appear before a Congressional committee that wanted to discuss muni default issues. Nouriel Roubini is a skilled economist. He knows this rule. He, therefore, used modifiers to adhere to it.

Let's talk about Whitney's forecast first. With great media fanfare, she predicted "50 to 100" sizable muni defaults, totaling about $100 billion, in 2011. That is correct: she said this year. The year in which the economy is in some sort of recovery and when the interest rate is held near zero by the Fed.

Ms. Whitney did not know about any oil shock when she made this forecast. While the current MENA turmoil is a serious new development, the resulting oil price shock will not help her be right in her forecast. In our view, there is nearly zero chance that there will be 50 to 100 sizable muni defaults amounting to $100 billion in the calendar year of 2011.

Nouriel Roubini suggested that there may be "close to $100 billion of defaults over five years, but typical 80% recoveries are far higher than on corporate bonds." Nouriel outlined his view of trouble in the muni world and attempted to measure the exposure in a very thoughtful way. He noted that most of the bonds he expected to default were in the high-yield or junk-bond category. His base-case estimate of defaults over five years for the investment-grade sector was under $30 billion, with "ultimate recovery" of nearly all the losses. Nouriel reminds us that "governments cannot be liquidated" like corporations.

Bloomberg's Joe Mysak observed the following about Roubini:

> *And so noted doomsayer Nouriel Roubini joins the numerous commentators who have opined about the municipal bond market, the most famous, of course, being Meredith Whitney, who in December on the CBS show '60 Minutes" blurted out the prediction that there would be 'hundreds of billions" of municipal bond defaults in 2011. That $100 billion estimate from the Roubini firm isn't in the same league as the Whitney call. What's more, it may not be so outrageous, depending upon how you count defaults. The record year for municipal bond defaults was 2008, when 167 issues totaling $8.5 billion went bust, according to the Distressed Debt Securities Newsletter. In 2009, more municipal bonds defaulted, 207, on a lower dollar amount, $7.3 billion. In 2010, 82 deals failed to pay on $2.7 billion in bonds. The $100 billion over the next five years isn't outside the realm of possibility. How are you counting? The people at Distressed Debt Securities, who have been doing it for decades now and who are the only ones with a historical database over that time, and who use a consistent methodology in their approach, count new defaults only in their calculations, which I think is the correct way to do it. Some analysts, scanning the daily material event notices at the Municipal Securities Rulemaking Board's EMMA web site, count all notices of default that are posted by issuers. And by doing it that way, by counting bonds that are already in default, you can come up with many more billions of dollars in defaulted municipals every year. That's because it takes years to cure some of these things. In the case of so-called dirt-bonds, used to finance infrastructure improvements to real estate developments, for example, bondholders have to wait until the real estate is foreclosed upon and sold before they see any end to their money woes. Dirt bonds are the overwhelming majority of those that have defaulted over the past few years. The same long wait is true for bonds used to build speculative projects like toll roads, or de-inking mills, or aquariums, or any of the other various quixotic stuff that has been financed in the municipal market. Actual*

municipalities, that is, cities and counties, rarely default on their obligations. When they do, they usually cure them in pretty short order, in months if not weeks. Jefferson County, Alabama, which defaulted on almost $4 billion in sewer debt several years ago, is an outlier. If history is a guide, it probably will remain so. So, $100 billion over five years? That's the headline number. It's not impossible, especially if you count continuing defaults. Still, that's quite a crystal ball.

We believe it is important for readers to understand the term default. Here is the official definition from the Municipal Securities Rulemaking Board (MSRB). Remember, bondholders are concerned about monetary defaults. Non-monetary defaults are important because they tell you about the management of the organization or its political structure. These non-monetary defaults actually can provide a bond buyer with opportunity for a bargain if he is willing to do the homework.

DEFAULT—A failure to pay principal of or interest on a bond when due or a failure to comply with any other covenant, promise or duty imposed by the bond contract. The most serious event of default, sometimes referred to as a 'monetary' default, occurs when the issuer fails to pay principal, interest, or both, when due. Other defaults, sometimes referred to as 'technical' defaults, result when specifically defined events of default occur, such as failure to maintain covenants. Technical defaults may include failing to charge rates sufficient to meet rate covenants, failing to maintain insurance on the project or failing to fund various reserves. If the issuer defaults in the payment of principal, interest, or both, or if a technical default is not cured within a specified period of time, the bondholders or trustee may exercise legally available rights and remedies for enforcement of the bond contract.

MSRB reported a Fact Book on the hundreds of thousands of items and on the 10.5 million muni trades for 2010. There were 371 disclosures of a principal & interest delinquency; these involved 1951 securities. The overwhelming majority of them were in project-specific or otherwise non-rated or "junk" bonds. So if you count them on the default list, the list gets bigger.

Does that mean you have to buy any of these bonds? Certainly not. Does delinquency mean an actual monetary default will occur? Maybe yes, maybe no. Each case is different.

When it comes to actual defaults in 2011, the statistics, so far, are improving. "Municipal-bond defaults in the first two months of 2011 are down 50 percent from the same period last year, Standard & Poor's said. Eight bond deals totaling about $222 million have entered default this year, compared with 16 totaling more than $329 million during the same period of 2010," said J.R. Rieger, vice-president of fixed-income indexes for S&P in New York (Bloomberg, March 4).

The media has been filled with talk about municipal bankruptcy. This is a serious subject, of course. But it, too, has been overblown. Evidence from the 2008 Vallejo, California bankruptcy demonstrated how costly this is for a city or county. Vallejo has spent nearly $10 million so far and has nothing to show for it. The Bond Buyer, a trade publication, reports that "Vallejo bonds backed by non-general fund revenues amount to $62 million of debt. They have been paid in full and on time throughout the bankruptcy proceeding. They include securities with dedicated income streams including water revenue bonds, tax allocation bonds, and assessment and improvement district bonds."

So far, in 2011, there has been just one Chapter 9 filing. Bloomberg reported it:

> *Boise County, Idaho, with a population of about 7,450, filed for bankruptcy, making it the first U.S. municipality to file Chapter 9 this year. The county sought protection after a federal jury in December found the county violated federal fair housing law in its conduct related to a developer's plan to build a 72-bed residential treatment facility for teenagers, the Idaho Statesman reported. The jury awarded a $4 million judgment to a developer, which hasn't been paid. The county's budget this year is $9.3 million. The county estimated its liabilities at less than $10 million, according to a March 1 filing in U.S. Bankruptcy Court in Boise. Alamar Ranch LLC, the developer, was the largest unsecured creditor with the $4 million claim. Idaho is one of 26 U.S. states that authorize municipal bankruptcy. Like Chapter 11 under the federal bankruptcy code, municipalities allows debtor to adjust debt. Unlike corporate bankruptcies, creditors can't force municipalities into liquidation and the bankruptcy court has little oversight of municipal operations. Six municipal entities filed for Chapter 9 last year, most of them small utility or sewer districts. The capital of Idaho, Boise, is in adjoining Ada County.*

Whitney's report does not delve deeply into the recovery history of munis and into the technical details of default. Nor does she examine the complexities of Chapter 9 Bankruptcy. That is a shame, since she does deserve credit for publicizing the important issue of budget stress in Muniland.

Roubini does examine recovery. He offers estimates and methodologies. And he thoroughly describes the issues involving Chapter 9. His conclusion is that muni recovery is much higher than markets seem to be pricing and that the widespread use of Chapter 9 is unlikely.

We believe the Roubini report is straightforward and worthy of respect. It is serious research work. It examines nearly two centuries of development in state and local government debt in the United States. It explains the methodology that it used to reach conclusions and estimates.

Roubini also attempts to estimate the price adjustment needed in the market in order to normalize the muni-Treasury spread. He notes that the financial crisis sell-off brought munis to "absurd panic levels." He reminds readers that, while things are improved since these wide spreads, the muni market is still under "extreme strain."

Cumberland agrees with Roubini's conclusion that the "ratio of muni yields to Treasuries remains elevated." We continue to be buyers of well-structured, high-grade, tax-free municipal bonds and of corresponding taxable municipal debt. They remain cheap, and spreads still have a ways to go before normalcy in pricing is attained.

24

The U.S. Downgrade and the Muni Bond Market

John R. Mousseau
August 10, 2011

The downgrade of the United States from AAA to AA+ this weekend affects a number of municipal bonds—more than 11,000. They fall broadly into several categories:

Housing bonds (bonds that enjoy the backing of federal agencies like GNMA and FNMA) will see their S&P ratings affected.

Certain lease bonds with the federal government as a tenant will see their ratings downgraded, depending on the proportion that the federal government is responsible for on the leases

Pre-refunded and escrowed municipal bonds: These are generally older, higher-coupon bonds that have been defeased by their issuers. Proceeds of "refunding" issues are placed in Treasury securities to pay interest and call the older bonds at the first call date. This results in significant cost savings for the municipalities, and the older bonds are often (but not always) re-rated AAA based on the U.S. Treasuries, which are now backing the older bonds. These bonds will see a downgrade.

What does this mean from a portfolio management sense? In our view, it should not affect the muni market greatly. In our opinion, the United States is still the premier sovereign credit in the world. We will continue to own pre-refunded bonds in the shorter-maturity end of our barbell strategy, and we believe that state housing agencies offer some of the best value in the municipal marketplace.

The charts below compare the pre-refunded municipal bond scale, with the Municipal Market Analytics AAA scale on August 1st and then on August 8th—after the passing of the debt ceiling, but just before the S&P downgrade of the U.S. (though in the marketplace that was a given). There was no budge in scale.

It is important to remember that both Moody's and Fitch continue to rate the U.S. as "AAA." Thus those ratings are still in place on housing bonds backed by the federal government or pre-refunded bonds or bonds backed by federal leases.

Because state and local governments and their agencies are rated on different criteria than sovereign governments, it is likely that a number of high-grade municipal issuers will have S&P credit ratings higher than that of the federal government.

In total, in our opinion, the municipal marketplace will still react to the same forces it has in the past: demand for tax-exempt interest, flows in and out of municipal bond funds, and perception of credit on an individual credit basis.

Monday, August 01, 2011		
	Pre-Re	**MMA - AAA**
2012	0.20	0.33
2013	0.40	0.58
2014	0.63	0.87
2015	0.84	1.21
2016	1.16	1.48
2017	1.52	1.77
2018	1.90	2.11
2019	2.23	2.39
2020	2.49	2.63
2021	2.67	2.86
2022	2.88	3.05
2023	3.05	3.25
2024	3.19	3.38

Sources: Bloomberg, Municipal Market Analytics

Monday, August 08, 2011		
	Pre-Re	**MMA - AAA**
2012	0.20	0.30
2013	0.35	0.51
2014	0.49	0.77
2015	0.67	1.08
2016	1.00	1.35
2017	1.35	1.63
2018	1.69	1.93
2019	2.00	2.21
2020	2.22	2.47
2021	2.38	2.68
2022	2.56	2.85
2023	2.73	3.06
2024	2.87	3.18

Sources: Bloomberg, Municipal Market Analytics

25

Policy Madness in Muniland

David R. Kotok
September 14, 2011

Policy Madness (inconsistency) in Muniland. Some bullets.

- President Obama proposes jobs creation by raising infrastructure spending. This is the purview of state and local governments. They finance their share with municipal bonds.
- Obama adds a reinstatement of the Build America Bonds program, which had a 35% federal subsidy of the taxable interest. The concept was to use the top federal income tax bracket as an equalizer. The BABs program was successful for the two years of its existence but failed to gain extension in the year-end political fight of the last lame-duck session. BABs was a nearly unique federal fiscal initiative. There was no monetary (Federal Reserve) component. It was used throughout the country. It financed infrastructure and met the needs of state and local government units. Its impact was equally divided among red states and blue states.
- Obama also proposes a reduction of the tax-free bond benefit for high-income Americans (over $250,000 annually for joint return filers, $200,000 for singles). The net effect is to reduce the value of tax-free income and thereby raise the cost of municipal finance. Poor people do not buy tax-free bonds. Wealthy American

taxpayers buy them when they are advantageous due to the tax arbitrage. Narrow the arbitrage and reduce the demand for tax-free bonds. Reduce the demand and lower their use. Lower their use and raise the cost of finance for every toll road, school board, and sewer plant in the United States.

- Let's examine this policy hodgepodge against some real-time, live market pricing. We will choose the NY State Thruway, since it is an infrastructure project and a toll road that nearly everyone can identify. They recently sold a tax-free issue and they have an existing BABs issue. Therefore, we are able to compare an apple with an apple. This is the same issuer with the same revenue securing the bonds. The maturity is nearly identical. The difference is that one is BABs and the other is tax-free. One gets 35% of the interest rebated by the federal government. The other gets no rebate, but the bondholder pays no federal income tax on the interest.
- Here is the market pricing. NYS THRUWAY 5.449s of 4/1/25 traded at 4.52% on 8/9/11 (most recent recorded trade). The CUSIP is 650014TF0. This is BABs. Compare it with NYS THRUWAY 5s of 3/15/26 priced at 3.28% on 9/9/11. The CUSIP is 650028TF0. This is federally tax-free.
- Let's do an exercise. We will assume that the NYS Thruway is going to finance today and could obtain this yield on a traditional new issue. We will assume the federal income tax top rate remains at 35%. In addition, we will assume that the BABs legislation passes and the program goes back into effect. Okay, 65% of a 4.52% yield is 2.94%. That is the rate the NY Thruway would actually pay (after federal rebate) if it were to sell new BABs bonds today and if the new BABs included a 35% rebate. Clearly, the BABs program would offer the NYS Thruway the lowest cost of financing for its infrastructure project.
- The existing market-based price of the tax-free bond has a yield of 3.28%. That is a very recent market-based new-issue price. If Obama reduces the value of the tax arbitrage on this bond, the yield in the market place will rise. That means the NYS Thruway will end up paying a higher yield to borrow with a tax-free bond.

Possible policy outcomes from Obama's initiative are: (1) Nothing changes and the political impasse in Washington prevails. Alternatively, (2) Obama reduces the value of tax-free bonds by raising the effective tax rate—the result is a higher cost of finance for the issuers. On the other hand, (3) if the Congress authorizes the BABs program to resume, then the cost of infrastructure finance declines.

Now, Congress: you decide the best way to create infrastructure jobs. The worst way is to continue to bicker and fight among yourselves and do nothing.

A final, unrelated note about another form of Muniland Madness. We have been a harsh critic of the Meredith Whitney scare, which predicted "hundreds of billions of dollars" of municipal defaults. She said it on 60 Minutes on December 19, 2010. So far, there has been less than $1 billion in muni defaults in the first 8 months of this year according to Distressed Debt Securities Newsletter.

We stand by our original and often-repeated position. High-grade muni credits are available and the notion of mass defaults is exaggerated. Whitney triggered months of muni bond fund redemptions. Billions were lost by investors who panicked and liquidated.

At Cumberland, we maintained that well-researched munis were cheap. Many muni investors went to the edge of the ledge. Fortunately for them we were able to talk them off. As you can see by the NYS Thruway example above, compared with their taxable counterparts, munis still are cheap.

Hat tip to Cumberland's Michael F. Comes, who helped research the bond details.

26

Infrastructure Plan—A Third Option

David R. Kotok
September 19, 2011

President Obama proposed $447 billion in a package designed to stimulate infrastructure spending and project-oriented job creation in the United States. House Speaker Boehner and House Republicans will offer an alternative plan. These plans then go through super-committee negotiations that are attempting to design a budget deficit, spending, tax-management proposition in a deeply divided Congress.

The outlook for any of the elements offered to lead to a successful compromise is considered bleak by many Washington observers. However, we want to place another option on the table, along with a concise way to pay for it without expanding the federal deficit.

Rather than a mixed package of $447 billion, we propose $535 billion in a five-year program to be allocated to infrastructure spending. The mechanics of this program are via Build America Bonds, a proven and tested method of infrastructure finance.

You may be asking yourself: why the number 535? That is the exact number of Senators and Representatives that comprise our Congress. If they vote no, they will each be taking responsibility for voting against one billion dollars of infrastructure spending.

We further propose that the moneys be distributed among the fifty states in proportion to the number of Senators and Congressmen in each state. Therefore, a small state with one Congressman and two Senators would receive an allocation of $3 billion of Build America Bonds. A larger state with ten Congressmen and two Senators would receive an allocation of $12 billion in Build America Bonds.

For what would the money be used? We propose that it must be spent on infrastructure, construction, and municipal development projects. Think of it as a way of funding schools, airports, sewer and water plants, toll roads, and bridges—all that is in the purview of government.

Who would determine what projects would be undertaken? Existing local and state-level agencies would decide their needs and how to structure their own projects. If a town needed a water company, they could use a Build America Bond to finance it. If a district needed a new school, they could do the same.

Fortunately, the structure would be the same as the Build America Bonds we already know. The federal government would pay 35% of the interest in the form of a rebate to the issuer of the bonds. We already have close to $200 billion of Build America Bonds issued. The disclosures and techniques in order to finance them are established, so there is no need to form a new federal agency, allocating to other agencies. A federal presence is not required, other than to define the use for which Build America Bond proceeds may be applied.

Would this create more federal deficits? Yes, if it was standalone, but we propose an alternative to pay for it. The interest subsidy on a Build America Bond at current market prices is somewhere around 1.5% per year. It works like this: a tax-free bond could be sold in conventional terms, and the buyers of such bonds would be limited to high-tax-bracket, wealthy Americans. Build America Bonds, on the other hand, are taxable instruments to the bond buyer. They are not tax-free municipal bonds, but the federal government rebates a portion of the interest to the issuer of the bond. So, the issuer of the bond makes a decision as to which method is less costly when it issues bonds. Does it use tax-free bonds? Does it use taxable bonds? Whichever one results in the least expensive finance is the one that is preferred.

So, how would the interest-rebate portion be paid out of the federal budget? The answer here is simple: repeal the ethanol subsidy, which is approximately the same amount of money as it would take to have a half-trillion-dollar Build America Bonds program. The Congressional Budget Office (CBO) would score ethanol subsidy and Build America Bonds at about the same amount of money per year for the next, say, thirty years.

What would happen if you stopped the ethanol subsidy? You would use that money instead to rebuild the infrastructure of the United States. You would stop driving up corn prices. You would free up almost half the corn crop, which is currently going into ethanol, and instead let it be applied for food. If ethanol remains economically viable because of the mandate that requires it to be part of the fuel system, so be it. If not, then there will be changes in different types of ethanol-like products. Even the most intense supporters of the ethanol subsidy admit that when the oil price is approximately $100 a barrel, the need for a subsidy for ethanol is really not justified.

Why five years instead of two, like the original BABs program? It takes time to plan infrastructure projects. If the project were approved tomorrow, for example, the school board would need to hire architects, contractors, and workers. It would have to go through the process of determining what type of school to build, how it would be built, and enter the process of bidding and construction and permit applications. The same would be true for the sewer plant upgrade or the reconstruction of a bridge. Infrastructure is a long-lead-time activity.

Would this create jobs right away? The answer is yes! Most projects create jobs immediately, because engineering firms, designer firms, architectural firms—those who do the preliminary work on a project—get employed quickly. The evolution of a project takes place over several years. Would it create the million jobs that the Obama Administration says are needed to rebuild the infrastructure of the United States? We do not know, but we do know what we have seen with Build America Bond-financed projects. We have acted as a financial advisor on a number of them, and we have determined from our experience that many construction, project, and infrastructure-related jobs result from them.

Would state and local governments have to use the Build America Bonds money? Absolutely not. This is not a wasteful program; it is an optional program. The money is available; the rerouting of ethanol subsidy money to Build America Bonds is there. The allocation goes to the states, and the states determine their level of participation.

Will these bonds stand on their own credit, since the federal government is not guaranteeing the bond principal? The answer here is yes. Market-based credit analysis and revenues have to be allocated to amortize the bonds—all that goes into the mix of each specific bond project. Each project must stand on its own merit. It must have the revenue, support, and economic research. This gets packaged into an official statement that can be presented to bond investors, who will determine on their own if they want to take the risk and buy this bond.

Who will buy these bonds? Build America Bonds are taxable securities. Therefore, they become desirable for pension plans, IRAs, institutions, charitable foundations, banks, and others who are seeking investments at yields that can justify those investments and who at the moment are thirsting to find them. In addition, foreigners will buy Build America Bonds. We saw that in the last round of BABs, when foreign buyers came into the market and started to participate in this form of finance.

In summary, here is our proposition. No federal deficit impact. Repeal ethanol subsidy. Reallocate ethanol subsidy to an interest subsidy in the Build America Bonds program. Launch the Build America Bonds program with a five-year time horizon. With the size of $535 billion, we can easily convince Washington that the math is simple. In Washington, if it is not simple it does not have a chance. That would enable each Congressman to stare down a vote of a $1 billion allocation for his or her state. A concise program that creates infrastructure spending, puts the incentives to do it where they belong, and allows for independent credit analysis, could be implemented immediately and does not interfere with the super-committee's work or any other committee's work. This is our option to rebuild the infrastructure of the United States.

27

Harrisburg Saga Continues to Unfold

John R. Mousseau
October 21, 2011

Reports last night from Bloomberg were that Pennsylvania Governor Tom Corbett and the Harrisburg City Council are in a standoff resulting from Harrisburg's filing of Chapter 9 Bankruptcy last week. The governor is looking to overrule the city council's action and have the Commonwealth of Pennsylvania take over the finances of the city.

The story—often reported by Cumberland—is that of an incinerator that was not needed, but built as a boondoggle. After failing to attract enough business, the city decided to spend much more money retrofitting the incinerator, putting the city's pledge behind the bonds used to finance and retrofit. This turned into a disaster. The city stopped making payments on the incinerator debt last year. With much consternation and discussion, they have continued to pay debt service on their general obligation bonds.

Last week the city council voted to declare Chapter 9 Bankruptcy for Harrisburg, even though the Mayor of Harrisburg was against it and the Commonwealth of Pennsylvania itself had passed a law declaring that it would be illegal for Harrisburg to declare bankruptcy.

There is now a court-mandated delay of a month to sort this out. On Monday, a judge for the U.S. Bankruptcy Court in Pennsylvania set a November 23 court date to settle the legality of the bankruptcy declaration by the council.

Why is the state moving as if the matter has already been settled in its favor? It's not just the politics, it's the state not wanting Harrisburg's woes to result in much higher borrowing costs for towns and cities in the rest of central Pennsylvania.

What do we see reflected in the municipal bond market, given the current state of affairs?

Most of the Harrisburg general obligation debt is insured. Ratings on Harrisburg itself have been withdrawn by the rating agencies. Bonds backed by Assured Guaranty, the healthiest of the bond insurers (AA3 Moody's and AA+ Standard and Poor's) are trading at 5.5% to 6%. Bonds from downgraded insurer MBIA (now National RE), rated Baa1/BBB, are trading in the 6.25-6.50% range, and bonds with other insurers who are below investment-grade and have no rating are all over the lot, with trades in the 7%-plus range (levels courtesy of Oppenheimer). This is in a world where longer-maturity, high-grade Pennsylvania debt is trading in the 4.5% range.

The one thing we know for sure is that the bond insurers come down squarely of the opinion that Harrisburg has NOT taken the necessary steps to avoid bankruptcy: raising taxes, selling assets, and using their full faith and credit to pay their bonds.

So far, this has not carried over to the state's own bonds, as far as any patina of higher yields associated with the problems of Harrisburg. The state sold bonds this week at their normal high-grade level.

Cumberland has not owned any Harrisburg bonds since January 2011. Stay tuned as this develops.

28

Jefferson County Finally Declared Bankruptcy

John R. Mousseau
November 10, 2011

Yesterday (November 9th), the Jefferson County, Alabama commissioners voted by 4-1 to file bankruptcy. It will be the largest Chapter 9 Bankruptcy in the United States and affects over $3 billion in municipal bonds. The process will start with hearings tomorrow. We have written about the ongoing turmoil in Jefferson County in the past. Here are two links to past Cumberland articles:

http://www.cumber.com/commentary.aspx?file=102411.asp

http://www.cumber.com/commentary.aspx?file=080311.asp

Is this a surprise?

Absolutely not. The municipal bond market has been expecting this for some time. For the past three years this situation has been deteriorating. Its roots involve a sewer system grossly expanded under federal mandate, and corruption among county officials. It also involves the downgrade of municipal bond insurers in 2008, which caused the county's many ill-advised swaps to skyrocket in interest costs.

Through much of the summer and fall, Jefferson County has been trying, to no avail, to negotiate a haircut on the principal of their bonds. With $3 billion involved, there will be some effects, mainly on lower-rated debt, but the market has been prepared for this. Most market participants were hoping that something could be worked out. The Governor of Alabama, Robert Bentley, had been trying to forge a solution between bondholders and the county. This solution would have included bonds backed by the state, but would also have resulted in much higher sewer fees in the county. The bankruptcy action may be an impetus toward crafting a solution.

Where have Jefferson County bonds been trading?

We expect to see little market impact on trading in Jefferson County bonds. The county has refunded most of its fixed-rate sewer debt with VRDBs and ARS in 2002 and 2003. The trades we have seen and local dealer quotes have been at high interest-rate levels. Participants most affected are the LOC banks that hold the failed remarketed debt and bond insurers, not bondholders.

Caa3/C FGIC Jefferson AL Swr 5.37% due 2/1/2027 Bid/Offer: 11.18% / 10.22%

B3/BBB- Jefferson AL Sales-Tax 5.25% due 1/1/2017 Bid/Offer: 7.14% / 5.94%

Baa2/B- Ambac Jefferson AL Lse Rev 5.0% due 4/1/2026 Bid: 12.62%

What does Jefferson County do next?

They need to demonstrate to the bankruptcy judge that they cannot pay their bills. The judge will then determine what obligations they must fulfill, and at what level. J.P. Morgan, as well as the bond insurers FGIC and Syncora (formerly XLCA), face the largest losses.

Does this morph into a Media Frenzy-like falloff?

We think not. Jefferson County has been developing for over three years. This is a result that almost happened in September. It was staved off by tentative settlements with creditors that did not get legislative approvals. Municipal bankruptcies are running at about 30% of last year's totals. Problems such as Harrisburg, PA and Central Falls, RI have been known for a while; they represent specific mismanagement. Furthermore, the improvement in municipal credit this year has been very good.

Through the courtesy of our friends at Raymond James, we show two graphs:

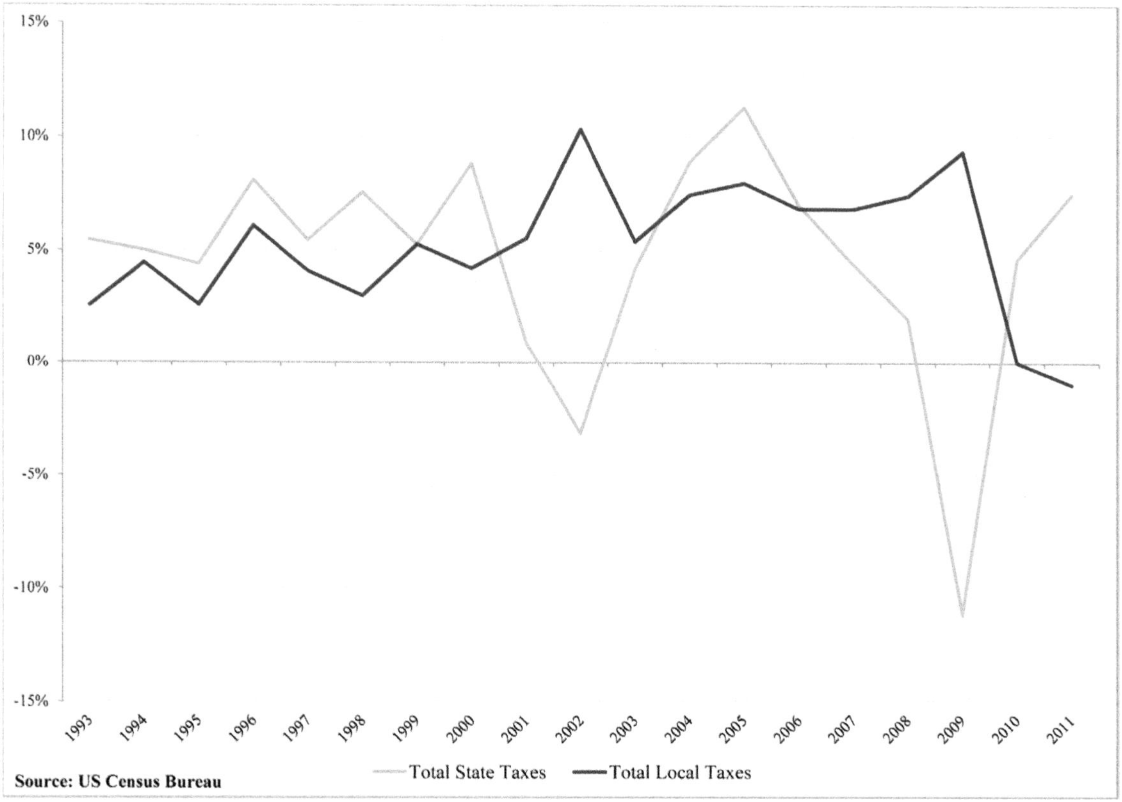
15%
10%
5%
0%
-5%
-10%
-15%
1993
1994
1995
1996
1997
1998
1999
2000
2001
2002
2003
2004
2005
2006
2007
2008
2009
2010
2011
Total State Taxes
Total Local Taxes
Source: US Census Bureau

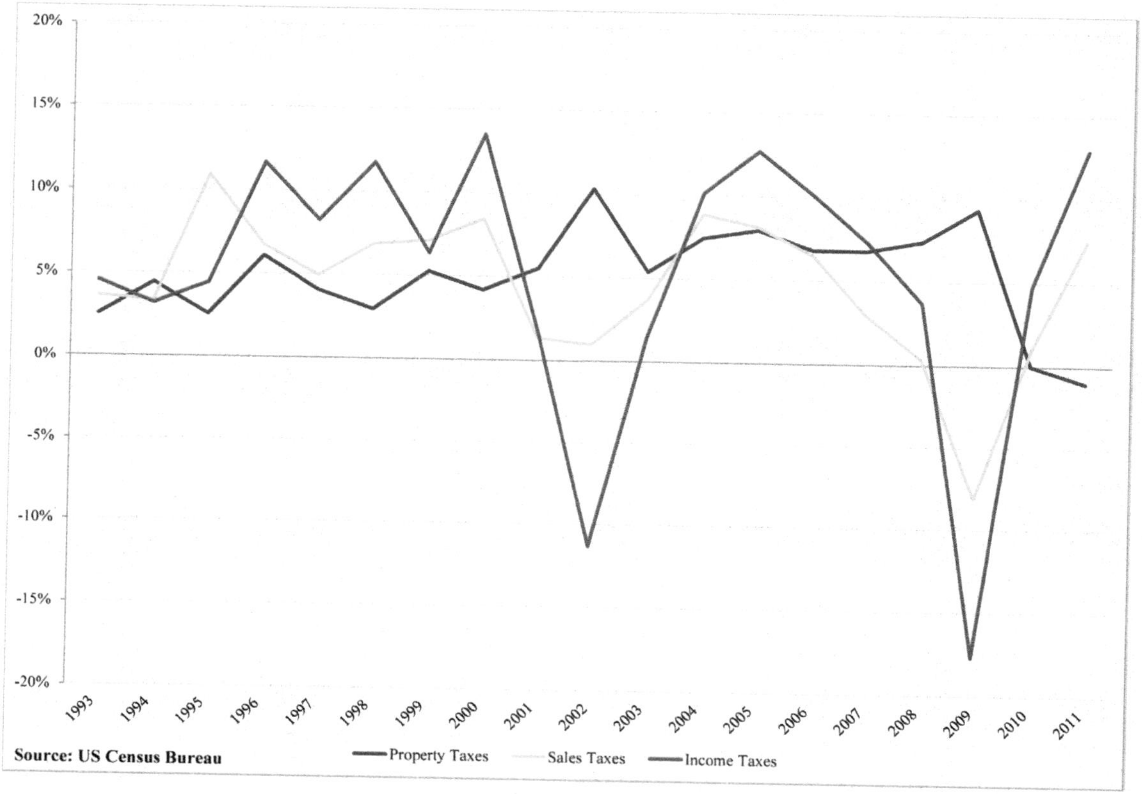

The first shows year-over-year changes in state and local taxes. The other shows specific tax revenue changes. You can see the strong rebound in state taxes, which are now back to pre-financial-crisis levels after seven quarters of gains (following five quarters of declines). Growth in local taxes—specifically property taxes—has been falling but held up better than other types of taxes when the recession hit, as it does in most recessions. The overall municipal market has rebounded smartly in the past nine months.

29

Meredith Redux—One Year Later

John R. Mousseau
December 19, 2011

December 19th marks one year since Meredith Whitney appeared on the CBS news magazine 60 Minutes and sent the municipal bond market into a tailspin from which it took months to recover. To recap that event: Ms. Whitney, a noted bank analyst, appeared on 60 Minutes and forecast "hundreds of billions" in municipal defaults during 2011. The result was a two- to three-month siege on the municipal bond market, which was already in the throes of a supply bulge because the Build America Bonds (BABs) program had expired.

As we have written previously, the first few post-Whitney months were marked by huge redemptions in municipal bond funds.

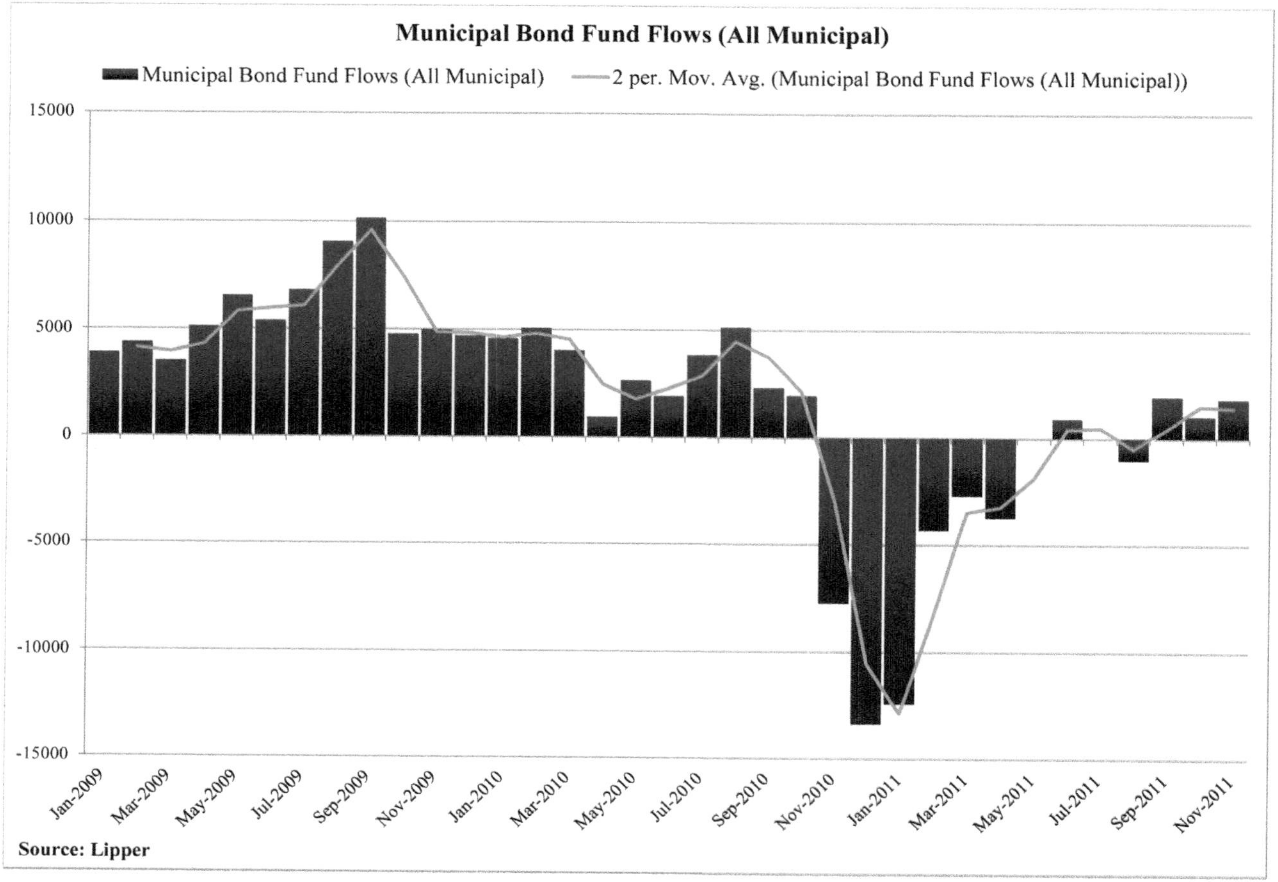

One can see that the redemptions approached hemorrhage levels in the early part of 2011. They got LESS negative as the spring wore on, and finally began to turn positive during the fall. It is important to note that while the mostly retail-oriented municipal bond funds were having crushing outflows, sending longer-maturity yields skyrocketing, the demand for the TAXABLE versions of the same credits (BABs) was sending BABs yields lower, as pension funds, foreign buyers, and charitable foundations scooped up the generous yields afforded by year-end 2010 BABs issuance. This was one of the clear signs that the Whitney-led meltdown was one related to liquidity and not to overall credit concern.

MMA				
	2	**5**	**10**	**20**
12/18/2010	0.77	1.66	3.18	4.88
01/15/2011	0.89	1.92	3.49	5.28
12/14/2011	0.48	1.19	2.37	4.33

Sources: Municipal Market Analytics

One can see from the chart that the skyrocketing of intermediate and LONGER term yields that occurred due to the 60 Minutes broadcast continued unabated through mid-January. This, of course, correlated with the massive amount of bond fund liquidations. And then began the long trip down in longer yields that has continued until now.

What were the keys to the turnaround?

Credit

State governments recently finished the seventh consecutive quarter of rising tax receipts. This followed five straight quarters of declines from the fall of 2008 through the end of 2009. To be sure, many states and cities are still struggling to rein in rising pension costs, as well as dealing with the loss of federal dollars. But many states have made deep cuts in expenses and, in most cases, budget gaps have been closed without reliance on one-time solutions. The market dealt with the bankruptcies of Harrisburg, PA and Jefferson County, AL without seeing a backup in overall tax-free yields. It treated these bankruptcies as "one-off events, caused by specific problems of municipal malfeasance, and not as being indicative of overall municipal health. As we have also written, overall financial health is better at the state level than at the local level—but all levels of government have been learning how to do more with less.

Supply

The sharp decline in long-term interest rates has spurred on issuers in recent months. However, even with robust issuance at year end, 2011 is poised to finish with under $300 billion in total municipal bond issuance, a far cry from the $433 billion of issuance in 2010. There is clearly a greater air of austerity at many different levels of municipal government, from the state level down to towns. Certainly, in many cases, additional bond debt is being voted down by electorates. In addition, many issuers decided to forego issuing bonds at the very high interest-rate levels that Meredith-mania caused in the early part of this year. And, once the Build America Bonds program expired at the end of 2010, many officials decided to forego projects that might have been financed with the federally subsidized BABs.

Demand

Again, the municipal bond mutual fund flows tell a lot of the story. Much of the bond fund selling was replaced with INDIVIDUAL bond purchases earlier in the year. But now bond fund flow has turned positive and should show overall positive flows for calendar year 2011. Volatility in the equity markets has caused money to be pulled from stock funds and, presumably, some of this has found its way into the municipal bond market. In addition, the prospect of higher taxes has also pushed investors toward tax-free municipals. Although the rise in federal marginal tax rates now looks like it might be on hold until AFTER the 2012 election, northeastern states like New York, New Jersey, and Connecticut have seen a hike in marginal income taxes, thus raising demand for tax-exempt income. We expect more states to raise income taxes at the margin in 2012—and, no doubt, to aim the increases at higher-income individuals.

Saturday, January 15, 2011				
	2	**5**	**10**	**20**
MMA	0.89	1.92	3.49	5.28
US Treasury	0.58	1.94	3.42	4.52
Ratio	1.53	0.99	1.02	1.17

Sources: Municipal Market Analytics

Friday, December 16, 2011				
	2	**5**	**10**	**20**
MMA	0.46	1.14	2.33	4.30
US Treasury	0.27	0.87	2.02	2.94
Ratio	1.72	1.31	1.15	1.46

Sources: Municipal Market Analytics

So as we head into the last two weeks of 2011, we can look at how tax-exempt yields stack up against US Treasuries on a relative basis now and in the middle of the Meredith meltdown last January. There is no question that munis are cheaper, on a relative basis, across the whole yield curve, particularly on the front end. But it is extremely important to note that municipal yields have moved in the same direction (down) as Treasuries—just not as much. The Congressional squabble over the debt ceiling, the downgrade of the United States by Standard & Poor's, and the Federal Reserve announcement of its "Operation Twist " in September all led to drops in Treasury yields, and munis—begrudgingly, in some cases—followed along. The muni market fought those events off, along with the Harrisburg and Jefferson County situations, and made the long trip back from the despair of a year ago. And for that we are thankful.

30

Land of Lincoln Follow-Up

John R. Mousseau
May 2, 2012

Our piece from Monday April 30th highlighted the State of Illinois' budget woes, and some of the steps they are taking to close their budget deficit.

Illinois brought their $1.8 billion general obligation deal to market yesterday, starting with an order period on Monday. How did the state do on the deal, on a relative basis?

Here are some selected maturities on the deal and where they were priced on a final scale, versus the Municipal Market Data AAA scale:

2019: +178
2022: +175
2025: +176

Overall, the deal had a good reception, and most maturities were repriced lower in yield by 2-5 basis points after the initial order period. Thus, the deal in general priced approximately 16-18 basis points cheaper to the AAA scale than the $500 million dollar deal brought in March. Clearly some of this is due to the larger size of this deal and the need to clear the market, but it is very evident that the price the state is paying for its fiscal woes is moving in only one direction: HIGHER. An unmistakable sign of how cheap the state's debt is getting is the fact that this week's issue attracted TAXABLE bond buyers who were buying the tax-exempt debt because it came so cheap.

To reiterate, Cumberland does not believe that any of the fifty states, including Illinois, would default on their debt. The question is always whether, as an investor, we are being compensated for the risk. And that risk is not just financial or based on the ability to pay. In the post-Lehman world, headline risk, whether from approaching hurricanes or approaching pension woes, is just as important to calibrate. We think there is more reckoning to come.

31

Muni Market After Sandy

John R. Mousseau
Michael F. Comes
November 8, 2012

The muni market was moribund last week in the wake of Superstorm Sandy. Almost all deals were postponed as both buy-side and sell-side participants were sidelined by this terrible storm. We take a look at the muni market post-Sandy from three different perspectives: market technicals, credit, and future developments.

Market Technicals

Last week saw most issuance postponed. For example, the state of New Jersey canceled a $2.6 billion Tax and Revenue Note issue. Many other issuers canceled deals and are bringing them back this week or next. The week after next is Thanksgiving and is traditionally very quiet.

Market participants tend to be wary of buying credits from affected areas in the period immediately following natural disasters such as hurricanes and earthquakes. Think of this as group apprehension: investors waiting for someone else to make the first move. This is usually reflected in higher yield spreads on bonds issued from affected areas. We witnessed this phenomenon in a number of different incidents: the San Francisco/Oakland earthquake of 1989, Hurricane Andrew in South Florida in 1992, and Hurricane Katrina in the gulf area, especially New Orleans, in 2007. These are only three very large examples; there are many more small ones.

In all cases there was spread widening in almost all credits, and the more affected the credit—think of New Orleans Water Authority—the wider the spread. In most cases the spread widening that initially occurred after the crisis started to narrow as the yield spreads of the affected credits reverted to the mean. Generally speaking, incremental yield in the face of a natural disaster has been an opportunity.

Credit

Superstorm Sandy is the most damaging storm to ever hit the New York/New Jersey area. Connecticut, Massachusetts, Rhode Island, Delaware, Pennsylvania, Maryland, and Virginia were affected but much less so. New Jersey is particularly affected, with 50% of north Jersey homes still without power one week after the storm. The long-term record of municipalities dealing with natural disaster is very good. Most of the time there has been little or no impact on bond ratings of issuers. Moody's states that budget strains are likely to come if recovery costs exceed budgeted contingencies and there are lags in aid from higher levels of government.

There are usually two offsetting effects from natural disasters on issuers. The first is an initial sharp decline in demand and output. Think about fewer people using bridges, roads, tunnels, or subways, as in New York, or fewer people driving and paying tolls or gas taxes, as in New Jersey. Or the attendant costs of cleanups and restoration being imposed on the many municipalities in the New York area, especially in Long Island and in northern New Jersey.

Generally speaking, in federally-mandated disaster areas, the federal government pays up to 75% or more of emergency costs, with the state having a hand in allocating the non-federal share. Certainly, in the New Jersey and New York areas, the risk is that state and local municipality costs are going to be much higher than original estimates. Fund balances will be drawn down. There is also the prospect of higher mortgage delinquencies in New York and New Jersey, as homeowners who are already somewhat strapped face higher costs of recovery plus likely delays in insurance reimbursements. From a pure bond perspective, bonds that are revenue-oriented (tolls, fare boxes, sales taxes, etc.) will feel the most immediate impact. Moody's states that debt-service coverage may decrease due to lost revenue during periods of inoperability and high cleanup costs for mass transit systems. Also vulnerable are debt classes such as sales taxes, special taxes, and housing bonds, due to appropriation risk and revenue cyclicality.

The second, offsetting effect is the bounce-back effect. State and local governments rebuild damaged or lost enterprises, resulting in a boost to output, often times in excess of pre-disaster levels. We have seen this time and time again, and there is no reason to think it won't happen in the areas affected by Superstorm Sandy. One of the issues, of course, is that much of the area was really just starting to recover from the financial crisis.

We maintain a bias toward larger credits with strong insurance risk-management practices and contingency plans. We use as a case study the Metropolitan Transportation Authority (MTA), a public provider of mass transit that services the New York City area. The transit system's large cash balances and reinsurance portfolio act as a financial cushion for bondholders during prolonged service stoppages. As some of our readers can attest, the gridlock experienced in New York City during the last few days, post-Sandy, highlights the essentiality of this system.

Before the storm, MTA made necessary preparations, such as moving 1000 railcars and locomotives to higher ground. Sandbags were deployed, as well. As of now the Brooklyn-Battery tunnel is the only tunnel not in operation; however this accounts for only 6% of revenues. Most MTA train lines are operational, including the Port Jervis line and New Canaan branch, which has had to substitute bus service for rail service. The Metro North line is an exception.

As a firm, preservation of a client's capital is the framework from which we make all decisions. When analyzing a credit we examine possible future events and their likely outcomes. For MTA, a credit we favor, this entails an analysis of bondholder safety during a possible interruption in system operations. The MTA's largest revenue bond credit, the transportation revenue credit, is a gross revenue stream pledge with 10x debt-service coverage. The bonds are senior to operations and maintenance expenses. The system has $1.3 billion cash on hand and can operate for five weeks without revenues. Total non-reinsured and non-FEMA exposure is $180mm. The system has a $30mm-deductible pre-reinsurance and $150mm maximum liability, concentrated in Flood Zone A, the area of mandatory evacuation designated by Mayor Bloomberg. These metrics and others that indicate an adequate bondholder safety margin formed the basis of our decision to hold this credit, and possibly add to our position at cheaper levels.

Future Developments

It makes sense that we will see more municipal bond issuance to help rebuild the areas affected by Sandy. In addition, it would not surprise us to see a consensus-building effort in the new Congress, or even in the lame-duck Congress, after the election. Though a return to issuing Build America Bonds is a long shot, there is a case to be made for issuing them on a regional basis to help towns, counties, and other affected jurisdictions rebuild. This could also be done through a larger regional bond bank structure that would allow smaller municipalities to borrow without having to absorb higher issuance costs due to their small size. In addition, Congress could also allow municipalities to advance refund existing higher-coupon REFUNDING issues. This was allowed during the post-financial-crisis period and certainly should be called for now. Allowing banks to reenter the arena and buy CURRENTLY issued bonds and deduct the carrying costs (as with 2009 and 2010 issues) would also help to lower costs for municipalities.

Nationwide, the storm's effects on economic growth are expected to be similar to those expected on the local level. An analysis by Goldman Sachs points to two important and offsetting effects on nationwide economic activity: sharp declines in demand and output in the short term, followed by a boost back to pre-disaster output and baseline growth. Goldman estimates a ¼-½ point reduction of GDP growth in the 4th quarter. The storm will likely have larger effects on higher-frequency indicators to be released over the next two months, such as retail sales, jobless claims, and nonfarm payrolls. Goldman states that during this time sentiment indicators such as confidence may paint a more accurate picture of the economy's growth.

A separate analysis by Eric Strobl, The Economic Growth Impact of Hurricanes: Evidence from U.S. Coastal Counties, published by Ecole Polytechnique in Paris, suggests that a county's annual economic growth rate will fall by 0.45%, on average, in response to a large hurricane strike. This is not insignificant, as economic growth in the NY-northern NJ-Long Island MSA has averaged only 1.43% annually since 2001.

Sandy was quite a wallop for the area, and it will be, at a minimum, weeks and probably months before anything approaching normality returns. But we do feel that higher yields resulting from post-Sandy developments will most likely be an opportunity.

32

The Fed & Munis—Quite a Stretch

David R. Kotok
June 26, 2013

It has been quite a stretch. Two Fed (Federal Reserve) meetings, lots of Fed-speak, turmoil in financial markets, and re-pricing of certain asset classes to levels unexpected—all done in a violent and volatile way.

As my colleague John Mousseau just wrote, high-grade, tax-free municipal bonds have been trading above 5 percent. Taxable-equivalent yields on instruments like that are between 8.5 percent and 9 percent depending on your state residency and tax bracket. Think about it: if you are a U.S. dollar-based American citizen in a higher tax bracket, where else can you get a compounded 8.5% on a fully taxable investment for a period of years? The question pertains to high-credit-quality alternatives. We see no more attractive alternatives.

At Cumberland, we have lengthened duration while moving to the buy side. We are buying where we can and altering accounts and mixes of accounts as we can. We are taking advantage of this very opportunistic time.

Why this bargain basement pricing occurred is a separate question. John Mousseau covered some of the reasons in his missive. Let me keep my comments directed at the Fed, since they were part of the problem. Hard as it is for them to admit an error, some in the Fed would now say they miscommunicated by sending a poor or confusing message. Others in the Fed would argue that is not the case and that the markets "misinterpreted" their message.

Misinterpreted? Hmmmm!

If you send a message to an audience and they do not interpret it the way you think they should have, who is wrong? Is it their fault because they did not hear you properly? Or is it your fault because you did not say it clearly? We can debate this forever. It is not important now. What is important is what happens next.

What do we know? We know that over the course of the last year the Fed has pointed to various unemployment rates ranging from 5.5 percent to 7 percent (most recently) to identify the point at which it will stop, taper, or diminish its purchasing of assets or stabilize and act to withdraw stimulus. Over time and taken together, the messages have been mixed to a disconcerting degree. At this point the unemployment rate target for the Fed is a mixed bag, and few market agents have confidence in any single number.

What else do we know? We know the present unemployment rate is higher than any one of those numbers. And we know that if you dig into the employment statistics deeply, you see that the recovery in employment, hence the recovery in labor income, is not robust. It is slow. Furthermore, we know that the federal budget sequester is about to cut the data-gathering enterprise along with much else, which means the numbers will be fewer and the picture they piece together perhaps less complete.

We know the Fed has a threshold in mind with regard to inflation. It said its longer-term target is 2 percent inflation, but it will permit inflation to go to 2.5 percent before it begins to trigger policy changes.

Ok. Where is the inflation rate now? It is a lot closer to 1 percent than 2 percent. It is headed down, not up. St. Louis Fed President, Jim Bullard, has articulated some worry about this. Bullard asks a valid question: Do we want to institute a policy change that markets will interpret as a reduction in the rate of stimulus when the inflation rate is below our target—and headed down? Notice how commodity prices are falling (copper is a clue to this price weakness).

Unfortunately, the rest of Bullard's colleagues on the FOMC (Federal Open Market Committee) have not addressed the question. We do not see consistent comments coming from the members of the FOMC about where they stand on this complicating factor of inflation's being below the FOMC target and falling.

What will the FOMC do if the inflation rate drops below 1 percent? What will they do if they are tapering while the inflation rate remains at 1 percent? How close to zero will they permit it to go before they change the way they are approaching monetary policy?

Can anyone answer those questions? Clearly the answer is no. Can anyone predict—with any pragmatically useful degree of precision—the policy pathways they will take through the unemployment-employment statistics? The answer is no. So we have confusion among market agents as a result of very mixed messages from the members of the FOMC.

Lastly, the U.S. President knocks the knees out from under the outgoing Fed Chairman in a statement that appalled many. In our view, Ben Bernanke does not deserve such treatment by the President who appointed him. Bernanke has served his country as well as he could under severe circumstances and from a critical position. It is apparent when you see him that he is tired. He has worked diligently as a patriot. It appears that he wants to stop at the end of his term on January 31, 2014. He is attempting to pave the way for his successor, as he should.

So why, then, did the President need to kick him hard in a very uncomfortable spot? Markets saw that. Now they have no idea what is coming. They know there will be a new Fed Chairman. They expect the appointment to be announced sometime after Labor Day, because there is a confirmation process that must get underway.

Discussions center on current Fed Vice Chairwoman Janet Yellen, former Fed Vice Chairman Roger Ferguson, former U.S. Treasury Secretary Timothy Geithner and, perhaps, former Fed Vice Chairman Alan Blinder. Lawrence Summers can be added to that lineup, although many observers believe his confirmation would not be possible in the U.S. Senate.

What do markets do when faced with rising uncertainty? How do they react to a confusing message as opposed to a clear one? A 6.5% percent unemployment rate and 2.5% percent inflation are clear milestones. Those numerical targets have now morphed into something quite slippery and confusing. So markets sold off and interest rates went up. The impact on the economy will slow the housing recovery. Just how much remains to be seen. Today's GDP revisions point to how fragile this recovery seems to be.

We are going to talk more about this soon. We are currently scheduled to guest host Bloomberg TV's Surveillance on Friday, June 28, 2013, at 6:00 AM EST. The Fed will likely be the topic of our discussion with Sara Eisen, Scarlet Fu, and Tom Keene.

Between now and then, we are on the buy side of tax-free bonds. They are cheap. It is time to back up the truck and own them.

33

Cheap Munis, Not Detroit

David R. Kotok
July 22, 2013

We thank Michael Wilson of Morgan Stanley Wealth Management and FactSet Research Systems for a compilation of returns. Michael's commentary in July talked about how "There was no place to hide in fixed income." We agree, although we think hedging dampened volatility so that the damage was minimized.

Michael's compilation of returns from May 1, 2013, close to the June lows in various markets reveals that all categories of fixed income had negative returns during this brief, less than two-month, period of time. The returns were as follows: bank loans down 0.45%, U.S. short-term down 1.34%, U.S. Treasuries down 3.46%, U.S. high-yield down 4.48%, international bonds down 4.71%, global high-yield bonds down 5.04%, U.S. municipals down 5.47%, U.S. investment-grade down 6.30%, global inflation-linked down 8.15%, U.S. TIPS down 9.73%, and emerging-market debt down 13.05%.

Clearly, bonds suffered a rout. Any bondholder who looked at the June 30, 2013, statements saw the effect of the global sell-off in fixed income. The sell-off did not happen in the U.S. alone, and it was not unique to a specific sector. There was a broad and wholesale abandonment of fixed-income markets. The strategic impact was to force liquidation by holders, hedge funds, mutual funds, and institutional structured finance. All the action was on the sell side.

The construction is simple. When mutual funds as a group are getting redemptions, all of them become sellers. That is what happened in the bond sell-off. There were also some hedge funds and structured finance agents in some bond dealer-supported institutions that failed and had to be forced or liquidated. Rumors exacerbated the sell-off.

When such bond sell-offs occur, buyers stand aside and let the blood flow. We were one of those.

Now what happens after this rout? Bond markets start to recover; things start to normalize; and liquidity returns to the markets. There are now questions about institutional liquidity because of rule changes dealing with the capital necessary for banks and dealers to support their inventories. Essentially, liquidity provided by that capital is dry, and the basis on which inventory positions can be held by dealers is limited.

In our view, this situation creates tremendous opportunity in some of the bond-market sectors. We have written many times about how the highest-grade U.S. tax-free municipal bonds are being priced in outrageous bargain structures. The entire curve of tax-free municipal bonds is now trading above the yields of taxable U.S. Treasury obligations. We are making this comparison using the MMD scale versus the Treasury scale. We examine and compare these measures every day. We look at the spreads between tax-free and taxable bonds and compare them at the highest credit quality. This we do in order to remove the issue of default or credit risk from the calculation.

We are not talking about comparing Detroit tax-free bonds with Treasury bonds. There is no comparison. Detroit is a mess, in default—the latest poster child of financial trouble. The Treasury is a riskless U.S. obligation subject only to political whim with regard to the extension of the debt limit. We presume that the U.S. Treasury obligation is default-free.

We have obtained permission to post Natalie Cohen's (Wells Fargo) excellent analysis on Detroit as a guest piece in the Special Reports section of our website. The link is:

http://www.cumber.com/content/special/detroit_public_pensions.pdf.

Readers may find this superb work of assistance as they sort through Detroit-related issues.

We also have our research colleague Michael F. Comes' Bloomberg Radio interview about Detroit on our website. The link is:

http://www.cumber.com/content/special/mcomes.wma.

Let's get back to the matter of munis being very cheap. Take the true and natural AAA credits available in the municipal bond market and compare them with Treasuries. The tax-free bonds yield more than the taxable Treasuries do. These bonds come from a sector, category, or subsector of tax-free municipal bonds that have a history of zero defaults in the last century. The comparison is almost as close as apples to apples. The U.S. Treasury obligation is technically a superior credit to a natural AAA tax-free municipal bond, but not superior by very much. History is 100% on the bond buyer's side when it comes to this debate.

What do we mean by a true and natural AAA credit? An example might be bonds issued by the state of Utah. Those bonds have particular budget coverage and requirements under Utah law; furthermore, they have an unblemished history of making all payments in a timely way. It is almost inconceivable that the state of Utah would default on the true AAA credit of its state's general obligation bond.

Another example of a tax-free bond in that category would be an education bond issued by Yale University, also a true AAA credit. Let's think about it for a minute. The university has been there for centuries and has a huge endowment fund. Its credentials as an academic institution are paramount and well established. It is almost inconceivable that Yale University would default on its debt obligations. Well-financed as it is, Yale does issue bonds under certain structures. There are Yale tax-free education bonds.

When you compare the performance of Yale, the state of Utah, and similar credits with the U.S. Treasury curve, you are very nearly comparing apples to apples in terms of their creditworthiness.

The present pricing of tax-free bonds makes sense only if we happen to think that the income tax code of the U.S. is going to be repealed. The present market dysfunction is irrational. Such pricing would work only if there were no advantages to a tax-free bond versus a taxable bond. Only dysfunction can explain why these high-grade tax-free bonds are yielding more than the taxable Treasury securities.

Now, we know without a doubt that the tax code is not going to be repealed. We also know that taxes on incomes falling in the middle and upper income tax brackets in the U.S. have gone up by a large amount. In addition, investors are now subject to the 3.8% Obamacare tax, on top of other taxes that may be particular to individuals in various jurisdictions.

What is causing this dysfunctional pricing in the market? There are two different sets of investors that determine these bond prices. In the U.S., about 20 or 25 million Americans determine the price at which they will buy or sell a tax-free municipal bond. They compare it with other investments and make judgments individually. They are the portion of our population that pays higher taxes. The other 90% of Americans ignore tax-free municipal bonds. They do not think about them.

The U.S. Treasury curve and its interest rates, on the other hand, are determined by the entire world. An investor in Singapore or Dubai is attuned to the yields and term structures of U.S. Treasury obligations; however, those investors have usually ignored the U.S. tax-free municipal bond market. That is no longer entirely true. There is evidence that some sophisticated bond buyers outside the U.S. are purchasing tax-free municipal bonds because the raw yield is higher than that of Treasuries. Such investors believe that sooner or later the present dysfunctional pricing will return to a more normal spread.

Logic would suggest that a high-grade, tax-free bond should yield less than a taxable Treasury bond. It usually has in the past and is likely to do so again in the future. Between now and then we are seizing on this bargain provided to us by market dysfunction.

The bond market sell-off was a rout. It rattled and terrified investors, and the process of healing is still underway. Tax-free municipals in the U.S. high-credit categories are very cheap.

We shall soon assemble in Maine for the annual fishing expedition, discussions, incantations, debates, and wagers at Leen's Lodge. Bloomberg Television is scheduled to cover the event and broadcast live on Friday, August 2, 2013. Tax-free and taxable bonds, Federal Reserve policy outlook, and markets will be among the intensely reviewed topics.

34

Puerto Rico Update

David R. Kotok
October 9, 2013

There has been a recent flurry of activity regarding Puerto Rico, involving their debt, rating agency views of that debt, the bond insurers that have been insuring their debt, the state-specific mutual funds that are holding Puerto Rico debt, and the projected plans of the Puerto Rican government to improve their deteriorating credit picture and economic situation. We have new (August) economic information from Puerto Rico. And we have the October 18 detailed financial report linked below.

In this commentary we wish to add a few additional points to what is already an intense and public debate. At the end of this note we will offer our firm's position on Puerto Rico's debt. Many of the professional folks we spoke to about Puerto Rico's debt situation asked for anonymity. They are under constraints from their firms, and we respect those restrictions. So our citations here will be from publicly available resources or our own computations.

We cannot say that Puerto Rico will default on all or some of its debt. Nor are we saying that it will pay all or some of its debt. We are saying the risk of default is high. As a skilled Washington-based expert said to me, "Puerto Rico might become an Argentina; and it might be able to turn itself around like Brazil." Right now the best guess is that we do not know which outcome will prevail. However, we must add that the pressure to roll existing debt maturities and pay liabilities is nearing a critical point.

We've heard from debt holders who point out that hedge funds are buyers of Puerto Rico's debt. They take that information as a positive indicator. We agree with the hedge fund purchase information. We disagree that it is a positive indicator. UBS's Mike Ryan sums it well. "I would be really careful to play Puerto Rico or trade it" he said. "Hedge funds don't own Puerto Rico. They rent." (*Barron's*, October 28)

My colleagues Michael F. Comes, John Mousseau, and I took apart a hedge fund trade. We reconstructed ways in which hedge funds can buy Puerto Rico and also hedge the other side of the trade for their profit. They can take long positions in Puerto Rico debt. They offset the risk through either a short position or put option on Assured Guaranty stock. Assured Guaranty is the major bond insurer of some Puerto Rico debt. Alternatively, the hedge fund can use a credit default swap on Assured Guaranty. In either case they try to neutralize their Puerto Rico default risk by using Assured as a proxy.

The theory behind this is that Assured Guaranty would be hurt if Puerto Rico defaults. So, the hedge fund's long position would lose from a Puerto Rico debt downgrade or default, but it would have an offsetting gain from the credit default swap position or short position on Assured Guaranty stock. The offsetting neutralized position could result in a profit to the hedge fund. In fact, my colleagues and I calculated that the hedge fund could assume a neutral duration position and thereby create about 350 basis points in an annualized tax-free yield. That yield would also be a tax-free yield to the hedge fund's investors. So the typical hedge fund investor can derive a taxable-equivalent yield of about double the tax-free yield, or about 7% on a maturity structure that can be unwound in only a few days. That is without leverage. My colleague John Mousseau noted that some hedge funds may be able to lever this up to 20 times.

There is still counterparty risk when putting such a trade together. And the position needs continuous rebalancing, since it has three or more moving parts and constantly adjusting weights. But that is exactly what a hedge fund is supposed to do. What we want to show is that there are ways to do it. Furthermore, note that the starting point of the trade is buying Puerto Rico debt, not because you like it but because it offers a hedging opportunity in a distressed market.

We want to demonstrate this with a chart that we have posted on our website for all to see (*http://www.cumber.com/content/special/puertoricocomplexity.pdf*). (We suggest that you view the image as you follow this discussion.) We have used Bloomberg data and constructed three series. (1) The Assured Guaranty stock price is in orange; that company is the bond insurer that has the dominant position with respect to Puerto Rico credit enhancement. (2) The Assured Guaranty credit default swap is depicted in green; it is inverted so that it can be visually compared to the stock price. (3) The price of the general obligation bond of Puerto Rico is in blue. The similarities in price change are obvious to the eye and well supported by the math that one would use to determine how tightly these are correlated. That is the math that helps to guide the hedge fund as it rebalances the weights. We've also marked the Detroit bankruptcy date and the Barron's Puerto Rico article date with respect to the front-page description of Puerto Rico. These two dates are important because they introduced headline risk. Please note that Assured Guaranty also has exposure in Detroit.

Readers can now make their own determinations about this so-called "bullish" hedge-fund trade. We will move on to the issue of credit risk.

At www.cumber.com, underneath the chart of the hedge-fund trade, readers may find the "Commonwealth Of Puerto Rico Financial Information and Operating Data Report," dated October 18, 2013. Here is a direct link: *http://cumber.com/content/special/october18commonwealthreport.pdf*. One can peruse it and see that about 40% of the revenue for the government of Puerto Rico is coming from the federal government of the United States. The details are in the report. The report is very comprehensive, and that is a positive from this beleaguered bond issuer. Such reports are now required under the newest versions of disclosure rules.

Read the details about the pension systems, which are in horrible straits. Various retirement funding liabilities of Puerto Rico are estimated at $37 billion by methodologies that include a 6% discounting rate to get to present value. The reports show that the pension system is only 8% funded, meaning it is 92% unfunded. On digging deeper, one can find that a substantial amount of the funded portion is in the form of assets consisting of small loans, mortgages, and certain cultural loans to participants. Those "assets" substituted for what otherwise would be cash or investments in the pension system.

We excerpt this quote from the report:

> *Another cause for the current situation of the Employees Retirement Systems is its personal loan program. The Employees Retirement System offers and manages a program that offers personal loans, mortgage loans and loans for cultural travels for retirement plan participants. Participants may obtain up to $5,000 in personal loans for any use. In 2007, the System increased this amount to $15,000, which reduced the cash in the System by approximately $600 million between 2007 and 2010. This deficit has been covered by funds from the System itself and has required the liquidation of assets that would have otherwise been available to make pension payments. Due to the amount of personal loans originated during recent years, the System's loan portfolio now has a significant amount of illiquid assets. In an effort to improve the situation, in 2011, the Board of Trustees of the Employees Retirement System lowered the maximum loan amount back to $5,000 and, in 2012, it approved the sale of approximately $315 million in loans. With a balance of $539 million as of June 30, 2013, personal loans are equivalent to approximately 76% of the Employees Retirement System's net assets.*
>
> *Finally, in 2008, the Employees Retirement System issued $2.9 billion in pension obligation bonds ("POBs"). The purpose of this offering was to increase the assets of the System available to invest and pay benefits. Unlike some other U.S. jurisdictions that have used this strategy, POBs are obligations of the Employees Retirement System itself and government employer contributions constitute the repayment source for the bonds.*

The Commonwealth and other participating employers are ultimately responsible for any funding deficiency in the Retirement Systems. The depletion of the assets available to cover retirement benefits would require the Commonwealth and other participating employers to cover such funding deficiency. Due to its multi-year fiscal imbalances previously mentioned, however, the Commonwealth has been unable to make the actuarially recommended contributions to the Retirement Systems. If the measures taken or expected to be taken by the current Commonwealth Administration fail to address the Retirement Systems' funding deficiency, the continued use of investment assets to pay benefits as a result of funding shortfalls and the resulting depletion of assets could adversely affect the ability of the Retirement Systems to meet the rates of return assumed in the actuarial valuations, which could in turn result in an earlier depletion of the Retirement Systems' assets and a significant increase in the unfunded actuarial accrued liability. Ultimately, since the Commonwealth's General Fund is required to cover a significant amount of the funding deficiency, the Commonwealth could have difficulty funding the annual required contributions if the measures taken or expected to be taken to reform the retirement systems do not have the expected effect. There may also be limitations on the Commonwealth's ability to change certain pension rights afforded to participants in the Retirement Systems."

There is no way we can predict when a pension system will fail to pay its pensioners. We can say that this is a terrible funding situation for promised retirement benefits. Puerto Rico is essentially operating on close to a pay-as-you-go basis. It has far worse pension funding than any of the 50 states in the U.S.. We have not included the promise of post-retirement health benefits, which only make the funding ratios worse. These are among the reasons why *The Economist* calls Puerto Rico a "Greek-like crisis on America's southern doorstep." (*The Economist*, October 26)

There is a second derivative at work now in dealing with state-specific mutual funds. Remember that Puerto Rico debt is tax-free in the various states and cities. State-specific funds can and do hold Puerto Rico debt as part of their composition. We think the involvement by states makes the exposure to Puerto Rico debt a nationwide issue, as opposed to the narrowness of exposure to the debt of Detroit, Stockton, or Harrisburg. A person in Arizona is not likely to own a tax-free bond from Detroit. Such a bond would be subject to taxation by Arizona. But a Puerto Rico bond could be held by any state-specific investor, because it would be tax-free. Mutual fund investors in state-specific funds may not know the exposure their fund has to Puerto Rico. The Oppenheimer Rochester funds have been mentioned by Lipper as having "the highest concentration of Puerto Rico bonds in the industry." (Reuters, October 16)

Rating agencies have Puerto Rico debt on negative watch and have it rated at the lowest level of investment grade. The ratings story is in the report and is available to those who subscribe to the rating agencies. There is not much we will add to it. But in our internal rating work at Cumberland we also consider population shifts and crime rates. This data is not positive for Puerto Rico.

Puerto Rico has a financing plan that it is trying to advance in order to raise between $500 million and $1.2 billion in the next round of bond issuance. The subject of Puerto Rico has been explored by a number of Wall Street firms and research houses and has been a topic at several conferences. We cannot say whether Puerto Rico will successfully be able to roll its debt. We can project that any financing will be at a high cost, imposed upon an economy beset by questionable growth, a history of chronic deficits, a huge per-capita debt load, and a nearly exhausted pension fund.

Since we have written about Puerto Rico and taken a hard-line negative position on its debt, naturally we have received emails regarding our position on Puerto Rico. We wish investors well. And we certainly hope that the Commonwealth of Puerto Rico finds a way to avoid any defaults and to keep its promises to pensioners. We are not cheering for the demise of this beautiful island, where 45% of its 3.5 million inhabitants live below the poverty line and where the debt-to-GNP ratio is estimated at about 140%, if the pension liability is included.

That said, we think there is additional headline risk of trouble in Puerto Rico; there is risk of a debt-service-payment miss in the event that Puerto Rico finds itself with insufficient cash flow to meet debt-service payment; and there is market risk if the Commonwealth fails to obtain sufficient market access so that it can roll the debt. At Cumberland, we are not holding Puerto Rico debt—we do not own it, and we would not buy it today. The same is true for any mutual fund with exposure to Puerto Rico.

35

Motor City Finally Hits Bankruptcy

John R. Mousseau
December 4, 2013

Yesterday, December 3, 2013, a federal judge ruled that the city of Detroit meet the legal criteria to file for relief under chapter 9 of the Bankruptcy Code and win protection from its creditors. The city filed for bankruptcy this past July.

United States bankruptcy judge Steven Rhodes effectively ruled that the city had demonstrated enough evidence to meet the test of insolvency. As a recap, remember that this is a city that has seen its population shrink from 1.8 million to 700,000 people in 35 years. The pension costs of earlier generations are being supported by a diminishing work force; there are ballooning annual deficits, a tax base that is decreasing substantially, and borrowing on top of borrowing. Detroit is by far the largest U.S. city to declare bankruptcy. It is struggling with approximately $18 billion in debt and long-term obligations.

Among the judge's findings were that (1) the city is, for all purposes, insolvent and has filed bankruptcy in good faith (this is important, as it means that cities cannot resort to bankruptcy on a whim) and (2) that pensions can be impaired (like other contracts) during a bankruptcy proceeding.

Clearly, the key in the bankruptcy language is that creditors will be treated fairly and equitably. When the city comes back with a further plan of adjustment, the negotiations will start. For most of the time period since the city filed in July, municipal unions have argued that pensions are protected under Michigan law. In this case, it would seem that the judge is saying that federal law supersedes state law.

What does this federal ruling mean, going forward?

Our first-glance opinion is that the city will continue to enjoy the protection afforded by chapter 9 of the Bankruptcy Code without being impeded by creditors. It also means that all unsecured creditors—pensioners, unsecured (read: general obligation) bondholders, and vendors—are subject to haircuts. The judge did go out of his way to say that the court will be very careful in exercising the power to impair pensions. This is an important point since, in some other states (notably California), some cities in bankruptcy proposed paying pensions even though they were cutting other debt.

The idea is for the city to be able to provide basic services—fire, police, and emergency services, as well as basic municipal services—and to be able to get back on a more solid financial footing and begin rebuilding. The kind of investments in the infrastructure that Detroit will need—from businesses, universities, and the state itself—will remain problematic. But to the extent it can happen, that investment will take place in an environment that is less financially crushing than the current one.

Bondholders, at first glance, would seem marginally better off as a result of the ruling. In other words, it doesn't appear they are being put behind other classes of creditors (read: unions). There has been very little trading in Detroit's general obligation bonds since the city filed in July. Five-year general obligation bonds (unsecured) are trading in the 6.90-7% range, compared to 1.25-1.50% for high-grade tax-exempt bonds. The general trend over the past two months has been a slight decrease in yields and a pickup in prices from the low levels going into bankruptcy. At the margin the ruling would also appear to benefit municipal bond insurers who have insured some of the city's debt. They now have another partner (unions) to help craft a solution.

The ruling does reinforce the benefit of having liens on essential services such as water, sewer, and transportation. General obligation bonds of all sorts have for years been considered among the safest classes of debt. But as we see with Detroit, in the case of the unthinkable—bankruptcy—

the general obligation bondholder becomes essentially an unsecured creditor. However, water and sewer bonds, secured by revenue streams, continue to be paid (although, as we have often mentioned, this provision doesn't forestall a drop in the value of bonds due to headline risk).

We will be watching developments closely. It would appear that this decision will reinforce some discipline among all parties involved in trying to craft a solution for Detroit, and will also affect other municipal entities grappling with problems such as pensions and other post-employment benefits. The State of Illinois passed a $160 billion pension rescue bill yesterday. The bill includes a number of measures, including limiting cost-of-living adjustments (COLA) in pensions and raising the retirement age for workers. In our opinion, the best aspect of the Illinois plan is that the legislature actually passed it. It was their sixth attempt in 16 months to approve some sort of pension reform in the state with the worst problems. If a solution can begin to be crafted in Illinois—even if it will certainly be challenged in the courts—then there is reason for optimism going forward.

Cumberland Advisors has not owned Detroit general obligation municipal bonds in portfolios in many years because of the clear credit risks and headline risks. We recently started to own Illinois state general obligation bonds again this summer as it appeared that progress was being made and that bonds were priced appropriately given the risks.

36

The Good, the Bad, and the Ugly—Muni Bonds in 2013

John R. Mousseau
December 17, 2013

The Good

After the bond market sell-off in June and July, which saw unprecedented bond redemptions, intermediate- and longer-maturity bond yields are the most attractive they have been in years. Even after some improvement in the market since September, there are plenty of 3%+ ten-year, 4%+ fifteen-year, and 5%+ twenty- to thirty-year tax-free yields. All but the highest of municipal credits in these ranges are trading higher than corresponding U.S. Treasury yields. At the same time that yields have spurted up over 100 basis points (1%), inflation has been declining. Trailing headline inflation, which had been at 2% at the end of February, is now at 1%. The math is simple: yields up over 1%, inflation down 1%. This is the cheapest that tax-free bonds have been on a REAL basis in quite some time. Locking in SOME book yields that are so high relative to current inflation is prudent.

And though Detroit and Puerto Rico have grabbed most of the credit headlines, the real story on municipal credit is that most municipalities are in the best shape they have been since the financial crisis, and in many cases they are better off than they were before the crisis. Most municipalities have undergone dramatic belt-tightening in the past five years. But the austerity has paid off. This should mark the 16th consecutive quarter of RISING overall municipal receipts. And there has been progress on the pension and other post-employment benefits (OPEB) front, even in states with the biggest problems, like Illinois. For the first time since the financial crisis, municipalities are NET hirers of workers this year.

The Bad

In our opinion, the panicked reaction of bond fund investors to the notion of Fed tapering was dramatic and greatly exaggerated. There was nothing orderly about the backup. Yields climbed on intermediate- and longer-term municipal bonds at an INCREASING rate during June/July. This trend was further compounded by an almost complete lack of support by Wall Street firms during the worst part of the meltdown (which, of course, helped CREATE the meltdown). For all purposes, it is as if the retail holders of bond funds mistook TAPERING (buying fewer bonds on a monthly basis by the Federal Reserve) with SELLING. Outright selling by the Fed could be years off. And with the federal deficit falling rapidly, the need to ISSUE Treasuries could be quite small. Right now it seems reasonable to conclude that the FEAR of tapering is much worse than TAPERING itself will turn out to be. Bond fund flows have continued to be negative—though not nearly at the pace of June and July.

The Ugly

Detroit and Puerto Rico have been the poster children this year for failure to address fiscal problems.

In the case of Detroit, the bankruptcy (filed in July and upheld this month) marked the culmination of years of downward spiraling. In a city that saw its bustling population of 1,800,000 some thirty-five years ago dwindle to an anemic 750,000 today, a steadily declining workforce found itself shouldering the pensions and benefits of an ever-increasing group of retiring workers. This unworkable equation meant that it was only a matter of time before the city's budgets buckled into fiscal collapse.

In the case of Puerto Rico, there is concern about whether the Commonwealth will be able to access the debt markets going forward. Puerto Rico has actually made real progress in cutting its deficit and addressing its pension issues. The cover of an August issue of Barron's, highlighting Puerto Rico's financial woes, points out how headline risk can rapidly escalate market risk.

Puerto Rico's financial problems have been well-known for some time. What the Barron's story pointed out was the fact that many municipal bond funds held 20-30% of their assets in Puerto Rico paper because of its exemption from income taxes in all fifty states. This "revelation" begat fierce selling of Puerto Rico paper, and the market quickly backed up over 200 basis points (2%) on many issues. While federal officials have been meeting with Puerto Rico officials to see if an enhanced level of cooperation can help to ease the financial crisis, the outcome on Puerto Rico is still up in the air. The Puerto Rico fiasco points out the need for as much vigilance with regard to headline risk as for outright financial risk itself.

So as we head into 2014, our viewpoint is that—away from the problem areas—intermediate and longer tax-free municipal bonds offer the best values they have in a long time. We feel the combination of now-higher interest rates, lower inflation, and better overall municipal credit affords investors a very good bargain for the assumed risk.

37

Build America Bonds—A Year in Review

Nannette L. Sabo
Vice President & Portfolio Manager—Fixed Income
December 27, 2013

Build America Bonds (BABs) are taxable bonds for which the U.S. Treasury Department pays a 35% direct subsidy to the issuer, offsetting borrowing costs. BABs are target-efficient. This means that for each dollar of revenue forgone by the federal government, a dollar's worth of benefits are received by state and local governments. The BABs program started on April 3, 2009, and offered new bonds in the primary markets until December 31, 2010. (Bonds continue trading today in secondary markets.) The first Build America Bond issued was a University of Virginia bond on April 5, 2009. BABs were created through the Economic Recovery and Reinvestment Act of 2009 (ERRA) and were designed with the intent to reduce the cost of municipal borrowing. They provided relief to struggling state and local municipalities by offering a new financing tool for public capital projects that could be successfully sold to investors at lower rates of interest. In the first year, new issuance amounted to $106 billion. This represented more than $90 billion of municipal financing and more than $12 billion in savings for that period. BABs did indeed enable municipalities to issue taxable debt and receive a federal tax subsidy (35% of interest expense); furthermore, they stimulated economic activity during the recession. BABs were well-received by 48 states, the District of Columbia, and two U.S. territories in the first year of issuance and constituted more than 20% of all new issuance in the municipal bond market from April 2009 through March 2010.

Like most fixed-income assets, BABs were cautiously scrutinized by investors in 2013, particularly during the first quarter. Sequestration talks were looming, and the congressional appetite for significant cutbacks had the stomachs of many investors and BABs issuers queasy, since the hands holding the budget-deal knife were positioning their blade to carve away at the BABs 35% federal subsidy. Anxiety continued to mount in the minds of investors when they realized that the asset class's unique ERP (extraordinary redemption provision) allowed issuers to call and refund issues in the event the BABs subsidy was lost. Essentially, this would take away the attractive lower financing costs for the issuer. The market initially expected to see an unprecedented number of calls and the pricing of BABs to drop significantly; however, we saw very few calls from issuers. Just two notable issues were called: Monona, Wisconsin, $7.67 million; and Columbus, OH, $476 million.

Approaching the end of the year, continuing conflict in Washington and still-lingering sequestration concerns resulted in the budgetary knives finally falling, confirming a 7.4% reduction to the 35% subsidy, leaving 32.41% for 2014. This less-than-favorable news was delivered to issuers in October. Another damaging punch to the belly of Build America Bond issuers was the news that during the government shutdown there would be no payments of BABs subsidies. This payment delay came as a surprise to most issuers. The government chose to view the payments as tax refunds and therefore did not distribute them during the shutdown. The market did not, however, take these developments as hard pressure points, since only the payments scheduled during the shutdown would be impacted; the payments would be delayed, not canceled; and the total amount of payments involved meant there would be limited fallout for investors. With respect to the ERP, most felt the ERP calls had already been triggered in April, and so further calls proved to be a nonevent. Refinancing would make sense for issuers only if BABs coupons could be replaced with lower-coupon tax-exempt issues. This, of course, would prove to be challenging since the tax-free markets had moved into a higher-yielding environment.

Let's now shift gears to examine how BABs spreads were impacted by the events of 2013. BABs experienced significant widening of spreads in April as a result of sequestration. Spreads rebounded only a little as we went into the summer months. Of course, there were unprecedented outflows from fixed-income funds in June and July after Ben Bernanke's implied statement that

Fed "tapering" was to commence in 2013. These outflows were an extreme overreaction, as the market seemed to hear that the Fed would taper, when Mr. Bernanke actually indicated that tapering would commence only if certain economic indicators (lower unemployment, higher GDP, higher inflation) were strong enough to support such an action. The clarification of Mr. Bernanke's statement came too late for many, and we saw a hurried flight out of fixed-income.

The selloff created exceptional opportunities to pick up assets at attractive prices paired with attractive yields. BABs continued to experience market-pricing drops as the entire municipal market confronted fears generated by the headlines about the bankruptcy of Detroit and troubles in Puerto Rico. The market seemed to throw all municipal issuers into the same stewpot of tainted assets—assets many investors simply no longer had the appetite to ingest.

Moving into the last quarter of 2013, taxable spreads moved slightly wider from their September mark; however, spread differentials between corporates narrowed by 2 bps. Bullets seemed to outperform, but callable BABs provided a higher relative value fit. Callable BABs were trading at lower prices by about 10-20 pts, with much higher yield pickups (50-90 bps) than non-callable paper. Based on the belief that most BABs are not expected to be called, these securities continue to offer a kick-up in yield and price to maturity after call dates. Primary risks to stay in front of (for callable BABs) would include: further cuts to or the elimination of the federal subsidy, resurrection of the BABs program (which could essentially offer opportunities for issuer refunds of outstanding callable bonds), or an extreme decline in tax-exempt rates (which would make tax-exempt bonds more tax-efficient).

Approaching the holiday season, taxable munis recovered much of their widening from April, making the week of Thanksgiving the best week of the year; and strong buying of thin offerings pushed spreads tighter. High-beta GOs and revenue bonds were observed to have performed extremely well, at times rallying 15-20 bps. Taxable munis rallied as we entered December, assisted by a treasuries sell-off that pushed yields back up by 5-7 bps. Strong buying resulted in strength in taxable munis: high-beta GOs continued to outperform, tightening 15-20 bps; and BABs traded just 10 bps wide to April's lows. The tightening of BABs spreads can be attributed to the calming of market volatility, the reclaiming of faith in underlying credits, and the need for spread product offering relative values in yields. BABs continue to offer limited upside, and there is still room for further tightening.

We like Build America Bonds in our portfolio construction as they add diversification. They represent slightly over 25% of our taxable assets. With wider spreads than comparable alternative assets, they provide more pick-up in yield. Furthermore, the asset class has proven to weather challenging times better than comparable alternatives, resulting in fewer defaults and bankruptcies. Historically, municipal bonds have exhibited lower default rates and higher recovery rates than comparable corporate alternatives. In a recent analysis by Moody's examining cumulative defaults rates averaged over the period of 1970-2012, municipal issuers with ratings of A and Baa experienced default rates in the 10th cumulative year of .05% & .305%, respectively, while corporate issuers with the same A and Baa ratings experienced default rates in the 10th cumulative year of 2.48% and 4.74%, respectively. Finally, BABs can be used in both weights of our taxable fixed-income barbell strategy, and BABs continue to be our favored asset in the long end of the barbell. Generally, we favor positioning BABs in our longer weighting; however, when we can find the right fit of liquidity, quality, and yield, we will also place them in the short-term end of the barbell as well. Certainly, these assets were not immune to market volatilities in 2013; however, they have remained a nice relative-value buy over most of the comparable alternatives.

38

Municipal Credit in the New Year

Michael F. Comes
January 9, 2014

As we enter 2014, we are faced with mixed developments affecting municipal bond issuers. Our firm-wide thesis is that the present slow, uneven recovery will continue, creating both challenges and opportunities for municipal bond investors. As a top-down manager, we have identified the following broad-based macro themes that will likely impact municipal issuers in the year to come.

Household net worth on a nominal basis is higher than in 2007, but it is lower on a real basis. Consumer deleveraging looks to have subsided as households have started to take on more debt.

1. Bonds backed by dedicated taxes (e.g., sales and income taxes) will likely benefit as incomes and discretionary spending increase.
2. Improving home values have stabilized property tax revenues to local governments in well-entrenched areas. We recommend local general obligation bonds with greater than $30 million in revenues, as idiosyncratic risk is greatly reduced once this threshold is crossed.

With roughly 6 million fewer people currently employed than in 2006 and low levels of business investment and capital expenditures, real GDP growth will likely remain sub-3%.

1. Essential service bonds backed by water and sewer revenues have proven to be resilient investments and have held up well throughout the cycle.
2. Debt issued by public higher-educational institutions with low reliance on state appropriations have performed well due to higher enrollments as demand has increased for relatively lower-cost public schools.

We are unsure of the extent to which federal budget cuts due to sequestration will manifest themselves in lower transfer payments to local governments. Transfers to state governments are meaningful, as roughly 40% of state revenues come from the federal government (Moody's Investors Service). CBO projects the budget deficit will increase to 3.5% of GDP by 2023 after declining to 2.1% next year. We expect further cuts and some impact to be felt at the local level.

1. The sector least exposed to the federal government is the infrastructure sector (source: Moody's). Issuers with monopolistic enterprises usually have adequate margin to increase fees, due to inelastic demand for their services. We recommend issuers who can raise fees without government intervention. These include airports, toll roads, and ports.
2. Several issuers have recently raised fees without reductions in user volumes. We view this as enhancing bondholder security. In December, the Port Authority of New York and New Jersey reported higher tolls on its bridges and tunnels without reduced usage. Going forward, we do not expect sequestration to directly impact Port Authority's ability to raise tolls.

Municipal buyers are fortunate in that the tax-exempt landscape is diverse and variegated. Bonds backed by sales taxes, tolls, water and sewer revenues, and tuition revenues all fall under the umbrella of "municipal bonds" yet bear little direct relationship to each other on a sector-wide level. This greatly enhances the diversification potential of municipal bond portfolios throughout the economic cycle. As we start the new year, we continue to look for these attractive opportunities for our clients.

39

More on Puerto Rico Debt

David R. Kotok
February 9, 2014

IRS Notice 2011-29 & Puerto Rico

An as-yet legally untested U.S. tax credit for the excise tax U.S. multinational companies pay to Puerto Rico essentially functions as a form of ongoing back-door financial aid to the economically distressed Commonwealth.

To delve into the details and determine what to make of them, we will begin by excerpting from the IRS notice regarding the Puerto Rican excise tax, linked here: *http://www.irs.gov/pub/irs-drop/n-11-29.pdf*. Research credits and additional informational links follow at the end of this commentary.

On October 25, 2010, Puerto Rico enacted legislation amending the Puerto Rico Internal Revenue Code of 1994 ("PR IRC")…Technical corrections to the legislation were enacted on October 28, 2010, and January 31, 2011. Final regulations relating to the Expanded ECI Rules and the Excise Tax were published on December 29, 2010. The Expanded ECI Rules and the Excise Tax are generally effective for income accruing and acquisitions occurring, respectively, after December 31, 2010.

Some other key points are excerpted, and the boldface is ours:

Section 901 allows a credit against U.S. income tax for the amount of any income…tax paid or accrued during the taxable year to any foreign country or to any possession of the United States."… The IRS and the Treasury Department are evaluating the Excise Tax. The provisions

of the Excise Tax are novel...The determination of the creditability of the Excise Tax requires the resolution of a number of legal and factual issues.

And here is a key additional paragraph:

Pending the resolution of these issues, the IRS will not challenge a taxpayer's position that the Excise Tax is a tax in lieu of an income tax under section 903. This notice is effective for Excise Tax paid or accrued on or after January 1, 2011. Any change in the foreign tax credit treatment of the Excise Tax after resolution of the pending issues **will be prospective**, and will apply to Excise Tax paid or accrued **after the date that further guidance is issued**.

Here are some key points in bullet form.

- PR collects the excise tax on so-called foreign companies with local manufacturing operations, and the paying companies then take a credit against their U.S. federal tax liability. Note that 33 of the 34 companies paying the tax are American; all but 300 of the 17,000 workers in these firms are employed by U.S.
- For the current PR fiscal year, the amount of revenue derived from the excise tax is estimated at about $2 billion, or about 20% of the PR general fund budget.
- The IRS has had nearly 3 years to study this "novel" excise tax and has not yet issued an opinion as to whether it should actually qualify for a tax credit. In the meantime, it does, and almost every dollar companies pay to PR is a dollar they don't otherwise pay in U.S. taxes.
- As of 2013, in light of continuing economic weakness, PR has not only extended the tax but raised it; it is now set to expire at the end of 2017 (an interesting coincidence, given the 2016 election cycle).
- According to writer Martin Sullivan of Tax Analysts (*www.taxanalysts.com*), five attorneys contacted by Tax Analysts "seriously" doubt the constitutionality of the tax; yet constitutional questions about this tax and credit remain untested. The tax is levied based on an 84-page legal opinion from the law firm hired by PR when PR Governor Luis Fortuño held office. He is now a partner of the Washington law firm that issued the opinion. See: h*ttp://www.steptoe.com/professionals-Luis_Fortuno.html.*

- On January 6, 2014, Treasury and the IRS stated they are continuing to evaluate the excise tax. They also affirmed that any change will be prospective.
- Neither Moody's (Feb. 7) nor Standard & Poor's (Feb. 4) mentions the overhanging and unresolved tax issue in their recent credit downgrades of PR; both rating agencies continue to keep PR on "negative" watch status.

Enough bullets! Let's step out of the weeds to look at the big picture.

Here is how we see it. (1) By not issuing an opinion the IRS and U.S. Treasury postpone the constitutional test litigation and perpetuate a policy that funnels an indirect subsidy of $2 billion a year to PR. (2) U.S. taxpayers are consequently funding almost one-fourth of the PR general fund budget without congressional approval, under the public radar screen, and based on an administrative deferral technique. (3) The actual cost to the businesses that pay the tax to PR is very small since they take a direct credit for that tax on their U.S. federal tax returns. (4) The rating agencies know that this is a fragile financial operation, and they also know that PR is collecting the tax and will continue to collect it until the IRS gives an opinion. (5) The amount involved each year is about equal to the annual interest payment on ALL of PR's outstanding debt. (6) This tax structure is based on a special provision of U.S. law enacted in 1921. (7) By continuing to "evaluate" the tax, the Obama Administration avoids a possible embarrassing default by PR; however, it simultaneously raises uncertainty for the businesses that do not know how to plan their PR tax policy. Thus debt markets price PR bonds as junk, and rating agencies maintain a negative outlook. The uncertainty premium in PR debt just grows and grows.

Cumberland does not hold PR debt in its managed accounts that call for investment-grade credit. We view PR bonds as a distressed debt in the junk category. The tax structure outlined above has not been enough to stabilize or revive PR, though it has no doubt assisted PR in avoiding, thus far, an outright default on its debt. PR's troubles in gaining market access at a reasonable interest rate continue to intensify.

Many thanks to Erin Arvedlund of the Philadelphia Inquirer for some research help. We applaud Martin Sullivan at Tax Analysts for his detailed January 27 paper entitled "The Treasury Bailout of Puerto Rico." See *http://www.taxanalysts.com/www/features.nsf/Articles/1F974381895173AC85257C6D005F0128.*

Cumberland's Michael F. Comes offered invaluable assistance in the research effort that led to this commentary.

40

Detroit Update

Michael F. Comes
February 27, 2014

On Friday of last week, Detroit Emergency Manager Kevyn Orr released his bankruptcy plan of adjustment detailing how the city will emerge from bankruptcy. This is a key step in the city's bankruptcy process as it lays the groundwork for how the city's finances will look after negotiations among stakeholders. A Chapter 9 municipal bankruptcy plan's purpose is to detail the haircuts, restructurings, and new investments in city services that will have to occur in order to realign the city's expense base with its current financial resources. The element which distinguishes this case from other forms of bankruptcy is "the new investments" part of the plan, which ensures that the bankruptcy will not only satisfy the claims of creditors but also meet the needs of city residents by providing improvements in city services, with the goal of making the city an inhabitable place again.

The marketplace has labeled the plan as "controversial" for its treatment of general obligation bondholders as unsecured creditors. The muni market has long viewed the general obligation pledge as a "senior and secured" pledge which compels an issuer to use its "full faith and credit" to repay the bonds by raising taxes—before paying other creditors. The plan contains no tax increases and instead proposes haircuts of 80% on GO bondholders, greater than the 70%-80% cuts for pension beneficiaries, effectively subordinating GO debt to claims of pension beneficiaries. Bond insurers, who have insured $641 million of general obligation debt, have argued in mediation that under state statute and existing case law, general obligation unlimited tax bondholders should receive preferential treatment over other creditors because of their secured status. Not so in this case.

The emergency manager's viewpoint is that the city's residents have paid a hefty price in the years leading up to bankruptcy in the form of reduced health and public services, high crime, and urban blight. As is, with 30% of its residents living below the poverty line, Detroit is the second-highest-taxed city in the state of Michigan; thus the capacity for further tax increases to repay bondholders is limited.

Other post-employment benefit (OPEB) beneficiaries will likely receive 10% of original value, and holders of Certificates of Participation or COPS (see Detroit Bites Again) are offered a low settlement with drastic haircuts typically not seen in Chapter 9 Bankruptcy cases. The plan also addresses Detroit Water and Sewerage Department debt, classifying it as bankruptcy-eligible and thus subject to automatic stay provisions—a questionable interpretation, as Chapter 9 states that special revenue debt is not legally direct debt of a bankrupt entity. Instead, it is self-supported by a dedicated revenue stream as part of a bankrupt entity's ongoing operations. In this case, Detroit water and sewer bonds are impaired by an exchange for notes in a new authority and subordination of debt service payments to payments back to the city.

The plan will have far-reaching consequences for how municipal bond investors perceive risk and return in the marketplace. Spreads on general obligation debt are likely to differ by state based on statutory authority to raise taxes, and the market's perception of "safe-haven asset" may switch from general obligation debt to self-supporting debt not subject to automatic stay. Detroit's emergence from bankruptcy will likely be a long, litigated process that could take years, with high direct and indirect costs. We will follow closely and keep readers apprised of new developments.

41

Puerto Rico Update

David R. Kotok
March 5, 2014

The PR GO curve is inverted and shorter maturity GOs are trading cheap to CCC corporates. Thus, if the Commonwealth is able to access sufficient long-term borrowing in a timely manner, the curve could flatten or even revert to an upward sloping one and GOs will richen vs. comparable maturity distressed corporates.

While the Attorney Generals have opined that COFINA's revenues are not considered available Commonwealth revenues and thus not available for clawback, the Supreme court has not ruled on constitutionality of segregating COFINA revenues as it does not have the jurisdiction to provide advisory rulings…

—Vikram Rai, Mikhail Foux, George Friedlander,
"U.S. Municipal Strategy Special Focus: A SWOT analysis of
of Puerto Rico's general obligation (GO) debt."
Citi Research,. March 4, 2014.

We fly to Paris in hours. Our first meeting there is Thursday late morning. Ukraine and the cross border effects on Europe's banks are a serious issue.

Meanwhile PR is in focus again. The Citi team listed above has issued a superbly done report. Here are Cumberland's bullets:

- It looks as though Puerto Rico will get the new financing done next week. It will be at a high cost with a junk rating. Governance may be NY law, not PR law, for whatever that means if they default down the road. Size is $3 to $3.5 billion. Rate on it will be 8.5% to 9.5% on the low and 10% to 11% on the high end. We think it comes on the low side. Tax-free, PR GO debt with dispute adjudication under NY law. Our best guess is 9% on the longest piece. Remember, the NY law issue is untested for PR debt issuance. There are many theories, but there are zero precedents.

- It buys Puerto Rico about two years' time to get their house in order. Will they do it? No one knows. Does the present young Governor Padilla want to? Yes, if he can. Will this be a turning point for PR? Maybe.

- The new money means cash needs are met for the next two years and no default occurs on most of the present bonds. Be careful here. Most is not all. Some of them are still at risk, and the research needed to sort this out really means getting into the weeds. Remember, this is still a junk credit so undocumented and un-researched assertions and assumptions may be dangerous to an investor's health.

- Temporary removal of the default threat temporarily helps bond insurers and most existing PR debt.

- A MUNI RALLY IS AT HAND. Why? Three reasons. 1.Muni funds hold more than one standard deviation above mean in cash because of the fear of redemptions (source: Ned Davis Research). 2.Detroit is resolving slowly; the losses and haircuts for bondholders are becoming known. 3.PR probably doesn't default. The long-term muni yield in the highest grade is still higher than the taxable Treasury. This will not last forever. It may change very soon.

- We think that the muni rally from this level can be fierce. We are very bullish on high-grade U.S.-dollar-denominated tax-free bonds. We are long and stay long. Furthermore, we think the upside yield levels where the highest grade tax-free bond yields more than the taxable treasury is about to reverse. Finally, the partial hedges on long munis may show results.

- Additionally, and only for those who have the risk tolerance for exposure to junk rated credits, we are also managing a special type of separate account in only PR debt. It is not high-grade. It is currently positioning. We are long junk credit in PR in these special researched accounts.

I am heading to Paris. À bientôt.

42

Muni Green Shoots

Michael F. Comes
April 4, 2014

During the first quarter of 2014, state and local government fiscal conditions have improved in line with what would be expected during a "new-normal," low-growth period. The aggregate demand-dampening effects of the recession and its flow-through to state and local government budgets has manifested itself in a continued subdued growth in tax receipts and greater demand for non-discretionary entitlement spending. The challenge in 2014 and beyond will be recovery from the effects of the recession and a continued commitment to cost containment.

From 2008–present, higher outlays for Medicaid and unemployment compensation, coupled with a 17% decline in tax revenues from the contraction in the national economy, forced across-the-board reductions in budget areas such as appropriations for K-12 education, higher education, transportation, and corrections. Without help from the federal government under the American Recovery and Reinvestment Act (ARRA), state budget cuts and tax increases would have been much more substantial[1]. Among the fifty states, the accumulated budgetary shortfall from 2009-2011 was $431 billion. States received approximately $140 billion in stimulus funds from 2009-2011, most of it distributed in 2010 when the total state budgetary shortfall was $191 billion, allowing states to temporarily maintain most of their funding levels[2]. When stimulus funding expired, in the face of weak sales and income tax collections, governors were forced to raise income and sales taxes and cut expenditures.

In 2013 and continuing into the first quarter of 2014, we saw a reversal of these trends. Given the severity of the conditions, the ability of states to bounce back in such short order is a testament to their flexibility. In recent quarters, enacted budget cuts and budget gaps have substantially declined while revenues have continued to outperform projections[3].The National Association of State Budget Officers' "Fiscal Survey of States," fall 2013, shows that enacted fiscal 2014 budgets reflect an aggregate increase in expenditures of 3.8% over 2013, a strong indicator of states' new focus on stimulus and investments instead of austerity. Anecdotal evidence such as New York Governor Andrew Cuomo's $300 million budget surplus in his proposed 2014 budget, which includes outlays for new programs such as universal pre-K without use of tax increases, suggests somewhat of a return to normalcy and a positive contribution from the state government sector to the overall economy[4].

The improving fiscal outlook for states has positive implications for other areas of the municipal market as well. We expect local government finances to improve in conjunction with the outlook for states, since the costs of several major expenditures such as K-12 education funding are borne by both state and local governments. The challenge in 2014 will be gaining access to funding from lesser-used revenue sources such as user fees and sales and income taxes, in the face of a continuing decline (albeit, at a decelerating rate) of property taxes. Since costs on the local level are much "stickier" than on the state level, because they cover provision of services and associated personnel costs rather than fiscal transfers to other entities, the cuts will be more difficult to enact and will involve workforce cuts and contract renegotiations.

Lastly, the subject of entitlement spending by state and local governments is a concern. Medicaid enrollment has tripled in the past three decades, from 20 million in 1980 to 53 million in 2011, accounting for, on average, 24% of state expenditures, making it the single largest expenditure item in state budgets. The expansion in eligibility for Medicaid under Obamacare and the declining federal government funding structure associated with these increases points to an increasingly larger burden of these costs having to be funded by states. This will likely crowd out other major budgetary priorities such as education and create additional funding pressures.

We will watch closely to see how states respond to these challenges. Tax revenues are likely to continue their upward climb at a subdued pace, as would be expected in a 2.5% real-growth environment. The recession created a void that put pressures on the rest of the market by taking away funding for important priorities while increasing demand for entitlements. We expect state and local governments to take the needed steps to address these patterns, as they have done in the past, through some combination of revenue diversification and cuts to expenditures. We will keep readers apprised of future developments.

[1,2,3] "Fiscal Survey of States Fall 2013" National Association of State Budget Officers.

[4] New York Seeks Upgrade after On-Time Budget; featured in Bloomberg Brief 3.31.14; Klopott, Freeman; Chappatta, Brian.

43

U-Turn

Michael F. Comes
April 12, 2014

It turns out there is a strong possibility losses to bondholders from Detroit's bankruptcy won't be as painful as had originally been thought. Emergency Manager Kevyn Orr has made a U-turn on how General Obligation Unlimited Tax (GO ULT) bondholders are going to be treated in this bankruptcy. Given the magnitude of insolvency, the irony is that Detroit's bondholders may fare better than other creditors in post-2008 vintage bankruptcies—and roughly in line with historical norms.

On Thursday, Judge Jerald Rosen, who is presiding over mediation between the city and bond insurers National Public Finance Guarantee, Ambac, and Assured Guaranty, announced a negotiated settlement whereby bond insurers would have their claims reinstated in the amount of $287.5 million of their $388 million original claim (a recovery of 74%) and exchanged for obligations of the Michigan Finance Authority. This new claim would be secured by an unlimited tax general obligation of the city, which is further secured by distributable state aid payments from the state of Michigan. The balance of the claim, 26%, will go to an income stabilization fund for vulnerable pension retirees. In layman's terms, general obligation unlimited tax bondholders in the Detroit bankruptcy, most of whom are insurers, will recover 74% of principal value, up from an offer of 20% in February and 15% as of March 31. This is a very fluid situation.

So why the drastic increase in recovery from 15-20% to 74%? It appears that Emergency Manager Kevyn Orr has had a change of heart.

Orr's original plan of adjustment classified GO ULT debt as unsecured, or not having a lien on the city's ability to raise taxes by the amount needed to pay debt service. We have written extensively in previous commentaries on the subject, arguing that GO ULT debt is in fact secured and that his degradation of this security structure impacts how local general obligation debt is treated relative to other types of securities in a typical local issuer's capital structure, namely to revenue debt like water and sewer bonds, which continue to be paid during bankruptcy and are not subject to automatic stay.

The new agreement states that UTGOs do in fact have a lien and that the UTGOs millage constitutes special revenue under Section 902 of the bankruptcy code.

In a Bloomberg Brief interview dated April 11, 2012, Kevyn Orr states that if the millage weren't enforced to repay bondholders, that it might not have been collectible by the city in the first place, forcing Detroit to forgo a key revenue stream into its general fund. The change in treatment has been prompted by the willingness of bond insurers to give up 26% of their dedicated revenue stream to pension beneficiaries, an arrangement which Orr supports. His interpretation of the bankruptcy law has changed based on his ability to extract concessions from bondholders in the form of distributable state aid payments.

The implications for this U-turn are vast. First, if in fact payments to general obligation unlimited tax bondholders do constitute a special revenue because they have an actual lien on taxing power, this solidifies the seniority of the GO ULT pledge versus other general fund pledges, a contentious issue prior to the announcement of this settlement agreement. Also, pursuant to Section 902 of the Bankruptcy Code, since special revenue indebtedness is not subject to automatic stay provisions, what would be the purpose of filing for Chapter 9 if the creditor could not seek relief from such obligations? Would unlimited tax general obligations be left intact while all other obligations not considered as having special liens, such as lease-backed, limited tax, and miscellaneous revenue bonds, be restructured?

As our friend Natalie Cohen of Wells Fargo has pointed out in her writings, the question of use of proceeds is also of interest. If Detroit used proceeds from GO ULT or GO LT indebtedness for specific projects, instead of just "general purposes," the revenues may be considered "special revenues." If not, this argument is less valid. Because the city of Detroit does issue GO ULT bonds for specific projects and not general purposes, they may be classified as special revenues.

Although this mediation agreement is just that, and not part of a court-approved plan, these terms could change; however, Emergency Manager Kevyn Orr, who during the course of this bankruptcy has had significant negotiating leverage over creditors, was party to this agreement. Given his desire to fast-track this process, we believe this agreement has a high probability of approval and incorporation into the plan of adjustment.

Analysis of post-2008 vintage bankruptcies shows that Detroit's GO ULT creditors will fare relatively well in this process, contrary to the market's prior perception. Harrisburg's general obligation bondholders recovered 75% while Jefferson County's holders of sewer warrants recovered 55-60%. Vallejo's creditors recovered 50%. If this agreement goes through, it will help cement the seniority of GO ULT creditors over other classes of debt in Chapter 9 municipal bankruptcy. This is a welcome event for a chapter in the bankruptcy code with little case law to guide its interpretation, a reflection of its lack of usage (annual Chapter 9 filings in the mid single digits versus roughly 11,000 annual Chapter 11 filings). This begs the question: "Was a Chapter 9 filing really necessary?" Kevyn Orr sought to classify GO ULT debt as unsecured, when in fact it was widely believed that it was secured. After tens of millions in legal fees, a river of negative press, and ripple effects to other local municipalities, we have taken a U-turn and are back to where we started.

44

The Cold Shoulder

Michael F. Comes
June 30, 2014

Last week was a difficult one for the Commonwealth of Puerto Rico.

On Wednesday and Thursday, the governor and legislature passed a law creating a statutory framework for the Commonwealth's public corporations to restructure their debt and contractual obligations. This legislation is analogous to U.S. Chapter 9 laws and dispels prior notions held by market participants that the Commonwealth would come to the rescue to bail out its public corporations. It appears that the ratings agencies were caught off guard by these changes as well and downgraded the Commonwealth's public corporations (in some cases multiple notches) as a result.

In years past, the demarcation between what constituted GO vs. agency debt was blurred. Ratings agencies and the marketplace treated Puerto Rico GOs and enterprise debt as being on parity with each other and assigned a slightly better value to the enterprise debt, given its "double-barrel" appropriation-backed and enterprise revenue pledge. The government's recent shifting stance marks a "sea change" in how it views its corporations. No longer will they be treated as within-arms-length conduits acting on behalf of the Commonwealth; instead they will function as independent enterprises, with more autonomy. The current governor, Alejandro Garcia Padilla, ran in 2012 on a mandate to turn the public corporations into enterprises independent from the Commonwealth.

Governor Padilla introduced the Recovery Act to preempt what he sees as inevitable at this point: restructurings of public corporations and possible forbearance agreements. The sudden shift in stance, which comes at the expense of bondholders, ignores an institutional framework that has been in place for the past 60 years. The governor's tactics in reneging on what was effectively an unspoken agreement between bondholders and the Commonwealth obscures the fact that the prior actions of the Commonwealth, using public corporations as conduits for debt issuance, are what got us here in the first place. Investors have now been given the cold shoulder.

We note the following characteristics of Puerto Rico debt as evidence of the "within arms-length" relationship that has existed between the Commonwealth and its corporations:

1. Bonds of the Puerto Rico Highways and Transportation Authority (PRHTA), and other public corporations are secured by revenues of their various enterprises but subject to prior claims from the Commonwealth's GO bondholders. This "constitutional clawback" allows the Commonwealth to dip into revenues to repay its general obligation indebtedness.

2. Annual operating subsidies are granted to Puerto Rico Aqueduct and Sewer Authority(PRASA) equal to 10% of revenues; subsidies are granted to Puerto Rico Electric Power Authority (PREPA); these corporations are required to make offsetting payments back to the Commonwealth in lieu of taxes.

3. Low collections rates and high receivables balances from the Commonwealth (by far PREPA's largest customer) for services rendered to it by public corporations would not occur under normal arms-length business transactions. PREPA's accounts receivables balance from the government sector hovers around $400 million, equal to 8% to 10% of revenues.

4. Prior to 6/27/14, Moody's had rated Puerto Rico Electric Power Authority (PREPA) as equal to or better than the Commonwealth's GO credit quality. The same does not hold true for PRASA, but buyers may have lumped those two together as being similar. The notching differential by Moody's where PREPA is rated lower than the Commonwealth is a new phenomenon that has occurred as a result of Moody's view of the "de-linking," in their own words, between the Commonwealth and PREPA and the public corporations.

5. The following excerpt, taken from a Moody's report dated 2/6/2012 for a PRASA new issue, highlighted the fact that a PRASA bond was issued to finance the Commonwealth's own budget deficit:

Proceeds of the... bonds will be used for refinancing $1.1 billion in lines of credit that had been extended by the [Government Development Bank] GDB and a $241 million bond anticipation note that was issued to repay a syndicated loan maturing in January 2012.... Furthermore, given the historical level of support from the commonwealth, Moody's views this financing as essentially a deficit financing of the commonwealth.

The law also opens up a broad discussion regarding the legal apparatus in place in Puerto Rico, which resembles Swiss cheese. Since the U.S. took control of the island in 1901, there have been efforts to "recodify" or "harmonize" the Commonwealth's government, based in Spanish civil code, with the U.S. legal system. True reforms have been slow to come, but a large step in the process was last Wednesday's passage of this new act which, quoting from a press release, will allow such public corporations to "overcome their financial obstacles, through a statutory process that allows them to handle their debts fairly and equitably, while ensuring the continuity of essential service and infrastructure upgrades." This is no doubt a page out of U.S. Chapter 9 Bankruptcy Code, which also stipulates a "fair and equitable" settlement under a bankruptcy.

Going forward, we believe in the need for purchasing credit-enhanced paper when buying Puerto Rico public corporation debt. The market is currently pricing insured paper at around 5.25%, whereas uninsured paper across the curve is trading on a recovery value of $44-47. Yields on insured versus uninsured paper have diverged in the past few months on questions of the credit erosion of public corporations and upgrades of AGM and Natl-RE by Moody's and S&P (when monolines insure a bond they are effectively selling their rating, the value of which increases as the rating increases). Other Puerto Rico debt, such as GOs and sales tax bonds, have traded higher in price since the restructuring legislation announcement, as they are specifically addressed as not being able to be restructured under this law. They will likely be kept intact to allow for future financing needs. We do not own uninsured paper issued by the Commonwealth's public corporations, as the risk of restructuring has increased substantially since last week.

In the coming days, weeks, and months, we expect new developments to occur which will create more of a divergence between Puerto Rico GO debt and bonds issued by PREPA, PRASA, and PRHTA. As obligations from these entities comprise roughly 40% of total public debt outstanding in the Commonwealth, the governor has found a convenient way to reduce the island's debt burden without an ugly sovereign restructuring. Other steps will have to be taken to reduce the island's energy costs and regain competitiveness, but this is likely the first of many steps to be taken in deleveraging and reducing the government's footprint on the economy.

45

HQLA & Munis

David R. Kotok
September 8, 2014

High Quality Liquid Assets (HQLA) is a term that now applies to the implementation of the Liquidity Coverage Ratio (LCR) in the Basel III Rule. This highly technical mouthful of acronyms and rules specifically applies to banks, their liquidity requirements and the rules governing the securities in their investment portfolios. The targets of the new rules are the big banks.

According to an analysis by BMO Capital Markets, "In general it will require banks with more than $250 billion in assets to hold enough HQLA to cover 100% of a projected 30-day cash outflow in a stressed scenario." BMO notes that banks holding over $50 billion will have to meet a "lighter version" of the requirements than will banks with over $250 billion. Small banks with under $50 billion are in a different category and are not considered by regulators to be systemically risky institutions, so the new rules do not apply to them.

What does all this have to do with municipal bonds?

The HQLA rules as defined by the Federal Reserve (Fed) for U.S. banks have excluded municipal bonds from this category of securities that must meet the LCR. Corporate bonds, certain equities, conventional mortgages, federal agency securities, and U.S. and other OECD sovereign debt are included.

Multiple issues arise for investors in the wake of the new rules, though readers must note that this is a fluid rulemaking determination and things may change. We will address some issues as we see them in this current and evolving regulatory structure.

It is important to note that investment-grade corporate bonds have a default rate that is 36 times higher than the default rate on investment-grade municipal bonds. This determination is based on information from Moody's compiled on investment-grade defaults from 1970 to 2013. In other words, the Fed has defined into the rule those corporate securities that have 36 times the default rate, historically speaking, of investment-grade municipal bonds that the Fed has excluded from the rule.

To give an example: the bond of Johnson & Johnson, a corporation headquartered at Exit 9 of the NJ turnpike is included, but NJ Turnpike Authority debt is not. Both bonds are quite liquid and easily traded, and both are high-grade ratings. Why the Fed made this decision, which would include JNJ and exclude NJ-TPKE, is still not completely clear. There is discussion underway among market professionals who are attempting to get the Fed to change its view.

What the rule means for municipal bonds is that a support mechanism in the marketplace that would have facilitated the issuance of municipal debt is weakened by a new rule. As a result, it will cost municipal bond issuers more to achieve their financing. There are various estimates of how much more it will cost—these issuers are all guessing. The fact is that it will take time to determine exactly how banks will hold municipal debt in the future, after the market has adjusted the price or yield to make up for the difference made by the rule.

There is an area in which municipal bonds will surely be impacted. That is in the "bank-qualified" smaller issues. BQ was an exception made in the Tax Reform Act of 1986 to facilitate the issuance of municipal debt by smaller issuers. Those bonds are not highly liquid and it would have made sense for the Fed to exclude them in a liquidity calculation. In most cases, the banks holding BQ debt are servicing local customers that are municipal entities and assisting them with financing. That is why the Tax Reform Act of 1986 provided special incentives for banks.

We now have a situation resulting from a change in a tax-law incentive that had been in place for decades. The Fed has issued a rule that has offset or reduced that incentive. A tension between incentive and disincentive is at work in the small-bank qualified-issuer municipal bond market.

In the United States, a large number of the 90,000 municipal bond issuers fall into in this BQ category. Their cost of financing will certainly rise by some amount.

Let's get to what the new HQLA rules mean for investors. In one way, this is good news. We are taking bond buyers (large banks, for instance) who traditionally participated in parts of a bond market, and removing some of those buyers or imposing a new cost on them. The impact raises tax-free yields to offset the change.

Individual municipal bond investors will like this new rule because it results in a higher tax-free interest rate for them. There is more prospective tax-free income for owning municipal bonds. As attractive as municipal bonds may have been in the past, they will be even more attractive because a competing buyer (the larger banks) is being removed or reduced.

How this ultimately plays out in a $3.7 trillion U.S. municipal bond market remains to be seen. We know the rule currently impacts municipal bond issuers in a negative way. At the present time, there is no indication that the rule is going to be changed.

In the U.S., at intermediate and long maturities, the tax arbitrage available in the income tax code for tax-free bonds is minimally applicable. Market forces are pricing municipal bonds of long maturities at relative bargain rates. We see that today when we compare a long-term, true-AAA, highest-grade, tax-free bond with an equivalent long-term U.S. Treasury taxable obligation. When we do that, we find the interest rate paid on those tax-free bonds in current market conditions is approximately the same as that paid on the taxable bond. In other words, market agents and forces are pricing the municipal bonds as if there is no income-tax code. This makes no sense.

We also know that when we get to the shorter-maturity end of the yield curve, we see the yield on tax-free way below the taxable yield. In the shorter end the tax arbitrage is almost fully applied. In the middle of the yield curve, the tax arbitrage of the U.S. income tax code is somewhat fully applied, while at the longest maturities it is virtually nonexistent in market pricing. So, as one goes from shorter to longer maturity, the tax arbitrage component diminishes. We think HQLA will only exacerbate this anomaly.

The bottom line of HQLA is that a change has occurred that will alter market-pricing references by some amount. We do not know how much. HQLA rules will benefit the individual investor who selectively manages municipal bonds and chooses them skillfully. The individual investor will gain at the expense of the large banks, which will be adversely affected to some degree. Small banks are not affected. The details will be revealed as markets adjust to this new paradigm.

Meanwhile, there are still relative bargains in the tax-free bond space. Investors who worry about rising rates can use hedging devices to dampen the volatility they would experience if and when rates eventually rise.

46

A Win for Muni Investors

Michael F. Comes
October 3, 2014

One of the unforeseen consequences of the financial crisis has been the phenomenon of municipal governments in distress. Prior to the financial crisis, Chapter 9 municipal bankruptcy was a topic hardly germane to municipal investors: it happened sometimes, usually for one-off reasons (e.g., a legal judgment or poor internal controls) but was not widespread. The infrequency of municipal distress made municipal bankruptcy an issue that was overlooked by investors, and untested. Annual Chapter 9 filings number in the single digits and are concentrated in small, non-rated issues; in contrast, there are roughly 10,000 Chapter 11 filings annually.

The biggest "credit" issue is the municipal capital structure, and the recent emergence of pension obligations and other post-employment benefits as long-term liabilities—the result of poor stock market performance and the graying of the population. Since this is a new problem, it raises unanswered questions. In the case of Detroit and California municipalities, which used bankruptcy as a tool to restructure, we've asked ourselves, "Who is first in line to get paid in a bankruptcy?"

On Wednesday, Judge Christopher Klein, the federal judge overseeing Stockton's bankruptcy, ruled that CalPERS and GO bondholders are both unsecured creditors. Payment of claims to CalPERS will not come prior to those of bondholders in a plan of adjustment; they will be equally secured on the same basis. This is a big deal for three reasons. First, it asserts the power of the federal government in the relationship between state and local governments. We take Klein's decision to mean that state and local fiscal relationships fall within the jurisdiction of federal courts. This has been called into question by CalPERS who has argued that state law and constitutional protections cannot be altered by federal government. This is very much a 10th Amendment issue. Second, the ruling reinforces the government's power to amend, modify, and break contracts, a power reserved solely to the federal government under the "Contracts Clause" of the U.S. Constitution. Third, it is a positive for bondholders.

It does not solve a primary problem we've seen, and that is the principal-agent problem inherent in local government finance—namely, will Stockton's elected officials do what is in the best interest of bondholders, or themselves? Stockton's proposed plan of adjustment haircuts creditors but not pension payments to unions. The plan is much less likely to be confirmed now. Hearings on the city's plan of adjustment start on October 30th.

This ruling is different from other bankruptcy rulings because it speaks to the foundations of federalism in the entire country. If state constitutional protections of pension benefits are invalidated, cities like Chicago, for example, can more easily negotiate benefit reductions with unions using federal law as leverage. Illinois constitutional protections would be an afterthought.

Last, we think the ruling helps the trading value of bonds. In weak areas where investors trade bonds based on likelihood of default, the market's loss-given-default assumption is reduced. We also think it serves as a fiscal management tool in the setting of pension benefits. It removes the incentive of filing for bankruptcy as a way to continue paying pension benefits at the expense of bondholders. Haircuts will be set for both types of entities, such that one is not greater than the other.

The ruling provides clarity in an otherwise untested chapter in the U.S. bankruptcy code. We have studied cases of municipal bankruptcy and find this issue to be a pressing one in need of resolution.

47

The Muni Supply Spike—Bond Buyer Visible Supply

John R. Mousseau
December 1, 2014

The Bond Buyer Visible Supply represents the amount of municipal bonds to be offered by dealers over the next 30 days. This week we have seen a spike of over $18 billion in supply. This spike is in a market that has been averaging about $8 billion in new issuance. It averaged much less earlier in the year.

A large amount of this issuance will be used to refund older higher-coupon bonds that were issued in 2005. Those bonds are now approaching their 10-year call. New bonds with lower yields can now replace those older ones. This is a tried and true method for issuers to manage and lower their overall debt-service costs. Many of these 2005 issues were bonds issued to advance-refund even older higher-coupon bonds (issued at around 6%) in the late 1990s. During that time interest rates were much higher and were reflected in the stock market tech craze. IRS rules prohibited the issuers from advance-refunding these 2005 issues. Issuers can refund the bonds once the call date is reached, and that is what they are doing. We think this activity puts pressure on the municipal bond market. Even though the amount of net new issuance does not drastically change (example: selling $100 million new bonds and calling in $100 million older higher-coupon bonds), the issues still have to clear the market. There is clearly some money rolling over at year-end to absorb some of this, but the sheer size of the calendar should allow for some softening of prices.

This phenomenon should continue through much of 2015 and into 2016—not all the time but most acutely at the junctures of large maturities of bonds—that is, January and July. We expect this to be a fairly good opportunity to buy longer-dated municipal bonds at municipal-to-Treasury yield ratios approaching 135–140%. This is excellent value in our opinion, given the ratios and the extreme difference in yields between shorter-term and longer-term bonds. We will keep readers informed.

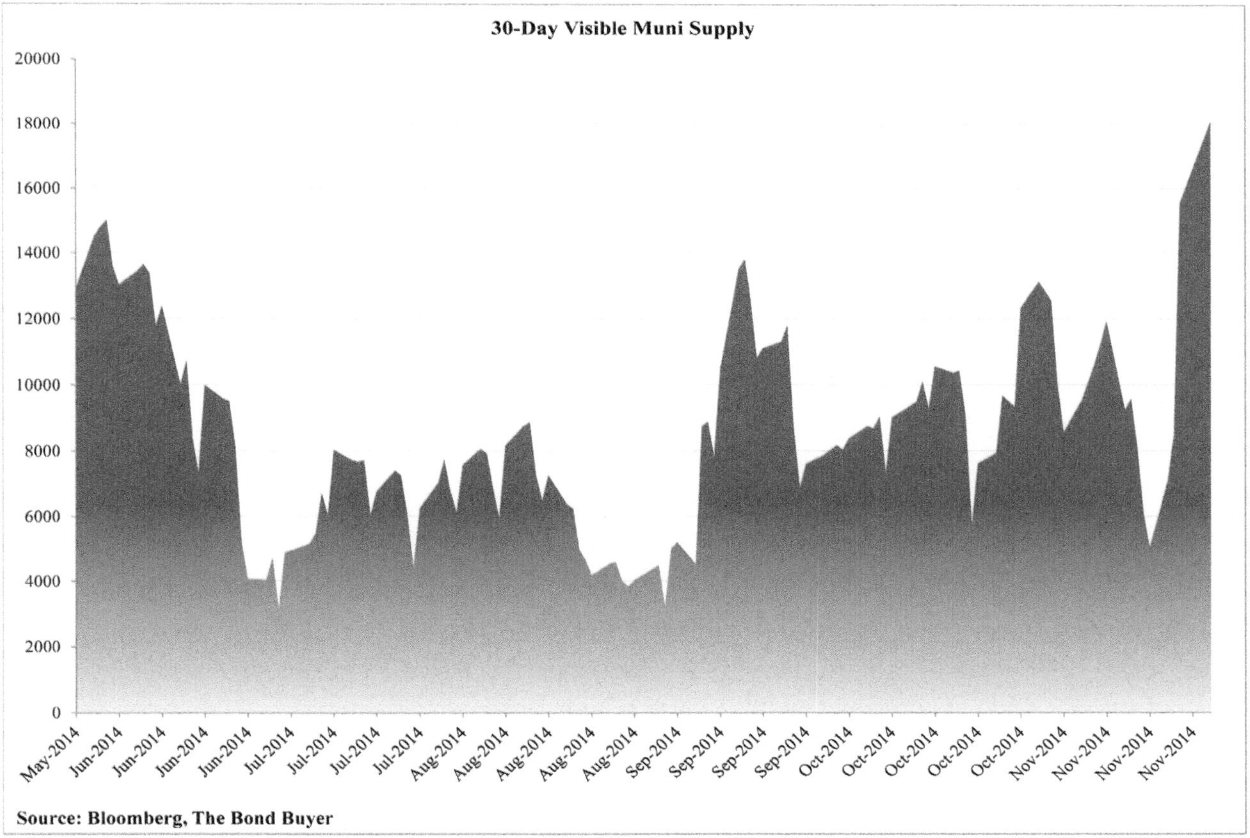

Notes

Section I: The Transformation of an Entire Asset Class

Chapter 1: The Changing Face of the Municipal Bond Market

1 Tender option bonds are investment vehicles whereby a sponsor such as a hedge fund or investment bank would purchase long-term bonds and partially finance the purchase with sale of short-term floating-rate bonds to money market funds. With the widespread downgrade of bond insurers starting in 2007, many banks were unable to continue rolling the short-term notes to money market funds, leaving them on the hook to redeem them from money market investors. Because of restrictions on proprietary trading under the Dodd-Frank Act, tender-option bond financing has come to a virtual standstill.

2 MMA's research services can be accessed by subscribers on the World Wide Web. More information can be found on their homepage at the following URL: http://www.mma-research.com/.

3 We highly recommend that interested readers visit the website of *The Bond Buyer*, a daily publication covering the municipal bond market. The newspaper's journalists have provided valuable analysis and commentary on important events as they transpired. http://www.bondbuyer.com

4 The authors would like to credit Natalie Cohen, Managing Director and Head of Municipal Research at Wells Fargo Securities for constructing the historical narrative presented in these paragraphs.

5 Municipal Market Analytics, *Monthly Overview: September* (2008), 2., The authors would like to thank certain bond salesmen and traders at broker-dealer firms for informing our judgments about these events as they occurred. These professionals have chosen to remain anonymous.

6 Municipal Market Analytics also provides historical municipal bond yield data. Their data is used throughout the book for historical comparisons and analysis.

7 The term "wrap" refers to a financial guaranty insurance policy. A "wrapped bond" is a bond with financial guaranty insurance. For more information on bond insurance see Chapter 6, "Bond Insurance: A Comeback in the Cards?"

8 *Municipal Bond Insurance Ratings at a Glance,* Raymond James Fixed Income Services (2013), 2.

9 Ibid.

10 Richard A. Ciccarone, "Managing a Buy-Side Municipal Bond Research Department," in *The Handbook of Municipal Bonds* (John Wiley & Sons, 2008), 775.

11 Dan Seymour et al., "2014 Outlook—U.S. Local Governments" Moody's Investors Service (2014), 6.

12 Ibid.

13 Ibid.

14 Ibid., 1.

15 Ibid., 6.

16 Gabriel J. Petek, "U.S. State and Local Government Credit Conditions Forecast: 2014 Will Be a Balancing Act" (McGraw Hill Financial, Standard & Poor's, 2013), 17.

17 Ibid., 16.

18 Ibid.

19 Ibid., 18.

20 *The Fiscal Survey of States: Fall 2014*, National Association of State Budget Officers, (2014), 1.

21 Richard Ravitch and Paul A. Volker, *State Budget Crisis Tax Force: California Report* (State Budget Crisis Task Force, September 2012), 13.

22 Donald J. Boyd and Peter J. Kiernan, *The Blinken Report: Strengthening the Security of Public Sector Defined Benefit Plans* (Nelson A. Rockefeller Institute of Government, 2014), 10.

23 Alfred Medioli et al. *U.S. Municipal Bond Defaults and Recoveries 1970–2013* (Moody's Investors Service, 2014), 5.

24 Cristin Jacoby et al., *Recent U.S. Local Government Defaults Point to Lower Recovery Rates* (Moody's Investors Service, 2013), 1.

Chapter 2: A Profile of the Municipal Bond Market

1 Sylvan G. Feldstein and Frank G. Fabozzi, eds., *The Handbook of Municipal Bonds* (John Wiley & Sons, 2008), xxxi.

2 Eric Friedland, "Top 10 Differences Between Municipal Bonds and Corporate Bonds," Fitch, www.fitchratings.com, (2010), 1,5.

3 Feldstein and Fabozzi, *Handbook of Municipal Bonds*, 17.

4 Ibid.

5 Ibid., 18.

6 *Federal-State Reference Guide Publication 963 (Rev. 11-2013)*, Internal Revenue Service (2013), 14. http://www.irs.gov/pub/irs-pdf/p963.pdf.

7 A well-known test of an entity's status as a government was the IRS's determination in 2014 that the Villages Center Community Development District was a for-profit entity instead of a state instrumentality. We recommend interested readers visit the Villages Community Development District's website for more information at http://www.districtgov.org/IRSupdate.aspx.

8 "Instrumentalities," *1990 EO CPE Text*, Internal Revenue Service, http://www.irs.gov/pub/irs-tege/eotopice90.pdf., *Federal-State Reference Guide Publication 963*, Internal Revenue Service, 14., "Definition of 'Governmental' Employer," New York State Teachers' Retirement System, accessed 15 March 2014, http://www.nctr.org/pdf/NYSTRS_Schneider.pdf.

9 Feldstein and Fabozzi, *Handbook of Municipal Bonds*, 9.

10 *Federal Grants to State and Local Governments*, Congressional Budget Office (2013), 12.

11 Ellis Katz, "American Federalism, Past, Present and Future," U.S. Information Service, *Issues of Democracy* 2, no. 2 (1997), 1.

12 Ibid.

13 "Local Government Authority," National League of Cities, *NLC.org*, accessed March 16, 2014. http://www.nlc.org/build-skills-and-networks/resources/cities-101/city-powers/local-government-authority.

14 Ibid., 4.

15 "Policy Basics: Where Do Our State Tax Dollars Go?" Center on Budget and Policy Priorities, updated March 27, 2014, http://www.cbpp.org/cms/index.cfm?fa=view&id=2783.

16 *Federal Grants to State and Local Governments*, 10.

17 Ibid.

18 Information from Census Bureau Survey of State Government Finances, United State Census Bureau, https://www.census.gov/govs/state/.

19 *Federal Grants to State and Local Governments*, 16.

20 Ibid.

21 Ibid.

22 Ibid., 6.

23 Ibid., 9.

24 *State Budgeting and Lessons Learned from The Economic Downturn*, National Association of State Budget Officers (2013), 8.

25 *Federal Grants to State and Local Governments*, 9.

26 Ibid.

27 Ibid.

28 *Fiscal Survey of the States*, 8.

29 Annual Census Survey of State and Local Government Finance, United States Census Bureau (2014), http://www.census.gov/govs/local/.

30 Federal Reserve Bank of St. Louis FRED Database, Congressional Budget Office, Census Bureau Survey of State Government Finances.

31 Ibid.

32 Annual Census Survey of State and Local Government Finance, Census Bureau.

33 Liz Schott, LaDonna Pavetti, and Ife Finch, "How States Have Spent Federal and State Funds Under The TANF Block Grant," (Center on Budget and Policy Priorities, August 7, 2012), http://www.cbpp.org/cms/?fa=view&id=3808.

34 Ibid.

35 *Fiscal Survey of the States*, 1.

36 *Federal Grants to State and Local Governments*, 16.

37 Ibid.

38 Schott, Pavetti, and Finch, "How States Have Spent," 2.

39 *State Higher Education Finance FY 2012*, State Higher Education Executive Officers Association, www.sheeo.org (2013), 21, http://www.sheeo.org/sites/default/files/publications/SHEF%20FY%2012-20130322rev.pdf.

40 *State Higher Education Finance FY 2012*, 43.

41 Ibid.

42 Annual Census Survey of State and Local Government Finance, Census Bureau.

43 *State Higher Education Finance FY 2012*, 43

44 We thank Natalie Cohen, Head of Municipal Research at Wells Fargo Securities, for providing these contributions in her manuscript review and various phone conversations.

45 *Postsecondary Education Through the Budget Process: Challenges and Opportunities*, National Association of State Budget Officers (2013), 5, http://www.nasbo.org/higher-education-report-2013.

46 As John Quinterno has written in his report "The Great Cost Shift: How Higher Education Cuts Undermine the Future of the Middle Class" (Demos.org, 2012), the states have cut higher education funding when students and their families need education subsidized the most.

47 *State Higher Education Finance FY 2012*, 10.

48 Ibid.

49 Ibid., 11.

50 Information accessed from Elementary & Secondary Education page on the National Association of State Budget Officers website, http://www.nasbo.org/budget-topics/elementary-secondary-education.

51 Ibid.

52 Kevin Carey, "Overview of K-12 Education Finance," Center on Budget and Policy Priorities (2002), 2, http://www.cbpp.org/cms/index.cfm?fa=view&id=1427.

53 Ibid., 3.

54 Ibid., 6.

55 Ibid., 6.

56 Ibid., 10.

57 Ibid., 8.

58 Phil Oliff et al., "Recent Deep State Higher Education Cuts May Harm Students and the Economy for Years to Come," Center on Budget and Policy Priorities, cbpp.org, (19 March 2013), http://www.cbpp.org/cms/?fa=view&id=3927., Annual Census Survey of State Government Finance, Census Bureau.

59 Data retrieved from the *Bond Buyer*'s Primary Market Statistics at bondbuyer.com.

60 John Medina et al., "U.S. Public Finance Special Tax Methodology," Moody's Investors Service, January 31, 2014, 6.

61 "Local Government Authority," National League of Cities, *NLC.org*, accessed March 16, 2014, http://www.nlc.org/build-skills-and-networks/resources/cities-101/city-powers/local-government-authority.

62 Ibid.

63 Ibid.

64 Ibid.

65 Ibid.

66 "Overview of County Government," National Association of Counties (2010), 1.

67 We thank Natalie Cohen for providing these contributions in her manuscript review and various phone conversations.

68 Ibid. "Overview of County Government"

69 Ibid.

70 "Instrumentalities," Internal Revenue Service, IRS.gov, http://www.irs.gov/pub/irs-tege/eotopice90.pdf.

71 Osborne M. Reynolds, Jr., *Local Government Law*, 3rd ed. (St. Paul: West, 2009), 24.

72 Ibid.

73 "How NC Municipalities Work," North Carolina League of Municipalities, NCLM.org, accessed April 4, 2014, http://www.nclm.org/resource-center/Pages/How-Municipalities-Work.aspx.

74 Dan Seymour et al., "2014 Outlook—U.S. Local Governments," Moody's Investors Service (2014), 5.

75 "An Economic Analysis of Transportation Infrastructure Investment," National Economic Council and the President's Council of Economic Advisors, White House, July 2014), 2, http://www.whitehouse.gov/sites/default/files/docs/economic_analysis_of_transportation_investments.pdf.

76 Medina et al., "U.S. Public Finance Special Tax Methodology," 6.

Chapter 3: General Obligation Bonds: The Backbone of the Municipal Bond Market

1 Data retrieved from *A Decade of Municipal Bond Finance* database, Bond Buyer, *BondBuyer.com,* http://www.bondbuyer.com/marketstatistics/decade_1/#dataTable.

2 Ibid.

3 Ibid.

4 "State Budgeting and Lessons Learned from the Economic Downturn," National Association of State Budget Officers, NASBO.org (2013), 9.

5 USCourts.gov states that general obligation debt is considered "general debt" and therefore subject to bankruptcy negotiation, whereas special revenue debt will continue to be paid during bankruptcy process. General debt is senior to contractual obligations. We recommend that interested readers access the U.S. Courts website for more information. The following URL lists relevant information: http://www.uscourts.gov/FederalCourts/Bankruptcy/BankruptcyBasics/Chapter9.aspx.

6 Information gleaned from conference call hosted by the National Federation of Municipal Analysts on 10 December 2014, titled "Hot Legal Topics in Restructuring and Chapter 9 Bankruptcy: The Lessons from Detroit's Now Approved Plan of Adjustment." Speaker was William W. Kannel, member and Bankruptcy Section head, Mintz Levin.

7 Ibid.

8 We credit Natalie Cohen, Managing Director and Head of Municipal Research at Wells Fargo, for highlighting the distinction between general funds and debt service funds.

9 Data accessed from U. S. Census Bureau's "Quarterly Summary of State and Local Taxes," http://www.census.gov/govs/qtax/.

10 "Changing Tampa's Economic DNA: Comprehensive Annual Financial Report of the City of Tampa, Florida, for the Fiscal Year Ended September 30, 2013," Department of Revenue and Finance, City of Tampa, Florida, 29, http://www.tampagov.net/sites/default/files/accounting/files/2013CAFR.PDF.

11 Merritt Research Database accessed using Investortools' Creditscope software.

12 Dan Seymour et al., *2014 Outlook—U.S. Local Governments*, 5.

13 Ibid.

14 "S&P/Case-Shiller 20-City Composite Home Price Index," S&P Dow Jones Indices, McGraw Hill Financial (2014), http://us.spindices.com/indices/real-estate/sp-case-shiller-20-city-composite-home-price-index.

15 ibid.

16 Richard Ravitch et al., *Report of the State Budget Crisis Task Force: Illinois Report* (State Budget Crisis Task Force, 2012), 31.

17 Ibid.

18 Congressional Budget Office, *Federal Grants to State and Local Governments*, (Congressional Budget Office, 2013), 9.

19 Robert Lamb, James Leigland, and Stephen Rappaport, *The Handbook of Municipal Bonds and Public Finance*. (New York: New York Institute of Finance, 1993), 128.

20 Ibid.

21 Emily Raimes et al., "U.S. States Rating Methodology," Moody's Investors Service (2013), 3, http://www.nasra.org/Files/Topical%20Reports/Credit%20Effects/Moodys_State_Methodology_April_2013.pdf.

22 Data retrieved from U.S. Census Bureau's State Government Finances database, https://www.census.gov/govs/state/.

23 Eric Scorsone, "Municipal Fiscal Emergency Laws: Background and Guide to State-Based Approaches," *working paper*, (Mercatus Center George Mason University, No 14, July 21, 2014), 13.

24 Constitution of the State of Alabama, accessed from website Ballotpedia.org on April 4, 2014,,http://ballotpedia.org/Alabama_Constitution.

25 *The Fiscal Survey of States Fall 2013* (National Association of State Budget Officers, 2013), 26.

26 Ibid., 26.

27 Phil Oliff, Chris Mai, and Vincent Palacios, "States Continue to Feel Recession's Impact," Center on Budget and Policy Priorities, CBPP.org (2012), 7, http://www.cbpp.org/cms/index.cfm?fa=view&id=711.

28 Raimes et al., "U.S. States Rating Methodology," 8.

29 Ravitch et al., *Illinois Report*, 16. Ravitch and coauthors discuss Illinois' use of some 600 special funds to account for the state's expenditures outside of the general fund to meet balanced budget requirements. The state also uses conduits such as the Metropolitan Pier & Exposition Authority to issue special revenue debt separate from its GO pledge.

30 Alan Walter Steiss, "Revenue Bonds." Retrieved from the website of Professor Alan Walter Steiss at the University of Michigan. His webpage speaks in-depth about the types of revenue bond debt and the history of Mello-Roos financings. An instructive primer on the revenue bond sector accessible at http://www-personal.umich.edu/~steiss/page63.html.

31 Ibid., Medina et al., "U.S. Public Finance Special Tax Methodology," 2,

32 Ibid.

Chapter 4: Revenue Bonds: How America Builds Infrastructure

1 Data retrieved from the *A Decade of Municipal Bond Finance* database on *The Bond Buyer* website, http://www.bondbuyer.com/marketstatistics/decade_1/#dataTable.

2 Steiss, "Revenue Bonds."

3 Ibid.

4 Ibid.

5 Ibid.

6 Ibid.

7 Medina, et al., "U.S. Public Finance Special Tax Methodology," 2.

8 Maria Matesanz et al., *Government Owned Toll Roads* Moody's Investors Service, 2012), 3.

9 Medina, *Special Tax Methodology*, 3.

10 This structure is used to circumvent debt restrictions written into New York State's constitution.

11 Robin L. Prunty and John A. Sugden, "Illinois Sales Tax," Standard & Poor's Ratings Services, McGraw Hill Financial, March 6, 2014., Edward Hampton and Edith Behr, "Moody's Assigns A2 Rating, Negative Outlook to Metropolitan Pier and Exposition Authority's $1.18 Billion Expansion Project Bonds in Three Series," Moody's Investors Service, September 27, 2010.

12 Ibid.

13 Ibid.

14 Ibid.

15 Ibid.

16 Ibid., 18.

17 Ibid., 2.

18 Anticipation Revenue Vehicles (GARVEEs)," Transportation Finance Clearinghouse, AASHTO, *http://www.transportation-finance.org/funding_financing/financing/bonding_debt_instruments/municipal_public_bond_issues/garvees.aspx.*

19 Ibid.

20 Marcia Van Wagner and Julius Mavro, "Moody's downgrades 17 GARVEE ratings vulnerable to federal payment interruptions; outlook remains negative," Moody's Investors Service, (2014), 1.

21 "GARVEEs," Transportation Finance Clearinghouse, AASHTO.

22 Ibid.

23 Ibid.

24 Steiss, "Revenue Bonds."

25 Ibid.

26 Ibid.

27 Mary Francoeur et al., "Analytical Framework for Water and Sewer System Ratings," Moody's Investors Service (1999), 4.

28 Ibid., 5.

29 Data were retrieved from the *A Decade of Municipal Bond Finance* database on *The Bond Buyer* website. <http://www.bondbuyer.com/marketstatistics/decade_1/#dataTable>

30 Francoeur, Mary, et al., “Analytical Framework,” 5.

31 Ibid., 4.

32 Ibid.

33 Theodore Chapman et al., “U.S. Municipal Water and Sewer Utilities 2014 Sector Outlook: Learning To Do More With Less,” Standard & Poor’s Ratings Services, McGraw Hill Financial (2014), 2.

34 Ibid., 4.

35 Ibid.

36 New York City Municipal Water Finance Authority, http://www.nyc.gov/html/nyw/home.html.

37 Karen Kedem, “U.S. Not-for-Profit Private and Public Higher Education,” Moody’s Investors Service (2011), 2.

38 Ibid.

39 Ibid.

40 Ibid.

41 Jessica Matsumori, et al., _“Many Factors Burden The U.S. Higher Education Sector in 2014,” Standard & Poor’s Rating Services, McGraw Hill Financial (2014), 2.

42 Ibid.

43 Ibid., 7.

44 Ibid., 4.

45 Ibid.

46 Ibid.

47 John Quinterno, “The Great Cost Shift: How Higher Education Cuts Undermine the Future of the Middle Class,” (Demos, 2012).

48 State Higher Education Executive Officers, 48.

49 Ibid.

50 Quinterno, 15.

51 Kedem, 18.

52 Florence Zeman et al., “U.S. Housing Finance Agency Single Family Programs,” Moody’s Investors Service (2013), 2.

53 Lawrence R. Witte et al., “Loan Performance Gap Widens Between U.S. Housing Finance Agency and Single-Family Programs and State Prime Pools,” Standard & Poor’s Ratings Services, McGraw Hill Financial (2013), 2.

54 Ibid.

55 Ibid., 3.

56 Ibid.

57 Ibid.

58 Peter V. Murphy, “For U.S. Public Transportation Issuers, Funding Questions And Budget Strains Cloud The Stable Outlook For 2014,” Standard & Poor’s Ratings Services, McGraw Hill Financial (2014), 3.

59 Ibid., 3.

60 Ibid., 4.

61 Ibid., 5.
62 Ibid., 3.
63 Ibid., 9.
64 Ibid., 7.
65 Ibid.
66 Ibid.
67 Ibid.
68 Kurt Krummenacker et al., "Rating Methodology: Airports with Unregulated Rate Setting," Moody's Investors Service (July 21, 2011), 10.
69 Maria Matesanz et al., "Rating Methodology: Government Owned Toll Roads," Moody's Investors Service (3 October 2012), 9.
70 U.S. Department of Transportation Federal Highway Administration, Bureau of Economic Analysis.
71 Ibid.
72 Matesanz, 16.
73 Ibid., 7–8.
74 Ibid., 16.
75 Ibid., 10.
76 Ibid.
77 "American Public Transportation Association Ridership Report, Q2 2014 Report," American Public Transportation Association, APTA.com, http://www.apta.com/resources/statistics/Documents/Ridership/2014-q2-ridership-APTA.pdf.
78 Ibid.
79 "Ridership Report," American Public Transportation Association statistical database, http://www.apta.com/resources/statistics/Pages/ridershipreport.aspx.
80 Merxe Tudela et al., "U.S. Municipal Bond Defaults and Recoveries, 1970-2011," Moody's Investors Service, (March 7, 2012), 9.
81 Ibid., 1.
82 Kevin J Holloran et al., "The Outlook for U.S. Not-for-Profit Health Care Providers Is Negative From Increasing Pressures," Standard & Poor's Ratings Services, McGraw Hill Financial (2013), 6.
83 Ibid., 4.
84 Ibid.
85 Ibid.
86 Martin D. Arrick, "Current Credit Considerations For The U.S. Healthcare Sector," Standard & Poor's Ratings Services, McGraw Hill Financial (2013), 7.

Chapter 5: Ratings Agencies: The Shadow Regulators of the Muni Market

1 Egan-Jones Ratings Co., "How to Improve the Credit Rating Agency Sector," (American Enterprise Institute Presentation on June 24, 2008), 1.
2 Ibid.
3 "Standard & Poor's Ratings Definitions," (New York: Standard & Poor's Ratings Services, 2014), 4.
4 Edward A Rabson, "The Role of Rating Agencies," published in The Handbook of Municipal Bonds (John Wiley & Sons, Inc., 2008), 233.

5 "Rating Symbols and Definitions," Moody's Investors Service (2014), 39.

6 Frank Partnoy, "The Siskel and Ebert of Financial Markets? Two Thumbs Down for the Credit Rating Agencies," Washington University Law Review, Volume 77, Issue 3 (1999), 635.

7 J. M. Pimbley, "Bond Insurers," Journal of Applied Finance, Volume No. 22, No. 1 (2012), http://www.maxwell-consulting.com/Finance-Articles.html.

8 Moritz Kraemer et al., "Credit FAQ: Factors Behind Our Rating Actions on Eurozone Sovereign Governments" (Frankfurt: Standard & Poor's, 2012), 1.

9 Ibid.

10 Ibid.

11 Rebecca C. Moses et al.,¬ "Fitch Downgrades Beaumont ISD, TX's ULTGOs to BBB+; Outlook Negative," (Austin: Fitch Ratings, 2014) 1.

12 Ibid.

13 Chandra Ghosal, et al., "Upgrades Reign in 2013, but Par Value of Upgrades Reach Highest Level Since 2010," Moody's Investors Service (2014), Appendix.

14 Ghosal, 2.

15 Ibid., 11.

16 Ibid., 5.

17 Merxe Tudela et al.,¬¬ "U.S. Municipal Bond Defaults and Recoveries," Moody's Investors Service (2012), 3

18 Holmes, Chris, "The Great Credit Shift: U.S. Public Finance Post Crisis," Moody's Investors Service (September 21, 2011), 14.

19 Tudela, et al., 17.

20 "Rating Symbols and Definitions," Moody's Investors Service (2014), 34.

21 Standard & Poor's Ratings Definitions, 3.

22 Ibid.

23 "Ratings Symbols and Definitions," Moody's, 34.

24 Ibid.

25 Ibid.

26 Partnoy, 635.

27 "Competition and Credit Rating Agencies," Transcription of Hearings taking place on 5 October 2010, Organization for Economic Cooperation and Development, 8

28 Ibid., 19.

29 Organization for Economic Cooperation and Development, 54.

30 "Alternatives to the Use of External Credit Ratings in the Regulations of the OCC Docket No. OCC 2011-0019," Office of Comptroller of the Currency (2011).

31 Office of Comptroller of the Currency, "Alternatives," 5.

32 Ibid.

33 Ibid.

34 Ibid.

35 Organization for Economic Cooperation and Development, 39.

36 Ibid., 70.

37 Ibid., 18.

38 Tudela, 11.

39 "Office of the Attorney General Settles Public Finance Lawsuits against Moody's, Standard and Poor's, and Fitch," accessed at the website of State of Connecticut Attorney General George Jepsen on May 5, 2014, http://www.ct.gov/ag/cwp/view.asp?A=2341&Q=488608.

40 Ibid.

41 Gail Sussman et al., ¬"Recalibration of Moody's U.S. Municipal Ratings to its GlobalRating Scale," Moody's Investors Service (2010), 1.

42 Ibid., 3.

43 Organization for Economic Cooperation and Development, 42.

44 Christopher Alessi, "The Credit Rating Controversy," Council on Foreign Relations (2013), 3.

45 Organization for Economic Cooperation and Development, 41.

46 Ibid.

47 Ibid.

48 Ibid., 7.

49 Ibid., 41.

50 Ibid.

51 Ibid., 8.

52 Organization for Economic Cooperation and Development, 10.

53 Ibid.

54 Partnoy, 704.

55 Organization for Economic Cooperation and Development, 14.

56 Partnoy, 656.

57 Ibid., 628.

58 Ibid.

59 Ibid., 655.

60 Ibid., 623.

61 Antoine Gara, "S&P, Moody's Shares Surge on Fraud Lawsuit Settlement," The Street (29 April 2013), accessed 6 May 2014, http://www.thestreet.com/story/11908039/1/sp-moodys-lingering-legal-risks.html.

62 Pimbley, J.M., "Bond Insurers," Journal of Applied Finance, Vol. 22, No. 1 (2012), 36-43, October 10, 2014, http://www.maxwell-consulting.com/Bond_Insurers_JAF_Pimbley.pdf.

63 James P. McNichols, "Monoline Insurance & Financial Guaranty Reserving," Casualty Actuarial Society Forum (2003), Casact.org, 231-304 (October 10, 2014), https://www.casact.org/pubs/forum/03fforum/03ff231.pdf.

64 Partnoy, 655.

65 Organization for Economic Cooperation and Development, 14.

Chapter 6: Bond Insurance: A Comeback in the Cards

1 Feldstein and Fabozzi, Handbook of Municipal Bonds, xxxi.

2 The authors would like to credit J. M. Pimbley, author of "Bond Insurers," for insights that have informed our writing on this subject. Pimbley's analysis of the demise of the bond insurance industry in 2008 is a must-read. This in-depth look into the

financial guaranty insurance industry can be found in the Journal of Applied Finance, Volume No. 22, No. 1 (2012) or on his website at the following URL: http://www.maxwell-consulting.com/Finance-Articles.html.

3 Roy A. Howard, "Bond Insurance," W.M. Financial Strategies, BondAdvisor.com, http://www.munibondadvisor.com/BondInsurance.htm.

4 Ibid.

5 Rich White, "Fatal Seduction of the Bond Insurers," Investopedia, accessed October 10, 2014 at http://www.investopedia.com/articles/bonds/08/municipal-bond-insurance.asp.

6 McNichols, "Monoline Insurance & Financial Guaranty Reserving."

7 History," MBIA Insurance Corporation, MBIA.com, http://investor.mbia.com/GenPage.aspx?IID=103405&GKP=207756.

8 Ibid.

9 Ibid.

10 Pimbley, "Bond Insurers."

11 Ibid.

12 Ibid.

13 McNichols, "Monoline Insurance & Financial Guaranty Reserving."

14 McNichols, 264.

15 Pimbley, "Bond Insurers."

16 McNichols.

17 McKnight, Michael, "Reserving for Financial Guaranty Products," Casualty Actuarial Society Forum (2001), Casact.org, 255-280, accessed October 10, 2014 at http://www.casact.org/pubs/forum/01fforum/01ff255.pdf.

18 McNichols, 265.

19 Ibid.

20 Ibid.

21 Pimbley, "Bond Insurers."

22 Ibid.

23 Ibid.

24 Ibid.

25 Rich White, "Fatal Seduction of the Municipal Bond Insurers."

26 Ibid.

27 Jon Barasch, moderator, -"State of Bond Insurers," panel discussion at the National Federation of Municipal Analysts 2014 Annual Conference on May 8, 2014 in Kissimmee, Florida.

28 Ibid.

29 McKnight, Michael, "Monoline Insurance & Financial Guaranty Reserving."

30 Ibid.

31 Pimbley.

32 McNichols, 235.

33 Ibid.

34 Pimbley.

35 Ibid.

36 Feldstein and Fabozzi, Handbook of Municipal Bonds, 1090.

37 Ibid.

38 Ibid.

39 David S. Veno et al., ¬"U.S. Municipal Bankruptcies May Cause Bond Insurers to Change Up Their Game Plans," Standard & Poor's Ratings Services (2013), 4.

40 Ibid.

41 Ibid.

42 Ibid.

43 Ibid.

44 Ibid.

45 Ibid.

46 Pimbley.

47 Ibid.

48 Ibid.

49 Ibid.

50 Ibid.

51 Ibid.

52 Ibid.

53 Ibid.

54 Norris, Floyd, "After Years of Battling, Bank of America and MBIA Settle Mortgage Dispute," *New York Times* (May 6, 2013), http://dealbook.nytimes.com/2013/05/06/bank-of-america-and-mbia-said-to-agree-to-1-7-billion-settlement/.

55 Pimbley, 10.

56 Ibid.

57 Ibid., 2.

58 McNichols, "Monoline Insurance & Financial Guaranty Reserving."

59 Ibid.

60 Ibid.

61 Ibid.

62 Ted Collins et al., "Moody's Rating Methodology for the Financial Guaranty Insurance Industry," Moody's Investors Service (2006): 10.

63 Ibid.

64 Ibid.

65 Ibid., 14.

66 Alfred Medioli et al., "U.S. Municipal Bond Defaults and Recoveries 1970-2013," Moody's Investors Service (2014): 16.

67 McNichols.

68 McNichols, 236.

69 Barasch, ¬"State of Bond Insurers."

70 Ibid.

71 Ibid.

Chapter 7: Municipalities in Recession

1 Data accessed from Census Bureau's Quarterly Summary of State and Local Tax Revenue, within Census' Federal, State and Local Governments page at www.census.gov/govs/qtax/, accessed October 10, 2014.

2 Dan Seymour et al., 2014 Outlook—U.S. Local Governments, Moody's Investors Service (2014), 4.

3 Data accessed from Census Bureau's Quarterly Summary of State and Local Tax Revenue, within Census' Federal, State and Local Governments page, www.census.gov/govs/qtax/.

4 Ibid.

5 Ibid.

6 Ibid.

7 Ibid.

8 Ibid.

9 Data accessed from Census Bureau's Quarterly Summary of State and Local Tax Revenue, within Census' Federal, State and Local Governments page <www.census.gov/govs/qtax/>

10 Ibid.

11 Seymour, Dan, et al., "2014 Outlook—U.S. Local Governments," Moody's Investors Service, (2014), 10.

12 Ibid., 8.

13 "A Widening Gap in Cities: Shortfalls in Funding for Pensions and Retiree Healthcare," The Pew Charitable Trusts (January 16, 2013), 2, http://www.pewtrusts.org/en/research-and-analysis/reports/0001/01/01/a-widening-gap-in-cities.

14 Ibid., 21.

15 Ibid., 41.

16 Data retrieved from the Public Plans Database at The Center for Retirement Research at Boston College, http://crr.bc.edu/data/public-plans-database/.

17 Ibid.

18 Ibid.

19 Ibid.

20 "Widening Gap," 23.

21 Ibid., 13.

22 Ibid., 23.

23 Ibid.

24 bid., 33.

25 Ibid., 23.

26 Ibid.

27 Ibid., 22.

28 Ibid., 21.

29 Ibid.

30 Ibid., 23.

31 Ibid.

32 Ibid.

33 Ibid.

34 Ibid.

35 Steven Hochman and Renee Boicourt, "Comment: New Jersey Pension Board Proposal," Moody's Investors Service, (March 26, 1997).

36 "Widening Gap," 26.

37 Donald J. Boyd and Peter J Kiernan, "Strengthening the Security of Public Sector Defined Benefit Plans," The Blinken Report. The Nelson A. Rockefeller Institute of Government (January 2014), viii.

38 "Widening Gap," 27.

39 Ibid.

40 Ibid.

41 Ibid.

42 Catherine Saillant et al., "Salary 'spiking' drains public pension funds, analysis finds," Los Angeles Times (March 3, 2014).

43 Ibid.

44 Ibid.

45 Ibid.

46 Ibid.

47 Ibid.

48 Ibid.

49 Ibid.

50 Boyd and Kiernan, 13.

51 "Widening Gap," 30.

52 Ibid.

53 Ibid., 8.

54 Ibid., 8.

55 Eileen Norcross and Frederic Sautet, "Institutions Matter: Can New Jersey Reverse Course?" Working Paper, Mercatus Center at George Mason University (July 2009), 22.

56 "Widening Gap," 26.

57 Ibid., 14.

58 Ibid.

59 Ibid., 8.

60 Ibid.

Chapter 8: An Overview of Municipal Bankruptcy

1 Gregory W. Lipitz, "Key Credit Considerations for Municipal Governments in Bankruptcy," Moody's Investors Service (2012), 1.

2 Lipitz, 1.

3 Alfred Medioli et al., "U.S. Municipal Bond Defaults and Recoveries 1970-2013," Moody's Investors Service (2014), 16.

4 Medioli, 16.

5 Ibid.

6 James E. Spiotto, "Chapter 9: The Last Resort for Financially Distressed Municipalities," in The Handbook of Municipal Bonds, eds. Sylvan Feldstein and Frank Fabozzi (New York: John Wiley & Sons, 2008), 146.

7 Ibid., 8.

8 Lipitz, ¬"Key Credit Considerations," 8.

9 Ibid.

10 Ibid., 1.

11 Ibid.

12 David G Heiman, Bruce Bennett, and Jonathan S. Green, "Disclosure Statement with Respect to Plan for the Adjustment of Debts of the City of Detroit," filed in United States Bankruptcy Court, Eastern District of Michigan, Southern Division on February 21, 2014., Natalie Cohen, "On Detroit, General Obligations and Public Pensions," Wells Fargo Municipal Securities Research (July 19, 2013), 1.

13 Anne Van Praagh, "Recent Local Government Defaults and Bankruptcies May Indicate a Shift in Willingness to Pay Debt," (Moody's Investors Service (2012), 1.

14 Shelly Sigo, "Jefferson County Officials Readying Counteroffer for Creditors," Bond Buyer, August 5, 2011, http://www.bondbuyer.com/news/-1029687-1.html.

15 "Proposal for Creditors," Office of the Emergency Manager, City of Detroit, June 14, 2013, 6.

16 Cohen, 1.

17 Vikram Rai et al., "Alert: Detroit—Potential Long Term Negative Impact on the Full Faith and Credit Pledge for Local GO Debt," Citi Research Municipals (July 19, 2013), 1.

18 Ibid.

19 Ibid.

20 Freddie Mac House Price Index Riverside-San Bernardino-Ontario CA MSA, data, accessed using Bloomberg.

21 City of San Bernardino, "Budgetary Analysis and Recommendations for Budget Stabilization," City of San Bernardino, California Finance Department (2012), 6.

22 Ibid., 14.

23 Ibid., 22.

24 Van Praagh, "Shift in Willingness to Pay," 4.

25 Ibid.

26 Matthew A. Jones, "Rating Methodology: U.S. Local Government General Obligation Debt," Moody's Investors Service (January 15, 2014), 17.

27 Romy Varghese, "Pennsylvania Capital Harrisburg Files for Bankruptcy, Council Lawyer Says," Bloomberg News, October 12, 2011.

28 John Buntin, "Harrisburg's Failed Infrastructure Project," Governing the States and Localities, Governing.com, November 2010, 2, http://www.governing.com/topics/transportation-infrastructure/Harrisburgs-failed-infrastructure-project.html.

29 Ibid.

30 Josellyn Yousef, "Harrisburg, Pennsylvania's Default on Insured General Obligation Debt is Credit Negative," Moody's Investors Service (March 19, 2012), 1.

31 Buntin, 2.

32 Cristin Jacoby et al., "Recent U.S. Local Government Defaults Point to Lower Recovery Rates," Moody's Investors Service (2013), 2.

33 Don Spatz, "Philadelphia company to guide Reading through Act 47," Reading Eagle, December 9, 2009, http://www2.readingeagle.com/article.aspx?id=174937.

34 Lipitz, 3.

35 Ibid.

36 Ibid.

37 Buntin, 6.

38 Spiotto, 150.

39 Interested readers are strongly encouraged to read Mr. Spiotto's chapter in The Handbook of Municipal Bonds, titled, "Chapter 9: The Last Resort for Financially Distressed Municipalities" (New York: John Wiley & Sons, 2008).

40 Spiotto, 151.

41 Accessed from the United States Courts website on October 31, 2014, http://www.uscourts.gov/FederalCourts/Bankruptcy/BankruptcyBasics/Chapter9.aspx.

42 Spiotto, 150–155.

43 United States Courts.

44 Ibid.

45 Ibid.

46 Ibid.

47 Ibid.

48 Ibid.

49 Ibid.

50 Spiotto, 156.

51 Ibid.

52 Spiotto, 170-174.

53 B. Summer Chandler and Mark S. Kaufman, "Maybe Taxes Aren't So Certain: What Is Fair and Equitable in a Chapter 9 Plan," American Bankruptcy Institute Journal, Vol. XXXII, No. 1, February 2013, https://www.mckennalong.com/media/resource/1984_American%20Bankruptcy%20Institute%20Journal.pdf, 1.

54 Ibid.

55 Ibid.

56 Ibid, 2.

57 Ibid.

58 United States Courts.

59 11 U.S. Code § 904—Limitation on Jurisdiction and Powers of Court, United States Code, 2006 Edition, Supplement 5, Title 11—Bankruptcy, U.S. Government Publishing Office.

60 Ibid.

61 Ibid.

62 Ibid.

63 Donna Shalala and Carol Bellamy, "A State Saves a City: The New York Case," Duke Law Journal, Vol. 76:1119), 1129.

64 Matthew Dolan, "Cost of Detroit's Historic Bankruptcy Reaches $126 Million," *The Wall Street Journal*, September 12, 2014.

65 Shalala, 1125.

66 Spiotto, 149.

Chapter 9: Case Studies of Distressed Local Governments

1 Anne Van Praagh et al., "Recent Local Government Defaults and Bankruptcies May Indicate a Shift in Willingness to Pay Debt," Moody's Investors Service, 2012), 1.

2 BLS Employment Data retrieved from Bloomberg, LP; Housing data retrieved from Truilia, www.trulia.com.

3 Kevyn D. Orr, "Recommendation Pursuant to Section 18(1) of PA 436," City of Detroit, Emergency Manager's Office, July 16, 2013, 2.

4 Data retrieved from Census Bureau and Bureau of Economic Analysis.

5 Ibid.

6 Ibid., 10.

7 Natalie Cohen, "On Detroit, General Obligations and Public Pensions," 1.

8 Lisa Lambert, "Major Settlement Puts Detroit Closer to Bankruptcy Exit," Reuters, 16 October 2014, accessed on January 4, 2015, at http://www.reuters.com/article/2014/10/16/us-usa-detroit-bankruptcy-fgic-idUSKCN0I51RN20141016.

9 Jay Reeves, "Bankruptcy Real Possibility in One Alabama Count," ¬Associated Press, July 28, 2011.

10 Dan Seymour et al., "How Moody's Calculates 55%-60% Proposed Recovery Rate for Jefferson County Sewer Warrants," Moody's Investors Service (2013), 2.

11 Ibid.

12 Ibid., 7.

13 Jefferson County Commission, Audited Financial Statements, September 30, 2009, 63.

14 Ibid.

15 Jefferson County Commission, Audited Financial Statements, 46.

16 Shelly Sigo, "Bankruptcy Over, But Jefferson County, Ala., Will Remain in the News," The Bond Buyer Online Edition, December 31, 2013, accessed on December 15, 2014, at the http://www.bondbuyer.com/issues/123_1/bankruptcy-over-but-jefferson-county-ala-will-remain-in-the-news-1058616-1.html., Seymour, 1.

17 Christopher Coviello, "Jefferson County's Bankruptcy Increases Bondholder Uncertainty," Moody's Investors Service, 2011), 1.

18 Ibid., 1.

19 Ibid.

20 Ibid.

21 "CalPERS at a Glance," December 2014, accessed from CalPERS website on 15 December 2014 at http://www.calpers.ca.gov/eip-docs/about/facts/calpers-at-a-glance.pdf.

22 Michael B. Marois, ¬"California Insolvencies Mount as Atwater Votes Emergency," Bloomberg News, October 4, 2012). Accessed on October 4, 2012, at http://www.bloomberg.com/news/2012-10-04/california-mayor-asks-for-prayers-as-bankruptcy-looms.html.

23 Meeting Minutes of Atwater Public Financing Authority, June 28, 2013, 23.

24 Ibid.

25 Ibid.

26 Ibid.

27 Ibid.

28 Ibid.

29 Gabriel J Petek, ¬"Case Study: The Vallejo, Calif. Bankruptcy," Standard & Poor's Ratings Services, McGraw Hill Financial (2012), 2.

30 Van Praagh, 3.

31 Petek, 2.

32 Misty L Newland and Lisa R. Schroeer, "Summary: Vallejo, California; Appropriations," Standard & Poor's Rating Services, McGraw Hill Financial, June 30, 2014.

33 Ibid., 3.

34 Susan Corson and Lisa Schroeer, ¬¬"Summary: Mammoth Lakes, California; Appropriations," Standard & Poor's Ratings Services, McGraw Hill Financial (2012), 1.

35 Ibid, 2.

36 Town of Mammoth Lakes, "RAW: Mammoth's View of the MLLA Mess, How It Started and What Has Happened Since," Mammoth Times, March 28, 2012, accessed on October 10, 2012 at http://www.mammothtimes.com/content/raw-mammoths-view-mlla-mess-how-it-started-and-what-has-happened.

37 Ibid.

38 Corson, 2.

39 Mammoth Lakes.

40 Ibid.

41 Andrea Travis-Miller, Jason Simpson, and Michael Busch, "Pendency Plan City of San Bernardino," November 27, 2012, 3.

42 Ibid.

43 Ibid.

44 City of Stockton, CA, "Public Hearing Adopting The Proposed Fiscal Year 2012-2013 Annual Budget," June 26, 2012, 19

45 Ibid.

46 Ibid.

47 bid., 8.

48 Van Praagh, 1.

49 Buntin, 6.

50 John Luciew, "¬Harrisburg Incinerator: History of the Project and How Taxpayers Got Saddled with the Debt," The Patriot News, pennlive.com, October 28, 2007.

51 Ibid.

52 Buntin, 2.

53 Luciew.

54 Ibid.

55 Buntin, 2.

56 Minutes from Dauphin County Board of Commissioners Workshop Meeting, December 3, 2008, 10:30 A.M., 2.

57 John Medina et al., "Moody's Downgrades to B2 from Ba2 The City of Harrisburg's (PA) Long-Term GO Rating; Rating Removed from Watchlist and Negative Outlook Assigned," Moody's Investors Service (February 11, 2010), 3.

58 Ibid.

59 Michael H. Frost, "States as Chapter 9 Bankruptcy Gatekeepers: Federalism, Specific Authorization, and Protection of Municipal Economic Health," Mississippi School of Law, February 4, 2014. Available at SSRN: http://ssrn.com/abstract=2390758 or http://dx.doi.org/10.2139/ssrn.2390758, 1.

60 Michael D'Arcy et al., "Harrisburg's GO Creditors Get Wide-Ranging Recovery Rates Averaging 75%," Moody's Investors Service, (2014), 2.

Chapter 10: Build America Bonds to the Rescue

1 Figure retrieved from Bloomberg database of Build America Bond new issues on Bloomberg Terminal.

2 Municipal Market Analytics, Monthly Advisor, September 2008, 1.

3 Ibid.
4 Municipal Market Analytics yield data and U.S. Treasury data retrieved from Bloomberg Terminal.
5 New York City bond yield data retrieved from Bloomberg terminal. Yields derived from Bloomberg matrix pricing.
6 Municipal Market Analytics, Monthly Advisor, April 2009, 1.
7 Municipal Market Analytics yield data retrieved from Bloomberg terminal.
8 Vikram Rai, "Build America Bond (BAB) Callables, Defensive Strategies for Convexity Moves," Citi Research Municipals, September 18, 2012, 1.
9 Ibid.
10 George Friedlander, U.S. Rates Special Topic: The Build America Bond Program is a Classic "Win-Win" for Federal, State and Local Governments, Citigroup Global Markets, November 23, 2010, 8.
11 Douglas W. Elmendorf and Thomas A. Barthold, ¬"Subsidizing Infrastructure Investment with Tax-Preferred Bonds," joint study, Congressional Budget Office and the Joint Committee on Taxation, October 2009, 25.
12 Ibid.
13 Ibid.
14 Ibid., 10.
15 Ibid., 31.
16 Ibid., 32.
17 Ibid.
18 Ibid. ,
19 Ibid.
20 Ibid.
21 Ibid.
22 Ibid.
23 Alfred Medioli et al., "U.S. Municipal Bond Defaults and Recoveries 1970–2013," Moody's Investors Service (2014), 16.
24 BofA Merrill Lynch Build America Bond Index data and Bloomberg Index data retrieved from Bloomberg, LP.

Chapter 12: The Puerto Rico Conundrum

1 At the January 2014 GIC Conference on Puerto Rico, Robert Kurtter, Managing Director of U.S. State and Regional Ratings at Moody's Investment Service, presented with David Hitchcock, Senior Director of Standard & Poor's Public Finance Ratings, for a discussion of rating agency views. Each of their presentations is posted on the GIC website. The link for Robert Kurtter's presentation is http://www.interdependence.org/resources/robert-kurtters-presentation-puerto-ricos-debt/#.Utbd4mTTIqs. The link for David Hitchcock's presentation is http://www.interdependence.org/resources/puerto-rico/#.UtgDJ_RDsfU. Both participants discussed their own rating agencies' methodologies and how they view debt in general and Puerto Rico debt specifically.
2 At the January 2014 GIC Conference on Puerto Rico, Don Rissmiller, founding partner and chief economist at Strategas, presented his views on "Puerto Rico: The Island's Economics." The link for his presentation is as follows: https://www.interdependence.org/resources/puerto-rico-islands-economics/#.
3 At the January 2014 GIC Conference on Puerto Rico, Natalie Cohen, Managing Director and Head of Municipal Research, Wells Fargo, presented her views on the health of the Commonwealth's finances and its pension system. The link for her presentation is as follows: https://www.interdependence.org/resources/municipal-securities-research/#.VGP6VPnF-Qt.
4 Ibid.

5 Cohen.

6 Rachel Barkley, "The State of State Pension Plans 2013: A Deep Dive into Shortfalls and Surpluses," Morningstar, September 16, 2013.

7 At the January 2014 GIC Conference on Puerto Rico, Joseph Engelhard, Senior Vice President, Capital Alpha Partners, presented his views on Washington's role in fixing the Commonwealth's finances. The link for his presentation is as follows: https://www.interdependence.org/resources/puerto-rico-can-washington-anything-help-2/#.VGlZrfnF-Qt,

8 At the January 2014 GIC Conference on Puerto Rico, John Mousseau, Executive Vice President & Director of Fixed Income, Cumberland Advisors, presented his views on systemic impacts of the sell-off in Puerto Rico debt. The link for his presentation is as follows: https://www.interdependence.org/resources/john-mousseaus-presentation-puerto-rico-debt/#.VGlavPnF-Qt.

9 Ibid.

10 Kurtter and Hitchcock.

11 $3,500,000,000 COMMONWEALTH OF PUERTO RICO General Obligation Bonds of 2014, Series A (Government of Puerto Rico, 2014), http://www.gdbpr.com/investors_resources/documents/CommonwealthPRGO2014SeriesA-FinalOS.PDF.

12 Preliminary Official Statement, "$3 billion Commonwealth of Puerto Rico General Obligation Bonds," Government of Puerto Rico, March 6, 2014, 23.

13 "Can Puerto Rico Reinvent Itself as a Global Competitor?" Knowledge @ Wharton, The Wharton School of the University of Pennsylvania, August 22, 2012, accessed on June 22, 2014, http://knowledge.wharton.upenn.edu/article/can-puerto-rico-reinvent-itself-as-a-global-competitor/, 4.

14 Ibid.

15 Ibid.

16 Eugenio J. Aleman, "Puerto Rico: Failure of the State," Economics Group Special Commentary, Wells Fargo Securities, May 24, 2012, 6.

17 Ibid., 8.

18 Ibid.

19 Wharton, 2.

20 Ibid.

21 Ibid.

22 Ibid.

23 Ibid.

24 Ibid.

25 Martin A. Sullivan, "Economic Analysis: The Treasury Bailout of Puerto Rico," Tax Analysts, TaxAnalysts.com, January 27, 2014, accessed February 6, 2014, http://www.taxanalysts.com/www/features.nsf/Features/1F974381895173AC85257C6D005F0128.

26 Ibid.

27 Ibid.

28 Aleman, "Failure of the State,"1.

29 I bid.

30 Ibid.

31 Ibid., 8.

32 Wharton, 1.

33 Aleman, 5.

34 Ibid.

35 Ibid.
36 Ibid, 17.
37 Ibid.
38 Wharton, 2.
39 Aleman, 8.
40 Ibid., 7.
41 Ibid.
42 Ibid.
43 Ibid., 17.
44 Ibid., 11.
45 Ibid., 17.
46 Natalie Cohen.
47 Data retrieved from Puerto Rico Annual Financials compiled by Merritt Research Services, accessed from Creditscope database.
48 Ibid.

Chapter 13: Pension Problems and the Land of Lincoln

1 Data retrieved from Puerto Rico Annual Financials compiled by Merritt Research Services, accessed from Creditscope database.
2 Richard Ravitch and Paul Volcker et al., "Report of the State Budget Crisis Task Force: Illinois Report," State Budget Crisis Task Force, October 2012, 16.
3 Judy Baar Topinka, Comptroller, State of Illinois Comprehensive Annual Financial Report, Fiscal Year ended June 30, 2013, State of Illinois, February 28, 2014, 142.
4 Ibid.
5 Ibid.
6 "$3,700,000,000 State of Illinois General Obligation Bonds, Taxable Series of February 2011," Official Statement, State of Illinois, February 23, 2011, 58.
7 Ibid.
8 Ibid.
9 Ibid.
10 Ibid.
11 Ibid.
12 Ibid.
13 Ibid.
14 Ibid.
15 Ibid.
16 Ibid.
17 Data retrieved from Puerto Rico Annual Financials compiled by Merritt Research Services, accessed from Creditscope database.
18 Ibid.
19 Ibid.
20 Ted Hampton et al., "Illinois Pension Reform Legislation is Credit Positive," Moody's Investors Service (December 6, 2013), 1.

21 Ravitch, 30.
22 "$3,700,000,000 State of Illinois General Obligation Bonds, Taxable Series of February 2011," Official Statement, State of Illinois, February 23, 2011, 58.
23 Ravitch, 20.
24 Ibid.
25 Ibid.
26 Ibid.
27 Ibid.
28 Ibid., 67.
29 Ibid., 60.
30 Data retrieved from Puerto Rico Annual Financials compiled by Merritt Research Services, accessed from Creditscope database.
31 Ravitch, 9.
32 "$3,700,000,000 State of Illinois General Obligation Bonds, Taxable Series of February 2011," Official Statement, February 23, 2011, 21.
33 Ibid.
34 Ibid., 68.
35 Ibid., 54.
36 Data retrieved from Puerto Rico Annual Financials compiled by Merritt Research Services, accessed from Creditscope database.
37 Hampton, 3.
38 Robert Kurtter, "New Issue: Illinois, State of," Moody's Investors Service (March 11, 1992), 2.
39 Ibid.
40 Data retrieved from Puerto Rico Annual Financials compiled by Merritt Research Services, accessed from Creditscope database.
41 Ibid.
42 Ravitch, 16.
43 Ibid.
44 Ibid.
45 Ibid.
46 Ibid., 7.
47 Ibid., 45.
48 Ibid.
49 Ibid., 29.
50 Ravitch, 31.
51 Ibid.
52 Ibid., 13.

Chapter 14: The State of State Infrastructure Spending

1 "Pension Funds Investment in Infrastructure: A Survey," Organization for Economic Cooperation and Development (OECD), International Futures Programme, September 2011, 1.
2 Sylvain Leduc and Daniel Wilson, "FRBSF Economic Letter: Highway Grants: Roads to Prosperity?" Federal Reserve Bank of San

Francisco, November 26, 2012, accessed on June 24, 2014, http://www.frbsf.org/economic-research/publications/economic-letter/2012/november/highway-grants/.

3 Data retrieved from Census Bureau's The Value of Construction Put in Place Survey as of the date of this writing.

4 Ibid.

5 Ibid.

6 Ibid.

7 Ibid.

8 John Quinterno, "How Higher Education Cuts Undermine The Future Middle Class," Demos.org, March 2012, 12.

9 Michael Mitchell et al., "States Are Still Funding Higher Education Below Pre-Recession Levels," Center on Budget and Policy Priorities, May 1, 2014), 1.

10 Ibid., 4.

11 "Investing in Our Future: Returning Teachers to The Classroom," Executive Office of the President, report prepared jointly by the Council of Economic Advisers, the Domestic Policy Council, and the National Economic Council, August 2012, 3.

12 "State Budgeting and Lessons Learned from The Economic Downturn," National Association of State Budget Officers, 2013, 22.

13 "A Widening Gap in Cities," Pew Charitable Trusts, 2013), 18.

14 Data retrieved from Census Bureau's The Value of Construction Put in Place Survey as of the date of this writing.

15 Ibid.

16 Accessed from American Society of Civil Engineers homepage, http://www.infrastructurereportcard.org/.

17 Susan Lund et al., "Game Changers: Five Opportunities for U.S. Growth and Renewal," McKinsey Global Institute, July 2013, 2.

18 Klaus Schwab, "The Global Competitiveness Forum: 2013-2014," World Economic Forum, 2013, 18.

19 Chris Edwards, ¬"Infrastructure Investment: A State, Local and Private Responsibility," Cato Institute Tax and Budget Bulletin, No. 67, January 2013, 1.

20 Ibid.

21 ata retrieved from Census Bureau's The Value of Construction Put in Place Survey as of the date of this writing.

22 Ibid.

23 Ibid.

24 Organization for Economic Cooperation and Development, 2.

25 Edwards, 2.

26 Ibid., 4.

27 Ibid.

28 Organization for Economic Cooperation and Development, 109.

29 Edwards, 3.

30 Ibid., 157.

31 Ibid., 35.

32 Information about the TIFI program accessed on 24 June 2014 from Federal Highway Administration's website at the following URL: http://www.fhwa.dot.gov/ipd/tifia/.

33 Ibid.

34 "Capital Budgeting in the States Spring 2014," National Association of State Budget Officers, NASBO.org, 2014.

35 Ibid., 3.

36 Ibid.

37 Ibid.
38 Ibid., 2.
39 Ibid., 1.
40 Data retrieved from Census Bureau's The Value of Construction Put in Place Survey on June 24, 2014.
41 NASBO, "Capital Budgeting," 2.
42 Ibid., 45.
43 Ibid.
44 Ibid., 53.
45 Ibid., 40.
46 Ibid., 42.
47 Ibid., 22.
48 Ibid., 61.
49 Ibid.
50 Data retrieved from Census Bureau's The Value of Construction Put in Place Survey as of the date of this writing.
51 Sarah Puro, "The Highway Trust Fund and Treatment of Surface Transportation Programs in The Federal Budget," Congressional Budget Office, June 2014, 6.
52 Ibid.
53 Ibid.
54 Ibid.
55 Ibid.
56 Ibid.
57 Ibid., 8.
58 Ibid.
59 Ibid., 8.
60 "Lower residential energy use reduces home energy expenditures as share of household income," U.S. Energy Information Administration, accessed on June 24, 2014, at http://www.eia.gov/todayinenergy/detail.cfm?id=10891.
61 Joe Wiesenthal, "A Simple Rule Of Thumb Regarding Oil And How It Impacts The Economy," Business Insider, 24 February 2011, accessed on June 24, 2014, at http://www.businessinsider.com/oil-impact-on-the-economy-2011-2#ixzz3M5h947zv.
62 Puro, "The Highway Trust Fund," 8.

Chapter 15: A Tale of Broken Promises: Trouble in the Garden State

1 Eileen Norcross and Frederic Sautet, "Institutions Matter: Can New Jersey Reverse Course?" Working Paper, Mercatus Center at George Mason University, July 2009, 1.
2 Ibid.
3 Richard Ravitch and Paul Volcker et al., "Report of the State Budget Crisis Task Force: New Jersey Report," State Budget Crisis Task Force, September 2012, 13.
4 Data retrieved from state of New Jersey annual financial statements compiled by Merritt Research Services, accessed from Creditscope database.
5 Norcross and Sautet, 40.
6 Data retrieved from New Jersey Annual Financials compiled by Merritt Research Services, accessed from Creditscope database.

7 Norcross and Sautet, 40.
8 Ravitch, 65., Norcross and Sautet, 40.
9 Ibid.
10 Norcross and Sautet, 45.
11 Chris Christie and Kim Guadagno, "The Governor's FY 2015 Budget: Budget Summary," State of New Jersey Fiscal 2015 Budget, 5.
12 Ibid.
13 Rajashri Chakrabarti and Sarah Sutherland, "New Jersey's Abbott Districts: Education Finances during the Great Recession," Federal Reserve Bank of New York, Current Issues in Economics and Finance, Volume 19, Number 4, 2013, 3.
14 Ibid.
15 Ibid., 1.
16 Bill Wichert, "Chris Christie Claims 31 Former Abbott Districts Receive 70 Percent of the State Aid," Politifact.com, December 1, 2011.
17 Norcross and Sautet, 19.
18 New Jersey State Constitution, Article VIII, §II ¶ a, http://www.njleg.state.nj.us/lawsconstitution/constitution.asp.
19 Data retrieved from New Jersey Annual Financials compiled by Merritt Research Services, accessed from Creditscope database.
20 Norcross and Sautet, 43.
21 Ibid., 19, 22.
22 Ibid., 21.
23 Norcross and Sautet, 15.
24 Norcross and Sautet, 46.
25 Ibid.
26 Data retrieved from New Jersey Annual Financials compiled by Merritt Research Services, accessed from Creditscope database.
27 Ravitch, 31.
28 Ravitch, 30.
29 Ibid., 30.
30 Norcross and Sautet, 30-31.
31 Ibid.
32 Ibid., 31.
33 Ibid., 31.
34 Ibid., 30.
35 Timothy Blake et al., "New Jersey (State of)," Moody's Investors Service, August 2002, 8.
36 Chris Christie and Kim Guadagno, "The Governor's FY 2013 Budget: Budget Summary," State of New Jersey Fiscal 2015 Budget, 39.
37 Blake, 8.
38 Charles V., Bagli and Richard Perez-Pena, "For Xanadu Mall, Stalled and Scorned, Deal May Offer New Life," *New York Times*, April 28, 2011.
39 Data retrieved from New Jersey Annual Financials compiled by Merritt Research Services, accessed from Creditscope database.
40 Norcross and Sautet, 4.
41 Norcross and Sautet.

42 Ibid., 49.

43 Ibid., 4.

44 State of New Jersey Division of Pension Pensions and Investments, Financial Statements and Schedules, State of New Jersey, June 30, 2013, 54.

45 Ibid.

46 Ibid., 23.

47 Data retrieved from State of New Jersey annual financial statements compiled by Merritt Research Services, accessed from Creditscope database.

48 Norcross and Sautet, 22.

49 Ibid.

50 Ibid.

51 Steven Hochman and Renee Boicourt, "Comment: New Jersey Pension Board Proposal," Moody's Investors Service, March 26, 1997.

52 Ibid.

53 Marcy Block, "Fitch Downgrades New Jersey's GO & Appropriation Ratings: Outlook Remains Negative," Fitch Ratings (September 5, 2014), 4.

54 Data retrieved from state of New Jersey annual financial statements compiled by Merritt Research Services, accessed from Creditscope database.

Section I—Conclusion

1 Frank Partnoy, "The Siskel and Ebert of Financial Markets? Two Thumbs Down for the Credit Rating Agencies," Washington University Law Review, Volume 77, Issue 3 (1999), 655.

2 Ibid.

3 Gabriel J. Petek and John A. Sugden, "How Might the Oil Price Plunge Affect U.S. States' Credit Quality?" Standard & Poor's Ratings Services, McGraw Hill Financial, January 27, 2015.

4 Ibid.

5 Gabriel J. Petek et al., "U.S. State and Local Government Credit Conditions Forecast: For 2015, the Future is Now," Standard & Poor's Ratings Services, McGraw Hill Financial, December 10, 2014.

Glossary

This glossary draws heavily from the definitions found in the MSRB Glossary of Municipal Securities Terms. We recommend to interested readers the more comprehensive glossary on their website at the following URL: http://www.msrb.org/glossary.aspx. The authors would also like to thank Joe Mysak of Bloomberg L.P. for guidance in assembling this glossary. Our glossary draws heavily on the glossary found in his work, *Handbook for Muni-Bond Issuers* (Bloomberg Press, 1998). We highly recommended this work to interested readers.

ad valorem tax A tax levied on property; in the case of munis, real property. The amount of tax levied is derived from the property's assessed value. Local governments typically budget for a needed amount of tax revenues then levy based on these revenue needs. See assessed valuation.

additional bonds test (ABT) Required minimum debt service coverage ratio an issuer must meet in order to issue additional parity bonds. This contract provision is typically found in revenue bond indentures. See debt service.

advance refunding A process by which an issuer will refund higher-coupon debt by issuing lower-coupon debt and investing proceeds into SLGS, or "State and Local Government Series," special Treasury securities sold by U.S. Treasury specifically for this purpose. The SLGS will be placed into an escrow account and used to make payments until the call date or maturity on the refunded higher-coupon bonds. See state and local government series.

Alternative Minimum Tax (AMT) bond Subject to the alternative minimum tax, this bonds typically trades at higher yields than tax-exempt, non-AMT bonds to compensate the buyer for the cost of the taxation.

American Recovery and Reinvestment Act of 2009 (ARRA) Also known as the "stimulus act," passed in 2009. Contained many programs pertaining to state and local governments, most notably BABs and QSCBs. Expanded the scope of securities meeting bank-qualified and bank-eligible criteria. See Build America Bond.

appropriation pledge Commitment by an issuer to the repayment of bonds from legally available funds appropriated annually by a governing body's legislature. An appropriation pledge typically backs certificates of participation (COPs) and lease-revenue bonds.

assessed valuation Value of property set by a government from which payment of taxes will be derived. Assessed valuation rates vary by state and are limited by statute as to their amount.

authority An agency established by a government or governmental entity in order to serve a defined purpose. Typically authorities are established to issue debt, operate an asset, or construct a facility.

bank-eligible New money bonds issued in 2009 and 2010 that are eligible for IRS 2% de minimis interest expense deduction by banks. Authorized under ARRA. See American Recovery and Reinvestment Act.

bank-qualified (BQ) Bond issue with total face amount of less than $10 million ($30 million from 2009–2010, per ARRA), such that a commercial bank can deduct 80% of the interest cost used to finance purchase of the position. See American Recovery and Reinvestment Act.

basis point (bp) A unit equal to 1/100th of 1%, or .01%, equivalent to .0001 in decimal form. Quoted as a measurement unit of yields and returns by financial market participants.

bond anticipation note (BAN) A short-term financing vehicle issued by state and local governments, payable from the proceeds of a future long-term bond issue.

bond bank An authority or instrumentality created by some states to purchase loans from small local governments. Purchases of loans are financed with the proceeds of a municipal bond issue, providing a low-cost source of financing for small local governments.

bond insurance A guarantee by a bond insurer as to full payment of principal and interest in a timely manner for a given security.

bond insurer A company that issues bond insurance policies. See bond insurance.

Build America Bond (BAB) Taxable municipal bonds authorized under the American Recovery and Reinvestment Act, issued from 2009 through 2010. See American Recovery and Reinvestment Act.

call A contractual provision attached to a bond allowing the issuer to redeem the bond prior to maturity. Typically exercised when new debt can be issued at a cost savings to existing callable debt.

call price The price at which a bond is called for redemption. Typically $100 per bond (or par). See call.

capital appreciation bond (CAB) A municipal bond, resembling a zero coupon bond, which makes full payment of compound interest and principal at maturity. On the maturity date, the owner receives a lump sum payment of compound interest and principal.

capitalized interest A portion of bond proceeds deposited into a special fund to pay interest on those bonds for a specified period. Interest is typically capitalized during a project's construction period, prior to monetization of the asset being constructed.

certificate of participation (COP) A financial instrument giving the holder the right to a pro-rata share of lease payments from an issuer, typically subject to appropriation. Also subject to abatement risk.

comprehensive annual financial report (CAFR) A financial report disclosing an issuer's annual financial performance. The report contains audited financial statements that must conform to standards set forth by the Governmental Accounting Standards Board (GASB). See Governmental Accounting Standards Board.

conduit financing A municipal bond financing done by a governmental issuer or instrumentality on behalf of a third party such as a private enterprise or another governmental entity.

continuing disclosure Release of material information that a bond issuer is obligated to make to the marketplace. Includes annual financial disclosure and various other operating information, defeasance, and credit rating downgrades.

covenant Obligations set forth in a bond indenture that an issuer must follow in order to protect bondholder interests. Examples include rate covenants, additional bonds tests, and tax covenants. See rate covenant, additional bonds test.

credit default swap (CDS) A derivative instrument allowing a counterparty known as the protection seller to transfer credit risk to another counterparty, the protection buyer, in exchange for periodic payments.

credit enhancement The use of another entity's credit to guarantee or provide a second source of payment for a given bond issue. Examples include bond insurance, letters of credit, and state intercept programs. See bond insurance, letter of credit.

credit watch A notification by a credit rating agency that an issuer's credit rating will likely change. See nationally recognized statistical rating organization (NRSRO).

current interest bond A bond that pays interest periodically. The term is used to differentiate from capital appreciation bonds, which pay compound interest at maturity. See capital appreciation bond.

debt service The amount an issuer pays in principal and interest annually.

debt service reserve A fund with moneys deposited in it that can be applied to pay debt service in the event revenues are insufficient to pay the required amount for debt service.

dedicated taxes A pledge of taxes securing a bond issue. Typically transaction-based taxes.

default An issuer's failure to pay principal or interest when due. Can also refer to noncompliance with covenants as set out in a bond indenture, known as technical default. See technical default.

defeasance The removal of an issuer's obligation to make debt service payments, typically associated with a refunding. See pre-refunded bond.

derivative A financial instrument whose value is derived from the value of another financial instrument. Examples include options, swaps, caps, floors, and futures.

dollar price The price of a security quoted in dollars per $100 par value.

double-barreled bond A bond that has as its source of payment both a defined revenue source from operation of an enterprise and the taxing power of the government issuing the bond. See revenue bond, general obligation bond.

downgrade When a ratings agency lowers the credit rating of a bond issuer. Downgrades typically result in higher yields on outstanding debt.

duration The time-weighted value of a bond's cash flows. A measure of a bond price's volatility with respect to changes in interest rates.

enterprise fund A fund established by a local government to account for activities of businesslike enterprises such as water and sewer or mass transit systems. Typically found in the fund financial statements section of an issuer's comprehensive annual financial report (CAFR). See comprehensive annual financial report, revenue bond.

escrow An account established by an issuer to hold Treasury securities used to repay principal and interest on a refunded bond. See pre-refunded bond, defeasance.

fiscal year A 12-month period, not coinciding with a calendar year, at the end of which an issuer's financial statements are prepared.

flow of funds The order in which cash flows are received and disbursed from the time they are received by the issuer to the payment of debt service. Flow of funds structures are specified in revenue bond indentures of businesslike enterprises.

full faith and credit A phrase used to describe an issuer's commitment to repay bondholders with all available funds and legal powers to raise revenues.

GARVEE bond Also known as Grant Anticipation Revenue Vehicles. Issued by state and local agencies for transportation projects and secured by future grant moneys from the federal government.

general obligation (GO) A pledge of an issuer's general funds with the additional promise to levy taxes sufficient to repay the obligation.

Governmental Accounting Standards Board (GASB) A standard-setting organization that sets financial accounting and reporting practices for state and local governments.

high-grade Bonds considered virtually riskless, with de minimis default risk. Typically rated in the highest ratings categories by Moody's and S&P.

indenture A comprehensive document specifying the legal rights, remedies, and duties of the issuer and the specific security structure backing a bond. The trustee is able to enforce the provisions of the indenture on behalf of bondholders.

industrial development bond A tax-exempt bond issued on behalf of a taxable issuer such as a business or corporation.

instrumentality A governmental entity created to fulfill a specific purpose such as meeting special financing needs or operating a businesslike enterprise.

interest rate swap A derivative instrument utilized by local governments to convert floating-rate bonds into fixed-rate bonds and vice versa. Typically done to reduce debt service costs relative to issuance of fixed-rate debt. See derivative.

investment-grade A security that is considered to be low-risk by a ratings agency. Typically, bonds rated Baa3/BBB- or higher. See nationally recognized statistical ratings organization, ratings.

junior lien A bond whose priority of payments falls after that of another bond in the flow of funds structure. Junior lien bonds are typically utilized in revenue bond financings.

junk bond A bond that is not rated or rated below investment-grade. Such bonds carry substantially higher risk of default than do investment-grade bonds.

lease-backed bond A bond typically issued to build a facility, whereby cash flows to repay the bonds come from rental payments.

legal opinion A letter written by bond counsel in the official statement certifying that the bonds are valid and that interest is excludable from income for tax purposes. See official statement.

letter of credit A commitment made by a bank to honor demands for payments on debt. Typically issued in conjunction with notes and commercial paper as additional security for noteholders.

limited tax general obligation (LT GO) bond A bond payable from ad valorem taxes limited by statute as to rate or amount.

make-whole call (MWC) A type of call provision allowing an issuer to call a bond at any time, while protecting bondholders from losses. Different from a stated call. The call price is determined by a formula, typically quoted as a spread in basis points, over the comparable Treasury security. Make-whole calls are common in taxable securities. See call.

maturity The date upon which the final payment of principal is due and payable to bondholders and the issuer's obligation to bondholders is defeased.

maximum annual debt service (MADS) Within a bond's debt service schedule, the maximum payment amount due in a given year through the life of the bonds. Rate covenants can be set as some multiple of MADS. See rate covenant.

millage (mill) 0.1 cents or .001 dollars. This is the rate applied to a property's assessed valuation to calculate taxes. See assessed valuation.

miscellaneous tax bond A bond secured by some combination of sales, use, or excise taxes. A popular financing source in the years after the Great Recession.

moral obligation bond A bond that has, as additional backing, a nonbinding pledge from a governing body to appropriate funds to make up debt service deficiencies. See debt service, appropriation pledge.

nationally recognized statistical rating organization (NRSRO) A company that assigns bond issuers ratings based on their perceived credit quality. Designated as a NRSRO by the Securities and Exchange Commission. See ratings.

new-money bond A bond whose proceeds are used to construct a new project or facility, not to refund prior indebtedness. See refunding.

obligor Typically, the issuer ultimately responsible for full payment of principal and interest in a conduit financing. See conduit financing.

official statement (OS) A document prepared on behalf of a bond issuer in connection with the offering of securities that will contain required disclosures such as the pledge of revenues securing the bonds, use of proceeds, and the issuer's financial and economic characteristics. See indenture.

original issue discount (OID) In everyday bond parlance among market practitioners, the term OID refers to the yield at which bonds were priced at issuance. OID can also refer to the dollar price discount from par at issuance.

pledged revenues The revenues set aside to pay debt service for a given bond issue. See debt service.

pre-refunded bond A bond whose source of payments are State and Local Government Series U.S. Treasury securities in escrow, in connection with an advance refunding. See advance refunding, escrow, refunding.

private activity bond (PAB) Bonds whose proceeds are used by private entities to finance various facilities. Typically subject to AMT (see AMT bond).

public-private partnership (PPP or P3) An agreement between a private-sector entity and a government to operate a piece of infrastructure. Control of the asset is typically transferred to the private-sector entity in exchange for a lump sum or ongoing payments.

qualified school construction bond (QSCB) Tax-credit bonds authorized under the American Recovery and Reinvestment Act, with proceeds used for qualified purposes such as school capital improvements or construction of new facilities. See American Recovery and Reinvestment Act, Build America Bond.

rainy day fund Amounts held by state and local governments as reserves in the event revenues fall below budgeted levels.

rate covenant The obligation by a bond issuer to charge rates sufficient to exceed a specified threshold. Typically associated with essential-service bond issuers such as water and sewer systems. See covenant.

ratings Categorical scores assigned by nationally recognized statistical ratings organizations, reflecting their opinions of the credit quality of bond issuers. See nationally recognized statistical ratings organization.

redemption When an issuer repays a bondholder full principal and accrued interest on a security. Can occur on a call date or maturity.

refunding When an issuer refinances existing indebtedness by issuing new bonds. Done to reduce interest costs or remove burdensome covenants associated with the prior indebtedness. See covenant, pre-refunded bond, advance refunding.

revenue anticipation note (RAN) Short-term securities issued in anticipation of receiving revenues in the future. Issued as a short-term cash management tool. See tax anticipation note.

Revenue Bond A bond payable from a specific stream of cash flows, either from the operation of a businesslike enterprise or dedicated taxes. To be distinguished from the general taxing power securing a general obligation bond. See dedicated taxes, unlimited tax general obligation bond, limited tax general obligation bond, miscellaneous tax bond.

special purpose district A governmental entity established to operate a public asset such as a library, hospital, or water system. Given independent power to levy taxes, set rates, and issue debt; typically independent from overlapping general-purpose governments such as school districts, towns, or counties.

special tax bond A bond whose pledged revenues are derived from transaction-based taxes, typically sales and use, excise, or income taxes. See miscellaneous tax bond, revenue bond.

split ratings Divergent credit ratings assigned to a bond by two or more of the nationally recognized statistical ratings organizations. For example, a bond rated AAA by S&P and Baa1 by Moody's. Typically occurs as a result of differing philosophical approaches to rating bonds. See nationally recognized statistical ratings organization, ratings.

tax anticipation note (TAN) A note issued payable from expected tax revenues. Similar to a revenue anticipation note but payable from a pledge of future tax collections instead of defined revenues. See revenue anticipation note.

tax increment bond A bond payable from the increase in tax revenues associated with greater economic development within a specified area. Used to finance development in blighted areas. Also known as tax allocation bonds.

taxable-equivalent yield (TEY) The yield a taxable bond needs to exceed in order for its after-tax yield to exceed that of a tax-exempt bond. Varies based on an investor's tax rate.

technical default An event whereby an issuer violates a covenant listed in the bond contract. Bondholders are typically given enforceable remedies in the event of technical default. A technical default is distinguished from the colloquial meaning of default in that the issuer typically has not missed payments in a technical default. See covenant, default.

trustee A financial institution granted special fiduciary powers to work on behalf of bondholders and to enforce remedies of bondholders.

underlying rating The credit rating assigned to a bond's issuer. Distinguished from a credit rating assigned to a bond's credit enhancement or guarantor. See ratings, credit enhancement.

underwriter A securities dealer who will purchase securities from an issuer and reoffer them to investors in a primary offering.

unlimited tax general obligation (ULT GO) bond A bond payable from taxes, not limited in rate or amount.

variable rate bond Also known as a "floating rate" bond. The bond will have a long final maturity, with a coupon that will reset periodically (daily, weekly, or monthly).

warrant A type of debt security used in some jurisdictions, without the legal remedies afforded by traditional bonds.

yield spread (spread) The amount, expressed in basis points, by which a security's yield exceeds that of a benchmark. Used by market practitioners as a measure of credit risk or relative value. See basis point, yield to call, yield to maturity, yield to worst.

yield to call (YTC) The return an investor will receive if a bond is held until its call date, presuming that the bond is called at the call price and coupon payments are compounded semi-annually at the yield to call.

yield to maturity (YTM) The return an investor will receive if a bond is held until its maturity date, assuming coupon payments are compounded semi-annually at the yield to maturity and full repayment of principal is received at maturity.

yield to worst (YTW) For a given dollar price, the lower of the yield to call or yield to maturity. See yield to call, yield to maturity.

zero-coupon bond A bond, issued at a discount, that pays no coupons and will accrete to par at maturity.

Index

Note: page numbers in *italics* indicate figures and tables.

CPSIA information can be obtained
at www.ICGtesting.com
Printed in the USA
LVOW05s1922051115
461222LV00004B/8/P

9 780985 344740